Around the World in 80 Days

My World Record Breaking Adventure

Mark Beaumont

CORGI BOOKS

TRANSWORLD PUBLISHERS
61–63 Uxbridge Road, London W5 5SA
www.penguin.co.uk

Transworld is part of the Penguin Random House group of companies
whose addresses can be found at global.penguinrandomhouse.com

Penguin
Random House
UK

First published in Great Britain in 2018 by Bantam Press
an imprint of Transworld Publishers
Corgi edition published 2019

A CIP catalogue record for this book
is available from the British Library.

ISBN 9780552175494

Typeset in 9.57/12.85pt Times NR MT by Jouve (UK), Milton Keynes.
Printed and bound in Great Britain by Clays Ltd, Elcograf S.p.A.

Penguin Random House is committed to a sustainable
future for our business, our readers and our planet. This book
is made from Forest Stewardship Council® certified paper.

1 3 5 7 9 10 8 6 4 2

With love to Nicci, Harriet and Willa

Contents

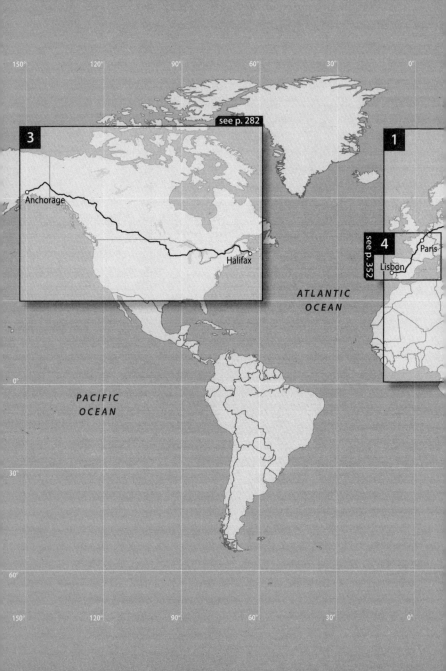

see p. 282

3

1

see p. 352

4

Anchorage

Halifax

Paris

Lisbon

ATLANTIC
OCEAN

PACIFIC
OCEAN

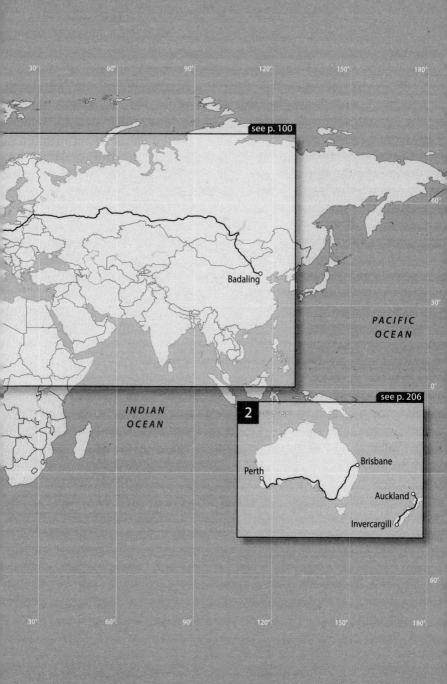

see p. 100

Badaling

PACIFIC
OCEAN

INDIAN
OCEAN

see p. 206

2

Perth

Brisbane

Auckland

Invercargill

Prologue

I'd like to think that Jules Verne would have laughed and loved the audacity of someone powering himself around the planet on a bicycle in fewer than eighty days.

The 145-year-old fiction of *Around the World in 80 Days* has now become a reality in a way Verne's Victorian readership wouldn't have believed possible. But it has to be said that an audience in the first half of 2017 remained hard to convince, even though the plan, on paper, looked simple enough.

To get around the world in 80 days, I needed to average 240 miles a day. Imagine pedalling from the Forth Road Bridge to Liverpool, or London to Plymouth, or more than New York to Boston, every day for two and a half months. To make this sustainable, every single day you'd have to be in the saddle for sixteen hours and get about five hours' sleep.

My team set about obliterating the previous 18,000-mile circumnavigation world record of 123 days. And we came full circle in a time of 78 days, 14 hours and 40 minutes, working off a plan of seventy-five days' riding, three days of flights and two days' contingency – we just didn't use the entire contingency.

Now that I have written the conclusion on the first page, we can get down to business. Behind the headlines and the hype, and before I have told the story a thousand times, I want to catalogue what this project actually felt like, how glorious but terrifying it was – and that was before I turned a single pedal. I also want to acknowledge properly that, like the front man in a band, I get the lion's share of the profile and credit for what was actually an amazing team performance.

As I write this prologue, just months after the finish, there is already a sense of inevitability about the 80 Days, as if it were always on the horizon, the next prize to be claimed in endurance cycling. No, it wasn't. People thought it was a crazy ambition. Success only looks inevitable with the privilege of retrospect. There was no reference point for riding this fast, nothing in the history of endurance cycling that people could latch on to and say, 'Well, if that was possible, this should be possible.' I was asking people around me to believe in a massive leap in performance, and that takes a quiet confidence in your ability, a healthy dose of obsession and a bloody good plan.

The romantic notion of record-breaking is that you throw everything at 'the impossible' and figure out what is possible. You figure out physically what you are capable of and mentally how strong you are in the heat of battle. The reality is that after years of planning, we read a plan from a script. That rather mundane description doesn't seem to account for all the rotten luck, including four crashes, serious storms and delays on borders, not to mention the uncertainty of even getting to the start line. Being more objective, we must have had as much 'good luck' as 'bad luck'.

Let me say up front, I will not be cycling around the world a third time. This is the first time in my career I feel like I have nothing to prove to myself in terms of endurance, that the 80 Days was not a stepping stone to 'what's next'. Despite the self-limiting logic of our target, this really does feel like my personal best. I suffered hugely, and my team's commitment to the task was incredible to witness. Furthermore, I would happily mentor anyone who wants to break my record. I am not precious about it in the slightest. In fact, I applaud the audacity of whoever comes next.

Since my return to Paris on 18 September 2017, the reaction from the world's press and the public has been extraordinary. After living in a performance bubble for months, to stop and appreciate the wider perspective on my team's furious progress, and the interest in it, has been incredible. But why would so many people care how fast I can ride a bicycle around the world? And I am not talking about the cycling press. Why would the *Financial Times* write five features on this human endeavour, and why would the finale be watched by over 300,000 people on Facebook? Maybe because we are all fascinated by human aspiration, with one eye on the mirror, wondering what *we* are capable of. It's a perspective on our own personal milestones.

Pedalling the planet in under eighty days makes our world seem both gigantic, when I remember the endurance and suffering, and somewhat smaller than before, when I zoom out to consider the entire race. I certainly hope it is a journey that gives people confidence of their own to be bold, to be disruptive (in a good way), to attempt to redefine what is possible.

Part One

Before the World Began

1

Why the World?

Full circle, back to the bike.

At home in Scotland, the newspapers always refer to me as a cyclist and adventurer, normally in that order. However, for the decade since graduating from Glasgow University with a perfectly useful Economics and Politics degree I have been pedalling for a minority of that time, having spent years rowing boats, exploring the Arctic, climbing mountains, fundraising for charities, working with corporate businesses and being a TV person in numerous guises.

In August 2014, when I first floated the idea with my wife Nicci to come back to life on two wheels, I was in the worst shape of my adult life. The eleven days of sport at the Glasgow Commonwealth Games had just come to a close and I had spent the preceding nine months abroad, following the Queen's Baton Relay to sixty-eight nations and territories, telling the inspiring stories of hundreds of competitors for BBC World. Elite and aspiring athletes constantly surrounded us, but for my cameramen, director and me, this was a feat of airport and hotel endurance, red carpets and the corresponding feasting. I did attempt to run 10km in every Commonwealth country, but looking back, this was a two-year sabbatical in my athletic career.

The word 'floated' is aptly chosen, because I very nearly didn't. At the end of January 2012, as part of a team attempting to break the world record rowing across the Atlantic from Morocco, we capsized 500 miles from the finish line in Barbados. Spending fourteen hours treading water in high seas fighting for your life tends to induce, if only temporarily, an epiphany over what's important about living.

Just eight weeks after being dropped off by our rescue vessel, the cargo ship *Nord Taipei*, in Gibraltar, I got married, and my two daughters Harriet and Willa have since appeared on the scene. For clarity, I should stress that getting married was not a knee-jerk reaction to nearly drowning, but I had definitely been putting off the idea of children for some time in the future.

For those few years 2012 to 2014, then, being a sports presenter was the stepping stone from filming my own expeditions to turning the camera the other way and telling others' stories. As a twenty-seven-year-old I would tell anyone who wished to know it would be 'a few more years' before I stopped the major expeditions and found a new 'job'. I have now turned thirty-five and completed the Everest of my career. And I have learnt the fallacy of prophets, not to be so grandiose as to suggest retirement. Life is best kept in the now, the future left unmade, a balance struck between your own grand plans and opportunities that come your way.

My coming back to being a professional bike rider was difficult on a number of fronts. Firstly there was the simple mental and physical battle to get back into shape. Performance sport inevitably involves incredible discipline in terms of eating and training, and as creatures of habit I believe we are all by nature rather lazy, so new habits are hard to acquire. Not doing something, or more often postponing it, is always easier than doing what is most important right now.

There is also the matter of how you see yourself and how others see you. We are all hugely shaped by perceptions and assumptions, so to reimagine ourselves takes persistent effort and confidence. Adventure cycling has not historically been seen as part of professional cycling, but my ambition is that the circumnavigation world record by bicycle will soon be as coveted and as professionally regarded as the circumnavigation world record by sailing. There is no reason why it shouldn't be, considering the scale of the task, the money involved and the talent within cycling.

It's worth recapping briefly the history of this world record, for those who are new to the concept of cycling around the world against the clock. It is not a linear journey through the decades and the records, as the Guinness World Record rules have changed a few times; in fact there was a time when you didn't have to go around the world at all to hold the record. In 1981, before I was born, Nick Sanders cycled 13,609 miles in 138 days, taking a route around the northern hemisphere. A few years later two Americans, Jay Aldous and Matt DeWaal, beat this in a time of 106 days. Nearly a decade after that, Polish rider Andrew Slodkowski completed the 'Around the World in 80 Days'. None of these routes was a circumnavigation by the modern definition as they did not pass through opposite sides of the world.

The GWR rules then changed considerably, stating that the journey should be a minimum ridden distance of 18,000 miles (29,000km), and that the total distance travelled (including transfers between continents – you can't cycle across the sea!) should exceed the length of the equator, in other words 24,900 miles (40,100km). There is also that stipulation that you must pass through antipodal points on opposite sides of the world. This can make for tricky logistics, with many riders choosing Madrid in Spain and Wellington in New Zealand.

GWR hold distinct world records for team and solo, male and female, but not for supported and unsupported. Therefore, circumnavigations have inevitably become increasingly supported as the years have gone by, in order to go faster. GWR consider 'supported' as a sliding scale, so it is hard to define what is either completely supported or unsupported. I think it is inevitable that all ultra endurance cycling records will become supported, with unsupported riding returning to the realms of adventures rather than races.

Steve Strange set the first world record under the new rules in a time of 276 days in 2005, while I was in my penultimate year at Glasgow University, ruminating about becoming an accountant. Phil White, who tried and failed to beat this time, was one of the people who helped me plan my first cycle around the world a few years later.

The Man Who Cycled the World was based on a simple sum: cycling 100 miles a day for 18,000 miles with a day off every fortnight. Including flight times, this equals 195 days, and I came home in 194 days and 17 hours. A BBC1 documentary on the journey was a success, which put circumnavigation by bicycle into the mainstream and launched my career. I went from pulling pints in a Glasgow bar and working the photocopier in interim office jobs to being offered TV adverts,

follow-on documentaries, public speaking engagements and, more rel-
evantly, a publishing deal to write my first book. It has been tough at
times to make this career viable, but there was a definite honeymoon
period after the world cycle when I rode the wave of that success.

I remember the headlines after breaking the world record by over
eighty days, and the speculation about whether that time of 194 days
would ever be broken. This seems rather disingenuous now, especially
when you consider how much faster Jay, Matt and Andrew had gone
before, albeit over a shorter distance. Now, 194 days seems positively
pedestrian. Rather than launch a career, this achievement probably
wouldn't be enough to warrant a mention in the national papers these
days. This evolution fascinates me and inspired me to come back and
have another crack. However, the profile I achieved after my first time
around in some ways made it difficult to go again. When speaking to
would-be sponsors, the assumption by many was that I still held the
record.

But there have been a number of magnificent rides since 2008,
though none of them were televised or managed to break out of the
niche interest of adventure cycling fans and local press. James
Bowthorpe got around in 175 days, and Julian Sayarer, with a particular axe to grind, finished in 169 days, but to the best of my knowledge
GWR did not verify either attempt. Vin Cox, a real gent who I have
enjoyed following over the years, officially pedalled around in 163
days in 2010. Just four days later, Alan Bates, a Brit living in Thai-
land, with the backing of its king, completed his ride, a huge leap in
performance to 125 days.

In 2012 a group of riders set out at the same time from Greenwich in
London in a head-to-head race for the Guinness World Record, which
was the first serious foray of the adventurer Sean Conway. This was won,
completely unsupported, by the late and great Mike Hall. I first met
Mike during one of my UK talk tours, when I was in Durham. I remember, like so many others, him coming over after the talk to tell me about
his big cycle plans. I answered his questions and wished him well, not
realizing the force for good he would become within endurance cycling.

Tragically, Mike lost his life in a cycling accident during the 2017
Indian Pacific Wheel (IndiPac) cycle race across Australia. He was the

only other person I knew who had been speculating about the possibility of cycling around the world in 80 days. After his totally unsupported circumnavigation of 91 days and 18 hours, completed in June 2012, Guinness World Records changed the rules to include total travel time. Under the new regulations, Mike's time was 107 days, 2 hours and 30 minutes, and sadly it was not ratified. Other fast hopefuls were also disappointed not to take the crown, including Lee Fancourt and Thomas Großerichter, despite getting around in 105 and 103 days respectively. Lee also passed away in January 2018 – another great loss to the world of ultra endurance cycling.

It was the spirited New Zealander Andrew Nicholson who set the previous verified benchmark of 123 days and 43 minutes, in a mainly unsupported ride (he only used a support vehicle across the Australian outback). *Road Rage*, Andrew's brilliantly candid account of the ride, tells of his lifelong fight for recognition, first through his professional Olympic career as a speed skater and then afterwards as a teacher. His cycle around the world sounded like his escape valve for all life's frustrations, hence the title. His raw emotions and at times volatile personality made for an enthralling race.

It is perhaps odd that the UltraMarathon Cycling Association, who would have more knowledge of the sport than Guinness World Records, are not seen as the governing body for the circumnavigation world record. GWR work hard, but have the fairly thankless task of verifying all world records under the sun, from the world's largest strawberry to this 18,000-mile pedal.

So, after the spate of attempts in 2012, GWR's new rules stated, quite simply, that the clock never stops, which meant transit times were now included. This tweak to the regulations may sound like small change, but here is the knock. Getting around the world in 80 days, according to the old rules, meant riding 225 miles a day. Under the new rules the average needs to be about 240 miles a day, once you work out that you'll lose about three days to travel time between continents, and allow a small contingency of twelve hours per continent. This is a detail I will come back to, as it became the blueprint for our entire world adventure. And if the difference between 225 miles and 240 miles sounds minor, I'd encourage you to pedal for 225 miles then see how you feel about that final 15 miles – and then consider repeating that average every day for the next two and a half months!

Paola Gianotti currently holds the women's circumnavigation world record, at 144 days, although controversially her route was not ridden consecutively. I am in touch with and helping where possible an Indian, an Irish and a Scottish woman all training to claim this crown.

I say controversially as I feel that there are two criteria missing in the rules. Firstly, the ride should be continuous. If I crash, even if it isn't my fault, and I'm unable to carry on, the race is over as far as I am concerned. I can't recover and return to finish the route at a later date. The second missing criterion, in my humble opinion, is that you should be able to look at a world map and immediately say that the route *looks* like a circumnavigation. While it is not always possible to ride to the water's edge, every effort should be made to ride in an unbroken line across continents. If flights are taken across the middle of a continent, you can tick all the rules, but if you look at a map of a route like that, it doesn't visually add up to a circumnavigation.

The extreme example of this could be cycling as few miles as possible through Asia and then doing big north-south loops in North America to make up the miles. Typically riders have missed big chunks of Asia with a flight that crosses the landmass instead of an ocean. I understand both the challenges that GWR face governing such a record and also the natural desire for cyclists to make the most of the rules, especially when parts of the route are more dangerous, so these comments aren't a criticism of riders or of GWR; they are more the criteria I had for my own ride, and that I hope future riders honour. If this was a social media blog, I can only imagine the opinions and comments that would follow that carefully worded explanation! Endurance cycling, like anything worthwhile and very personal in life, is filled with hell-bent opinions.

Ultimately, can we all agree that there is no wrong way to ride your bicycle. Just get out there and ride.

The final insecurity I had about getting back on my bike was simple, and it's one I'll come back to: the fear of failure. I could live with people's opinions of me (although we all like to be liked), but I did worry about putting all my cards on the table and failing. What would this mean for my work, for my ability simply to pay the mortgage and look after my family? I wasn't a new graduate any more, without a care or financial burden to my name. To put all my experience and reputation on the line was bold. If I was coming back, it was to take endurance cycling to the next level, not to try but fail, or, worse still, to be a shadow of my younger self.

I had loved presenting the Queen's Baton Relay, and from Usain Bolt and Sally Pearson to unknown heroes like Kent Gabourel and Nijel Amos, I had met and interviewed hundreds of athletes. The truth of the matter was that by the end of Glasgow 2014 I was utterly inspired and inevitably jealous: I wanted to be doing what they were doing, not asking the questions.

While I was emotionally pulled towards being an athlete again, I was also pushed back into the saddle by the lack of follow-up opportunities within the BBC and other networks. The QBR had been a huge personal and family commitment; I had been away from my daughter Harriet for the best part of nine months of the first year of her life, with the idea that it would be a launchpad for a career in broadcasting, yet it seemed to be a journey that led nowhere, professionally at least. Perhaps I didn't invest the time that is needed to develop new documentaries and presenting jobs, but the numerous meetings I did take with TV executives I would describe as enthusiastically noncommittal. Everyone knew me, liked me, wanted to work with me, and wanted to keep in touch. Which left me feeling like I might spend years floating about telly-land being encouraged, but ultimately remaining homeless. So while I felt somewhat unfulfilled being a 'gob on a stick', as one cameraman neatly put it, I also felt the pressure of making ends meet, to create another major project and not just try to live off past successes.

On the flipside of any financial and career worries there was the kid inside me who simply wanted to ride his bike fast and far. Let's not pretend that cycling around the world is the safest career move; there were plenty of other paths I could have taken if paying the mortgage was the sum total of my ambition.

I'll always remember the drive to my mum Una's house in Fife when I broached the subject of 'the World' with Nicci. She did not seem altogether surprised, which made me question how public my thoughts were. And on a positive note, she also didn't seem too upset.

The big factors were my safety, which we both had a different view on since the Atlantic capsize – Nicci has always been fearful of the oceans ever since a scare when sailing as a child, so it shows the strength of her support that she had never tried to stop me rowing the Arctic or the Atlantic – and also long periods of time away from home. But both risk and time away seemed a lot less compared to previous expeditions, especially if I was to cycle around the world fully supported and at the speeds I was suggesting. The agreement we reached was that I could have until Harriet went to school to shoot for the stars and take on the World. Harriet, at the time, was two years old, so this gave me three years.

This conversation was in fact a lot more protracted and inconclusive than it may appear on paper, but this was the crux, which I felt happily coincided with my optimal years as an endurance athlete, given that I was thirty-two at the time. I felt that there was only one time in my life to really put all my cards on the table and figure out what my personal best was. I tried to convince myself that it didn't matter whether I succeeded or failed, that I, or we as a family, should never regret risking big and taking on the World again.

My previous three books, *The Man Who Cycled the World*, *The Man Who Cycled the Americas* and *Africa Solo*, were essentially personal travelogues, about the people, the tapestry of cultures, and that slide-show view on the world you can only have from the saddle of a bicycle. The last of those journeys, undertaken during the spring of 2015, was the first big test of how I could perform back on the bike again.

Cairo to Cape Town is about 6,000 miles, nearly a third of the world in distance. I have long considered the Pan Americas, Cairo to Cape Town and the circumnavigation as the ultimate hat-trick of ultra endurance cycle rides. Africa was my missing journey, and after spending a few months in 2014 visiting the eighteen Commonwealth countries of that great continent, albeit with a red carpet, I was fascinated to go back and explore from the asphalt. Although southern Ethiopia and northern Kenya didn't boast such luxury when I sped through – dirt roads at best, mud most afternoons when the heavens opened with angry rains. My world record of 41 days and 10 hours must be ripe for the taking now that there is tarmac in an almost unbroken line from top to toe.

Africa Solo was very much a stand-alone expedition, but in the back of my mind I was already dreaming of coming back to take on the World. I was riding a KOGA Solacio, a carbon racing set-up with Di2 electronic gears, tri-bars and frame bags – a far cry from my earlier World and Americas trekking bikes. Going as light as possible meant I could average 160 miles a day, although my mileages had a very wide span from as little as 80 miles to topping out at what felt like a whopping 240 miles. Anything over 200 miles felt like an epic day, and I am on camera in Zambia boasting that I wonder if I will ever cycle so far again in a month.

Looking back, Africa was simply a training ride for the World. If I was going to cycle around the world in 80 days, it would not be what I have come to term a 'wild man' adventure. This time I had to convince sponsors and the public that this was not a version of what had gone before. These comments are not to diminish the achievements of those who went before, not least because that would also mean shooting myself in the foot, but with every respect, I was not interested in repeating history a wee bit faster.

This time, in order to break the record by such a margin, I would need a team – and the best one whatever money I could raise would buy.

2

Building the Team

There was an evolution of thinking that brought me to believe I could cycle around the world in 80 days. The risk in writing this book is to reverse-engineer and make each course of action sound within my control, and the outcomes seem inevitable. I wish this had been the case, but we are all human, insecure, fallible and lacking such omniscience.

While I have always been in a hurry, as opposed to being from the Alastair Humphreys school of nomadic travelling (Al's first big adventure was a four-year cycle journey around the world), for me the bike is still a vehicle to get between and travel through interesting situations. However, *Around the World in 80 Days* is not a story about the people of Mongolia whom I did not meet. This cannot be a traditional travelogue as this was a mission about exact planning and logistics, about cycling performance at the extremes of endurance. As the athlete at the heart of such a complicated project, I have a limited perspective. So much happened around me that I had no awareness of at the time, so my task here is to faithfully represent the events that were crucial to the journey. All told there were about forty people involved, so not everyone is going to agree on every point. My aim is to recount points of friction factually, without bias. Because I have a public voice and my team does not to the same extent, I hope that I can tell stories accurately, keeping in mind that this is a first-person narrative and doesn't pretend to disclose everyone's truth, the whole truth and nothing but the truth.

On that disclaimer, I would add that I am not the easiest person to work with. Like many people driven to achieve sporting success, I can be furiously obsessed and intolerant of diversion. I can excuse any and all behaviours because of sleep deprivation, pressure and some downright ridiculous situations, but I don't wish to. Friction is sometimes important. While it is worth striving for perfection, let's hope we never get there. The magic often happens when you feel uncomfortably on the edge and when the stakes are high. Accountability, creativity and emotion can get lost when we aren't pushing hard.

On balance, I used to blissfully think I was an all-round nice, easy-going guy, but now I realistically hope my moral compass is in the right place. I feel battle-scarred by the trials of the past few years, but out of the struggles have come friendships that will last a lifetime and some painful lessons that will make me less naive the next time. Once again, I aim to avoid talking with the advantage of hindsight about anything that happened during the 80 Days, instead focusing on how things appeared and felt at the time.

16 August 2016

Hi Laura,

I am looking for someone with your impressive skill-set to support a mega expedition July/September 2017. Have you got the interest and availability? Happy to call tomorrow or Friday to let you in on the secret!

All the best,
Mark

Laura Penhaul would become the most important lady during the World (as I like to call it), apart from Nicci and Una obviously! She was my performance manager, and as everything about the 80 Days came down to performance, this was my most critical selection for the team I needed to complete the journey. Oddly, despite not knowing Laura that well, I never considered anyone else for the role.

At the same time as I pedalled off from Cairo down the length of Africa, Laura had cast off from San Francisco leading an all-female crew aiming to row across the Pacific Ocean, via Hawaii and Samoa, 8,556 miles to Australia. This six-month ambition turned into an incredible nine-month odyssey, captured in the documentary *Losing Sight of Shore.*

I had first met Laura and an early version of her Coxless Crew in 2010. At the time I was working closely with the sports brand Kukri, who were making noises about moving into adventure sports. Rather than just launching a range of kit, we decided to commit a modest budget to an adventure scholarship to help seed-fund expeditions, the rationale being that the story you tell is the product you sell. Over the course of a long day, our panel, including TV presenter Ben Shephard and ocean rower Sarah Outen, conducted a *Dragon's Den*-style interview process with all nature of would-be adventurers. My favourite was Nick Hancock, who converted a water tank into a sleeping pod and lived on Rockall, a remote rocky outcrop in the North Atlantic 286 miles off the coast of Scotland, for forty-three days. The other judges felt that occupying a rock was daft and not a journey and therefore not an adventure, but I just love such British eccentricity. If you have to ask 'Why?', you'll never understand.

Laura's was by far the most ambitious and impressive pitch of the day. An all-female crew to row the Pacific? Adventures don't get much bigger than that. However, they needed a huge amount of money, more than our meagre scholarship could make a dent in, and I had concerns about the fact they hadn't spent many nights training at sea, and that the scale of the ambition was bigger than they imagined. Over time, I was happy to be proved wrong. I know that not being funded was a big blow for Laura. While I had looked forward to giving help and hope to novice adventurers, I hadn't been prepared for tears of disappointment.

Laura and I managed loosely to stay in touch, and a few years later, after my Atlantic capsize, she asked if I could meet or have a Skype call with her team, whose line-up had changed slightly since I'd first met them. She wanted me to explain, warts and all, what had gone wrong, how we had capsized and how we had survived. I guess Laura wanted her team to think beyond the fun of the training courses, when you swim around in a wave pool trying to inflate a life raft and keep each other above water. After that video call one of her team-mates left. Whether the reality I painted was the reason or it was simply the straw that broke the camel's back, I clearly didn't help with the cohesion of the Coxless Crew. So in real terms, turning Laura down for funding and in part causing a team-mate of hers to leave her crew mightn't seem the strongest foundations for the most important friend and ally on my team.

Laura had worked at the past three Paralympics – Vancouver, London and Rio – so I thought it was unlikely that I could lure her away from Team GB. I certainly couldn't pay the same. But to my surprise, Laura was looking for a new challenge, and obviously missing the wilder side of adventure sports.

Other key members of the 80 Days team came from more accidental encounters in the great outdoors.

Now, I have a ridiculous dog called Monty. This was my own nickname, in fact my only used name outside my family throughout high school and university – much to the amusement of Nicci when friends now call and apparently ask to speak to the dog. He is a cross between a Jack Russell and a red squirrel judging by looks, although we were led to believe he was a Jackadoodle as a pup.

One very wet day I drove up to Loch Turret in the heart of Perthshire and attempted to go for a trail run. The saturated moorland was bursting across the gravel track in regular torrents, so that the normal streams were wide and freezing cold. Apart from disliking long runs, Monty also hates water, so my training run was cut short as I lolloped along, carrying him under one arm. While Monty simply refuses at any watery obstacle, I had also been through that daft process where you jump enthusiastically across the first series of such obstacles until you realize how futile such vanity is and you start ploughing happily through every watercourse. So I must have been an odd sight when I arrived back at the car park, drenched and mud-splattered, clutching a drowned squirrel.

I was startled by a shout from a family starting their dog walk: 'Hello, Mark!'

It was Phil Mestecky. We had met before, although I didn't know that at the time. In 2013, I ran and swam 240 miles across Scotland from Arran to Aberdeen in a televised charity challenge for the STV

Children's Appeal, and when I had run through Crieff in Perthshire, Phil had arranged for the Strathearn Harriers, the juniors from the local running club, to join me. After a fleeting chat in the rain, we now agreed to meet for some fell runs, and it was on these long explorations of Strathearn that I shared early plans for the World, and eventually Phil came on board as my researcher for about a year.

Nicci was a housemistress at Glenalmond College, near Crieff, which is an independent senior school set on a beautiful rural estate. Across the River Almond and over two fields was the nearest hamlet of Harrietfield. It was only a small cluster of houses so it came as a huge surprise to find that one of the support team from my 2011 expedition Rowing the Arctic, Lt Col Justin Holt MBE, had bought a holiday home there. In June 2015 I was on a five-mile run around the valley while pushing a sleeping Harriet in her chariot buggy when I came across Justin limbering up in the road for a jog. So in another unlikely rendezvous we caught up for the first time in years and I explained my plans for the World, which led to his involvement, albeit not for the duration.

Perhaps I should have carried on running around Perthshire until I had recruited the full cohort.

The Etape Royale is a stunning sportive that starts close to the Queen's Scottish residence at Balmoral Castle and takes in 103 miles of Aberdeenshire, including a challenging section over the Lecht ski resort. The first time I rode the course was also the first time that the event organizer, my good friend David Fox Pitt, had ever ridden a century on any bicycle, and we decided to recce the route on penny farthings. I can't recall why we chose these dangerous and difficult contraptions, but I do remember it as one of the most painful days I have ever spent on a bike. I had persuaded ITV4's *The Cycle Show* to drive up from London to film this spectacle and so we put on a brave face and wobbled sore-arsed into Ballater after fourteen hours.

The second time I rode the route was on the event day itself and I soon buddied up with Rob Wainwright, the former Scotland rugby captain and British Lion. Rob, a retired military doctor turned sheep farmer, is also now an avid bike rider, having completed the Race Across America (RAAM) a few times. Rob agreed to put me in touch with an organization called Leadership Challenges, who had ably manned his RAAM rides.

And so my recruitment drive led me to a man called Mike Griffiths. But rather than come back with a list of able bodies whom I could contact, Mike said, 'We love the idea of supporting such an inspirational challenge, we have a huge amount to offer.' The 'we' he referred to included Jeff Thomas, a digital entrepreneur who had been moved to help set up Leadership Challenges after tragically losing his nine-year-old daughter Antonia to asthma. Their *raison d'être* is to create events that give people from all backgrounds life-changing experiences, challenging their comfort zones and teaching them the power of teamwork and leadership. They are simple but very powerful ambitions, while also raising money for charities, most notably Asthma UK.

It's never that straightforward, there must be a catch – that's what I was thinking as I left a meeting with Mike and Jeff in Glasgow a few weeks later. Sponsorship involves such hard miles; I'm well used to networking tirelessly and chasing enquiries that go unanswered. Yet here was Leadership Challenges travelling up especially to see me and offering to take over the logistical planning for the entire World attempt, to coordinate the lot, at their cost. It seemed too good to be true.

Mike saw this as the ultimate calling card, the event that would define the capabilities of Leadership Challenges, and he took my opportunity and ran with it. But running logistics for the World was a massive job, both complicated and critical, and not something I was going to hand over lightly.

Mike is a British Army veteran who served for twenty-six years in operations around the world. He has provided engineering solutions in all kinds of extreme environments, leading searches for improvised explosive devices and specializing in diving projects too. After serving in places including the Balkan states, Angola, the Falklands and Northern Ireland, Mike was selected as regimental sergeant major and deployed to Afghanistan with the Explosive Ordnance Disposal and Search Task Force. His career was recognized in the 2014 Queen's New Year's Honours. But you wouldn't guess all that from the man I met, who seemed very down to earth and keen to impress, speaking quickly and enthusiastically. Only his formality gave a hint of his military past.

For the World in 2017 Mike would assume the role of overall logistics manager, as well as team leader for the last two legs, 3 and 4. But the part of the route that was giving me most sleepless nights in terms of logistics was the second stage of leg 1 (what we called leg 1b), all the way across Russia to Beijing. Mike was the first to admit that these border crossings, language barriers and cultural unknowns were not his forte. So I needed a team leader who could both handle the diplomacy and navigate the bureaucracy of Russia, Mongolia and China, while also understanding the performance requirements of a bike race. It was Dr Andrew Murray, my friend and our team doctor, who had connected me a number of years earlier with David Scott, Honorary Consul for Mongolia in Scotland, who also happened to run an expedition company called Sandbaggers. An ex-policeman who is as comfortable working in the refined company of ambassadors as he is having a wrestling competition beside the campfire in the wilderness, he was a good man for the job.

Leven Brown is an old friend from my ocean rowing days, and while far more comfortable on the waves than cycling on tarmac, I knew how well he worked under pressure – always with a wry smile, looking out for others. So it was a real shame that his work commitments meant he couldn't spare the time that was needed to lead leg 2, but his involvement in the Around Britain cycle – our 'Warm-up to the World' – was invaluable, and he certainly helped shape the team for the World itself.

A key member of both the Around Britain and World teams was former British cross-country mountain bike champion Alex Glasgow, who now designs forests for a living. His skillset as a mechanic and navigator was a huge asset, not to mention his ability to inject humour and enthusiasm into even the weariest crew. There was only one issue with his unbounded energy. Whereas most people slow down when they get tired or stressed, Alex has the tendency to go the other way, completely manic, which could be amusing but also something the rest of the team learnt to watch out for!

Alex so nearly didn't get the job. I first met him in 2012 when a chap called Stuart Doyle got in touch through social media saying he was doing twelve twelve-hour challenges for 2012. He had played tennis for twelve hours, then football, and so on. His plan was now to cycle across Scotland in twelve hours and he wanted to know if I could help. Certainly, I said, but it sounded a bit easy, so I suggested mountain bikes. I knew nothing about mountain biking routes across Scotland so I brainstormed with the well-known round-the-world cyclist Al Humphreys, and he suggested getting in touch with his friend Alex Glasgow.

Stuart, Alex and I set out from Buckie, near Aberdeen, on a 170-mile route which we had sorely underestimated. Stuart had certainly bitten off too much and was in the support van within an hour. Alex and I finished after seventeen hours – an epic day off-road, and a great way to make a new friend.

We had shared other adventures since, but when I emailed to invite him on to my crew he didn't reply and I assumed he wasn't interested. While searching for something else in his spam folder a month later, my invitation popped up, and I received a hasty response asking if he was too late. A lucky find.

Over the autumn of 2016 my training was building quickly and I had less time to commit to the growing task of taking all Phil Mestecky's research and turning it into a workable plan. I needed Leadership Challenges, but as I didn't know them apart from by recommendation, it felt like I would be outsourcing the entire logistics operation, which was too much of a risk.

So I interviewed and recruited another ex-military chap called Keith to work alongside Mike. Within weeks there was a huge difference in output, which is slightly unfair on the new recruit who simply didn't have the same relevant experience. With one of them based near Newcastle and the other near Bath, myself in Perthshire and Una desperately trying to keep tabs on everything from her home in Fife, it unfortunately wasn't going to work.

Team-building is not easy, but decision-making is vital. I had to act quickly, to try and treat everyone fairly while having to let a few people go. I placed a huge amount of trust in one person, Mike, to build the plan for the ultimate bike race, albeit under the ever-watchful eye of

Una, who became overall project leader, although that hadn't been my intention.

I can't overstate the importance of this mother–son working relationship. As I set out for my first pedal around the planet in 2007, I handed Una – aka Mum aka Base Camp – my laptop and said, 'You're going to need this, Mum.' On her drive home from the start in Paris she stopped at her brother's house in Folkestone and had a session with my cousin to learn the ABC of computer skills. After a lifetime of working with horses and on the farm, an office job was, and still is, Mum's idea of hell. Yet in support of my expeditions and business we have worked shoulder to shoulder for over a decade.

It hasn't always been easy. We are both strong, slightly obsessive characters and perhaps we wouldn't have lasted as colleagues if we weren't related – but therein lies the strength. Una has the admirable control never to put on the 'mum' hat and ask me not to do something. If she worries about me, she doesn't tell me. This is a character trait I have noticed a lot more since having my own children: it's hard to imagine going from those early years, watching their every move and setting their boundaries, to working together like Una and I do.

There was a time in my twenties when I was a bit sheepish about working with Mum, thinking it looked amateur. But that was my insecurity, and I grew out of it. Having family at the heart of what I do is a great strength. Who better to look out for your interests? As a result of my progress from being slightly embarrassed to fiercely proud, there were a few male team members on the 80 Days project who didn't last, simply because they didn't respect Una's role – they just saw her as my mum – whereas I needed to know that whenever I left the room, they would understand that Una represented my interests, that she called the shots. This was sometimes a difficult distinction to spot, when I personally got on well with the people concerned.

It wasn't just Mum; we had a few challenges with some men on the team over respecting the experience and responsibility of women. Nearly half my final team was female, by accident and talent rather than design. As time went on, especially once we were on the road, I needed a team that respected professional boundaries, understood where their job ended and others' started, and had the same goodwill and respect for everyone else, regardless of their age or gender. In short, I needed people who would acquit their roles with expertise, efficiency, energy and tactfulness, because there would be no room for passengers on the World attempt.

3

Money, Money, Money

The mountain that needed climbing before I turned a single pedal stroke was fundraising – and this was a seriously big mountain. I've spoken to people who say 'it's incredible to pull this off for less than half a million quid'. A hotelier I met commented glibly, 'I could just about refurbish one of my kitchens for that!' But 'expensive' is all a matter of perspective. Half a million may be a fraction of the cost of sailing around the world, but I'm pretty confident it's by far the most expensive expedition to cycle around the world, and in my head it's an insane amount of cash to spend on a bike ride.

If I'd buggered my knee on day 1 and it was over, most of the money would still have been spent. The initial budget to go 18,000 miles fully supported and with a film crew totalled around £600,000. Like most preliminary figures, this was met with a sharp intake of breath, which led to a severe whittling down, and then it grew again gently as the true costs replaced the estimates. The final number was almost bang on £500K. Put simply, I could pay for every other expedition I have ever planned for this sum.

But this was a professional expedition so I never wanted to rely on volunteers. Leadership Challenges rely on volunteers for the Race Across America, which is part of their model to develop people's skills, but while I was happy to give people the chance to step up and shine, I didn't want to take any risks. I wanted to recruit professional people who understood that this race was about making the bike go as fast as possible, and not about them 'finding themselves' as they ventured far out of their comfort zone. The only people who didn't get paid were myself and Mum, which is why during 2016 and 2017, right up to the start line, at least half of every week was still being given over to events and working with corporates – far from ideal when trying to train full-time.

There was a contradiction within me – the kid inside just wanting to figure out how fast I could go and wanting to do this regardless of the following, the fame, the future; but then again I was always well aware of the opportunities that would come if I became the first person to cycle the planet in fewer than eighty days. The security it would give my family, the doors it could open. But I felt I was risking big – all my cards were on the table. If I failed, I didn't know how my career would be perceived, where that would leave my work, especially if I failed quickly and without showing any promise of achieving the target.

I had a network of previous sponsors whom I could go back to, but this expedition was so much bigger. I had never asked for so much before without the security of a commissioned TV documentary.

One of my first sponsorship meetings, on 31 August 2016, was in St James Street with Lindsay Whitelaw and Derek Stuart from Artemis. Artemis were my title sponsors a decade earlier with *The Man Who Cycled the World*, and we had kept in touch over the years and I had supported some of their charity events, but they had not been involved in sponsoring any of the interim expeditions. Lindsay and Derek are refreshingly straightforward to work with, and Artemis is of a scale where decisions are made quickly and definitively. I knew there would be no committee meetings and long proposals. In fact they gave the impression that details on paper were of little importance compared to their belief and trust in me. On 14 September a short email arrived confirming that they would be title sponsor. I was making the kids dinner when Mum rang and told me to check my emails. The cooking was entirely forgotten as I raced through the house to find Nicci. We had got our break. This was really happening. Someone was willing to back me. The relief was incredible.

LDC were also a sponsor a decade ago, and I have continued to work closely with them as their corporate ambassador, hosting around a dozen events each year, and they in turn have sponsored some of the expeditions. While the title spot wasn't of interest, they definitely wanted to be involved in the biggest project of my career and came in quickly as a supporting sponsor. It felt like we had hit the ground running and I surprised myself having raised nearly half of the budget so quickly and without help.

From then, everything slowed down.

I knew I was neither qualified nor did I have the time to raise the rest of the vast amount of cash the team needed, so I set about recruiting a fundraiser. Through recommendation I met a chap who fitted the bill. After the meeting I gave him a copy of my *Africa Solo* book, which the following weekend he told me he had read. I was impressed with his commitment, and his long list of fundraising triumphs – millions for educational bodies, even name-dropping a network that made my current quandary sound like small fry. This charismatic chap had the smooth persistence of a salesman, but the deference of someone used to working with high-profile businesses and people. He even came up with a solution for his own pay, which seemed to completely de-risk the partnership for me. He asked a foundation to pay for his salary, meaning they would seed-fund the project, leaving him to raise the rest of the £500K. It was the perfect solution to my biggest challenge.

I'm not naming the people involved as I have no interest in making accusations or settling scores; I'm simply capturing what happened.

Because the only catch was, he didn't raise a single penny.

I was over-impressed for far too long. It was more than six months before I took back the reins. At that stage, with just months to go before the planned start, if I didn't go out personally and raise the funds myself, it wasn't happening. In January 2017, Nicci and I had serious conversations about putting back plans by a year, but there were already so many people working on the project, I was physically on track, and everything was gearing up for a July departure. The only thing we didn't have was money. I found those first months of 2017 incredibly stressful and in the end had to personally plug the gap in the budget. In for a penny, in for a pound. It was money that had been set aside for buying the family home.

My approach to fundraising has always been direct: asking friends, business contacts, anyone who shows interest, for introductions. I don't ask directly for sponsorship as that is a yes/no conversation. People are proud of who they know, but don't like giving away money – that is human nature – so it's much easier to ask people for their connections. Most of my sponsors over the years have come through a second or third point of contact, as opposed to the person I initially knew.

My newly appointed fundraiser's approach was the opposite of this, despite a very impressive contacts book, if anecdotes were to be believed. His method was about crunching the big numbers, taking a vast database and whittling it down. Not only did this lead to no sponsorship, it led to no real meetings with potential sponsors. For months there were lots of updates and stats and reassurance that he wouldn't leave the project until he had seen it through, and I should have had the confidence to say 'bullshit'.

There were a few meetings, one of them memorable. I was invited to a dinner in a penthouse apartment overlooking the Thames. Beforehand we met for a briefing in a nearby pub, where a bespectacled middle-aged man in a suit and a young Indian couple joined us. The host was a Chinese billionaire interested in investing in UK ventures and we sat down in her lavish dining-room for an impressive home-cooked meal. Thankfully I was invited to speak first, so while we worked through starters I engaged the table with my plans for Around the World in 80 Days. It didn't feel like there was much common ground with any of the other guests, but everyone nodded enthusiastically.

When the main course was served, it was clear my 'pitch' was over and attention turned to the young Indian chap, who without much introduction handed out some black boxes for us to open and explore. This electronics engineer had invented the next-generation vibrator, called the Mystery Vibe (if you are interested), which bends in many different ways and is remotely charged so both ends can be used. While on my best behaviour, fine-dining with a group of strangers, I found myself trying to engage with equal enthusiasm in conversation about the exponential growth of the sex toy industry in China.

Thankfully the vibrators were put back in their boxes and the main course was cleared. Over dessert the middle-aged besuited chap was pitching for investment in a hedge fund, which might have been the most data-led, futuristic, all-conquering creation of the decade, but after cycling around the world and sex toys he did struggle to make his proposal sound even vaguely interesting. I left, bemused and amused, around 11.30 p.m. and wandered back to Euston station to get the sleeper train back to Edinburgh.

The other meeting of note was with delegates from CCTV, the biggest TV channel in China, and *China Daily*, the major English-language newspaper. I was told that to impress them we should meet at China Tang at the Dorchester Hotel, by Hyde Park. It was a stunning meal, but being left with the bill when things were so tight did sting and left me wondering if I was being taken for a ride.

In the end there were further conversations with CCTV, but for them even to consider sharing the story and then the documentary they wanted me to re-route through more of China – in fact their initial first response was 'This sounds interesting, but would Mark consider making the ride and documentary just around China?', which shows the lens they were looking through. The Chinese government's economic development policy of 'One Belt, One Road' is about a modern Silk Route, connectivity and cooperation through Eurasia. But this goes west from China, not north into Mongolia and Russia, so to work for the Chinese my route would have to drop into Kazakhstan and then run the entire breadth of China to Beijing.

'Bear Grylls sold half a million books in China last year' and 'I'll make you famous in China' were the lines I was hearing. And on this question I was absolutely clear: if all things were equal with the route, it would be fantastic to create a major story in China. The research went back and forth for weeks, and we finally had a long and slightly heated meeting during which I drew a line under the deal. The topography was similar, so in terms of hills there was little to choose between the routes; in terms of road quality, supplies and ease of border crossing, again it was much of a muchness; but when you looked in detail at the wind patterns in western China they were hopelessly unpredictable, whereas coming in from the north across Mongolia and the Gobi Desert, there looked to be predictable tailwinds for a few thousand miles. It was impossible to say if the more southerly route through China would be an hour slower or a day slower, but it was definitely slower. So forget it.

This decision was not met with unanimous support. I could see the commercial pressure, the allure of fame and fortune, playing into the equation. But if I didn't get Around the World in 80 Days, all bets were off, so as far as I was concerned there was nothing left to discuss. After some very difficult months and false promises, this felt like the final straw and my fundraiser left the project. Una picked up conversations with sponsors I have worked with for many years and found they had also not been kept in the loop, so there was damage limitation to be done. It was a hard lesson and an expensive one. It nearly cost us the project.

The one success, which I am very grateful for, came through my would-be fundraiser's wife, a teacher, who suggested and created the initial work with Twinkl, an online teachers' resource with lesson plans that are translated and incorporated in school curricula around the world. Twinkl worked with us throughout the 80 Days and managed to take the story to thousands of classrooms, teaching everything from Aboriginal artwork as I pedalled across Australia to the physiology of endurance cycling. This at least has been a fantastic legacy.

Along with Twinkl, *Blue Peter* were also excited to follow the adventure. When I was young they only had a studio dog, but these days they also have a tortoise, called Shelley. I appreciate the metaphor – slow and steady wins the race! Shelley perhaps wasn't fit for the 18,000 miles, but we were to take her cut-out, a life-size model, and update the *Blue Peter* audience with 'Where's Shelley?' and her pedal around the planet. Between Twinkl, *Blue Peter* and my own social media channels, we would take the adventure to hundreds of thousands of children.

On the charity side, the fundraiser who didn't fundraise had plans to bring on board a major international charity in order to leverage celebrity endorsement. I was uncomfortable with the idea of using charity to further our aims; however, I bowed to the advice that this was how big-brand relationships work. I was told that it was our job to create a media story, a 'vehicle' for the charity to then leverage for fundraising and media gains. In my experience I have never known a charity to run with a story like this; they rely on you personally to do the fundraising, and might help a bit with media relations along the way. However, this advice led to an interesting six months, and a learning curve with one of the biggest of all charities.

I was open to partnership, but also still very much wanted my own charity, Orkidstudio, to benefit. James Mitchell, an architect, founded

Orkidstudio as a nineteen-year-old student to create buildings which were at the heart of communities, sympathetic to the environment, and employed the local workforce, in particular women. The impact of Orkidstudio over the past decade, especially in East Africa, has been brilliant, and I am proud to be their patron and chair.

The major charity, and my fundraiser, could not see the value of having Orkidstudio involved. While initially this partnership approach was accepted, the major charity soon insisted on exclusivity and that we needed to commit to a minimum of £250,000 of fundraising. This would justify them engaging their celebrity ambassadors and getting behind the marketing.

I felt that I had lost control of our core purpose. I would love to have committed to a quarter of a million quid's fundraising, but to be honest would prefer that to go to Orkidstudio, where I had that personal connection and trust about where the funds would go. But I was also a quarter of a million short for the expedition itself. At the same time my friend Carron Tobin was developing charity fundraising ideas, including a grand installation at Edinburgh Airport, a crowdfunding campaign, and corporate events. But in the end it all became such a distraction from our core purpose. Regretfully, feeling very stressed and preoccupied, I made the call to scrap it all, and focus on actually getting Around the World in 80 Days. If I did that, then I could refocus on making a big difference for charity.

I do understand the positioning of a large charity, with major fundraising targets and celebrity ambassadors to utilize but also to protect. But fundamentally it was the wrong tone of conversation: this was a commercial negotiation, whereas since I was twelve years old, working with charities alongside my adventures has been about working together, having a connection with the people involved and the people who will benefit. I wished I had been stronger with these convictions earlier on, but I was flattered by the conversations, trusted that this was a more professional level of working, and even took meetings with high-profile friends asking for this kind of support, which I regret. I so nearly let go of Orkidstudio, my own charity, in favour of a global giant. Thankfully it felt wrong enough for me to react and take back control. All in all we lost a lot of time on these conversations, but I have to look at the positives, I learnt a huge amount.

The new target was far more modest: a thousand pounds per day, so £80,000 for Orkidstudio. If we did that well, without detracting from the performance, then on the back of a successful race I should have the time and profile to do a lot more afterwards. But all in the right order.

I was so very grateful that Artemis were such an easy-going sponsor. They simply wanted me to succeed. There was no conversation about return on investment, contingencies if we failed, marketing plans and event days. They simply watched closely, checked in regularly, and helped with introductions, advice and use of office space whenever needed. Their payoff was in seeing me succeed, and being associated with such a monumental prize.

It's worth flagging the fact that juggling all these conversations was far more than I could do on my own. While the team was growing quickly, it was Una who remained my confidante, the person whom I knew better than anyone, so I knew she could pick up and coordinate even the most sensitive of conversations. I could see the strain it was putting on her as well; she shared the risk and reward from this dream, whereas anyone else could walk away at any time without such consequences.

I faced a few other stumbling blocks in how people perceived the 80 Days ambition.

Firstly, none of the men who have taken the circumnavigation world record in the past decade have done so with any profile outside the narrow adventure cycling world. So I soon realized that there was a widespread public belief that I still held the world record. By way of reminder, my seemingly pedestrian effort of 194 days and 17 hours had now been slashed to 123 days, so we weren't splitting hairs – my previous effort was obsolete. Yet for many people I spoke to Mark Beaumont was the only person they had ever heard of to have cycled around the world. Without a sense of competition and wider interest in the feat, this just seemed like one man's obsession to keep cycling around the world. I spent a lot of time filling in the back story and trying to give scale and gravity to the world record.

The second stumbling point was the 80 Days. It doesn't take a PR genius to get the media hook. However, for those who didn't accept without question my target there was the regular comment of 'Why do you think you can go over forty days faster, breaking the world record by a third?' For those who really thought about the practicalities of the race, there was a concern that I was risking too much. A more cautious approach would be to try and break the world record of 123 days, and if possible surprise everyone with a staggering sub-eighty days finale. To call the entire project Around the World in 80 Days was really placing all our cards on the table, because if I came home in eighty-one days, that might obliterate the world record but could still look like a failure.

I thought a lot about this and felt it would be disingenuous to claim that I was out there to break Andrew Nicholson's mainly unsupported circumnavigation while being fully supported. This was not a like-for-like race. Being fully supported, I was always going to create a significant leap in performance – and sub-100 days felt too safe. In contrast, sub-eighty days felt ridiculously ambitious, but I am a firm believer that you can never do better than what you set out to do. As a paper exercise, the 240 miles a day, sixteen hours a day, fifteen miles an hour, three days of flights and two days of contingency all made sense. But the margin of error was tiny: twelve hours of 'faff' time per leg of the journey.

Most good endurance bike riders can just about imagine a 240-mile day, being well rested, when the sun shines and you have a tailwind; well after the sun has set you tick over the magic number. But for this ride 240 miles is not your best day, it is your average day, every day for two and a half months, with the cumulative effect of sleep deprivation, not to mention the complexity and bureaucracy involved in crossing sixteen countries across four continents. This was the stumbling point for some would-be sponsors. In the real world, the chances of everything going so well that I could hit this average seemed highly unlikely. Even a contingency of a few more days would allow only for a few flight delays, tricky border crossings, illness and injury.

I understood their concerns, but I also felt that we would create so much media interest from the start that come success or failure, the profile for sponsors would be significant. Rather than just relying on a TV documentary and book to tell the story after the event, this was about taking a global audience on the journey from the moment we launched, and if we did that properly it would be a story about teamwork, endurance and taking on your biggest dream. I wanted this to be much bigger than a cycling story. So by being over-concerned about the finish line and the record, it felt to me like sponsors were missing the point.

This was the ultimate story about time, about how fast man can get around the world against the clock, so engaging a timepiece sponsor was top of my list. This became an example of one of the many setbacks. We had a deal agreed in principle with one of the big players. The company's European marketing director's final remark at our meeting was 'I don't take anything to the global director that doesn't get signed off, as it looks bad on me. We will make this happen.' Time passed but I was reassured by our conversation, so we didn't pursue any other brands . . . until an apology came back that their six-figure backing had not been approved.

Similarly, a major online retailer wanted to come in as a six-figure sponsor, sitting just underneath Artemis. This was perfect. Shortly before getting the paperwork sorted there was a change in their chief executive, the budget couldn't be signed off for the transition period, and my team threw a huge amount of goodwill into the relationship to keep everything on track. After months, word came back that they had changed their mind. It was another massive blow.

I was more annoyed with this latter situation as they had gone public with their support, gained media value, and then dropped out. I wasn't the only one feeling a bit used; the other fully paid-up sponsors felt the retailer had been given a freebie. To give them some credit, they threw a lot of kit into the project, but we were still left with a big hole in the budget.

However, a few important pieces of the puzzle were in the meantime falling into place. Having a strong press office and media hub was going to be crucial and I spoke to a number of candidates, ranging from freelancers to big businesses. They were all expensive. Ewan

Hunter, a friend who runs the Hunter Foundation (on behalf of Sir Tom Hunter, but no relation), helped with introductions and advice throughout the planning and at this particular hurdle put us in touch with the team at Muckle Media, who jumped at the opportunity and said that 75 per cent of their work would be pro bono. For the balance, I spoke to one of their clients, the EICC (Edinburgh International Conference Centre), and agreed to speak at a major homecoming event with them if they could add the balance of the PR costs to their bill. This solution saved between £30,000 and £50,000 from the budget.

The website and social media plan was another crucial pillar of the project and I got quite far down the road with a digital agency. But the costs, once again, were huge. A key moment came when I was leaving a major meeting in Edinburgh feeling very stressed and overwhelmed. I called Una and told her, 'We are out of options, out of time; regardless of the cost, we just have to bite the bullet.' Mum had this other company called 80 Days for me to go and meet. I responded, 'No, I don't have time.' 'Please, just take the meeting,' she said. I got in the car and drove off but stopped at some traffic lights, trying to decide whether to turn right or carry on. I took a deep breath and went straight into the city centre.

George Bowie owned the bike shop across from my flat when I graduated. I had walked in and told them about my plans to cycle around the world, and they had been both amused and helpful – and supporters ever since. Una was speaking to George to ask about some electrolytes I had used during the Africa Solo expedition when he mentioned that a friend of his owned a company called 80 Days, and that they did digital marketing. A few weeks later, when we were wondering which way to turn, Una called him back to get more information, and to ask for an introduction to Mark Forrester.

80 Days create website and occupancy solutions for top-end hotels and resorts; their world is a million miles from adventure and sport. All that connected us was the title '80 Days', so I sat down with Mark and his team, led by Chris McGuire and David Gardner, to discuss my need for a cracking website and digital plan. A few hours later they had offered to do most of the work pro bono. This meeting, which I so nearly didn't take, saved the best part of another £50K

from the budget – but I am sure for 80 Days it was a much higher chargeable fee than that, once the project grew to its final scale.

In reality, far from being a good PR opportunity, their being called 80 Days and my cycling Around the World in 80 Days was a terrible marketing match, because it was merely confusing – their sponsorship just didn't jump out of any press release. Thankfully Mark laughed about this and was so enthusiastic about the project that he got stuck straight into making it happen.

I was surprised by the lack of interest in the cycling world. A trip to Eurobike in Germany, the world's biggest bike show, produced only a few new leads. KOGA, my long-standing bike sponsor, were very keen to be involved again, but this time I was needing them to write a cheque as well as build me the dream machine. They eventually obliged.

Things were more straightforward on the kit front, as LDC owned ZyroFisher, who make Altura cycling clothing. I would have liked to stick with my previous Scottish sponsors, but this connection with LDC meant that I received an email from Jon, ZyroFisher's marketing director, pretty much saying 'we have been told to sponsor you'. And through them I was introduced to the lively Jeff Zell from Panaracer tyres. Over a rather scratchy Skype connection to San Francisco I sold the dream. It felt like such a speculative call, so I was amazed and delighted when they came back with a yes. These smaller sponsors, in the £20K to £30K range, slowly started to add up. But others, including brands I have used and therefore promoted for years, wouldn't put a pound in the pot; in fact it was difficult even to get kit sponsorship. At the lower end (it all adds up), Yellow Ltd sponsored Corima wheels, and Rudy Project my helmet and sunglasses with a bit of cash on top.

Visit Scotland, through Charlie Smith, had been involved in some short films and marketing that I had been the face of called *Wild About Argyll*. But being a public body it was difficult for them to sponsor an individual. They definitely wanted me to fly the flag though, so we devised a series of short films showcasing areas in Scotland and my training in the build-up to the World, in return for a fee which I put into the sponsorship pot.

Closer to the start, well after going public with the 80 Days announcement in April 2017, some final all-important sponsors were: Cardtronics, through Ana Stewart, who had just sold her business, iDesign, to them; Hiscox Insurance, through an introduction from Bruce Stevenson Insurance Brokers; XL Caitlin, through a friend to many adventurers, Duncan Sutcliffe; and Menzies Aviation.

The connection with Menzies Aviation would become one of the most important factors in our success: they are the one sponsor who in real terms can claim to have got us around the world faster, probably by at least half a day. Initial contact had come via a phone call about speaking at an event, by recommendation from a friend, Andy Rogerson. Forsyth Black, their chief executive, needed a speaker for a conference. During my call to discuss this, I realized that the fact that they had ground handlers in almost every airport I passed through could be invaluable. Forsyth made it clear that sponsorship was not something they normally did; however, if I could support a few of their conferences then they could top up the fee to a sponsorship amount, which would put them 'on the strip' and they would support logistics as best they could. This would become a massive part of our story – all from a chat about an event in Las Vegas.

Having lost well over £200,000 of what we had thought was agreed sponsorship, the final months before the start were very nerve-racking. With a month to go I had breakfast with Lindsay Whitelaw from Artemis in London and shared everything, including my personal investment, which I had written off, accepting I wouldn't get it back. He seemed concerned, and I received a call from his colleague Derek Stuart soon afterwards. They were worried about my level of stress and financial commitment, and inevitably I think they were concerned about the fate of their own considerable financial commitment if I was distracted from performance and underfunded. Derek was calling to assure me that because we were leaving with no contingency in the budget, Artemis would step in and cover any increases in spend and would also increase their sponsorship by 10 per cent. I was to stop fundraising and completely focus on the ride.

I was incredibly grateful and a bit embarrassed. But I could now concentrate exclusively on riding my bike.

4

Shaping Up

Nicci's job as a housemistress at Glenalmond College, looking after around forty teenage girls, not only brought the only salary into the household, it also provided us with a rather lovely Victorian house, set within a 300-acre estate. For seven years we had made the most of living in this country retreat, but the downside was that none of it was ours and Nicci's job included overnights and weekends and therefore an inevitable split loyalty between looking after the pupils in her care and our own children. So when Willa was born at the end of May 2016 we moved and rented a generous house in Crieff, the town 7 miles away from the school. Its large double garage would become my training dungeon for the next year.

Bleary-eyed, I would creep out of bed at 4 or 5 a.m., pull on my bib shorts, cycle shoes and a warm fleece, and clip into the WattBike for a lonely four-hour session. After ten minutes the fleece was off, but I could watch my breath crystallize in the cold, still air. Around 7 a.m. Harriet and Nicci would often appear at the door to say good morning, looking disapprovingly at this glistening, bare-chested sight surrounded by a growing puddle, slowly making his way through mindless box sets on the iPad. By 8 a.m. training was done, and the day could be dedicated to logistics, events, travel and meetings. I would be lucky if I managed to get out for longer road rides three times a week, often taking in my favourite loops over Lochearn, Loch Tay, then the Glen Quaich pass to Amulree and back down the Sma' Glen, or south through Gleneagles and Glendevon and into Fife, before looping back along the Tay estuary and through Perth. The options were endless; this is perfect road cycling territory. I just didn't have the time to train as much as I wished.

With so much still to sort, with the whole project uncertain, it felt very difficult to disappear to Spain for most of January 2017. But if I didn't prioritize training, and by that I mean proper endurance miles, all the planning and fundraising would be for nothing.

I had been working with Dr Lesley Ingram at Napier University for testing, alongside Ruth McKean, my nutritionist, and a number of bike fitters, but Laura Penhaul was now stepping up as performance manager and taking over all these conversations, trying to distil information on to a need-to-know basis. The training plan throughout 2016 had been a typical three-week build, one-week recovery, and repeat, training through the zones as opposed to just riding big miles, from zone 1 (easy, a pace you can hold all day) through to zone 5 (high-intensity work, up to an hour). Riding big miles at tempo gets very boring in training, plus it doesn't give you the all-round conditioning you need. Cycling around the world fast is not a test of power and speed, it is a test in not injuring yourself. Unlike most roadies, who are allergic to walking let alone running, I went for two- to four-hour fell runs most weeks to strengthen up all the small muscle balances in my knees and ankles. And most of the sessions I did on the road and on the WattBike were much, much harder than you would ever ride on expedition. I rode intervals till I cried out through pain, gasping for air. I did riding sessions where I would do pyramids from 50rpm (like a weights session on the pedals) right up to furiously spinning at 120rpm and back down, again and again. I would ride four hours at 250 watts, and do hour sessions at 310 watts. I made every session hurt, mentally and physically. I knew that my ability to ride 240 miles a day for two and a half months was going to boil down to my ability to suffer and my resilience to injury.

The start of 2017 was when I wanted to translate all that conditioning into endurance miles, to get used to the longer hours. I put a call out on social media for suggestions, having never before done a winter training camp in the south of Europe, and a ton of suggestions came back. But the small set-up of Rachel Paling and James Williamson, RJ Cycling Camps, on Spain's Costa Blanca, caught my attention;

I liked their simple offering. I would be staying in the same hotel as Team BMC, probably the world's second largest pro cycling team after Team Sky. They had booked out exclusivity of Hotel Denia La Selle Golf Resort – meaning no other pro cycling teams could stay there – whereas the nearby town of Calpe itself was a Mecca for other outfits.

For three weeks I was the odd stable partner for the road pros, and I certainly rode a hell of a lot more than they did. We ended up chatting. To start with I was that strange guy staying on his own, eating on his own, plugged into his laptop any moment he wasn't sleeping, riding or eating. But the intrigue grew, and BMC's team directors, the likes of Max Sciandri, started to wonder what I was doing. Why these mainly solitary mega miles?

During the first week in Spain I was ill. All I wanted to do was ride but for the first days I was under strict instructions to rest. Every morning I would wake, take my resting heart rate and some other data, fill in a monitoring app, hit send and wait for the feedback from my team back in the UK. The messages stayed the same: take another day off, and another, and another. I was going crazy. I was burnt out and had a bad cold and a temperature, but all I wanted to do was get out and ride. I hated being away from Nicci and the girls for weeks at a time, I could see the strain it caused, especially when I was rattling around a pretty empty hotel.

On one of these enforced days off I walked up the hill behind the golf course and filmed a rather desperate social media plea for sponsors. I couldn't say what for, as the plan wasn't yet public, but for the first time in my life I turned to the tens of thousands of followers and said, 'Please help.' I pressed send and got a huge number of replies. I could whittle quickly through most of them as people just wanted to know the big plan, but there were a few more intriguing leads, ranging from a men's underwear brand to a big insurance company. None came to anything in terms of sponsorship, but Richard Curtis, one of those who replied, worked for Universal Studios and ended up on the team, firstly as a driver to deliver an RV across Europe then using his talents to network on the broadcasting side.

In week two I was allowed out, albeit to build gradually in hours and intensity. The terrain around Denia and Calpe is utterly glorious for cycling, but initially I stayed near the coast, looping through orange orchards and exploring the labyrinth of backroads, often with James as guide. By midweek I was doing eight-hour gentle rides, starting early. I would tap-dance my way across the tiled hotel reception floor in my cycle cleats, wheeling my bike out at first light, and go for a pre-breakfast spin. By the time I got back around 10 a.m., the BMC guys, who had their own chefs and their own part of the restaurant, were ready to head out, to return normally by 2 p.m., to spend the majority of the rest of their day lounging around the lobby chatting to each other, chatting on Facetime, listening to music and, by the look of it, whiling time away. I am certain they trained incredibly hard, but to be cooped up like that as a young athlete in a hotel in the middle of nowhere with very little to do except eat, sleep and ride your bike four or five hours a day looked like a very boring existence. This was the pinnacle of the sport, they were one of the top teams in the world, what most aspiring young road cyclists dream of becoming – but from what I saw I wouldn't swap their lifestyle for the chance to explore the wider world on two wheels.

I was ready for longer rides, and I got dressed in the dark one morning, not bothering to look out of the window, then clattered my way across a deserted reception at 6 a.m., wondering where the staff were. They were at the door, staring out, snapping away excitedly on their phones, and I joined them to figure out what was going on. Under the streetlamps of the car park I watched in equal disbelief as a blizzard continued to pile up snow that was already inches thick. It hadn't snowed in Calpe since 1983, they told me – so for as long as I have been alive – and here was a proper snowstorm, which I could happily have stayed at home for. That day Team Sky posted photos of a blizzard at their training camp in Mallorca. At least the roads were clear there, whereas on the mainland it was impossible to ride. I treated myself to an extra slice of toast at breakfast – amid a six-month mission to cut weight – and considered my options.

After finding the maintenance man and a spanner, I changed the pedals on the very rudimentary spin bike in the hotel gym and settled down for an eight-hour session. From the lack of movement, my mind and my backside were equally numb when I limped off it. Whether it was effective training or not, I felt good for having committed to suffering so much rather than take the day off.

The evening before, the Swedish women's golf team had arrived for their winter training on the hotel's top-notch course, and perhaps it doesn't need explaining that they were not sore on the eyes. Neither the golfers nor the bike racers had anything to do that day, or the next as the arctic snap continued. So while I spent the rest of the day sitting in the lobby, online, chasing sponsors as usual, I amused myself watching the young BMC riders, who outnumbered the Swedish golfers three to one, doing their best to get acquainted.

Since starting testing in July 2016 and then again just before Christmas, the improvements we were looking for had begun to show. For a start, I had dropped in weight from 91.5kg to 88.4kg and my resting heart rate had gone from 48 down to 40. Lactate readings were encouraging too. Lactate is one of the natural by-products of the use of glucose by our muscle cells and is commonly used as a test marker in performance. In endurance, it's important to understand when there is onset of blood lactate accumulation in correlation to heart rate and power output (watts) on the bike because in long-duration exercise you want to keep blood lactate to a minimum. By understanding this, I would know what I could hold during the World without risking increasing lactate build-up and therefore muscle fatigue, which could lead to injury and a drop in performance. My peak lactate was 11.6mmol, up from 4.8, but I had gone a further three stages in the ramp test, showing that I was becoming more efficient on the bike, and could also dig deeper: the onset of the lactate rise was later in the incremental stages, meaning I could hold higher watts on the bike without creating too much lactate, and therefore cycle harder without fatigue. My VO_2 peak, or maximum oxygen uptake (a value widely used as an indicator of health), was 56ml per kg per minute at a peak power of 410 watts – considerably up over a six-month period – and VO_2 peak was lower for all levels of output, showing I was having to work less hard to produce the same level of output. My power-to-weight ratio increased from 3.8W/kg to 4.6W/kg.

Ruth planned to continue working on reducing my body weight, but without losing any power. Fuel utilization was also important – I wanted to be fat efficient. In testing, the Respiratory Exchange Ratio shows your use of carbohydrate and therefore fat as your main fuel source. My RER of 0.7 indicated that fat metabolism predominated, while any value over 1 would indicate a switch to carbohydrates as a main fuel source. My RER stayed below 1 until I was churning out 350 watts, at a heart rate of 150 beats per minute, showing I had definitely built a diesel engine. I was a fat-burning machine.

Laura flew out to support me for seven days, by which time the snow had begun to melt, but it had been replaced by torrential rain and high winds that were the talk of everyone I met. The BMC training camp had taken over the basement of the hotel with a bank of bikes on turbos, but I set out to explore the coastal roads past Benidorm and the endless cols of the region. It was some of the coldest riding I could remember – not why I picked southeast Spain in January for my winter training.

The most we ventured was three four-hour sets a day, but even this made for an epic day. Fitting in the final four-hour set to make up an average sixteen-hour day for the World seemed a step too far in the conditions, and so soon after illness. We set out in the dark and rain, rode for four hours, got back to the hotel in time for breakfast, into a dry set of kit, back out until late lunch, another set of dry kit, and back for dinner – twelve hours with Laura patiently driving behind me in her tiny hire car, endlessly cheery. Cycling from A to B, you don't have an option to stop short, but doing short loop after loop near the hotel (the longer routes were too snowy) meant having the discipline of getting close to home and forcing yourself to turn away, to do that extra loop to complete the time.

It was such a valuable experience, far more gritty than we had expected, and brilliant for getting the measure of each other. Regardless of whether this was ideal physical training, which it obviously was not, it proved to Laura that I would never wimp out, never stop, and it gave me the confidence that I had found a kindred spirit, someone who smiled more when the chips were down – someone who understood what Type 2 fun was, that life-affirming stuff that is miserable at the time but which becomes your fondest memories. We had a miserably wonderful time doing endless loops of those mountain passes on pretty much deserted roads. The locals weren't going to drive in those conditions.

The weather did improve though, and we got to see why the Calpe region is such a cycling Mecca – glorious roads and, I'm told, normally ubiquitous sunshine. James and Rach looked after me brilliantly, although James considered six hours a long ride, so he left me alone for the dawn and dusk shifts.

While I was in Spain there was a major breakthrough with my media plans. I had spent much of 2016 exploring options for how to film the 80 Days through every network you can mention and a lot of independent British TV companies, many of whom liked the idea, but the same old enthusiastic but noncommittal conversations were going nowhere. The BBC made it clear that they weren't interested in a journey for the sake of a journey; their tagline was now 'journeys for a reason', so unless there was a scientific, cultural or some other layer to it, it wasn't for them. It seemed that the likes of *The Man Who Cycled the World* and my earlier documentaries wouldn't be commissioned any more under the new remit. Even if we could make the second layer of the documentary about sports performance or something else they could justify as meaningful outside of the race, there seemed no way to create a co-production. I wasn't willing to find myself in the position where it was shown once on British TV, then sat in the archive forever and a day. I wanted to create some legacy from the journey and have access to my own story.

Tim Chevallier was my cameraman through much of the Africa Solo ride. He is a legend in the business, with a real passion for film-making and a love of adventure. We got on brilliantly; I will always remember meeting him in Kimberley in the north of South Africa where he had just driven from Cape Town. Everyone was expecting me to finish in another five days, and without hesitation he said, 'You're going to finish in four days,' and I smiled. How did he know my plan? Sleep less, ride more. We finished in four days, with Tim boundlessly enthusiastic, filming the sprint finish.

Tim connected me with MoonSport, a South African production company and offshoot company to Moonlighting, who are responsible for tons of films shot in Africa including *The Crown*, *Homeland* and *Invictus*. Trent Key runs MoonSport and his father Philip owns Moonlighting, and he happened to be on business in Italy during January. Without any hesitation Philip flew over to Spain, came to the hotel, and we met over dinner to discuss how MoonSport would take the 80 Days to a global audience. The whole tone of the conversation was so different to anything I'd experienced with British production companies – there was no discussion about 'if and when', it was immediately all about 'how'. They saw this as a massive calling card for their capability in sports broadcasting. It also soon became clear to me that it would be a lot more affordable to hire a media crew in South African rand than the British pound, which would help my budget, theoretical as it still was.

For my final days in Spain, quite by coincidence, Rob Wainwright and some of his cycling buddies came out and joined me, and it was great to have the company. They had this novel notion of cycling hard over a mountain pass and then stopping for a coffee and a spot of lunch while soaking up the sunshine. Stopping wasn't something I had practised so far, so those final days in Spain were far more sociable and a bit of a wind-down from the long, inclement miles in the middle.

On my penultimate night, I asked Rach and James if we could drive out and meet a guy called Aleks Kashefi, who was running the length of Europe barefoot. On my last UK talk tour I had heard about Aleks when I was in his hometown of Buxton, so got him onstage for ten minutes to introduce this unsung madman to his local audience. I gave him the proceeds from the book sales that evening and the next morning he pinged me a photo of the plane tickets to Norway he had just bought! I loved the lunacy and tenacity of the man. At the time he had recently run Land's End to John O'Groats barefoot.

When we found Aleks in a town about 100km from Calpe, he was in a bit of a state. He had been putting in massive miles through southern France and northern Spain to reach me before I flew home, and the night before had slept out in appalling conditions; everything was drenched and his phone was broken. Aleks also smelt like a man who had just had his first shower in weeks, then put back on his dirty clothes. Rach and James seemed quite bemused by this bearded, fragrant, shoeless wildman, but I took a lot from our conversation. In the face of insecurities and setbacks, and feeling like I was an outlier with mad plans, it was cathartic to spend a few hours in the company of someone who didn't think what I was doing was out of the ordinary.

Training hard and feeling like I was eating like a mouse was hard to maintain. I am 6ft 3in and naturally over 90kg, and having done so many sports over my life I have muscles that road cyclists simply don't need. My regular conversations with Ruth and the performance team were about cutting weight and increasing my power-to-weight ratio. Soon after returning from Spain I went to Stirling University for a DEXA scan, a full-body X-ray showing absolutely everything from bone density to intra-muscular fat. Rather than the good old skin fold test, there is no guesswork with the detailed numbers on a DEXA scan. I had a total body fat of 9 per cent, and all conversations about losing more weight stopped. While not quite Tour de France skinny, I was 88kg with 9 per cent body fat, and departing Paris with less wouldn't leave me with much to lose, either in the overall battle of attrition or in case of illness. The only way to lose more weight was to lose more muscle, which was happening anyway: my arms and chest, built up in the past through rowing and gym training, were starting to look comparatively scrawny.

As a fifteen-year-old, had I been able to catch a ball and had I had the interest, my natural build could have been developed into a rugby player. The most common remark when I meet cycle fans is 'you're bigger than I thought'. And indeed if I was naturally 10 or 15kg lighter, it would help a lot, but I'm not, and on balance perhaps being a big chap has made me more resilient to injury. You wouldn't design an ultra endurance racer to look like me; then again, I don't feel my size has worked against me.

While the team were busying themselves with preparations for my next massive training ride, there were ongoing developments to the World attempt to attend to, especially leg 1 across eastern Europe. We had the ride worked out down to four-hour blocks, with flight times and every single movement of people and vehicles factored in. If anything changed in leg 1, a lot of admin would be required to sort out all the knock-on effects.

As the plan stood, we were heading to Minsk, the capital of Belarus, and crossing at Krasnoe into Russia. But it transpired that there was a certain degree of posturing going on between the Belarus and Russian governments. As part of David Scott's ongoing checks and risk assessments, this was now escalating into a point of real concern. The latest development was reports of issues concerning visa-free travel for EU citizens in Minsk. The situation was evolving fast, so we needed to find a plan B that allowed us to re-route and avoid any problems.

The official Russian line to the Foreign Office was that UK citizens were no longer permitted to cross the border at Krasnoe. David sought clarification in writing from the Russian consulate to see if concessions for exceptional circumstances were permitted. But given the political nature of these developments he felt it was unlikely, and even then a concession in writing wouldn't assist us should the political situation deteriorate, and we could end up being re-routed south, with a substantial time implication and the risk of having to backtrack, which could break the Guinness World Record rules.

After much research and debate, the new plan was to re-route from Poland to Moscow via Lithuania and the Latvian border post with Russia at Zilupe. This was a distance of 1,750km which would add approximately 150km to my route, the equivalent of about six hours' ride time. This option would involve only one non-Schengen frontier, which would save time with border crossings, whereas if we re-routed south to avoid the Belarus issue, going via Ukraine to the Russia border at Veselivka, it would add slightly more kilometres to the route and involve two non-Schengen border crossings. This latter option was flatter, so possibly faster to ride, but a border that sees fewer EU vehicles and is close to the military zone in eastern Ukraine made it seem slower and so less favourable.

While this was going on spring arrived, and it was time to tell the world about the ride. Throughout 2016 and early 2017 there had been a lot of speculation online about what my next big plan was. It was obvious from my training and media silence that there was something major in the making but I'd asked everyone I was working with to be incredibly careful about who they told. I really wanted to keep the 80 Days dream under wraps. There were no non-disclosure agreements so if someone had spilt the beans there was little I could have done about it, but everyone did well to keep a lid on things despite the furious networking for sponsors.

On Sunday 2 April, working with the team at Muckle Media, I went public, going to London for a day of press before the story hit newsstands on the Monday morning. We first announced the plans on the red sofa of *BBC Breakfast*. Knowing how averse the BBC are to showing sponsors' names, I decided not to try and walk into Broadcasting House in normal clothes and then change into cycle kit, as they would just ask me to change back. Instead I walked through security and into the green room in my full lycras and road shoes at 6.30 a.m., which raised a few eyebrows. But no one was bold enough to say anything, so I got away with it. Luckily the presenter that morning was Louise Minchin, who is a UK age-group triathlete, and she had a huge interest in my plans. Off-air we carried on chatting, with me giving her tips for training. The sponsors, especially Artemis, were delighted with such prime-time branding.

As expected, the reaction in the press and online was considerable. The comments on forums and social media were a mixture of excitement and awe, but also inevitably some questioning. Overall, though, I was delighted; there was little negativity, very few naysayers. I don't think anyone was surprised that I was going back to take on the World again, but the 80 Days was a target that captured the imagination, got people talking and definitely divided opinion over what was possible.

While the 80 Days plan would be played out with sports science and hard-nosed pragmatism, the dream was a romantic one. I have grown up being continually inspired and enthralled by the history of British endeavour. In my days of ocean rowing, my favourite statistic was that, of the five-hundred-odd folk who had rowed an ocean at that time, about 350 of them were British. We Scots, British, however I may identify, live on a small island on the western fringe of the Eurasia landmass, and yet have always punched disproportionately hard in exploration and adventure. I have always been confused by why, within the small world of endurance cycling, Americans, other Europeans and indeed everyone else (with a few notable exceptions) are happy to race each other in continent-wide rides like RAAM, but leave it to Brits to race each other around the world.

In line with this romantic notion, I wanted to give a nod to the history of the 80 Days and in some way tie my attempt to Phileas Fogg's journey. Jules Verne's *Le Tour du Monde en Quatre-Vingts Jours* (if revision is needed) tells the fictional story of this rich British gent and his French valet Passepartout, who set out on a £20,000 wager to travel around the world in fewer than eighty days. The wager was set by friends at the Reform Club, 104 Pall Mall, one of London's original private members' clubs.

In modern money this wager is worth over £2 million, and I had early aspirations to try and raise this sum for charity. That would still be a wonderful legacy from the 80 Days, but I had to adjust these ambitions downwards as my time and focus became consumed with the race.

As is the way of these things, knocking on the front door rarely works, and it was from an initial introduction by Penny Dain from the London Marathon, through David Fox Pitt, that we were put in touch with Ian Kenworthy, the Reform's acting club secretary, who met our enquiry with caution. I now understand that the Reform Club is a very private place that does not crave publicity. In fact when I first visited, in February 2016, I quickly realized that I wasn't the first person with the idea of tying an Around the World in 80 Days adventure to the club. I have never held such a hushed meeting. Ian had an air that was both reverent and noncommittal, leaving me feeling that this wasn't a place to sell an idea, instead it was about getting to know and trust. Then Ian showed me around the incredible 1840s building and the vast library that runs through most of the rooms. I set myself the challenge of trying to get my own books included in the collection.

Michael Palin famously finished his *Around the World in 80 Days* documentary on the Reform Club steps having not been allowed to enter the building. It made for a memorable end to his journey – a series I had watched as a child – but I now discovered that this was a sore point, that the members felt this was a TV construct at the expense of the club. I'm sure someone knows the truth of this matter – whether or not the club was informed about the BBC's plans – but I understood that incidents like this had made them cautious of the media and that their priority was their members.

Over the months I built a relationship with the Reform Club. I committed to giving one of my first talks after Around the World in 80 Days to the members, and was allowed back to take photos on the front steps, although I think the portraits on the walls would come to life and revolt if a man in lycra were to enter the main hall. Nothing less than a shirt and tie, young man!

5

Keep the Water to Your Left

I needed a few weeks at 80 Days pace to really consolidate all my training – to physically adapt to the task that lay ahead and, more than that, to give my crew confidence in the plan. The only time I had ridden more than sixteen hours back-to-back was when I cycled the North Coast 500-mile route non-stop, completing it in thirty-seven hours. And that definitively had not been sustainable: it was a ride to oblivion, which took a good few days to recover from.

The Great Tour was an amateur cycle race around the entire coast-line of Britain, organized by the same team behind the Tour of Britain, and which I was asked to support on some stages a few years ago. The Great Tour took a couple of months to make its way around the intricate coastline of England, Wales and Scotland, and this gave me the idea for my training ride – a 3,000-mile route from London, clockwise, back to the start in about a fortnight. I planned to leave at the end of March, but after research and a few winter weather warnings we decided to push this back until after the clocks sprang forward, to early April, in the hope of slightly more daylight and spring-like conditions.

The purpose of the Warm-up to the World: Around Britain, as we called it, was clearly defined in our team manual: to train and test myself and the bike, to train and test the support team and all the support systems that had been designed, and lastly as a publicity stunt – a home-soil event to capture the imagination, to create earned media value from the moment that plans for the Artemis World Cycle: Around the World in 80 Days hit the newspapers. I would set out the very next morning, Tuesday 4 April, for my race around Britain.

The team had now grown, with team leaders for each leg of the World (of which there were four), and within each team a mechanic, drivers, cooks and general able bodies. On the Around Britain there would be a lot of people on the road, and they would have to rotate out pretty quickly so that everyone could build the experience they would need. But the main focus during January to March had been the World, so the detailed planning for Around Britain was not as thorough, the assumption being that routing and communications would be easier on the whole as we were on home soil.

The official world record for cycling around Britain was held by Nick Sanders (who also set the original Guinness World Record for cycling around the world, in 1981) in a time of 22 days, covering 4,800 miles. I contacted Guinness World Records to check this, but it is one of those records that they have archived and no longer verify. So for a number of reasons I ditched the idea of doing a like-for-like ride. Firstly it seemed unfair to go for and claim a world record that was no longer verified, and I felt that following every tiny C-road on the very edge of Britain, adding over 1,000 miles to our total, was not conducive to the sort of long, steady tempo riding that I was training for: 240 miles a day, sixteen hours in the saddle. There was also consensus that we should keep the focus for a world record on the 80 Days, rather than confusing matters with a world record for Britain. It was simply a training ride.

While I was doing my media rounds in London, the team had been camped out for a few days near Gravesend in Kent, about 20 miles to my east, across the Thames estuary from Tilbury in Essex, where I planned to finish my coastal jaunt. I felt completely removed from this beehive of activity, the packing, team training, first aid preparations and sorting of communications and mapping. Late on the Monday I drove out and found them in a field with an excited air of anticipation and purpose – a million miles from the soundbites and posing for photos I had left behind.

There were team members I had never met before, old friends I hadn't seen for ages, crew I had only been to meetings with, all of whom were sitting around enjoying a team stew, a moment of calm as the sun went down and it got pretty cold. After the food, everyone returned to their tasks, Mike Griffiths sorting the Garmins, Alex Glasgow tinkering with the bikes with another young mechanic, Leven Brown and David Scott packing the RVs – everyone busy. I felt like a spare part. It was strange to have nothing to do. Everyone was busy on my behalf and without my direction. What had I created? I stood back and watched.

We were staying in a very basic local inn. Perhaps I was spoilt by recent memories of the Chesterfield, the four-star hotel in Mayfair I had been staying in, but we would have enjoyed more luxury in the RVs. And I did not sleep well, very aware of the 3.30 a.m. start. But everyone was in the same mood, mentally switched on and ready before the alarms went off, and we were up and out in minutes.

For years now, to start my day on expeditions I had been taking Cherry Active mixed into home-made smoothies as an antioxidant. Another option for dietary nitrates is Beet Active, and this was part of my morning supplement list. Unbeknown to Laura I had never tried it before, and she gave it to me to down the shot. I did, and it was pretty vile tasting, but presumably good for me.

As we drove in the RV to the start point, Laura handed me a bowl of muesli and yoghurt, which I started before the first wave of nausea hit me. Leven, an old friend from ocean rowing days, was driving and I sat in the back, trying to look out of the windscreen into the dark, to compensate for everything else in sight moving. All eyes were on me, or so I felt, and I really didn't want to make a fuss. This was all about proving the plan. Everyone was here to support me and I had to step up and be strong.

'You're going to have to stop!' I said as Leven swung around another roundabout or took a sharp corner – who knows, as I was now staring at my feet. I just made it out of the side door before vomiting into the verge.

Still feeling awful but under control, I lasted as far as Gravesend, where it was starting to rain steadily as I made a sharp exit from the pool of streetlamps and walked over an embankment, searching for solitude to be sick again.

It was shortly after 4 a.m. when in unceremonial fashion I saddled up and rode off. I wasn't thinking about cycling over 3,000 miles around Britain, I was focused entirely on not being sick, on how awful I felt and on just breathing deeply and enjoying the cool pattering of rain in the darkness as I pedalled through the sleeping suburbs.

After a few miles I spotted a cyclist up ahead. Here was another nutter out cycling in the early hours! More than that, as Alan came alongside and started chatting, I understood that he was here to see me, and excited by the prospect of riding. I couldn't have wished for a better welcome. What a wonderful effort to come and ride at 4.30 a.m. as I set out around the coastline. I tried to forget about the nausea and get stuck into a pre-dawn ramble through Kent.

Alan was a soldier and keen roadie, training for the upcoming Transcontinental, the annual self-supported bike race across Europe. Just five days before, the event founder, Mike Hall, had died after being struck by a car while racing the IndiPac in Australia. The shock in the endurance cycling community was felt deeply and his tragic accident had been raised quite a lot by the press surrounding my launch. For Alan and the Transcontinental riders there was also uncertainty about whether the official event would go ahead. But already there was a stoic resolve that they would ride regardless, in Mike's memory. The hashtag #bemoremike was already growing in solidarity online – a fitting legacy. As Alan and I rode through that dreich dawn, we had a respectful and poignant conversation about why we ride our bikes, why we ride endurance.

Keep the water to your left. The theory is simple, yet the coastline of Britain contains a labyrinth of options. It was complicated by the fact that I could weave through suburbia a lot more efficiently than our two large camper-vans, which we called the Follow Vehicle (FV) and Media Vehicle (MV), especially once the world had woken up. The map of southeast England looks green enough, yet the allure of the coast means that a gazillion houses and a surprising amount of industry skirt this part of the country. In fact it felt like I barely left towns all day. Perhaps a few miles inland the roads would have been quieter, but the flow of my chosen route was constantly obstructed by traffic or traffic lights, by the big hills between Dover and Folkestone, or by hopping on and off the promenade and cycle paths through Hastings and Brighton. However the excitement and fresh legs of day 1 meant solid progress and by lunchtime I could even stomach some food. We all started to laugh about the Beet Active incident, which Laura has been teased relentlessly about ever since.

In my jersey pocket I had a tiny GPS tracker, 110×40×20mm, made by Helen and Bill Cussen at Trident Sensors, which weighed just 63g; it pinged every ten minutes so anyone could look online and see my exact location. Compare this to a decade ago, when they built me a cutting-edge tracking unit that weighed 500g. And throughout the day a surprising number of people came out and rode sections; other well-wishers shouted from the roadside, and even the regular sound of car horns I chose to translate as support. The level of public awareness amazed me, making this ride already feel like a victory lap before I had achieved anything. Even my support crew who had supported RAAM riders were unused to such attention and seemed to be enjoying it. There was a buzz of excitement as the months of planning finally came to fruition.

Late in the afternoon, a big team of riders from Wiggle came out and rode with me to their HQ near Portsmouth, so I could stop worrying about my route and enjoy the peloton. As I wasn't riding under the rules of the circumnavigation yet, when other cyclists would never be allowed in front of me, I was quite happy to sit on the wheels of riders, getting a slight rest, chatting away, which certainly made the miles pass quickly. The added thrill of a motorbike cameraman and more press made for an exciting ride, and in Portsmouth there was a huge inflatable finish line, a big welcome party and even a pizza van dishing out delicious free slices. It was a festival atmosphere and I was easily distracted from the discipline of the day.

After stopping for twenty minutes, and with the light starting to fade, Laura reminded me that we still had a good way to ride and I said my goodbyes and set off with the support of one of the Wiggle riders, heading for the New Forest National Park. It was so much harder to ride now, yet nothing had really changed; it was purely the mindset of stopping, being distracted, and then having to restart and refocus. It affects your momentum.

At 9.30 p.m., after clocking just over the target 240 miles despite the stop-start nature of the day, we pulled off the road on to a track, and promptly got lost. I was left in the dark as the Follow Vehicle tried to find the Media Vehicle, which had been sent ahead to set up camp. There were numerous tracks, and a total breakdown in communication. It was a valuable lesson – exactly why we were doing this training ride. After sixteen hours' riding the race was still on to eat, wash and sleep as quickly as possible. Losing valuable time finding each other and a camp spot was not acceptable. This was the kind of detail that couldn't be worked out in a planning meeting. Mistakes needed to be made now so they wouldn't happen on the World.

It was a late finish, gone 11 p.m. by the time I switched off the light and set my phone alarm for 3.30. There was the tired but excited chatter after a first day. The scale of each day, the massive miles and logistics, was hitting home, but also a sense of relief that we were finally on the road.

It was a rude amount of sleep. An ungodly hour to wake up. Nothing really happens at 3.30 in the morning.

Most people could attempt a day like this, fresh-legged and motivated by the monumental mile. But on day 2 the excitement lessens a little; you start tired with heavy legs. Day 3 even more so, and so on. You have been through the routine enough times and the novel absurdity starts to become normal. That's the real test, when the excitement fades and long before the light at the end of the tunnel appears. How do you find motivation because of what you are doing, instead of being motivated by the thought that it'll soon be over?

Day 2 was all about navigation and not making mistakes. We had placed too much trust in technology, which soon had me discovering the lanes and then dirt tracks of Dorset. Blindly following my Garmin, with no back-up mapping or awareness of route choices, soon had me taking serious climbs just inland from a flatter, faster route. I could put this all down to training, but a situation like this during the World would be a disaster. Not least because I was soon far from my support vehicles with no supplies, as we opted for the seat-of-our-pants 'just go through there, we'll go around' school of navigation. The stress levels rose alarmingly, showing the pressure everyone felt to get things right, already compounded by being tired and cooped up in the RVs all day. Keeping everyone calm was going to be tough. I realized that

while I set the tone in terms of seriousness and focus, I didn't want to
be seen as the leader on the road, so it was for Mike, Leven and David,
all in charge of stages of Around Britain, to make sure the mood in
camp was a positive one.

We lost a ton of time and miles on tiny roads, trying to find Devon.
We also realized the limitations of mobile phones. If communicating
was this tricky in the UK, where would that leave us in Mongolia? The
simple answer was that I couldn't be left alone – support meant full
support. Cycling up and down lanes looking for phone coverage would
really not help my chances of getting Around the World in 80 Days.

It was becoming abundantly clear that if any one thing went wrong
in any given day, causing a delay, then reaching 240 miles, let alone
making it an average distance within sixteen hours, was nearly impossible. If I had my wheels turning in the right direction for every minute
of the sixteen hours, then 15mph was not an ambitious target. But if I
lost any time at all, this average speed had to quickly escalate to make
up the miles and unless I was on flat roads with a tailwind, I couldn't
sustain such a pace without risking injury.

We made a disappointing 219 miles in a day that boasted just shy of
5,000m of climbing. The following day would entail even more, as the
southwest served up the toughest climbs around the UK's coastline.
In comparison, there would be nothing close to 5,000m climbing in a
single day on the 18,000-mile World route. Every effort had been
made to find the flattest possible roads around the globe.

We stopped just past Truro after another sociable day, with a lot of
well-wishers through Exeter and Plymouth, but the mood in camp
was subdued. We had lost miles mainly because of what happened off
the bike, as opposed to on it.

Laura was in the best spirits though as she was home in Cornwall
and had her family turn out in force to wave us by just before dark,
one relative in a tweed flat cap with a cardboard sign reading PROPER
JOB MARK, and in small brackets underneath HAPPY LATE BIRTHDAY
LAURA! Better still, her Aunty Marie provided a basket of pasties for
everyone's dinner.

Day 3 started with the aim of reaching Land's End in the first four-
hour block and it was a stunning crisp dawn ride past Penzance and

then down the winding road by the Minack Theatre, probably the
favourite place I have ever spoken at. The terraced seating is cut out
of the cliffs, and the backdrop to the stage is the English Channel.
Facing an open-air theatre, the audience wrapped in rugs and sipping
hot beverages, without the crutch of a screen to show photos and
video, it was adventure storytelling at its best.

I daydreamed, my mind starting to unwind after the intensity and
expectation of the first two days. After the stress of not covering 240
miles on day 2, my main emotion was 'oh well, it happened, move on,
keep it consistent'. This mental shift allowed me to appreciate the world
around me a bit more, to realize that this 'wee training ride' was a heck
of an adventure in itself, and worth savouring. The constant reaction and
support from well-wishers on the road was definitely helping me step
back and stop taking this quite so seriously. Just before dawn, a postman
came out to ride 5 miles with me before racing home to start his round.
We swapped stories as we headed west and the day woke up around us.

Land's End has tried very hard to make itself more than simply the
most southwesterly point on mainland Britain, but at that early hour
the coach park was empty, the toilets locked, and more importantly
there was no coffee on offer. There were people milling around, the
daily cohort of Land's End to John O'Groats travellers getting their
start-line photos. I stopped on the narrow road to allow a group of
cyclists to be filmed for their big moment without spoiling the shot,
before doing the same myself – the mandatory photo-call of sponsors'
banners at the first iconic location on the ride.

More impressively, another LEJOG starter was on foot, with a well-
decaled van in support as he aimed to run the 1,000 miles. As I rode
back down the road I had just come in on, passing the runner and the
cyclists, it occurred to me, rather obviously, that I was also about to do
Land's End to John O'Groats, albeit via the coastline of England, Wales
and Scotland. The last time I had completed this route, from top to toe,
I was fifteen years old, with Mum and Dad driving our Peugeot 406 in
support.

I turned off the main A30 and on to the smaller roads around the
north coast of Cornwall towards St Ives, enjoying the openness and
emptiness of the west coast, relieved to be on a northerly tack.

The north coast of Cornwall and then Devon are excused their unrelenting climbs because of their rugged beauty. It was an utterly leg-sapping day, with brief respites as I returned to sea level through towns like Barnstaple. I pedalled along for a few hours with a local greenkeeper, and he told me he had followed my adventures over the years and his bike had saved him from depression. His story took me out of my bubble; I was reminded of the wider impact, the unquantifiable value of sharing the journey. This was perhaps the most selfish endeavour of my career, it was all about me going far and fast, and yet it was such fuel to the fire to hear how others also felt it was important, that it gave confidence and perspective to their own ambitions.

A local rugby-playing lad then joined for a longer stretch and kicked on every hill, burning me off, then waited patiently at the top, talking on his phone. Time and time again. There was no malice in this, but the not-so-subtle oneupmanship got a bit wearing, and I made a point of not mentioning it. Perhaps it was genuine training for him, but for me, when in the hurt locker, trying to keep it steady, I didn't need anyone to keep reminding me how lead-legged I was.

If the morning was a rollercoaster, the afternoon was a comedy of terrain. If we hadn't laughed, as a team, we would have found it rather upsetting. It wasn't a day to worry about making the miles; it was a day about committing to doing the hours, about not getting off the bike. It was a lesson in how long-term averages work, in putting in the same effort on the toughest days as when it's flat and fast. The Exmoor National Park packs a serious punch and finishes with a climb that tops out over 17 per cent.

The Follow Vehicle had ignored the numerous signs stating NOT SUITABLE FOR LARGE VEHICLES, or words to that effect, so as not to lose me as it had on day 2. This led to them crawling back down to sea level several times and having to stop to let the brakes cool off. The B3234 Lynmouth Hill has sections which are 1 in 4, making it one of the steepest classified roads in the UK. I stopped at the bottom, to check I was going the right way, looking at the wall of a road in front of me. As I was midway up, out of the saddle, rhythmically rocking the bike, calves crying, the RV crawled past in a low gear, engine protesting loudly, wafts of burnt clutch assailing my nostrils. The road flattened out slightly towards the top just as Nicci called, so I turned a corner to find a concerned Mike and Laura, who'd stopped to check I was OK only to see me happily spin past chatting on Facetime. Mike's look of disbelief made me laugh.

The reward was another climb over Kipscombe Hill, gradually up and up, with the grassy verge disappearing steeply down to the white horses crashing ashore a long way below. The emptiness was beautiful, just me and the road as the sun slowly set, framing the horizon in a dramatic red. Near the top I found the team standing on the edge of the drop-off, snapping photos and waving me by.

Two hundred watts was the magic number; any day that averaged over that I considered as going into the red. It sounds suitably pedestrian, until you try it for sixteen hours. That day, and many that followed up the west coast of Britain, comfortably topped this; but if I could easily do it in the moment, afterwards I paid for it. Little niggles crept into my knees and ankles, aches in the morning that told me I had overcooked it the day before.

After two massive days of climbing my arms also felt pretty stripped. We had some custom-made compression sleeves and decided to give them a go while I slept to aid recovery. I was used to pulling on incredibly tight knee-high compression socks each night but hadn't used the sleeves yet. This seemed the perfect opportunity. Except I woke a few hours later with my left hand in a lot of pain, filled with fluid and blood, fingers like sausages. Laura had not been there to oversee this, letting another physiotherapist get experience supporting me. She knew my heart rate dropped a lot in sleep, and so compression on my arms was ill advised. The pain from the pressure was unlike anything I had felt before and I ripped the sleeves off, gently massaging my hands to try and drain the swelling. From then on the small fingers on my left hand never really recovered and stayed swollen and sore for the rest of the ride. A self-inflicted injury, but looking on the bright side, better to learn this lesson now rather than on the World.

In contrast to Devon and Cornwall, day 4 was the flattest day yet, as we completed the dogleg east to Bristol, across the Severn Bridge and then west along the south coast of Wales through Cardiff and Swansea to finish near St David's.

An old friend, Rob Pendleton, came out early doors to ride through Bristol, which was sociable but slow. Rob used to be the marketing director for LDC, one of my longest-standing supporters. When I first pitched sponsorship to their CEO in 2007 he quickly agreed, much to my surprise, and left me in the room with a slightly less enthusiastic Rob, who had somehow to work this into his marketing plans. We have had a lot of fun over the decade since, racing Pro-Am races in the Alps, taking a team from LDC from Land's End to John O'Groats, and most memorably completing London to Paris in twenty-four hours, a mammoth undertaking for a cohort of office dwellers.

Midway across the Severn Bridge, having waved Rob off home, I met another Rob – Rob Lutter – whom I had followed for years on social media as he pedalled around the world; he had cycled out and was waiting on the apex of the bridge, knowing it was the only point of the day where I couldn't take another route and so miss him. Just into Wales a local pro team mechanic rocked up, and the socializing continued. I was grateful for the distraction though as I was hurting despite the relative lack of hills.

And yet, despite the recovery-ride nature of the route, we covered only 220 miles, fewer than on day 3. It was another reminder that terrain, road quality and headwinds all mattered, but that the biggest factor in covering the miles was getting the hours in. What we could control was worth obsessing about, but worrying about what we couldn't affect was futile. We weaved slowly through the lanes and cycle tracks of Bristol and then stop-started through the towns of south Wales, so that my ride time was well under fifteen hours, at a slower average on these busier roads, despite being on the go from 4 a.m. until 9.30 p.m. as planned. The discipline was the detail. Losing an hour's ride time was so easy, and that meant losing 15 to 20 miles. Doing those extra miles seemed almost impossible within sixteen hours, based on our experience over the first four days of Around Britain, and it was a constant reminder of how ambitious and difficult the 240 average would be on the World.

6

Heading for Home

Mike dropped out in Cardiff – we would see him again in the north of Scotland – as it was important that he allowed others to step up and show their leadership. Almost every day there were crew changes, and at times we would have up to ten people on the road as everyone tried to get up to speed.

My legs felt stripped and I was experiencing pain in my neck that was becoming difficult to bear. I knew this first week would be about letting the body adapt, building the conditioning, but taking on the southwest so early on was not kind, and I was suffering more than I had expected. Laura strapped my shoulders to try and take the strain off my neck and also lightly strapped my right knee, which was protesting after the relentless climbs.

The graveyard shift at the start of day 5 through the Pembrokeshire Coast National Park was empty and eerie, through thick, freezing fog. I passed barely any houses, no cars for hours. My buff was over my mouth and nose, and my toes and fingers protested as they gradually cooled until they were numb.

As the day became light, and warmed slightly, I discovered a landscape of traditional farmsteads and little ports, beaches, bays and sea cliffs, a part of Britain I knew nothing about. There was a simple target for the day, to clear the entire length of Wales, and I was rewarded into the afternoon with a stunning clear day as we skirted Snowdonia National Park.

Mid-afternoon I was joined by a young chap called James, who put my efforts into perspective, having left his student home in Cardiff that morning long before dawn in order to find me. He was wearing cycling shorts and a jersey, no leggings, no thick base layers. I had nothing to complain about, as James recounted his tale of having to stop pre-dawn and buy a newspaper to stuff down his front to insulate himself against the same freezing fog I had come through. His family home was on the Lleyn peninsula, to the west of Snowdonia, and he had ridden well over 200 miles to join me and was in high spirits. Racing on at one point, I thought he had left without saying goodbye, but he found me again half an hour later, brandishing a clutch of Calippo ice lollies to share. What simple bliss.

We pedalled on to the peninsula and were soon joined by his brother, and the three of us rode past their house and back on to the road north towards Bangor. Near Caernarfon, Tommo, an RAF mechanic based in Anglesey, rocked up on his heavy mountain bike, but thanks to a cracking tailwind we sped along at a good pace, enjoying the flatlands of northern Wales after another day that had topped 4,000m of climbing. Home for Tommo was Norfolk and as he waved me off he shouted he would see me again for a few miles next week when I was coming back down the other side of Britain!

As it got dark we crossed the Menai Bridge on to Anglesey and started a clockwise loop of this windswept island, making camp by Llanfaelog.

The prevailing wind normally sweeps across the UK from the southwest and over the coming days this would grow steadily from the light breeze that saw me cruising through Snowdonia in glorious sunshine to a fully-fledged storm by the time I was midway up Scotland, causing gale-force wintry conditions and the cancellation of ferries. In contrast the flatlands of the A55 in north Wales on day 6 were time-trialling heaven – until Her Majesty's finest took exception and redirected me on to B-roads. I genuinely hadn't seen any signs saying NO CYCLING, but they were not amused. It was our second conversation with the law: the South Devon constabulary had also taken exception to the Follow Vehicle giving me protection on a busy stretch of road. This was all part of the learning curve; conversations with officials were going to happen, and they'd probably not be so simply resolved in countries like Russia.

Out of the relative wilderness of Wales and into Liverpool, Preston, Blackpool and Lancaster – I was in a busy corner of our island and once again lost the RVs. I could see from the WhatsApp chatter that came through on my watch that this was causing rising stress, but as long as I didn't have a puncture or breakdown I was distracted enough by the constant company and lively conversations.

I would spot a group of cyclists waiting on the road up ahead, and they would join me. After a week of this, I knew the routine: names, 'Can I join you?', a few pleasantries about the day and the weather, as per the British way, then typically people would talk about their longest bike rides, their greatest adventures, their dreams. Perhaps this observation is blindingly obvious, but it keeps you grounded. While people had come out to meet me, what many really wanted to do was tell me about themselves. That didn't bother me at all, I reflected when I was left alone towards the end of the day; the lens that many people saw my journeys through was often how it made them feel about their own ambitions. A few people took the other approach and treated the ride as a rolling Q&A, which I could sustain only for a while before starting to use my own questions as a form of defence! Normal conversations were more enjoyable than feeling like I was hosting a private event.

I mention this as I was often mulling over how better to share the 80 Days story with a global audience in a way that focused on the endurance, the teamwork and the excitement of the race as opposed to becoming a selfie storyboard. On social media I have become disillusioned with professional athletes and adventurers who constantly make the centre of the story themselves, rather than the engagement with what they are doing. It is not an easy perspective to get when you are essentially promoting what you are doing, but it boils down to the simple question 'Why should other people care?' – which rarely elicits the same answer as 'Why do I care?'

In terms of storytelling done well, I was enjoying following Alex Thomson in the around-the-world yacht race the Vendée Globe – here was a team managing to engage an audience outside their sport. I don't have any real affinity with sailing, yet the story he was sharing and the epic nature of his challenge was captivating. It was about him, but without ego, focusing on the race and the elements.

My other observation was that when people rode with me, whether for 10 miles or 100 miles, they experienced the same psychological journey as me – they started fresh and enthusiastic, they dug deep and went quieter in the middle, then showed relief at the end. The difference was that my daily psychological journey lasted sixteen hours. When they gave me the 'phew, that's me done, that was tough' I often had to have a word with myself to keep it steady, and not lose focus.

Laura was becoming a bit concerned about the amount of company on the road, not from a road safety position – she trusted me on that – but from the perspective of my mindset. It was a wonderful show of support, but I spent a lot of each day distracted, in conversation with members of the public, rather than thinking about the team, the plans, the miles. This was a hard balance to strike, as I certainly didn't want to be rude. But this time Around Britain was so precious as a means to learn all we could.

A big late push up into Cumbria meant that we did clear 240 miles for only the second time, and we found a beautiful camping ground by Ulverston. At least the excited owners told me it was beautiful, and I believed them as I dashed into the RV out of the dark, the cold and the gentle rain. When I met people like this I was always acutely aware of how frantic I must seem. Holidaymakers had approached me over the past few days – attracted by the liveried RVs and serious race set-up, and with time on their hands for a leisurely chat – but I was becoming good at delegating these conversations to the crew as I kept busy, counting every moment off the saddle for food, treatment and recovery. The only time I had for leisurely chats was on the bike. We must have always seemed very serious, but I just couldn't bring myself to stand around and chat. Apart from the feeling of always being behind the miles, I felt that if I stopped I would find it hard to get going again, so it was necessary and best to keep busy.

A week in, the 3.30 a.m. starts were becoming normal, but never easy, especially when stepping out of the warm RV on to frozen roads. But on day 7 a mate, Bruce Duncan, joined me from the off. Bruce, who lives in Kendal, is a former top-flight adventure racer and I rode the early miles with a down climbing jacket on, appreciating the familiar company. It was a particularly dark start in rural, tree-lined countryside. Bruce was more honest than other members of the public and just kept muttering how unpleasant it was to be out riding in the freezing cold at such a ridiculous hour. I was grateful for the banter, but jealous of the hot breakfast he kept talking about, and he turned for home around 7 a.m. I cracked on alone, refocusing on the next big milestone: home to Scotland.

After sailing north to the border near Gretna Green, it was a tough left tack into Dumfries and Galloway, towards Stranraer, into the full force of the wind blowing off the Irish Sea. It made for a very slow afternoon, albeit in stunning scenery, firstly inland through rolling dairy pastures, then dropping down to the bleak coastline, the marshlands and grassy dunes on the north side of the Solway Firth.

The following morning I turned north again around first light and pedalled past the Trump Turnberry golf course, wondering how business was faring, and was soon met by a peloton of riders up past Ayr to the Gourock Ferry, including my cousin Ramsay and a friend, Mike Kennedy, who was part of the team that first set the Cairo to Cape Town world record.

Physically I was starting to show unexpected side effects from the cold and wet. My left hand, especially the smaller fingers, was swollen painfully, making the fingers difficult to bend and hard to fit into gloves. It became a two-person job to put them on, and we had already resorted to trying latex glove liners, gardening glove-overs, climbing mitts, whatever it took, as none of our cycling glove options could keep out hour after hour of freezing rain. Tubs of talc were employed to tend puffy hands and feet that resembled wrinkled prunes. My right hand wasn't as bad, but the signs were also there of an injury.

It was a wonderful surprise to see Mum, who had driven across Scotland with her Rhodesian ridgeback, Neo, to find us, albeit for a matter of moments as the ferry was already loading when we rolled in. Her main concern was to meet my media team, MoonSport's Johnny Swanepoel and Helmut Scherz, as reports were reaching her about how tired they were. She wanted to suss out how they were coping, looking after their vehicle, staying safe.

If all went well it would be only three days until I was over the top of Scotland and back down the east coast, where we would pass near

Una's house in Fife. We raced straight on to the ferry for the short hop over the Firth of Clyde. I immediately relaxed in familiar territory, enjoying revisiting one of my favourite parts of Scotland. This adventure coast is incredible, and I immediately relished the quieter roads, still on the mainland but cut off from Scotland's central belt by having such an elaborate coastline – hence the ferry link.

A steep up-and-over through dense forests to the next ferry, across Loch Fyne from Portavadie to Tarbert, had me out of the saddle, legs aching, but even if this had been flat, making the next ferry would have been a time-trialling effort – and so for the first time in eight days, when I reached the end of the road I was forced to stop and wait, which felt very strange indeed. Home-made cakes from a lady called Helen Dick and a complimentary lunch in Portavadie made the team feel very welcome in Argyll, and Laura used the time to fit in treatment.

Sheltering from the weather inside the ferry port café, I must have made for a strange sight lying on the floor as Laura worked on my shoulders, neck and legs. My legs were painful when they were being treated, but weren't grumbling too much on the bike, whereas my neck pain was constant – but I'd been expecting this, and only hoped that as the weeks passed my body would adapt to the position. After eight hours sitting in an office chair, most people feel a bit stiff and round-shouldered; try doubling that on a bike, every day. The body was allowed to protest.

From Tarbert on the Kintyre peninsula it was headlong into the wind on tiny roads to Kilberry for a few hours, and I was counting down the miles until I could turn north, and pretty much double my speed. After rejoining the main west coastal road past Lochgilphead, the storm broke out and I was soon riding in freezing rain. I wished it was a few degrees colder so it would turn to snow, which would be much easier to bear.

Darkness came earlier than usual and it was a bitter final shift in the battering wind and rain. We set our sights on Oban, but doing so meant riding late. The payoff would be not starting again until 8 a.m., when the ferry left Oban for the Isle of Mull, so I focused on the very happy thought of seven hours' sleep to distract myself from the biting temperature. My hands were so cold that I couldn't really feel my fingers, so I was very careful on the brakes. At least my core was warm and dry.

A few hours from the finish, a car drove past, with a bike on the roof. It turned past me again, but I paid scant attention, lost in the world of my front light and the hammering rain on the road. Then a few minutes later I found a guy waiting eagerly at the roadside. I took a few seconds to take it in. He was wearing cycle shorts but had bare legs and no overshoes. He had on a decent-looking waterproof jacket but what looked like builders' gloves. And he was absurdly happy, in contrast to my deep grump.

'I was sitting at home having dinner, with the wind and rain battering off the window, watching your tracker on the phone,' he shouted over the storm, 'and I turned to my wife and said, "Let's go and find Mark."'

Steven Groom was a local joiner and had just started cycling a few years ago – and all credit to his wife who patiently drove with us in some of the most atrocious conditions I have ever ridden in. Steven seemed utterly oblivious, despite being woefully underdressed, ridiculously content to be out riding his bike. What a gent.

We parted from him on the outskirts of Oban and camped nearby. My left hand was not looking pretty, the capillaries on the back of a few fingers starting to burst from the inside. There was weakness there anyway from a couple of road-rash scars, the result of a crash the year before, coincidentally on Mull. But this scar tissue was now swollen, bloody and painful. Fingers seemed an unlikely injury from too much cycling.

I certainly felt renewed by the luxury of day 9's 7 a.m. alarm call. Rather than the usual scramble for the bike I had a ferry crossing, during which I slept some more. Inevitably my legs protested sharply when I did start riding; they had assumed the torment was over.

A stunning route lay ahead, across Mull and over to the remote Ardnamurchan peninsula, then east before heading due north to the Mallaig ferry to the Isle of Skye, back on to the mainland by the Kyle of Lochalsh bridge, around Loch Carron, and past the Applecross peninsula to Torridon and beyond. You couldn't devise a more beautiful day on the bike anywhere on the planet. I may be biased, of course.

Thankfully the start was a pretty flat spin to the main town on Mull of Tobermory, which cannot be said for the rest of the island, so I was glad to be skipping straight on to the Kilchoan ferry and back to the mainland, after another wait. It would be a low mileage day, what with missing the first four-hour block and with two more ferries, but it managed to stack up to well over 3,000m of climbing in a paltry 166 miles.

The Ardnamurchan peninsula was seriously windy again, unfortunately coming off the mainland for a change, so I was delighted when some riders from Fort William cycling club found me and we could take turns. We were averaging about 250 watts for hours on end, which was not sensible, but any less and we would stop in those conditions. More seriously, news reached my team that the ferry to Skye was off due to the stormy conditions, which meant a detour inland. Half an hour later, the next update was that a serious crash on the inland route had closed the road, meaning a detour of about 60 miles up Loch Ness, nearly as far as Inverness (on the east coast) and then back across.

I resigned myself to this, which meant going headlong into the weather for the rest of the day. Alex Glasgow, my mechanic for stage 1 of the journey, had other ideas, however, as well as good local knowledge. He had been with us for the first few days and then gone home, but would soon be joining us in Inverness for the rest of Around Britain. He scrambled a private boat charter, which we got news of just in time as we stopped briefly at a junction to decide if we would carry on east or risk it in the hope the ferries would resume. If we got to Mallaig and there were no boats, it was a U-turn and back south 40 miles to this junction – an 80-mile detour.

The small charter boat trip to Skye was an adventure, first handing the bike and kit down the vertical ladder on the side of the harbour, then holding on to our seats for a seriously rock-and-roll crossing. The local crew seemed unfazed – it was just another day on the west coast for them – but for us landlubbers it was the most exciting thing that had happened that day. As we carted our kit up the concrete landing ramp the rain and wind were lashing, and I dashed into a phone box to enjoy a brief respite as the team sorted kit. One of the RVs was now hightailing it across the north of Scotland and back, while the other waited for the ferry to restart. So Laura had grabbed the emergency medical bag and some bags of kit and Helmut the cameraman had joined her, trying to keep his kit free from salt. From here they would be bundled into Alex's Skoda until we could regroup with the RVs. It was all fantastic training for the team: so many logistics to sort, so many patches of no signal.

A seventeen-year-old lad called Fin Graham was waiting for me with his dad Drew, who had driven down from near Dingwall, 100 miles away. I didn't know Fin and have to admit I was concerned he had come all this way. He had all the kit, but he was young and I could see he had something going on with his legs; one was abnormally thin and covered up. I needn't have worried because Fin is one very able and determined rider. He was born with two club feet and has no muscles on his left calf, but bike riding was his passion, and that July, as I pedalled furiously across Russia, Fin took gold in the British Championship road race for his category of disability, and has his sights firmly set on the 2020 Paralympics in Tokyo. He stayed with me for about 60 tough miles and at last light, when I paused at the roadside to throw on a thick jacket, I could tell he was cold and very tired, so he called it a day. But it had been a stoic ride and I had enjoyed his company. With no real training facilities in the Highlands he was used to making weekly trips to the Glasgow velodrome – a 400-mile round trip. I loved his spirit, and the support of his parents; he reminded me of my own travels as a teenager.

The ride across Skye had been glorious as the rain stopped and the road dried. Once again I had more company, a local lady who like so many had moved to the area for the very obvious reason of its stunning scenery, and she gave me a running commentary on everything we came across. I then crossed back to the mainland and on to roads I knew well. At one point we passed Alex's family on the roadside, including his one-year-old daughter, waving enthusiastically (he lives in a house that he built himself, in the sleepy village of Plockton).

The road for the next few days would follow the route of the North Coast 500. In 2015, shortly after getting back from breaking the Cairo to Cape Town world record, I cycled the NC500 non-stop to set a record and create some publicity for the new route. I had first heard about this lap from Inverness around the north of Scotland when I was training with the Scottish development squad at the Sir Chris Hoy velodrome in Glasgow. They were brainstorming doing a training week on it. I asked to speak to the organizer and we devised a plan which meant starting at 6 a.m. at Inverness Castle on a Monday morning and finishing around 8 p.m. on the Tuesday evening. It is still my longest non-stop ride at 520 miles. I was quite looking forward to seeing some of the Caithness stretch in the light this time.

The imposing grandeur of the Torridon mountains was lost in the darkness as the road swung inland, but conditions improved and I flew along in the dark, listening to the burr of rolling over cattle grids at speed and navigating the odd sheep, determined to reach the end of the glen at Kinlochewe.

There was a buoyant relief but real weariness from Leven, David and Johnny, who had made the long trip east because of a crash that had closed the Fort William road. Both vehicles met in a lay-by shortly after the turn-off and we called it a day.

7

A Pain or an Injury?

By the end of our tenth day we reached John O'Groats, and so nearly cracked the magic 240. However, 240 miles in everyone's mind was no longer a realistic average; it had become the far-off horizon of success, an almost unattainable finish line each day that we strove for but had only managed twice so far. Another way of putting it was that in ten days we had made it across the bottom of Britain, up the left-hand side and along the top – a very respectable milestone, including Land's End to John O'Groats in eight days, via Anglesey!

Sutherland is hard to beat. Caithness tries but the west wins with views over the Summer Isles, the dome of Stac Pollaidh and the sheer wilderness from Ullapool to Durness. Alan Picken, a keen cyclocross rider whom I had ridden with before, was holidaying with his family and joined me for a long stint which went well until he stopped to investigate a wobble. The rear triangle on his carbon frame had completely snapped; I'd never seen such a major break without the impact of a crash. This was not a stretch of road you could walk home from, and he jumped in the FV.

The schedule had been gruelling for all the crew, but it was toughest for the media boys Johnny and Helmut. Over the months of developing plans with the MoonSport team in Cape Town, they had insisted that in order for the media team to do the job properly they would need the autonomy of going off and filming cultural stories and landscapes, plus the freedom to drive ahead and park up to do the editing and sending back of data. Being within the support vehicles didn't give them this flexibility. But the reality on the road was that

Johnny and Helmut had to drive themselves, film and photograph – by hand and by drone – and then when everyone else was grabbing their precious five hours' sleep they were still awake, editing. They could never get far enough ahead each day to edit without missing important milestones.

I grew hugely frustrated that they seemed to be flying by the seat of their pants, reacting to whatever happened rather than knowing what lay ahead. For example they had missed my crossing into Scotland. You could hardly blame them, being a South African and a German trying to get to grips with British roads, but there were a lot of lessons for the World. We needed a much better plan for their filming and better support for their safety. That said, the content they were creating was brilliant and I could see it was managing to share the story every day online in a way I had never done before. They were both very talented cameramen, Johnny more on the stills and editing, Helmut on the footage and drone, but I felt they lacked a director on the road, or at least a solid storyboard to work off.

Johnny in particular was heading for zombie mode with the schedule, which is why their safety on the road was becoming a concern. They also seemed to spend a lot of their time lost and trying to find us. Joking aside, they had in fact nearly driven off the road; there were conflicting reports about this, but the side of their van was badly bashed in. They blamed a soft verge, but the amount of damage suggested a bigger impact, and there was a serious team conflab about the wisdom of their driving while over-tired and possibly falling asleep at the wheel. Mike Griffiths, who rejoined us at the top of Scotland, took charge of this situation and started helping with their driving.

In terms of looks Johnny is somewhere between a surfer and a rocker, heavily tattooed with big rings on his fingers and a love of beanie hats and black hoodies, which he wore with the hood up for a lot of Britain. You could mistake Johnny for the hardman, but in fact he is a very sensitive guy, quick to smile, always so keen to please everyone, and always working.

Helmut is a wiry-looking German, just a few days younger than me, who had gone to South Africa to film the football World Cup and never gone home. His English is perfect, but he let Johnny take the lead in conversations, so he was hard to get to know. He flew the drone with the precision of a fighter pilot, normally with a fag hanging out the corner of his mouth, wearing an expression of deep concentration. He had a healthy disregard for the rules if they stood in the way of progress, but when he did speak it was always to the point, so in that sense at least reassuringly German.

We have done well to come this far without talking about bums. The hope was that I would spend most of each day in the tri-bars, leaning forward, dynamic, more aerodynamic and putting less weight directly on to the saddle. Admittedly, when you rotate forward in the saddle your weight is going through a smaller area, so you can get other types of pressure sores building up. However, with the near constant hills on the west coast of Britain I had been sitting upright almost all the time, hands on the brake lugs. This also wasn't helping the numbness in my hands, as many of the nerves in your hands meet in the fleshy pad at the base of your thumb and then the ulnar nerve wraps up the length of your arm, into your shoulder, meaning my hand numbing and neck pain were directly related.

Laura and everyone in the team with knowledge about bike performance were worried about this, wanting to see me in a more efficient position on the bike, concerned that I couldn't hold the time-trial position for long hours. I was still confident the issue was the terrain, as opposed to the bike fit or my flexibility. But the consequence of how I had been riding, upright, was that my backside was seriously painful. And the catalyst for taking this from a bearable pain to a rawness that was hard to endure was my being nearly constantly wet because of the rain.

While camped at John O'Groats (a very bleak spot in the night-time – only the lights on the horizon twinkling from Orkney remind you that you are not at the very edge of the world), the suggestion was made to pull on a second pair of bib shorts as an extra layer of padding. I'd never thought about doing this before, and once over the odd sensation of wearing a nappy, the comfort on the bike was wonderful. In fact it was revolutionary, and on day 11 I pedalled southwards far happier, enjoying the flatter roads of the east coast and so being able to find the time-trial position more often. Double shorts seemed like a great solution. But it turned out to be a serious mistake.

The wider lesson learnt over the coming days was not so much about clothing, it was about spotting more quickly when things go wrong. Any little niggles, any changes in form needed to be noted and analysed before they became a big problem. Laura in particular was very mindful of how difficult it was continuously to be objective and analytical in her role as performance manager, especially when tired, and when so focused on fairly mundane routines. The team needed to maintain the ability to step away from the coal face and constantly ask questions such as 'Why has that happened?', 'What has changed?', 'What caused that?' Tiny issues can escalate very quickly under these levels of endurance, whether they be dynamics within the team or something practical with the athlete or the bike; we had to be able to self-monitor and keep tweaking the plan. Far easier said than done when you are caught up in the race.

Riding in the dark makes you very aware of the bike, how it sounds and feels. But I didn't need to be in tune to hear the rasping chain as I pedalled towards Wick at 5 a.m. Calling back to the FV, I asked if the young mechanic had put oil on the chain. 'Oh no, I was tired,' he replied. That answer lost him his job. Not because he had forgotten to do something – we are all human – but because it was an attitude that demonstrated he was more of a burden than a boon to the team. He was a brilliant mechanic, so this was not about technical ability; it was simply about attitude, about taking a level of ownership. We needed people who were more than their particular expertise, who had the ability to smile when the chips were down, to look out for each other, to have discipline and systems for their jobs, and who had enough life experience to know what Type 2 fun was.

As the days crept by, the reality had hit home for some of my crew – this wasn't as much fun, or the sort of fun, as it looked like on the telly. A few had become more and more withdrawn, looking after themselves and doing the bare minimum to get through each day. Rather than putting the team and challenge first, they'd grown to feel sorry for themselves and were an emotional burden for the rest of the team to carry. I had ridden fifteen hours in the rain the day before and this chap hadn't bothered to put oil on the chain. I couldn't be thinking for my crew, checking they had done their jobs, and I reacted angrily, giving him a blasting when we stopped. I then felt ashamed as it seemed a bit of an overreaction. Then again small mistakes would easily cost us the 80 Days and we had no room for passengers.

The big dipper of the Berriedale Braes was the only real test on the first 120 miles to Inverness, which was a windy (if that fact isn't becoming inevitable) but dry morning's ride. There was almost constant company and much faster miles as I headed east around the coastline towards Aberdeen, which I hoped to reach by the end of the day. Some of the cycle clubs had come out in force and I was relayed from one group to the next, from Nairn to Elgin and then on the prettier B-roads to Fraserburgh. We ended disappointingly short of Aberdeen, at the old fishing port of Peterhead.

It was hard to imagine being back where we had started in just over three days' time, but the east coast of Britain is an altogether more straightforward place to cycle than the west. It was also about 10°C warmer so far.

If there was going to be a busy day, it would be day 12, on my home patch down the east coast through Dundee and Edinburgh. Well-wishers and fellow cyclists were all very welcome, especially on the Arbroath to Dundee stretch to the Tay Bridge and the St Andrews to Queensferry stretch to the Forth Road Bridge, because of the afore-mentioned winds. Going east was easy, and in the latter part of the day through Edinburgh and racing to the English border by the end of play I was barrelling along.

The only concern, and it was a growing subject for conversation, was my right hamstring. Laura was treating this almost every time I was off the bike, trying to release a painful spot about halfway between my butt and my knee. That is such a deep muscle, and the painful bit was hard to reach. On the bike I tried to spin a higher cadence, avoiding putting too much power through the pedals. My greatest worry was developing some daft repetitive strain injury, which could end it all. When you are generally sore all the time, it's important to figure out the difference between pain and an injury.

It was also a day to thank a few sponsors en route – early doors stopping off in Aberdeen with the John Clark Motor Group, and then in my school town of Dundee for the team at Cardtronics – posing next to cars and cash machines . . . odd ways to break up the day. Best of all I got to stop and see the family at St Andrews. The girls, Harriet and Willa, thought that exploring the RVs and eating ice cream was the best thing that had happened all week. After a quick cuddle we raced on. I thought about them a lot on the bike, and was sad only to have had a few moments. But ironically, Nicci and I had probably had longer conversations in the past fortnight than for years when I was at home: with such long hours on the bike, I actually had time to talk properly, albeit on the hands-free and only when the wind was behind me.

Late in the evening we passed Berwick upon Tweed, and to close off a very sociable day with dozens of cyclists and roadside supporters I heard and then saw in the darkness a lone piper standing by the roadside. A teenage lad, Euan Walker, had driven out with his parents in full-kilted regalia to cheer us by. What a wonderful departure from Scotland. I was humbled and blown away by the sometimes hundreds of people each day who wanted to come out and be a part of the ride.

I raced on from the border but we soon called it a day, parking in an industrial estate, which was far from ideal as an overnight spot. It is hard to go for a pee without feeling criminal under the watchful eye of security cameras.

At 3.30 a.m. I woke up feeling pretty wretched, and I tried not to think about sustaining a routine like this for over two months. In fact for the first half hour of every day I tried not to think too much. It was in those first moments that I felt most fragile, least capable, so it was best simply not to dwell on anything, certainly not to allow my mind to wander and contemplate the scale of the task. I always wondered what it would feel like to finally snap, not to have the mental willpower to carry on. I don't think I would even know if I was getting close to this actually happening, no longer being in control or being able to bully myself into more suffering. Because the deeper you go, the more you suffer and the less cognitive and objective you are. So I assume by the time you actually lose self-control, really lose the ability to go on, you're no longer yourself in any real sense. I reasoned that as long as I could keep having a bemused laugh at the absurdity of each situation I wasn't close to being lost in that type of situation.

I'm asked all the time if I ever consider giving up. And the answer is doggedly simple. No. But I am scared of failing.

Back to the old elephant in the room . . . and this was a fact I was definitely not thinking about at 3.30 a.m. We hadn't hit 240 miles again, and this elusive number was again feeling like an unattainable horizon. Nobody in the team expected to reach it any more when we set out each morning, and that in itself was a big problem. In that industrial estate I did all I could do and got busy with simple routines, as usual. Throwing on my thick down jacket, I stepped into the cold dark car park.

'Morning, Mark! Are you ready?'

A man was stood there, on his bike, ready to go. A moment before, Leven had popped in to forewarn me.

'Good morning,' I managed. 'You are keen. I'll be riding at four – keep warm.'

And I trundled off for some privacy.

It was a day of two distinct halves, the morning straightforward and rolling through Newcastle and Sunderland, the afternoon an unexpected battle across the North York Moors National Park and then to the Humber. We made camp as a band of very wet and weary travellers in suburbia, at odds with the scantily dressed night life on the street a few hundred metres away. As a Glasgow alumnus I'm used to out-of-season attempts to wear as little as possible, but these Yorkshire folk seemed to have taken it to the next level – an Ibiza bikini party on a cold, wet wintry night. Perhaps our distinctly middle-aged comments on this spectacle were designed to distract ourselves from the tension in camp. One of the RVs had been driven under a low bridge which had caused some damage, despite warnings to follow another route. Between that, the now multiple dings on the Media Vehicle and a side locker being tied on to my Follow Vehicle, our travelling circus was showing serious wear and tear after just thirteen days.

The chap who had driven out with his girlfriend at 2 a.m. from Newcastle to find me in that industrial estate car park had made the graveyard shift interesting. It was easy to forget we had a GPS tracker on us all the time. He struck me as a gentle man who had needed the sheer escape of the bike over the years to deal with what sounded like an unfair series of life events. I rode fairly quietly – I didn't have the energy to be hugely sociable. But I didn't need to because he shared and shared, as people often do. It's a surprising side of riding a bike: people feel like they really know me and can tell me their most personal stories. At 5, 6, 7 a.m. in the dark and cold I tapped along, wondering if there was a market for 'pedalling psychologists', a service to help people cope with life by sharing their problems from the comfort of a bicycle seat. I hope this reflection is not oversharing on his part; he was such an enthusiastic fan and I could tell how much it meant to him to ride those lonely hours into Newcastle together. For the last hour he was struggling a bit but he was determined to stick with me until the Tyne crossing.

Even the most coastal road through Yorkshire is brutal – all credit to those hardy locals. It makes my Scottish hills seem gentle, albeit grander. By mid-morning I had another buddy, a lanky, very able rider who had to remind me that we had met before. The London Marathon is the only organized marathon I have ever run, despite having completed the distance many times. Like most novice runners I set off in a wave of enthusiasm and was pulled along in the stream of people at a completely unsustainable pace. In fact I ran perfect reverse splits, so my first mile was my fastest and my last was by far my slowest. I ran a half marathon in under an hour and a half, then finished in three and a half hours, in absolute bits.

When you finish the London Marathon there is still a long way to go for those in as much pain as I was. The metal barriers carry on for hundreds of metres, eventually reaching the public by Trafalgar Square, but the charity I was running for had a welcome party, food and massage station about 400m away. I, rather pathetically, couldn't face the walk and in a stroke of genius spotted a rickshaw which I flagged down.

'Could you please, um, take me, um, over there?'

If there was any moment when anonymity was my wish, this was it. I thought I had got away with it, for a brief moment, but my cycling chauffeur turned to me and asked, 'Are you Mark Beaumont?' We ended up sitting in that rickshaw for ages outside the charity hub, chatting about all his adventures – how he had read *The Man Who Cycled the World* and soon after set out to cycle from London to New Zealand, where he had stayed for a long time, setting up a rickshaw business there.

This was James, now living in Yorkshire with his girlfriend and no longer riding rickshaws but showing his strength on the hills from years of lumping passengers around London and Auckland. He was welcome company, and I also didn't mind the distraction as my right hamstring was getting very painful. The hills obviously didn't help, but I felt it was just the sheer hours of repetitive strain that were niggling away, gradually worsening the problem. I was painfully slow on the hills, and mentally in a real slump as the day wore on. Despite the battle, and mainly thanks to the effortlessly cruisy start, we so nearly cracked 240, but not quite, and we were still a long way from making it a comfortable average.

Thankfully day 14 was as flat as the British coastline gets, through Lincolnshire and Norfolk. Tommo, the RAF mechanic who had buddied me across north Wales, came back out as promised, as well as a nine-year-old lad called Thomas, and many more. But we were soon receiving several annoyed comments from well-wishers who were waiting on the coastal road. I was making such painfully slow progress that we decided to cut inland in the afternoon on the faster roads through Norwich rather than stick with the tiny touristy roads. We hadn't advertised my route on purpose so we weren't committed to a particular destination, but people made fair assumptions that I would always be on the most coastal road, and I felt bad for letting them down.

It was Laura, as always, who reminded me that our core purpose was to train, not to entertain the public. And I was made acutely aware of how badly I was now cycling when a teenage lad joined me for a few hours. He didn't just drop me on the hills, he was dawdling to stick with me, though he was too polite to say anything. All the while I was experiencing a great deal of discomfort. My right leg was full of an acute, deep pain, right at the back, in the fattest bit of my thigh. It felt like someone was stabbing a knitting needle through the muscle.

'Take those second bib shorts off,' Laura suggested. It was mid-afternoon. Because of the saddle sores and wet conditions, I had been enjoying the double bib shorts ever since John O'Groats.

Off they came, I pedalled onwards, and immediately my right leg was spinning lighter. The pain was still there but it was no longer acute.

What an idiot. I berated myself all afternoon. Laura did the same, for being so focused on treating the problem that we hadn't stepped back from the situation and asked what had caused it to start with. We should have been asking what we had changed that could have caused an injury. I reflected, with the glory of hindsight, that it was surprising on the endlessly hilly west coast of Britain that I hadn't had any niggles or muscle injury, then down the relatively flat east coast this hamstring injury had suddenly appeared. I should have known my conditioning was robust enough for my muscles not to start failing – it was us who had done this. By wearing two sets of bib shorts, an extra tight band had formed around the hamstring and the compression had caused the muscle to tear. Back in Edinburgh weeks later, an ultrasound imaging scan by Dr Andrew Murray would show the extent of the damage we had done.

We finished the day on the coast northeast of Ipswich, with fewer than 100 miles to the finish. A lap of Britain in just over fourteen days. It would have been easy to lie in, start after daylight and complete the ride in the early afternoon, but everyone was keen to keep the discipline: up at 3.30, on the bike at 4, and get this done. Around Britain had been a lot tougher than I had imagined. I think it surprised most of us.

The final day's route was southwest through Colchester and Maldon to a far from iconic finish line at Tilbury Docks, across the Thames from where I had started. While only six hours of riding, this was a real test in route-setting for the team. At one point I found myself on a very busy dual carriageway with lorries thundering close by. It was no place for a cyclist and I pulled the plug for the first time. Jumping in the RV as quickly as possible, we backtracked to the last junction and found quieter roads. Yet again, this wouldn't be allowed on the World, but it was too dangerous to carry on here. I could see how hard the team were working trying to scout ahead, think ahead.

Our route had often changed from the planned one during Around Britain, and we had learnt as early as day 2 not to trust the suggested cycling routes, so we realized that the World route now needed a new level of detailed checks. We knew the overall topography, but every road needed checking to make sure bicycles were allowed, every rural stretch needed checking to make sure it wasn't a dirt track, and every junction needed checking through every town.

At around 10 a.m. I swung around the final few roundabouts, spotted the flags of the port and gingerly steered the bike on to a narrow metal bridge down to the water's edge. There, waiting and cheering, were the crew, Nicci and the girls. It was a huge bloody relief. Wonderful to stop. I was gaunt and shattered. Handshakes, hugs and smiles all around, everyone on top form.

But that was only the warm-up. That was a fortnight's cycling. We had averaged 225 miles a day, and I was injured. I would have been unable to carry on another day.

8

A Simple Plan

Seventy-five days' riding at 240 miles a day, three days of flights and two days' contingency.

It was, as I said, a simple plan.

Paris to Beijing was leg 1; Perth to Brisbane and then Invercargill to Auckland was leg 2; Anchorage to Halifax was leg 3; and then leg 4 was from Lisbon via Madrid to Paris. This 'sprint finish' was still a lot further than John O'Groats to Land's End, but on a world map it looked like a Sunday ride compared to the proportions of Russia, Australia and Canada.

After Around Britain we had ten weeks until Paris. If truth be told, I felt battered and looked terrible. For the first few weeks I didn't ride at all. Every focus was on repairing my hamstring. It had stopped getting worse the moment I stopped wearing double shorts, but the damage was already done and when I stopped riding, it seized up and I was left limping. Not an impressive entrance to sponsorship meetings. My left hand also slowly reduced in size, although my wedding ring wouldn't fit back on for another six months. Both these injuries were hard to deal with during Around Britain and very painful, but ultimately self-inflicted. And both needed rest before they would repair.

In theory I now had the necessary fitness and conditioning. In terms of the long-term training plan, Around Britain was the final test, and everything from then on was about maintenance. Apart from the obvious issues, Laura's main concern was to get me into a time-trial position more, and, for me to be able to do this for long

We live on a very hilly island! Final training ride, London to London, around the coastline of Britain – 3,200 miles in just over fourteen days, suffering with nerve damage and from the cold through my arms, as well as a tear in my right hamstring.

Above: The official sign-off from David Scott at 4 a.m., 2 July 2017, Arc de Triomphe, Paris.

Right: Averaging a country a day for six days through Europe.

Below: Uncertainty about how to get through Moscow.

Above: Organizing kit before the change of vehicles at the Russian border.

Above: Laura, Tony, Alex, David and Mike on stage 1a, through Europe.

Above: Settling into the routine of riding sixteen hours every day, starting at 4 a.m.

Below: David Scott getting to work digging the RV out of the mud.

Left and below: Laura (physio) with the help of Alex (bike mechanic) rebuild my broken tooth.

Left: Strapping the fractured elbow from crashing on day 9.

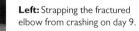

Left and above: Crossing the Asia–Europe divide and dealing with the daily deluge in Russia.

Above: Overnight camp by the spooky house in Latvia.

Below: After seventeen days across Russia, the scenery opens up towards Mongolia.

Above: The near constant trucks and tough roads of Russia.

Above: Taking Shelley, a cut-out of the Blue Peter tortoise, so children could follow the adventure.

Right: A makeshift mud guard for very wet conditions.

Below: The wilderness and utter expanse of the Mongolian steppe.

Above: The Mongolian Cycling Federation put the word out to support us.

Above: Getting stuck in the Gobi Desert.

Below: With my stage 1 team, not including the media boys, being presented with a traditional Mongolian blessing.

hours, to work on my core. At least this was something physical that I could focus on while not being able to ride.

The block programme is what we called the mega spreadsheet for the World. It showed the comings and goings of each team member, each vehicle and flight for every four-hour block of the 18,000 miles. Creating this had been a mammoth task for Mike Griffiths, and it had taken months, distilling a year's worth of research by Phil Mestecky, bringing in his experience of the practicalities of a bike race, and poring over minute details on Strava and Google mapping to figure out all the moving parts. Alongside this was the flight matrix created by Mike's colleague Jo Craig, as the transits between continents would be crucial in terms of saving time. The overall route and each airport had been chosen to give the most flexibility in terms of flight options per day and result in the least amount of transit time – but understanding all these options meant tackling a confusing amount of information. Assisted by Alex at Wexas Travel, who has run my travel logistics ever since my first pedal around the planet, we had all this information at our fingertips long before the race started.

While the block programme was the hymn sheet that everyone needed to sing from and work off, I stressed with the team that we were not riding to a set location each day, that we were not to be obsessed by the 240. The overview was needed for big-picture planning, but our focus day-to-day was to control those few things we could actually affect. Ride time, sleep time, calories and hydration – those four pillars were inputs, not outputs. If we did them right, consistently, then for the same inputs we would go 200 miles one day and 240 miles the next, because of the myriad of factors we could not affect such as wind, road quality and border crossings. I wanted to make sure everyone understood not to change the effort level, not to change the mood in camp regardless of how far we went each day. We just needed to trust the block programme, then get busy controlling the inputs. Conversely, if our happiness and motivation were dictated by the magic 240 then on days when we smashed it complacency could start to creep in, and likewise if we couldn't reach it we would feel demoralized.

The realization off the back of Around Britain was that every detail needed to be reviewed, and everything that could be decided upon and planned before we started had to be. We all now understood how limited our ability was on the road, not only due to sleep deprivation, but because of the incessant need to be moving. It was difficult for the team in the vehicles to work on anything that wasn't immediately in front of them. The team leaders had their work cut out being able to maintain the necessary overview.

We also had some difficult decisions to make with regard to team selection. For example, Leven was initially in charge of leg 2, but it became clear that his main work on his boatyard and supporting ocean expeditions was going to lead to a tricky balance with the responsibilities of leading a 4,500-mile stretch of riding on the other side of the world. I trusted Leven more than anyone to smile when the chips were down, to be the ultimate worker bee and get the job done, but I didn't have the assurances from the rest of the team that he had the capacity to lead and fully detail the logistics of leg 2. It was the right decision, albeit a very tough one, to find another team leader. Leven seemed completely onboard with this, and perhaps relieved.

A few others who had the necessary skillset but simply hadn't shown the right level of grit and accountability also left the project.

Tony Humphreys, who had been Laura's shore manager during her Pacific row, stepped in to lead leg 2 at very short notice. Another sea-lover, he had little experience of bike races but did have more availability to get stuck into the detail.

At the same time, off the back of mistakes made by everyone during Around Britain, we put a lot of pressure on David Scott, team leader for leg 1, to come back with very detailed plans and contingencies for how we would navigate the roads and possible bureaucracy of Russia, Mongolia and China. David, accustomed to running his own expeditions, obviously wasn't so used to having to report at a weekly planning meeting under such scrutiny.

David had a unique skillset within the team, as leg 1 was the one part of the World attempt where we had cultural unknowns. In Australia, New Zealand and North America it would be a straight bike race, but the different languages and culture, as well as fear of police interest in the race and the filming, made leg 1 somewhat unpredictable for the rest of the team. David, as Honorary Consul for Mongolia in Scotland, had the network to make things happen, as well as the cultural awareness of how to operate on foreign soil in this area of the world. My only concern was that he would be so focused on diplomatic relations and border crossings that he would miss the details of the day-to-day bike race. There was no point in him providing the diplomatic red carpet through Russia (in particular) if he couldn't grasp the details of what made the bike go faster.

From the start in Paris we would have all three team leaders with us – Tony Humphreys hadn't been on Around Britain so needed to learn the ropes, and Mike Griffiths as Logistics Manager wanted to see all his plans put into action and was needed as David Scott would only be with us until Hannover in Germany, from where he would fly forward to prep the Russian team. The western European part of leg 1, which we called leg 1a, through France, Belgium, Holland, Germany, Poland, Latvia and Lithuania, would be fast and exciting, seven countries in less than a week. It would allow all of the team leaders to share best practice.

David would carry on in charge from the Russian border, allowing Mike and Tony to return the RVs used for leg 1a to London, as he had informed us that taking vehicles with UK number-plates into Russia would be asking for police stops and delays. Using Russian vehicles and drivers created concerns about the language barrier and their reliability for working eighteen hours a day, but on balance gave us reassurance that we wouldn't be stopped. We would have in-country crew in Australia and New Zealand, too, who also hadn't been tested during Around Britain, but they were at least English-speaking. They had also come through Leven's trusted network.

One change to the overall plan was to leave Paris on the quietest day of the week, Sunday 2 July. Pushing back everything by a day caused a few headaches, but nothing close to the amusing, confusing and long-running conversations about how we would deal with time zones. Now, bear with me here.

Few people are aware, for instance, that Bristol is actually about ten minutes behind London. For simplicity's sake, it is lumped into the same time zone. Travelling nearly 1,000 miles every four days meant crossing a time zone in about the same time period. Doing nothing about this, assuming I could never compromise the sixteen hours' ride time, meant losing an hour's sleep, sometimes more, to compensate. We knew from Around Britain that if I and the crew dropped below four hours' sleep, our safety and performance were seriously affected. We committed to finding a better way to adjust.

As we raced eastbound, we would be catching the sun while it rose, progressing through time zones. When you are travelling overland you are catching the sun at a steady rate, shortening your day. The beauty of overland travel is that you don't normally experience jet lag, unless you push it to the extreme and are as sleep-deprived as we would be.

The geeky details are that 1° of longitude (the north/south lines around the world) at the equator is equivalent to 60 nautical miles (nm). These lines get closer together towards the poles, in contrast to lines of latitude (lines going horizontally around the world) which are parallel. Twenty-four hours is 1,440 minutes; divide by 360° and you find that 1° of arc around the planet is four minutes. One degree is 60nm (69 statute/land miles), so 240 cycling miles eastwards is approximately fourteen minutes' progress.

To add further complexity, I would be crossing Asia at roughly 50° north, where 1° is 40nm. I planned to ride 240 miles every day, which is 208nm. However, my route was never exactly eastbound, so a better approximation was 200nm due east per day, and 200nm at that latitude is 5°. This may seem counterintuitive, but time zones converge as you move away from the equator.

It became too complicated to work to the nearest minute, so we rounded up or down for each leg of the World.

We would experience time zones as follows:

- Leg 1 – Paris to Beijing, seven hours forward through six time zones.
- Leg 2 – Perth to Auckland, four hours forward through four time zones.
- Leg 3 – Anchorage to Halifax, five and a half hours forward through seven time zones.
- Leg 4 – Lisbon to Paris, one hour forward through two time zones.

So, over leg 1 we would go through six time-zone transitions, five of them of one hour each and one of them (east of Moscow) a two-hour leap. You can imagine the effect of sticking to local time and suddenly having just three hours' sleep.

My day would be made up of sixteen hours' riding, with half-hour breaks before and in between the four-hour blocks, with up to an hour at the end of the day, adding up to nineteen hours awake with five hours for sleep.

There was a period of conversation among the logistics team – mainly Mike and Alex, with Laura on the performance side – as to whether this adjustment per day should affect sleep time or ride time. The answer we settled on was neither, it had to come out of my break time during the day, so neither sleep nor ride time was ever affected.

Each day would start at 4 a.m., and at first break all watches would be moved back by a pre-determined time; for leg 1 this was fifteen minutes, for leg 2 it was ten minutes. So 'challenge time', or CT as it was always referred to on the vehicles' whiteboards, only rarely correlated with local time. Morning break was now shortened from half an hour to anywhere between ten and twenty minutes, depending on how far north or south of the equator I was.

So, if this explanation has baffled and confused you, all you need to know is that, roughly speaking, we would experience each day as only twenty-three hours and forty-five minutes.

The confusion that arises as you advance your way around the world of course formed the finale of the original *Around the World in 80 Days*, when Phileas Fogg thinks they have arrived late back to London but Passepartout, his French servant, figures out in the nick of time that they haven't. While you may feel like you have lived through an extra day as you work your way east, you have in fact lived slightly shorter days for eighty days, and that illusion of an extra day has disappeared in a blink of the International Date Line. Located in the mid-Pacific Ocean exactly halfway around the world from the prime meridian in Greenwich, it was established in 1852 but only formalized in 1884, so I have to confess it makes me even more baffled to work out how Jules Verne was able to make this the cliffhanger to his novel in 1873.

Suffice again to say that *many* hours of debate were caused by time zone confusion both before and during the ride!

May and June were a blur of activity. One of my great concerns, having experienced this build-up so many times before, was that the crew and I would arrive at the start line in Paris already tired. This is common in expeditions, given the excitement of packing, final training, the media circus and the emotions of leaving your family. When I pedalled out of Paris a decade earlier, I reached the outskirts near Charles de Gaulle airport and had to stop for a strong coffee because I was literally falling asleep on the bike. The adrenalin of the final week of preparation and the start had left me on the bike with 18,000 miles to pedal but feeling wiped out.

For the crew there was a swathe of final training courses – first aid, Di2 gearing and the full mechanics of the World bike, and a lot of familiarization with the IT, communications and data systems. If any one person got ill or dropped out, we needed others who knew how to cover their role.

In an ideal world the bike would remain untouched for the final few months so that I was utterly familiar and comfortable with it. In fact we were making tweaks and improvements until the last moments. I ended up riding out from Paris with a cockpit set-up (the drop-bars and tri-bars) on which I had done just one training ride.

KOGA, the top-end Dutch bicycle brand best known for trekking and e-bikes, have sponsored my ambitions since 2008, after my first pedal around the world. Pieter Jan Rijpstra from KOGA always makes a joke about how I had to buy my first World bike, albeit for a discount. But bike brands are bombarded with sponsorship requests and the answer is always no until you have actually proved yourself, built a story and value. Going on a big adventure in itself does not create value for bike brands, unless you can leverage that as a media story.

As a teenager I was a fan of the Saeco Estro cycle team, following the exploits of the charismatic Mario Cippolini, so I grew up dreaming of being a Cannondale bike rider. With the Artemis World Cycle I had created the Everest of endurance cycling stories and could have my pick of brands. But KOGA had never let me down, we had a decade of history, I was their main brand ambassador, and they are small enough to really care. So despite being flattered by the option to ride bigger brands, I realized I would be only one of hundreds of sponsored riders and be starting from scratch in terms of goodwill. The only downside for KOGA is that the UK is not a big market for them; it is pretty irrelevant having a brand ambassador who is Scottish. If only I was German, they often tell me, or at least German-speaking!

To launch the Artemis World Cycle bike I made a short trip to Amsterdam and appeared on *RTL Late Night*, their biggest live talk show, the *Graham Norton Show* of the Netherlands. There were six guests, myself included, and I was placed next to Rico Verhoeven, the world heavyweight kickboxing champion, trying to keep up to speed with a live conversation in Dutch as an American lady did simultaneous translations in my earpiece.

I had a great conversation with Rico afterwards about our commitment to training and the family sacrifices necessary to be your best, and we have followed each other's journeys since. Amid the months of hype and excitement I always take a lot from such moments, when I speak with someone who actually understands what it feels like to be in my shoes, as was the case with Aleks the barefoot runner. Perhaps it's hard to draw a comparison between a nomadic barefoot runner and the world heavyweight kickboxing champion, but trust me, they both have that same unbounded energy, that sense of purpose.

It took over a year to build that dream machine, which was an evolution of the Africa Solo bike. Going fully supported meant going lighter and more aerodynamic, so my position on the bike and wheel choice would be crucial. The frame was carbon, which is perhaps stiffer and less comfortable than titanium over such big miles but it is what I was most used to and trusted. It had bolt-through axles, an evolution taken from mountain bikes, making the ride even stiffer, as the forks and rear triangle barely flex. KOGA were given the colour palette from Artemis to work with, mainly blue and white, so I was surprised when their designers came back having chosen the colour of the Artemis coin, the company logo, making the frames a very striking bronze colour. The bike looked very bling, sleek and fast, even when motionless – a proper statement, which I was initially reticent about. In fact it was perfect – amid a peloton of race bikes it would still have stood out – it was just my reluctance to be so showy that I needed to get over.

We eventually opted to ride 47mm deep rim carbon wheels and for very windy days to have the option to swap for a lower-profile 32mm rim, a featherweight wheelset with just twenty spokes. For the helmet, riding with a visor rather than sunglasses felt like a marginal gain. Shoe covers would be worn whenever it wasn't too hot, to help airflow – all to lessen the effects of an 88kg body having the aerodynamics of a brick. The team from Altura took our feedback from Around Britain and made bib shorts with flatter seams and better foul-weather glove options. The colour tones of blue with white were switched around so that white was now the main colour for the 80 Days strip, with the idea that this would help in hot climates. It was also the tightest race fit I have ever worn, a skinsuit finish, which looked and felt fast. Now we just needed to fine-tune my connection with the bike.

The cockpit was changed because KOGA didn't want the brand I was using for Around Britain to be advertised on the bike. This was once again a commercial conversation impacting on performance, and Laura's aim was always to have everything tried out thoroughly, not to choose kit based on sponsorship. But the new brand, Profile Design, had a huge range, and we got busy finding a solution. The issue was finding a bar that gave my hands enough options. The three main positions were on the brake lugs, on the flats of the bars and stretched out on the tri-bars, but many tri-bar options meant giving up too much 'real estate' on the flats of the bars. So you need enough rise without compromising on the aero position.

It is relatively easy to find a saddle that is comfortable in one position, either in time-trial or a more upright road-riding position. Finding a saddle that has more than one comfortable position, where your hips can sit at about 60°, with weight on the middle part, but where you can also rotate forward to about 30°, without creating a pressure point where a man really doesn't want things to go numb, is tricky. Over the final year of training, two bike fitters had me trying a range of options, but I came back to what I knew, the Selle SMP Pro. With its broken nose, this odd-looking saddle is always a talking point, but saddles are a personal choice. None of my crew enjoyed riding this when they took the spare bikes for a spin.

When I first did a bike fit session on the new frame in the summer of 2016, it was quite distressing. I sat on the turbo trainer, rigged up with Velcro dots on each joint, with a pressure pad on my saddle, being monitored at every angle by the computer. The results showed considerable asymmetry and inefficiency. I went away disheartened, until I then went for a road spin and remembered that I was not a robot and knew how to ride a bike.

If the numbers and anecdotal feedback from that bike fit were to be believed, my back shape, hip angles, knee and ankle positions all needed to be changed. I did listen, I did adapt, and I did build my core strength – but I also changed my bike fitter to someone who had more endurance experience. We each have a unique physiology that needs to be taken into account when understanding the dynamic between a rider and the bike. I wasn't willing to accept that after cycling around the world, and top to bottom a couple of times, I now needed to learn how to ride a bike again.

So those final months of preparation became a huge juggling act, and when I couldn't sleep at night, overwhelmed by the scale and complexity of 18,000 miles in seventy-five days' riding, I reminded myself of the block programme, the daily routine and the simplicity of my job on the bike, and I relaxed. I actually couldn't wait to get started. I never did zoom out from imagining a single day. When I thought about a week or a month it was too scary, so I just thought about the smallest unit, the four-hour blocks, what any one day would be like.

A month before the start, we moved house. Not ideal timing. We had spent Nicci's maternity leave living in the rental house in Crieff, but it was not a good place to leave her and the children for months, away from friends and family. It had been a stop-gap, but while living in rural Perthshire was stunning, it was near to nowhere and meant 15,000-mile years of driving for me. We were only there because of Nicci's job, but her going back to work at the same time as I set off for the World seemed impossible, so she made the difficult decision to leave her job. We packed almost everything we owned into two shipping containers and moved into our tiny two-bedroom flat in Edinburgh, close to both our families and friends, with the city on her doorstep. It would be very cramped living, but the girls were young enough. The most often-used phrase in the Beaumont household was 'after the World'. Life could start again after the World – except none of my planning went that far. Whatever was going to happen after day 80, 19 September 2017, was a mystery.

On 20 June, I set out on my final 240-mile training ride. Visit Scotland had commissioned a series of short films to showcase my training and the What, Where, How and Why of my cycling. These themes took me through Perthshire, Fife, the Borders and Dumfries and Galloway, being filmed by Stefan Morrocco and Kieran Duncan. We had a lot of fun, but fitting in a long filming day in the final fortnight before the World once again wasn't ideal timing. This final hurrah across my home country was, however, a fitting finale to the years of build-up.

For this last ride, at 4 a.m. we left the ferry terminal over from the Isle of Gigha in Argyll and made our way through Loch Lomond National Park and then the Cairngorms National Park, a perfect 240 miles to Aberdeen. A glorious, clear, sunny day, it was my first long ride on the final set-up for the World bike. It felt fast and comfortable for most of the day. For Around Britain I had been riding a blue frame, which KOGA had made to look Scottish. In fact the dark colours did not stand out on camera in any landscape, whereas the new bright bronze and white bike was a bold statement. They had made seven of these frames, although I very much hoped we would only need a few. My signature was scrawled across the top tube, behind a neat logo for 'Artemis World Cycle 80 Days'. Another '80' was decaled in large font at the top of the fork. We had stamped the target on the bike; there was no plan B.

It was already light from the start at 4 a.m., and the sun was well up by the time I stopped briefly at the top of the iconic Rest and Be Thankful road and looked north. I felt relieved to be with my bike, in the sunshine, feeling that tingle of anticipation of a big day ahead. Everything else melted away, at least a little: the financial worries, the strained conversations, the juggling with my family. At this level, the task was incredibly simple – just ride. The day would be a real test for my injured hamstring. It felt strong, but only a long day would prove it. There were no back-to-back 240s planned for training, so today was the test.

On the west bank of Loch Lomond, the north shore of Loch Tay, and over the Mouilin Moor, I was thinking about the first 'long' road cycle I ever did at the age of ten, from our farm, over these 18 hilly miles to Pitlochry. The climb up from the Devil's Elbow to Glenshee would test any rider and the camera crew tracked gleefully alongside, relishing my discomfort, sweat stinging my eyes as I gently rocked the bike upwards to the ski station. From there, you are rewarded with the most glorious sweeping vista, following the Dee river gently downstream through Braemar and Ballater. If I sound giddy, I was. I was nostalgic about growing up here, about what the past twenty years had become, soaking up the full experience of home before taking on the World. We finished on the golf course overlooking Aberdeen as the sun dipped, but it never really gets dark that far north during summer solstice.

The reaction from Stefan, Kieran, Sam Weston from 80 Days and Carron Tobin – my film and support crew – was telling. It had been an epic day – but that was one day, one unit, and we had taken it on fresh-legged, well rested and with day 1 enthusiasm. I felt pretty good, considering. No discomfort from the right hamstring. My final tweaks would be to add comfort to handlebars and shoes – both hands and feet had been very painful towards the end. I blamed new custom-made insoles for the pressure sores under my cleats; they made it feel like I was riding on hot coals after more than twelve hours in the saddle.

From then it was just ten days until I flew to Paris, twelve until the start of the ride. My final week of training was all about acclimatizing to heat and getting rested, bolstering my immune system. I had three sessions in the heat chamber at Napier University under the watchful eye of Dr Lesley Ingram. By cranking the heat up to a very dry 35°C for sessions that lasted less than ninety minutes we could see how my body adapted quickly – a lower heart rate, sweating less. On my first session I dehydrated by 4kg; in my last, my weight remained the same, through adaptation and more regular, smaller sips of water.

So, Monday: heat chamber and travel clinic for final vaccinations; Tuesday: osteopath and stretching, core work; Wednesday: final training session, heat chamber and massage; Thursday: flying to Manchester for a live appearance on *Blue Peter* and lots more media interviews set up by my PR team; Friday: the 11.25 flight to Charles de Gaulle, where my team, who had all driven out, had been preparing for days with about enough supplies to start a bike shop, or more importantly to complete a month's expedition to Beijing.

Nicci and the girls had driven me to Edinburgh Airport on the Thursday morning and we had breakfast landside. It was a lovely moment to stop and enjoy being a family. There was absolutely no point in them coming out to see me before the end: 240 miles a day is not a fun road trip with a four- and a one-year-old. It wasn't the duration that worried Nicci – months on her own with the children is never easy, but we have done much longer trips – it was the intensity of what lay ahead. 'See you in Paris,' we said with forced smiles, and I set off through security. I was flying off for the World attempt with only a small carry-on bag.

On the other side of security, before reaching Duty Free, I stopped to have a look at my Africa Solo bike which was on a huge display stand, with three big screens telling the story of training in Scotland, adventures across Africa and the great work of Orkidstudio. Edinburgh Airport have supported my ambitions for years. This display is a big focal point, everyone who flies through the airport has to walk past it, and I amused myself by standing anonymously next to a group of businessmen who were talking about the bike, before carrying on to find a coffee.

The next day I flew out to Paris and walked out of arrivals to be met by Johnny Swanepoel and Helmut Scherz with cameras rolling. I then backtracked and walked out again, to get the right shot. Life on film for the coming few months. At least I had time to laugh about it now; once the race started, there would be no such second takes. Alex Glasgow was there too, bouncing with enthusiasm. Generally there was a jovial air of nervous energy.

I might have been the one who dreamt all this up and willed it to the start line, but I now watched with satisfaction as everything happened in spite of me. I was no longer a decision-maker, I was no longer the boss – the past few months since Around Britain had been a process of handing over the reins to my amazing team. It was now their job to get me around the world. This whole thing would fail if I was the default leader on the road. I knew very soon I wouldn't have the mental capacity or awareness to make important decisions. I was now just the bike rider. This is what I had always dreamt of, the chance to focus on pure performance. I wandered around greeting the team, observing a hive of activity that was happening because of me, but without any need for me. It was bizarre, but also wonderful.

However, despite these carefully laid plans not to be seen as the leader on the road, I could tell how people still looked to me for moral support. If I smiled, everyone was happy; if I was serious, likewise. Laura, used to working with athletes, seemed less affected, but I could see others looking for reassurance, for some banter to lighten the mood. I wanted to deflect this responsibility, for the team to have an even emotional keel, regardless of whether I was up or down. Hopefully that would come on the road. For now, as I said, there was just a lot of nervous energy.

Part Two

Paris to Beijing

Leg 1a: Paris to Russian border
David Scott – team leader
Mike Griffiths – overall logistics manager
Laura Penhaul – performance manager
Alex Glasgow – mechanic, driver, navigator
Tony Humphreys – as observer, in preparation for leading leg 2

Leg 1b: Russia, Mongolia and China
David Scott – team leader
Laura Penhaul – performance manager
Alex Glasgow – mechanic
Hishgue Khishgdulam Tumurbaatar – translator (to Chinese border)
Sasha, Aleksandr and two Dimitris – Russian drivers (to
    Chinese border)
Hajaa Khajidmaa – driver (from Nizhny Novgorod, east of Moscow,
    to Chinese border)

Film, camera, media
Johnny Swanepoel and Helmut Scherz from MoonSport Productions,
    Cape Town, covered the whole expedition, Paris back to Paris.

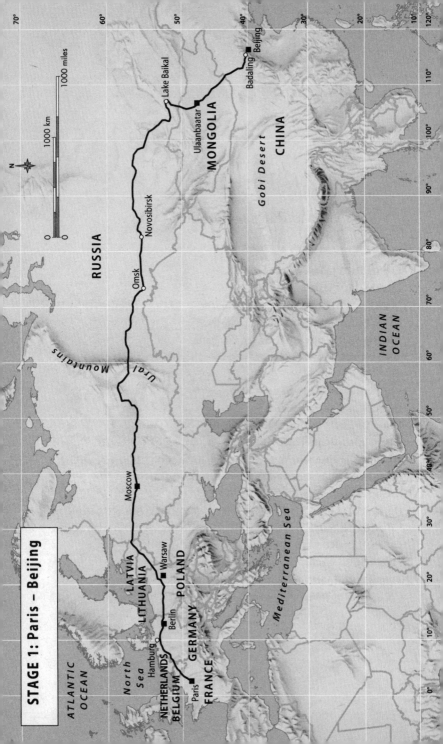

9

Another Day, Another Country

Day 0

Our base in Paris was at Camping International Maisons-Laffitte, situated on a small island in a large bend of the River Seine about half an hour's drive northwest of the Arc de Triomphe. Surrounded by French holidaymakers, our sponsor-decaled RVs and buzz of preparations were at odds with their more lethargic pace of life. I had a cabin on the other side of the camp, while the crew stayed on-board the RVs. I had complete space and privacy and just shut the door, and then my eyes. I was trying to stockpile sleep – easier said than done when your mind is in overdrive – but I was aware that tonight was the last time I would get eight hours of it.

On the Saturday morning, Si Richardson and the team from GCN (Global Cycling Network) turned up, straight from a busy few days before the start of the Tour de France in Germany. The race was starting that day, 1 July, in Düsseldorf, before the peloton raced towards France as I raced solo the other way. As the first three weeks of the Artemis World Cycle coincided perfectly with the Tour, I had linked up with ITV4, and the plan was for regular call-ins from my bike during their stage commentary. I would hopefully be nearing Mongolia by the time they sprinted down the Champs-Elysées. And over the course of the World I would cover about eight times the distance of the Tour de France in about four times the time, albeit at a much steadier pace.

With 1.2 million subscribers on YouTube, GCN is the biggest player in the online cycling community. I had spoken to them a few years before, when they wanted to branch into adventure and endurance cycling – I even got as far as writing some treatments for segments that they wanted me to film and present. But then the scale and focus of the Artemis World Cycle took over, and we postponed the plans. In fact I had got tied up talking to traditional networks like the BBC and the History Channel so had forgotten about GCN. It was Alex Glasgow and also James Robinson, a friend from LDC, who had both suggested I get them involved, a few months before the start.

I first met Si many years ago when I was presenting *Country Tracks*, the long-gone sister programme to *Countryfile* on BBC1. I had been filming a segment about Somerset, which one day had me making truckles of cheddar and then racing up Cheddar Gorge. At the time he was a UK pro, and after sportingly sticking with me for the first few corners he then kicked and I was left admiring his quickly disappearing beanpole of a figure. I am not, alas, a beanpole. For a big lad I can climb, but when you actually race uphill with a pro, you soon realize the gulf that exists between 'a decent climber' and a professional rider.

Now it was Si's turn to look nervous as he would be riding with me on the first day out of Paris and had never ridden over 200 miles in a day, not even once in his career. This was a common sentiment among pros I spoke to. A month earlier I had been hosting a corporate ride with David Millar. During our Q&A with Ned Boulting, David just laughed at the idea: 'Why would I ever ride 200 miles?'

Si and his team filmed the bike, the team and a short piece with me, but for the most part I was left alone all day, to tinker with kit, doze sporadically, and call home and a list of journalists. Apart from a big sit-down interview with Johnny and Helmut, my final day before an expedition had never been so restful. I felt like a spare part as the team worked furiously, running errands into Paris and checking and re-checking itineraries and communications.

The team looked superb in their new kit. This was one of the many safety ideas that came off the back of Around Britain, when the team were operating on the roadside all the time but were often hard to see. People didn't always remember to put on fluorescent bibs when tired and rushed, despite reminders, so we had simply made the team kit an unfashionably bright yellow.

There was a funny mood in camp. Everyone was busy with their list of jobs, losing themselves in details. No one was talking much about what lay ahead, at least not with me. Apart from how we would coordinate getting to the start, nothing in terms of the big picture was mentioned. 'How are you feeling?' was a well-meant question, but at the rate of tens of times a day . . . how are you meant to answer that? 'Fine thanks, it'll be good to just get wheels turning,' I kept answering. But after David Scott wrung my hand painfully and asked 'How are you feeling?' I light-heartedly banned the team from asking me that question, and Laura reminded them all that it was fist pumps only from now on. Handshaking was banned to avoid spreading germs.

The gates to the campsite were locked overnight – imagine, after years of planning, waking up and finding ourselves locked in, unable to get to the start! We made the decision to move the RVs to a car park by the bridge over to the mainland. And rather than stay in my cabin, I would sleep in the RV, so I could get an extra half hour's rest as we travelled to the start line.

We soon figured out why the gate was locked – young revellers, techno-playing boy racers, were out in force, and nobody got much sleep.

Day 1

It's ten to four, the second of July, and I am at the Arc de Triomphe and it's all about to kick off. Last night was . . . interesting, because we had to move the camper-vans outside of the campsite, because they close the barriers overnight, and it was like an all-night disco, so I don't think anyone in the team slept particularly well last night. But day 1, I am excited. The morning is basically getting up to the French border, the afternoon is riding through almost the entirety of Belgium, so a big day ahead – day 1!

Sleep or no sleep, everyone was raring to go and there wasn't any hesitation as engines started at 3.15 a.m. and we set off for the Arc. Coffee, some cereal, nothing fancy, and no beetroot this time. I watched from the back as we wound our way through the streetlights of a surprisingly busy Paris. As we turned a corner I caught a glimpse of the Arc, a good way ahead but a straight run. Trusting technology, Mike then followed the satnav, which bizarrely turned us away on to an underpass until we were soon at the Périphérique, Paris's ring-road, heading the long way round. It was comically ridiculous. Perhaps we only lost ten minutes with the mistake, but it was a funny way to settle everyone's nerves.

Mike on the bike and the team following in the RV had completed a successful practice run a few nights before, making sure the start and the first hour was scoped out. Everything had gone perfectly: navigation, communication, the works. Their main concern was the amount of traffic. At 3.50 a.m. on Sunday 2 July, I looked out at what must be Europe's craziest roundabout and it was relentless. When you choose an insurance policy for a car in Paris, there is a clause for coverage on the Arc de Triomphe. A single roundabout affects the price of your policy! Even in the middle of the night on a Sunday I could see why.

To my amazement, amid the locals were a motley crew of Brits who had turned out to wave me off. The 'official' start line, like a decade before, was a pedestrian crossing and there were the formalities and final media to rattle through. David Scott, in his role as Honorary Consul for Mongolia, seemed the best man for the official letter of adjudication, albeit he was crew, so not impartial. All being well, a Guinness World Records official would be on the finish line, but the start and all points along the way were for us to verify. Helpfully, the fans who had made the trek to be at the start were all delighted to add their witness signatures – which was a lot easier than trying to persuade drunk Frenchmen why we needed theirs. In 2007 I had stood on that start line holding a copy of *Le Monde* to verify the date and place, but this time it was too early for the day's papers.

So, moments before setting off around the world I was signing books, taking photos with the fans and chatting about how they'd all ended up here in the middle of the night. It certainly distracted me from the magnitude of the moment and I felt completely calm. One man had travelled by train the length of France and slept on a park bench to be there; @firsthippy and @malwinki were going to a Depeche Mode gig, so kudos for seeing this as a priority; and a chap called Michael Neville had cycled out from England over the past twenty-four hours, about 260km, to start with me. Which he did – literally the first mile, less than ten minutes, before turning around and cycling back to England! Amazing.

Ten, nine, eight . . . I started my watch and cycle computer, then glanced up, looking for a space between the traffic. Three, two, one . . . and I was off, with a wave and a smile, to a loud cheer from the small but elite group who had made the tremendous effort to be there.

Under the orange glow of Parisian streetlamps I exited the Arc and set off northeastwards, with Michael (very briefly) and then Si beside me, who was riding his most comfortable bike but still had a roadie set-up built for speed rather than comfort.

Navigating our way out of Paris at such an early hour should have been simple, but the pre-loaded navigation immediately failed, so we were straight back to the rudimentary one beep for turn left and two beeps for turn right. Perhaps there was an overload of data on the cycle computer. It didn't matter as long as we didn't have to stop to fix it or question our route.

As we left the last industrial throes of Paris behind and the day grew lighter, it started to rain. Nothing serious, just the heaviness of dawn causing a smirr, a drizzle in the air that did nothing to dampen spirits. I was jumping out of my skins and it was a task not to shift up the gears and burn off all those pent-up nerves and energy. I was also distracted from the task that lay ahead by having company and conversation in the form of Si. For the first six hours we blethered away, putting the world to rights, and for the ten hours after that Si mainly sat on my wheel, in silence. He wouldn't mind my saying that he found the morning a very gentle pace, which it was. By the end of the day he was utterly shattered.

Rain jackets were off by lunchtime and we were pushed along by a glorious tailwind. The north of France is pretty perfect cycling territory – long corridors of trees whose planting Napoleon is credited with having ordered, to enable his soldiers to march in the shade. These linear forests draw a line through the patchwork shades of yellow fields: oil-seed rape, sunflowers, the burning gold of the grains.

We would have made our first border crossing without knowing it, because it happened at a tricky junction, if Tony and David hadn't been standing there, one in France, the other in Belgium, madly waving small flags. One country down, fifteen to go.

After just fifteen hours' riding we clocked the magic 386km, the continental equivalent of 240 miles. But that figure was the average, not the target. Our only target was sixteen hours – that was all that mattered. On day 1 with fresh legs and a tailwind there was no way we were stopping. Si had other ideas; in his mind he was riding 240 miles as planned, so we stopped and had a quick interview, standing behind the RV in the late evening sunshine, with Si summing up his day: 'It's been incredibly hard, it's been an eye-opener. I knew what you were doing was a feat of endurance, but this has totally put things into perspective. That was me completely done, and you have eighty days of it. This is 240 miles to here. Until you have ridden that, it's hard to know. It rolls off the tongue quite easily, but it's a long way!'

I then carried on for another half an hour and we finished near the town of Bree, just shy of 400km and only a short distance from the Dutch border, but for the comfort of a campsite we detoured by nearly 3km, and made a note not to do that again. We would just stop wherever we were at the end of the hours. This was one of the small details to improve on, along with the issue of my Garmin 920XT watch freezing after the first hour, losing a short section of data. But all things considered it was a fantastic first day with nearly 250 miles in the bank.

Laura had been urging me to treat the first week as a warm-up, not to push too much until my body was completely used to the routine. She wasn't worried about hitting the 240 from day 1, in fact was realistic about the fact we may not. On the other hand, I was anxious to prove my plan, having failed to get close to this average on Around Britain. However, my other great fear was getting an injury during the first few days. I understood Laura's words of wisdom, but worried that 240 was such a high average that I had to be not far off it from the start.

With such favourable conditions, the miles had taken care of themselves on day 1. My compromise was to stop half an hour early. Despite having ridden carefully all day, there was a note of concern as my left Achilles was a bit crunchy – the first symptom of tendonitis. Laura treated it without comment, but there was an air of 'oh shit'. I went to sleep concerned. This was the sort of daft repetitive strain that could scupper everything from the outset.

Made it to the little town of Bree, in northern Belgium, and an awesome day 1. It's great just to get the first day in – I am stopping just before nine o'clock, 250 miles, that's further than I need to go for the average, so putting miles in the bank feels great. But even day 1 hurts; that's a lot of time in the saddle. Just getting back into it, so treatment and bed as soon as possible – I was up at half past two this morning. I tell you what, about two hours ago the fun nearly finished. Belgium is a labyrinth of cycle paths and I was flying along at about 25km/h and there were parked cars between the road and the cycle path, and a lady opened her car door into the cycle lane. I didn't really even see it; I reacted instinctively and I just threw my bike over to the right. If I had hit that car door, game over, day 1. I am serious. That was 300km into the ride. Si Richardson from GCN was right behind me, we were speaking about it afterwards, that was nearly a very serious crash. I can laugh about it, because nothing happened. I hope I have still got those fast reactions in a week's time.

Day 2

It's the start of day 2 and it's quite exciting, because we get to tick off some more countries. The body is just waking up to this, so I can feel my left Achilles. I am sure it will settle as the day goes on, but I am going to have to really watch that and try and take it easy on the bike. It's a bit colder out of the city this morning, so I will keep the jacket on for the first half hour.

Rolling out at 4.02 a.m. was just about acceptable, but it took another ten minutes to get back to our route, and that couldn't happen every day. If I lost just five minutes at the start of the day and every time I took a break, this would add well over a day to the record after seventy-five days' riding. Losing a few minutes might sound trivial over such a long day but it meant that we spent the day feeling like we were behind. We

needed to be off at 3.58 a.m. and straight back on to our route, and it
was good to see this level of detail being talked about within the team.

Laura had written up her notes and focused on the immediate concern, my Achilles: 'Mark has presented with Achilles tenosynovitis,
which is inflammation of the tissue/sheath around the tendon. It has
crepitus [a crunchy feeling] on the tendon glide, a warm feel to the
touch and a thickening. The cause I think was due to altering the foot
pressure because of experiencing pressure pain under the cleat of the
foot, therefore starting to grip with toes and holding the ankle angle
stiff while cycling. Treatment was ice, voltarol patch locally, offload
taping, compression garment, soft tissue release through the soleus
[deep under the Achilles/calf muscle], flexor hallucis longus [big toe
flexor] and intrinsics, plus acupuncture. We also changed orthotics to
provide a softer cushioning sole.'

It was the first thing I had thought about when the alarm went off
at 3.30 and I gingerly lifted my toe to feel how crunchy the ankle tendon felt. I couldn't believe I had picked up an injury on day 1.
Stumbling out of the starting blocks and not making it out of Europe.
Never even getting to prove that the 80 Days was not a pie-in-the-sky
dream.

Day 2 would be the only day on the World attempt when I would
cycle in three different countries, and while in theory it was advanta-
geous to have all the team leaders on the road from the start, it was
clear that David, in overall charge for leg 1, was having some difficul-
ties. It was a case of too many cooks, especially when Mike was seen as
the default leader, being the overall operations manager. The plan was
that David would jump out on day 3 at Hannover in Germany to fly
ahead to Moscow, to meet the four Russian drivers and two Mongolian
fixers and translators, who had travelled nearly 6,000km from Ulaanbaatar. But from the tranquillity of the bike I could see there was a bit
of friction and a settling-in process happening in the vehicles.

By dawn we were already into Holland, enjoying the flatlands, and
after first break I spotted Aloys Hanekamp, the manager from KOGA
who had worked with me to build the World bike, casually taking his
bike off his car and getting ready. I shot past, cruising in time-trial
position with the wind behind me. He jumped into action and raced

after me, forgetting his water bottles and some goodies he had brought along. It was fun to ride with Aloys, I appreciated his efforts to join me. The further he went, the further he would have to battle back into the wind, but after the last year's collaboration over this bike and at times difficult conversations about suppliers and deadlines, it was a relief just to ride some miles together and share the journey. As had been the case for Si, it was only now, actually riding a small part of one day, that the scale of the task began to make sense to Aloys. We had a laugh and I carried on, crossing into Germany.

Although Holland had taken a matter of hours to cross, and both Belgium and Holland are famed for their cycle networks, we had two issues with the police. Both times I was stopped because they didn't want me cycling on the road. While the cycle paths are ubiquitous, they are designed for cruising around town on a Dutch bike, going to the shops, not for road riding, and they are certainly not conducive to tapping out a fast average speed. But every time there was a path, not just when in towns, I was forced to follow these intricate bicycle lanes rather than carry on at good speed on the road. The first time the Belgian police stopped me it was before 6 a.m., when there was almost no one around, so the flashing lights, full pull-over theatrics and very stern telling off all seemed a tad overzealous.

After skirting the busy cities of Düsseldorf and Dortmund we made it to near Hannover by 9.30 p.m., and parked on the roadside. Just over 390 clicks – more miles in the bank. The evening before we'd had a campground shower, but without such luxury now I was a lot quicker to bed, wary of how to be efficient at the end of a day, how to eke out even an extra fifteen minutes' sleep.

In the heart of Germany now. Most of this afternoon has been trying to navigate through lots of little towns. The hardest part this afternoon is ending up on lots of roads where it is not clear where I am allowed to cycle or not. I was stopped by the police in Holland and Germany today, and they were fine, but said I was on the wrong road, so a bit of faff time coming off and finding another route. I am hoping east of here I am going to get on to clear roads, less towns, and I cannot be stopping and starting so much. But hey, 244 miles, great day!

Day 3

> Just about to set off, but with our time changes, that makes it feel a
> little earlier every morning. I am trying not to think about it too much.
> Our local time is now 3.30, although we are talking about it as if it is 4
> a.m., because we are losing fifteen minutes a day. So I got up at 3 a.m.
> local time, although that was 3.30 a.m. challenge time! Right, today is
> all about Germany, get as close to the Polish border as possible. Look
> at that . . . another cyclist, it's 3.30 in the morning!

Sure enough, I had company from the start, although it was limited
conversation given his broken English and my level of enthusiasm for
small talk through the graveyard shift. Top marks for effort after he
had heard about my journey through the day 1 video on GCN.

In the 3.30 a.m. wake-up routine, Alex had managed to walk into
the hatch window on the Follow Vehicle and split his head open so
Laura's skills and attention were diverted for a while. The next time I
saw Alex he looked like an extra in a war film, with a bandage wrapped
around his wild mop of hair, a stain of blood seeping through. He
assured us all he was fine, and a trip to A&E for stitches was decided
against. But joking aside, it was a sobering reminder of how easy it
was for any of the crew to get injured which, being entirely selfish,
could massively slow me down if not dealt with efficiently. Alex was
stoic and saw the funny side, so we cracked on – pun intended.

The first shift skirting Hannover was calm and straightforward, pedalling through a dawn landscape of wind turbines and low-lying mist
which reminded me of *War of the Worlds*. I then faced a series of tricky
navigation sections, partly because of the compulsory bike lanes and
also because of roadworks. Getting past Wolfsburg looked simple
enough on the map, but the bike lanes kept taking me into residential
areas, meaning that I lost time and track of the FV. Route 188, however,
was easy rolling with the continuing westerly wind behind me all the
way to Berlin, which was the major hurdle of the day, but which we cir-
cled without stopping.

Four road closures during the afternoon shifts made for stilted progress; the support vehicles were scattered across the landscape following long diversions while I ploughed on happily to take the most direct route. This meant about 10 miles of compacted gravel and then freshly laid road, as yet unopened to the public – it was a calculated risk that I could find a way through and that I wouldn't break down on a stretch where the FV couldn't reach me. But apart from these concerns it was bliss to have the best part of an hour on a road to myself and worthwhile as the diversion was twice the distance. I sensed Laura's concern when I just ploughed on in frustration at the 'closed road' sign, while Alex shared my sense of adventure and abandon. Mike simply followed my judgement call, but looked like he was about to tear up the road map.

It was Helmut, the local, who was kept busy advising me where I was allowed to cycle, and Alex did a great job of guiding me through these little roads, but at times it felt like I was in a labyrinth. None of the roads had 'no cycling' signs but when I was tooted at by lorries it was obvious I was in the wrong place.

This level of uncertainty at having to keep tweaking the route had come to a head at lunchtime when the Media Vehicle and Follow Vehicle were separated near the town of Rathenow, with Mike in the MV stating that they were setting up for lunch, so the FV and I should come back to them. I wasn't allowed to cycle on the highway, so this meant backtracking about a kilometre on a smaller road. I was absolutely fuming about this poor decision – the MV should have come to us. I ate lunch alone in the FV as the team had a conflab, clearing the air. But I made it very clear to Mike that this could never happen again. No backtracking and no prioritizing convenience for the crew if it compromised the progress of the bike.

I was unreasonably angry about this and got back on the bike in a fit of rage. The team could tell how I had blown this small mistake up; they seemed quite taken aback and nervous around me. I just wanted to be left alone and to clear my head on the bike. It was a blow-out for a lot of tension and focus over the past few days.

Mike was certainly doing his best, while trying to share leadership with Tony in preparation for him taking over for leg 2. Here's his log: 'Using the two vehicles, one stays with Mark, provides life support with performance manager and mechanic, and this second vehicle finds a route which allows Mark to keep going without any delays. Of course, the complication is we already had our own tasks for the day, [like buying] food; the fridge is broken in the other vehicle, so we need to find an ice-box, all that food is going warm and off. These are the sort of small niggles we will face every day. We need to find a way for Mark to get back on to a faster route, as obviously the backroads are not a problem for shorter periods, but ultimately every minute counts.'

In mid-afternoon, Laura had to stop the FV to be sick. I wasn't informed until 9.20 p.m. when we stopped outside the village of Seelow near the Polish border, by which time she was self-quarantined in the MV and everything in the FV had been deep-cleaned and sterilized. Alex was now in charge of performance, alongside Mike.

Laura looked very annoyed with herself as we made camp and she chatted to camera: 'I'm the performance manager who gives everyone else a load of chat about food and the quality that we are eating and how we are hygienic and how we look after ourselves and I am the one that becomes crook on day 3! So I am kicking myself a little bit, but unfortunately I've been vomiting a bit this afternoon so I have had to clear out of the van because I don't want to risk it with Mark. It could have been something I ate, it could be motion sickness because we were driving quite fast and swerving and I was busy in the back trying to prepare things, or maybe it was just because I am over-tired, but there is definitely something going on. However, this is also something we prepared for, and the key thing now is that I need to isolate myself, not touching too much in case it is a bug, and keep myself hydrated. I'd already written up everything I do for Mark from morning to evening, so anyone can step in and do that.'

Lunch had included processed sausages, the nasty sort you get in tins of beans. Such cheap meat was on the strict no-no list of food. But in the turmoil of the route dispute this hadn't been picked up on. It was a reminder to the crew that they must all eat like athletes – no short cuts, no junk food, no unnecessary risks. It also showed that when stress levels rose in the team, simple processes and standards were easily forgotten. It was the job of everyone to stay vigilant, to stick to the plans.

That was my first 400km day, 250 miles, which is utterly remarkable, because it has been a day of setbacks, just bizarre road closures and ducking on and off little cycle paths, and I am amazed that we have covered that distance. Hope Laura is OK, I need her, she is kind of a key player – just finished up my day and heard that she was ill, so she has taken herself off, so I don't get ill. We are a stone's throw from the Polish border here and will cross first thing in the morning. So, we have Alex here looking after me, but he is a wounded soldier as well. A good day though!

Day 4

Start of day 4. Hope Laura is OK this morning. She was pretty sick last night again, so she is keeping her distance to make sure she doesn't give whatever she has got to me and the rest of the team. Alex has done a good job of getting me up and out this morning. I'll roll across the Polish border pretty early this morning – pretty cool to have crossed Germany in a day and a half and we have a big day in Poland ahead. I am feeling OK; I mean I am feeling sore, but nothing to write home about. We are really clattering our way towards Lithuania, Latvia, and it starts to become quite crucial over the next few days at what time of day I reach the Russian border, so we can get across there efficiently – that's the next big milestone. If we get stuck there for three or four hours, that could undo a week's worth of good work and hard miles. So hopefully less roadworks and delays today. However we still made great miles yesterday. I certainly couldn't have hoped for a better start so far.

Laura was confined to the MV for the day, meaning that Mike was driving and Alex was in charge of nutrition and my admin. I crossed easily into Poland and on to long, straight, quiet wooded roads. Just after dawn a wolf trotted across the road right in front of me; it was a wonderful moment of calm and a glimpse into the wilderness – I was no longer in western Europe.

Alex seemed to be enjoying his new responsibilities and was working his way through the three-page log of food and hydration for the day: 'It's 9.30 a.m. and I now have to give Mark another water bottle, but I have just had a look and his bottle is still full, so I am off to tell him off! This can be an electrolyte or more carbohydrate-based drink. Next, I'll be making him a banana, peanut butter and Nutella wrap.'

Once the world woke up, it was a day on trunk roads with a ton of big trucks lumbering their way on the east–west commute. We came off the highway at a few points when the volume of traffic seemed to be getting dangerous, with smaller road options running parallel. But this ended up causing more confusion and at one stage the FV lost me. Alex jumped on the spare bike to chase me down while the FV was once again re-routed. Once we'd rendezvoused, we just took the risk and jumped back on to the big road to avoid losing more time.

The Achilles tendonitis had been Laura's and my main concern over the past forty-eight hours, and despite my fears of a painful injury that would have to be constantly managed for the next few weeks, it had eased brilliantly. What an incredible relief. In the past, the only way I could get rid of that crunchiness in the tendon was complete rest. Riding nearly 400km a day was not what the doctor would have ordered, and yet with proper management and consciously pedalling in a more fluid manner, not locking my ankle or gripping my toes, the tendon was free-flowing again. All round, apart from the discomfort from sixteen hours a day in the saddle, my body seemed to be adapting well to the routine.

Over lunch, Laura wanted to address tightness in my hip flexors and to release tension deep in my gluteus maximus (my bum). But because she was in isolation she delegated her duties to Alex who, bless him for trying, dropped his elbow and manoeuvred my leg and bum in a way I'm pretty sure made him rather uncomfortable. But it just wasn't hitting the spot, so I aborted the treatment; it would have to wait until Laura was back on duty. Alex might be good for a relaxing shoulder massage, but these deeper issues called for the expert.

The tailwind, which was with me all day, picked up beautifully into the evening and I was on a conveyor belt across the rolling country-side, making it 395km to just short of Plock.

Laura's sickness had abated by lunchtime and she managed to get a good block of sleep, and a bit later on to stomach some pasta. There was a ton of lovely messages of support online and I was heartened to see the social media audience appreciate the roles and commitment of the crew. I felt that Laura, Alex and Mike were all becoming known characters to the public following my journey.

246 miles, another good day. But I am quite sore. It has been a day of big trucks and lots of traffic. That first stint of the day, through forests, that feels like another week. After that first four hours I was thinking, wow, Poland is so quiet, but that is because I was riding from 3 a.m. local time (4 a.m. challenge time) until 7 a.m., so no wonder the roads were quiet. It's got very busy since then. I need to get some food in now. A good first four days – I can't believe we have made it from Paris in four days. I've gone about 990 miles in four days, not bad!

Day 5

Well, it's very early on day 5 and it's surprisingly cold. The mist is lying low on the fields and I'm just trying to wake up a tired body at this time of the day. I've just passed 1,000 miles, only 17,000 to go! But feeling very sore this morning and it doesn't help getting started in this mist; it's beautiful, it is atmospheric, but it is cold. It'll be quite nice when the day warms up a bit; this graveyard shift, this first one, is the toughest. I just think if I can get through four hours, I can have a cat nap, a little sleep and start the day properly.

The media boys had caught up with me already on the bike at first light, riding with knee-high compression socks which I normally slept in, and staying snug in my PrimaLoft jacket. We were now in the middle of Poland, near the capital Warsaw, and heading towards the Lithuanian border, so similar territory to what we had yesterday – pretty uneven but long, straight roads.

Laura was back on form and in charge of performance: 'Mark has woken up sore and stiff. I did a bit of treatment last night, more down through his calves, but wasn't getting too close to him obviously. He is definitely looking pretty tired so this first shift is going to be pretty tough for him. The area which needs daily maintenance is his neck and upper thoracic. Although this is an area that we addressed with training pre-cycle, the neck is going to take some time to adapt. Although these muscles are fairly fatigue-resistant in their architecture, holding sixteen hours of the same posture will place a great deal of stress on them. During the Ride Across America where cyclists are riding for twenty-three hours a day for nine days straight, there are often stories of the cyclists losing control of their neck muscles and therefore being unable to hold their heads up. They then have to rely on neck braces or equivalent contraptions in order to take the weight of their heads. This is something we want to avoid as riding with a neck brace is neither safe nor sustainable for eighty days. So daily maintenance is in place to offload these muscle groups, plus the option of altering the front end set-up of his handles to change the weight distribution and make small biomechanical adjustments.'

I forgot to start my Garmin watch for the first 10km – a little tell-tale sign of the mental fog that fatigue brings on. The morning routines needed nailing down so nothing was forgotten as we all tired. It wasn't a disaster, but we needed data to be as accurate as possible for Guinness World Record verification. My watches (the 920XTs) got changed at lunchtime every day – I wore a red one in the morning and a blue one in the afternoon, to keep it simple – as they wouldn't hold a full day of charge, and were our only back-up to the main cycle computer, the Edge 1000.

The early mist made for a memorable ride through Plock, over a wide suspension bridge, as if I were floating on a bed of cloud in the valley below. When the sun eventually appeared a long way above the horizon it shot out shards of colourful light that struggled to pierce the cloud, refracting off as if through the stained-glass windows of a dusty church.

After Ciechanów, heading on a more northerly tack through dense forests, the roads got smaller and prettier, but the quantity of trucks didn't lessen and I missed the comfort of a hard shoulder to duck into when they passed. The media boys tried some tracking shots but it was difficult to film me along such busy roads and they gave up after the following piece to camera, as we continued on the very hectic route 61 to Augustów: 'Well we are now getting into eastern Poland and what a difference. If I had gone due east I would have ended up in Belarus and Russia that way, but because I am cutting up between Lithuania and Latvia, I am starting to cut more northeast now and coming off the bigger roads. I am getting away from those big trucks which makes a massive difference. This is glorious. But what a difference it also makes because with a pretty strong westerly, every time I cut north I can feel that battering in, then every time I cut east again it is such a fantastic helping hand. After that really chilly start, it has turned into an absolutely glorious day.'

I kept my head down and soldiered on, but among the crew there was a lot of chat about the route ahead and the decision was made to get off this main corridor – it was just too busy and dangerous. A new route was set and the final shift of the day after Augustów was stunning and much quieter, along lakes and forest roads, and across the border into Lithuania without any delays, where we found a very rural roadside camp, surrounded by cows, after 390km.

Absolutely beautiful end to the day. I am actually really chuffed to make 242 miles today, because it got really hilly this afternoon and a few more issues. But new country in Lithuania and it has been an amazing day, thinking back to this morning when I felt absolutely rubbish pre-dawn.

Day 6

Last day riding through Europe, which is exciting – so, Lithuania this morning, Latvia this afternoon, and if all goes well we should cross into Russia at some point tomorrow morning. David has flown ahead to Moscow and met the Russian drivers and is coming back with the vehicles, and that is the next big milestone. I slept well, but a very sore neck from that riding position.

At 3.45 a.m. challenge time, Laura was working to release my headache and very tight neck as I recorded my morning video diary, but we had other concerns too. The main GPS tracker, Blue 1, wasn't working again. Una was watching the online tracking constantly and flagged this. The on-road team felt supported and checked up on in equal measures; but joking aside, the fact that Una never seemed to sleep and no mistakes would go unnoticed made for a very positive relationship with 'Base Camp'. Una fed back from the manufacturers Trident Sensors that we should check for water damage, and sure enough there was condensation inside the plastic housing, so we switched it for Blue 4.

These were bespoke GPS units, custom-made to be as small and lightweight as possible so that I could carry one in my cycle jersey back pocket, and the 80 Days digital team needed to redirect to the new mapping page, while also showing our progress so far. This was an improvement from Around Britain where online you could see where I was and the previous few 'pings', but not my entire route of data points. For the audience online, the story each day was book-ended with the morning and evening video diaries, and in between the GPS map updated my location every fifteen minutes, with photos being posted as often as we could. Before Around Britain, I had naively thought that I could still coordinate a lot of this day-to-day conversation – the Twitter and Facebook feeds – while leaving the Facebook page for bigger photo galleries and more blog-style video and written updates. But I simply didn't have the time, let alone the mental capacity, to be posting tweets and pictures.

On the rare occasion I had a safe stretch of road and was in the right mood, I would record a short video message from the bike. But I would usually send this straight back to the team at MoonSport in Cape Town, who would have it checked by Una and posted across social media. It was amazing how little time I had to do anything but eat, sleep and ride. I took a lot of support and confidence from my 'virtual peloton', and so every time I was cycling along, speaking with Nicci on the phone, she would read out some of the comments and questions, and I would dictate some replies. It was a welcome distraction from the hard miles and a connection with those who were following me – a good way to take me outside of my own head.

The roads got prettier and prettier, but it was a day of complex navigation to stay off the trunk routes. There were a few errors, some sections where the tarmac ran out and I could see the horror on the faces of the crew in the FV as I bumped on to long sections of dirt road, everyone hoping it would get back to tarmac quickly and that I wouldn't blow up at the mistake. I tried to stay pragmatic – it was a tricky section, and everyone was working hard to keep me on the fastest but safest route. We ended up taking a great course past the town of Utena and on to a much quieter main road, the A6, into Latvia.

We were then cruising happily along until hitting a 12km section of roadworks approaching Daugavpils: traffic lights, gravel and dust. I quickly lost the FV in the tailbacks, and regretted not taking Laura's advice to wear a buff as the dust clouds were terrible. I was left with a dry cough for days afterwards.

We camped down an overgrown lane next to an abandoned old house. Everyone else was much later to bed than me as there was all the kit to be sorted for the border crossing in the morning. And there was a slight issue with an unexpected local. While wandering away from the FV as I brushed my teeth, I had discovered, by the beam of my head torch, a pile of empty beer cans and some clothes by the open doorway of the house. Slightly spooked, I mentioned this to Laura, but thought nothing more of it and went to bed. The squatter appeared soon after to return to his ruined abode for the night and was not happy. Mike, taking charge of the situation and assuming that his smattering of German was closer to Latvian than English, tried his best to pacify the agitated tramp. Oddly, but very helpfully, one of the fans who had come out to cheer me on through Germany had given me some bottles of beer. How he thought this would fuel me Around the World in 80 Days I have no idea, but given the current predicament, they were the best bargaining chip we had. With a fresh stash of alcohol, the man carried on into his house. I knew nothing of this, so when I woke at just gone midnight, dying for a pee, and padded outside with my head torch on, I got the fright of my life to see the flicker of a campfire coming from within the house, just metres from where we were parked.

Very happy with that, 245 miles, but consider it was my biggest ascent day yet and involved a couple of sections of dirt roads in Lithuania and

then construction roads in Latvia. It was like being back cycling in
southern Ethiopia. I didn't expect that at all. I thought I would be chasing to get anywhere close to 240, but the last two to three hours opened
out, perfectly straight roads and just beautifully undulating, and I just
flew. It's a wonderful feeling. I'll take that, I've made it across Europe
in six days! Into Russia first thing tomorrow morning!

Day 7

Right, big day, day 7, about 70K from the Russian border. A lot of work
has gone into this bit, so I just hope we can get across without any
delays.

And with that I wheeled off down the track, back on to the road and
turned left, towards Paris.

'Wrong way!' The shouts came in unison.

'Ah yes,' I acknowledged with a self-deprecating chuckle.

'Wake up, Mark!' I muttered to myself as I turned and pedalled off
into the dawn.

I was away at bang on 4 a.m. and everything looked perfectly planned
until I reached a crossroads on my route at Rezekne. The Media Vehicle
with Tony and Laura was meant to jump ahead to the border to be
ready for the crossing. On the outskirts of town I took a right turn to
the border and immediately hit long sections of roadworks. First it
occurred to me that the MV hadn't passed me and then came reports
that they were already at the border, having encountered no roadworks.
It took a few minutes to work out what had happened. They were at the
wrong border crossing!

Tony had carried straight on northeast to a crossing at Grebnova,
whereas we were aiming for the border southeast of Rezekne near the
town of Zilupe. There was a classic pause in the WhatsApp conversation that was buzzing away on my watch every minute, a moment of
'ah, shit' and a few red faces, as they turned about and tested out the
top speed of the motorhome back down the road. Best-laid plans!
With a frantic redirection back to the correct border crossing via

Ludza, they avoided all the roadworks and caught us easily, overtaking with the pedal to the metal.

Speaking with Alex, his feeling was that this first week of sleep deprivation really seemed to be catching up on all of us. Combined with the complex, seat-of-the-pants navigation decisions, it had resulted in some pretty wired days. Alex had developed a strange left/right mix-up and it was most unlike Tony to disappear off to the wrong border.

On the other side of the border, one of my new Russian drivers, Aleksandr (aka Aleksei), was also being delayed crossing into Latvia in order for the two vehicles to swap all their kit over, after which the Russian vehicle would then cross back. So in fact our MV arriving late made no difference at all. When I arrived at 6.45 a.m. they were still waiting and it simply meant they would have further to catch up with me on the Russian side, rather than being with me from the start.

Alex jumped on the spare bike with the medical kit on his back and Laura waved me off, but I could tell she didn't like me being out of her sight, let alone in a different country. But on balance, it was more likely to be the bike that needed maintenance in the coming hours than me, so we opted for Alex to cross with me in support.

It took forty-five minutes for us to be allowed into Russia, and the unsmiling guards made sure we didn't feel welcome. I always feel a nervous energy around border crossings, and to be fair it isn't the job of soldiers to be nice to tourists, but there is something particularly austere about the Russian demeanour, and something particularly intimidating about the Russian border – it had been the most talked-about point on the entire route. But the delay was not unexpected, and I enjoyed the anticipation of pedalling into Russia. Ahead lay the big unknown, the wilderness, the part of the World route into which most research and worry had been invested. Alex shared my boyish sense of adventure, and we did our best to get a smile out of one young soldier, charged with directing traffic, who did at least lend us a pen to fill out forms.

The first person I saw on the other side was David Scott, wearing a 'Russia' T-shirt and beaming from ear to ear. 'Welcome to Russia!' he boomed, breaking into a jog as I pedalled away from the border building. 'We are parked up there.'

I had no intention of stopping for a meet and greet.

'I'll keep going,' I called back.

'OK.'

There were some bemused looks from the group standing next to our Russian RV. I glanced over and gave a wave, but no one responded. I could see that Alex thought I should say hello to the new crew, but he then waved me off as he pulled over to jump in the vehicle. I was on a mission, having lost forty-five minutes, and to be honest it didn't cross my mind to stop. It was only Alex's reaction that made me aware that this might be expected. I realized my mindset was not normal: on any previous cycling journey I'd loved the social side, the culture, the people I met, but I was in a more ruthless place now, and I had to be, so I made no apologies for it. I had the next fortnight and more for pleasantries with the Russians. I wasn't willing to lose another fifteen minutes now over polite small talk.

I had treated the border crossing as my first break of the day, so set out into Russia for my next four-hour block. I was in a corridor of fir trees with very little else so it was timely to reach a petrol station perfectly to break for lunch. The Russians stepped out of the FV as I pulled up and came over to say hello, stretching and lighting cigarettes in a relaxed manner. They assumed we were stopping for at least an hour. 'Thirty minutes!' I corrected them. 'It's a fast lunch!' It either hadn't been explained in detail or they hadn't taken the plan seriously. In any case, I could see they were in for a bit of a shock; it was going to be a tough job for them. There was not a lot of language in common between us, and I just hoped we had them onside for what would be a seriously tough race across Russia and Mongolia.

The MV caught up by 1 p.m. and we settled into the long, straight roads, being drawn east at a good pace and in good spirits by the strong following wind. The food was a bit sparse to begin with, but once the vehicles were together, the MV raced ahead to stock up for the long run across Russia.

It was about 600km from the border to Moscow and we managed more than half of that before the end of the day. Mike and Tony were now road-tripping back across Europe to the UK with the first two support vehicles, and I felt I owed them a big thank you for their support over the first week. I would see Tony again in Australia, and Mike in Alaska at the start of leg 3.

Paris to Russia in a week, crossing Europe at the speed of a country a day, had been as kind a start as I could possibly hope for. The inevitable and much-feared niggles of the first few days had come to nothing and my body and mind were reluctantly adapting well to this new normality. The routine – sixteen hours a day riding, five hours' sleep and 9,000 calories – hurt, lots, but it was possible. And I took a lot of confidence from having now done a week of it. Until now it had merely been a hypothesis, a dream. Around Britain had done little to reassure me. But Europe had been very kind and I hoped these conditions would remain. I had been willing to accept that for the first week I would be slightly behind schedule, making up miles once I was properly conditioned. But with a consistent wind from the west, by simply doing the hours I had hit the magic 240 every day without having to push the power, or risk overcooking it.

Russia looked as wild and empty as I'd imagined, the roads punctuated with stalls selling skins of bears and other beasts of the forest. There wasn't much else to notice for those first miles towards Moscow, but there was enough to remind me that I was now a long way from home.

An absolute dream start to Russia, 246 miles, but mentally tough. The focus for week one has just been to get to the border, to get to Russia, that has been my everything, so I crossed the border and mentally crashed for about six hours on the bike, because I had done it, I had got here, and I just needed to think it through and re-find that focus, figure out what is next, what is the next target. We've done it though, a great first week.

10

Fighting Tooth and Nail

Day 8

It's 3.55 a.m. challenge time, and 2.40 local time, but it's not worth thinking what local time is! Today is all about getting through Moscow. It is 283km from here and if all goes well we will get through by mid-afternoon. It's hard to imagine what is on the other side. To Moscow and whatever lies beyond, it is going to be an exciting day.

Indeed it was eventful and rather exciting, in a testing way. But the start was simple and quick from our roadside park and we had a steady first two sessions through the corridor of evergreen forests, on a straight road with a helpful tailwind as the dream conditions continued, allowing us to hit target while 'taking it easy'.

After lunch we were approaching Moscow, which shouldn't have come as a surprise, except in this utter wilderness it was hard to work out where the Russians were hiding this mega city of seventeen million folk. You went from a single carriageway through several hundred miles of forests suddenly on to a ten-lane highway and ring-roads with an intimidating volume of traffic. To this end David had spent months planning our best route across Moscow and his main task after flying ahead from Hannover was to recce the route.

The entry and exit routes into and out of Moscow were fixed and the plan was to link them using the northern ring-road, with a view to avoiding city-centre congestion and one-way streets. David had driven these stretches of ring-road and had arranged for a local cyclist to join me.

By the time we neared Moscow there was no cyclist and the ring-road option had been discarded. After experiencing European cities, David felt that the numerous junctions on the ring-road would cause delay and risk the FV loosing me. I also fed back that I wanted the most direct route. Therefore he looked again at city-centre options, discussing these with Alex. The most direct route involved a long tunnel, which was obviously not ideal and potentially illegal. They even discussed sandwiching me between vehicles through the tunnel for safety.

The tunnel was the pinch point before passing near Red Square and the Kremlin, but David thought that it seemed no worse than any other route, and it was shorter. It was right to be able to adapt the plan, but it was clear there was no detailed contingency. By this time Una had been called into action back in Scotland, examining aerial maps and quickly ruled out the new proposed route because of the tunnel. I didn't want to overrule David's decisions, but we were now within half an hour of the outskirts of Moscow without a clear route.

One of the Russian drivers, Alexei, a Moscow taxi driver, suggested the southern route, which we eventually took. But David and Alex were still concerned with the navigation on to it and whether I might not be allowed on part of it. They were urgently trying to decide, with Una's help back in Scotland, when the FV got stuck in the ditch.

The outskirts of Moscow were so busy that the FV kept leap-frogging ahead then pulling to the side to allow both traffic past and me to catch up. At one of these many stops the front right and then back wheels slid in the roadside mud and as the driver, Dimitri, tried to steer out, they slid further into the ditch. There was a bit of a panic. They thought they could be stuck for hours.

I told David to get into the Follow Vehicle, rather than trying to oversee this from the Media Vehicle. The Media Vehicle then got stuck in a very long contraflow, causing a period where the team couldn't join up. A three-way call with David, Laura and Una set the new plan, so credit to David for salvaging a very tense situation. We lost a few minutes at the roadside, but most of this lengthy period of frantic communication and research happened on the move.

After flagging down a passing lorry, the Russians finally managed to tow the RV, fishtailing its way up the siding, back on to the road. They caught up without too much delay and we managed to regroup and keep a fairly steady two-vehicle convoy through Moscow. It was very exciting, hair-raising even, and pretty smooth progress compared to what I had expected. Alex and I weaved through the dense stream of traffic on vast boulevards past luxury shops as we cut the fastest path, avoiding the inside lanes where buses were regularly stopping.

We crossed the Moskva river four times as its deep meanderings dissected the city, at one point pedalling down the mighty Zubovsky Boulevard, with seven lanes of traffic in each direction, then past the imposing Triumphal Arch on Kutuzovsky Avenue. We were limited to the speed of the traffic and so enjoyed slowing down, sitting up and looking around, taking in the imposing history and the scale of the Russian capital, experiencing the novelty of cycling through Moscow.

I felt certain we shouldn't be on such busy roads: there was no sign of other cyclists. When we did come across a policeman, monitoring the mayhem, I was certain our fun was over. But he barely glanced at us. It was amusing to compare this to the overzealous police a week earlier in Belgium, Holland and Germany; I sensed that the feeling was if you were crazy enough to be on these roads on a bicycle, that was your risk. There were no angry horns, everyone simply focused on their own business – and for that I quite liked Russia so far.

Before long, quicker than we'd imagined, I was clearing the eastern ring-roads, riding on my own again and being spat back into the countryside, although the scenery never reverted to the no-man's land of dense forests.

At the end of play we pulled into a large lorry park at the back of a garage. The crew half-expected me to carry on, but we were about to head into another remote stretch. We had cracked Moscow and clocked an incredible 262 miles, so we called it a day in a place where we had the luxury of getting away from the road for a quiet night's sleep, and somewhere we could resupply with water.

I could feel that there was immense relief, but also some tension in the team to be dispelled, some dented pride. Everyone was completely invested in the race and I could see how much it meant to them all; emotions were close to the surface. But the lesson from our route problems was that team leaders couldn't remain effective and in charge of complicated sections when working remotely; they needed to be where the race was, in the Follow Vehicle. Otherwise my performance team would end up taking operational decisions, stepping on the toes of the team leader. But I could see that David felt a responsibility to oversee the Russians in the MV, so I hoped this working dynamic would resolve itself in the coming days.

We were just lucky that on a day with a howling tailwind, it was only a few egos that took a battering and not the average mileage.

> So there we go, 422km, that is massive. I can't take all the credit, I have had a cracking tailwind all day.

Day 9

> It's drizzling a bit this morning, looks like it is going to be a wet one. Into the wilderness now, we are east of Moscow. We have just done 2,000 miles, another milestone, but I just need to keep playing the long game, because I am pretty sore, starting in the mornings like this. Some great miles, great successes, but a long way to go yet.

At 3.45 a.m. I looked bleary-eyed, with swollen lips from the days of sunshine and wind. As I pulled on my overshoes and set out, the rain started to come down a bit heavier. Over an hour later, when the day was just starting to lighten, far later than expected under the leaden skies, I pulled into a garage and the RV joined me. I was too cold, a bit shaky, and asked for an extra jacket. As I then pedalled down the exit lane from the garage to rejoin the main road, perhaps going 15mph, I looked over my left shoulder – a safety glance down the road, and back to the RV, which was still stationary.

Bang.

I hit the tarmac with my left hand instinctively outstretched, and then took the rest of the impact on my face.

Lying still for a stunned moment, I tasted blood and then felt shards of broken tooth in my mouth. My first thought was that I had knocked out all my front teeth. My mouth felt numb; there was no immediate pain.

I looked back at the RV, but there was no sign of movement. They hadn't seen my crash. As I started to stand up, pulling myself from the bike, my left arm protested at being used as a prop and I moaned. It wasn't a loud cry, just the noise that pain makes when it leaves you. My only thought was 'get to the RV', and I walked very gingerly back towards it, wheeling the bike. Halfway there, they spotted me, and Alex came racing out, grabbing the bike from me, and Laura took my arm over her shoulder. I felt completely spaced out.

I tried to mumble what had happened, but I didn't get very far. There was a lot of water on the road, and I had thought the pothole which had caused my crash was just more standing water – not that I had been paying close attention, as I was more immediately concerned with the junction to the main road, and I probably wasn't at my most agile, starting again, cold and wet.

Sitting down, I was oddly concerned about spoiling the cushions with my wet lycra and I also felt very cold and numb. Laura grabbed a plastic bowl so I could spit blood and shards of enamel out. She acted quickly but quietly, speaking calmly but directly to Alex and David. After peeling off my wet jacket, Laura plugged me into the TempusPro straight away, monitoring my blood pressure every three minutes, my oxygen saturation, heart and respiratory rates, while recording it all in the background, allowing her to get on with managing the trauma. This unit could also transmit this information directly to the team at World Extreme Medicine in the UK, who were quickly alerted to the accident. All my vitals were within normal range but continued to be monitored for any changes and the onset of shock.

The damage to my teeth was not as bad as I had feared: I had chipped off a good section of my upper left canine, it and the one behind it had been shunted upwards into the gum, and a couple of others were a bit wobbly. My lip was also cut, but Laura was more concerned about the force with which my head had hit the ground and the risk of a neck injury. This is what she checked first.

I started sobbing. It wasn't the pain, as I didn't feel much yet. Laura was leaning in, treating me, and I put my good arm over her shoulder and pulled her in. I felt very vulnerable, hurt and alone, just sitting there being filmed, the subject of an exciting moment in the story. I wanted to hide. The professional response from everyone was brilliant, but all I really needed right then was a hug.

The broken tooth was ragged and cutting the inside of my lip, but the pain was fairly dull, from it being loose as opposed to immediate nerve damage. It just felt like I had been punched in the mouth. I was sore, but ultimately it was not going to stop me riding the bike unless it developed into severe toothache.

Laura's immediate prognosis of my arm was that 'without imagery, we can say that Mark is able to tolerate weight-bearing through the arm and can grip the brakes/gears, so is therefore safe on the bike to continue to ride. Mark is happy to continue riding and doesn't feel it's bad enough to stop (that in itself is a strong indication of severity notwithstanding his mental strength). For now we ice it regularly, apply compression to be worn when riding, address any secondary stiffness above and below the joint and fundamentally monitor it over the next forty-eight hours. These next two days will give us a greater idea of its severity and presentation.'

After the release of emotion, I felt much better and quickly started thinking clearly again about how much time I was losing. We pulled on some dry kit gingerly and I tried to stand up. But Laura insisted that I stay put a bit longer so she could monitor me. David, used to dealing with incidents from his policing days, was also on hand, helping calmly. In total I was off the bike for thirty-five minutes.

By the time I carefully started out again, it was fully light. After navigating the pothole, which was now obvious once you knew where it was, I settled back on to the road and spun my legs lightly. Lifting my left hand off the bars, I slowly closed and opened the fingers into a fist, trying to ease the stiffening. This left side had taken such a battering during Around Britain and the nerves hadn't fully healed, so that during the first week of the World the numbing had already been worse than on my right side, and now I had an injured elbow.

After feeling shocked and upset, then regaining determination, my next emotion was anger. I was absolutely livid. Perhaps I needed an escape valve for all the pent-up pressure, but specifically I lost it at the filming boys who after the crash decided to disappear off in the Media Vehicle to the next town to do some laundry, not to be seen again for most of the day. Those first few hours back on the bike were crucial. If my injuries meant I couldn't carry on, the whole World attempt – the 80 Days – was over. I felt that pressure – 'Is this the end of the ride?' – and they buggered off to clean their clothes. If it all ended there, we would have nothing to show for it.

After forty-five minutes I had a rear puncture, and close support allowed a fast change of the rear wheel, moving from an 11-28 to a 12-25 block, as the roads were fairly flat with a gentle tailwind.

Meanwhile, while I stewed on the bike – a good antidote for the discomfort I was feeling – Laura was being more productive, recording the events and data. Through World Extreme Medicine she contacted Mark Hannaford to ask for a dental expert and was quickly speaking with Burjor Langdana, a former Antarctic Survey dentist. Within an hour of her sending photos of my tooth and gum, he sent back a plan, detailing the steps to take to manage the situation. This would involve filing down the tooth to smooth it and then applying a resin – all in a normal day's work for a physiotherapist!

While World Extreme Medicine were there for trauma and remote medicine, Dr Andrew Murray was on the team for anything related to performance. Andrew is an old friend from Edinburgh and an ultra endurance runner. He first came to my attention in 2012 when he ran the 4,300km from the north of Scotland to the Sahara Desert. Apart from being a very experienced sports doc, he also understands the repetitive strains and psychology of endurance sports, which saves a lot of explaining. Andrew had been in charge of taking my bloods for testing and some other pre-expedition checks.

Andrew and Laura spoke at length about the worst-case scenario of my having an underlying hairline fracture. In any normal situation you would get imaging and undergo further investigations to confirm a diagnosis; but we were not going to spend a few hours looking for and then sitting in a Russian A&E department. If it was diagnosed as an intra-articular joint fracture or a radial head fracture, what would our management of it be? Would that management change if we had the imagery? Could it be an injury that would have long-term negative effects if not treated correctly now?

We were careful about not saying too much on social media – not speculating, just stating the bare facts of what had happened. The response was incredible, but also amusing and useful in a few ways. Alex relayed with amusement that a lot of the comments expressed concern about the state of my bike rather than me. That's cyclists for you! The bike had taken the crash much better than I had, with just a few scratches on remote shifters, aerobars and the left brake lever. The Corima wheels would have taken quite a whack, but there were no broken spokes or damage to the rims, and the Panaracer tyres were fine as well, which was amazing.

Helpfully, an Irish friend, Jonathan Lamont, spotted the incident on Facebook and contacted Una to help. Jonathan had been put in touch with us by the British Embassy when we were looking for locals in Khartoum to show me through the Sudanese capital on Africa Solo. A keen cyclist, he had done this and a lot more. Since then he had moved back to the UK with Nina, his Russian wife, and had a son. Jonathan also knew all the right people at the British Embassy in Moscow. David had made contact with the embassy, but Jonathan knew them personally and it was his contact who immediately jumped into action, sourcing the resin that we needed to rebuild my tooth.

As the day wore on, the pain in my left elbow grew increasingly worrying. Laura suspected a fractured radial head, although she kept any speculation from me and just treated it as an unknown injury.

The roads remained wet with lots of grit, so though it stopped raining, the heavy truck traffic threw regular clouds of spray at me and I spent the day examining the tarmac in front of my front tyre, paranoid about missing another pothole.

I hit a big psychological low late in the morning and again after lunch. The fighting reaction from after the crash had passed, and the reality of what lay ahead began to hit home. I had two months to ride on a suspected fracture. But as the day wore on and the roads dried out, my spirits rose.

David was busy in the nearest big city, Nizhny Novgorod, on a massive laundry and shopping mission, but after my earlier angry complaint we now had both Helmut and Johnny in the FV. They were hoovering up everything in terms of filming, which also wasn't what I had meant – I just needed them to see and film important stories when they happened, to live the journey with us. I made a note to myself to try and avoid barking orders like this, showing my frustration when the team got it wrong, instead to relay any concerns through the team leaders and to avoid overreacting and taking back the reins. That wasn't my job and I undermined the leadership every time I did this.

We were also having issues with comms: both mobile and our vehicle internet connections were patchy at best. The world SIM cards that were meant to give both vehicles their own wifi spots were working but much slower than hoped, so the team were sourcing local SIMs.

During the evening our new Media Vehicle reached us. A black Land Cruiser Prado with Mongolian plates, it had been driven the thousands of miles from Ulaanbaatar by a lady called Hajaa. It had been rather cramped living for the crew since crossing into Russia, with four local drivers and a translator, Hishgue. From here until the Chinese border we would now have a three-vehicle convoy, which still seemed a lot to support one bike rider, but was unavoidable as the Brits couldn't drive Russian vehicles and their drivers were limited to eight-hour shifts. And as there was concern about bears, everyone needed to sleep inside the vehicles rather than camping out. It certainly felt like a lot of people on the road, and already three days into Russia I had barely spoken a word to some of them. I realized this would remain the case unless I made an effort.

We parked up at 9.30 p.m., up a small side road next to a field that smelt of fresh slurry, much to my amusement but not so much Alex's as he had to work outside on the bike. There was more to be done than usual at the end of the day, more medical checks and using the recovery pump on my arm to try and reduce the swelling. However, sheer relief meant that I was now in a chipper mood.

That was definitely the toughest day yet: 230 miles, which is a remarkable success, considering I started the day with a crash. I didn't have much of the help I had yesterday with the tailwind; it's been a really rolling day, big climbs and a cracking sidewind most of the time. But most of all this elbow: whether it is bone, or muscle or tendon, it is really painful on the bike, so I can ride, but I will get some treatment now. But considering that could have ended the whole expedition, I got away pretty lucky there. To only lose 10 miles, I'll take that. I am sure that I am going to hurt lots tomorrow morning. I have chipped a good amount of my canine tooth, but it's not the end of the world. I guess it will be a couple of months before I can get to a dentist. But I am OK, that is the main point, the ride goes on.

Day 10

It's a pretty mild start after we had heavy rain in the night. It is first light already. Had to wake up a bit earlier this morning because after the crash yesterday there was obviously a bit of treatment to be done. My arm is heavily bandaged – but do you know what, I am feeling OK, surprisingly OK. I am sore, but I am good to go. It's a mild start, it's dry, can't complain, hopefully in the next few days the aftermath of this crash can ease off so I can be less sore on the bike.

Laura was looking for evidence of whiplash and micro-trauma to my neck muscles and any effusion (fluid leaking into my skin tissue), especially swelling of the elbow. I had slept well, for a solid five hours. My range of movement was better than expected, and we kept the elbow compressed and heavily taped. Circulation to my injured fingers was an issue every time we taped or compressed an arm or shoulder, so we had to adjust this regularly.

It hurt starting out, and to ease this I found myself riding rather lopsidedly, protecting my left side. While lightening the pressure through my elbow, this asymmetry wasn't good. Sure enough, favouring my right arm quickly led to shoulder and neck pain, plus a tightness behind my right knee.

Into the afternoon I worked hard to try and sit in a more balanced position. It was less painful out on the tri-bars where my arms gave some suspension to the road, as opposed to sitting upright, when any bumps in the road were transferred directly up my arm.

The roads were rough and pretty busy, certainly a lot more than we'd expected. The next milestone was to reach the Ural mountains and head into Russia's empty expanses, skirting north of Kazakhstan and across the west Siberian plateau. I assumed this would be similar to riding the remote roads of Canada, but it had proved a difficult stretch to research. I had studied maps, but felt the lack of first-hand experience.

Just before lunch I took another call from the live coverage of the Tour de France as Ned Boulting and David Millar filled commentary time during a long, flat stage 11, their peloton racing to Pau in the Pyrenees. It was otherworldly to describe the contrast since we had last spoken, of leaving Europe behind and the fast change of riding in a new country almost every day and moving into these vast rolling landscapes of what felt like the middle of Russia when in fact I was still very much in the west of it, slowly making a dent on the world's largest country by landmass.

The afternoon was much easier to bear after treatment at lunchtime and taping that helped my shoulders. The sun also came out after lunch and the road surface got much better. But in the evening, as we approached the city of Kazan, the skies darkened and three incredible thunderstorms rolled through.

The capital of the Republic of Tatarstan, a semi-autonomous region, Kazan has been dubbed the sports capital of Russia. From my perspective it just had a very long ring-road, and as we approached a bridge high above the Volga river the heavens opened and torrential rain hammered down, causing all the traffic to slow abruptly, and visibility to drop dramatically in a veil of rain and spray. The crew filmed enthusiastically out from the windscreen, the wipers struggling to keep up with the deluge, my rear red light blinking defiantly in the storm. Conditions like these are crazy to ride through, and thankfully such intensity rarely lasts for long.

Alex had changed the chain at lunchtime – it had done a week – and thoroughly checked the bike, so he had been dropped off at a garage to clean up and sort himself out before the Prado picked him up later. In this short stint I punctured, around 8.45 p.m. as I was starting to dry out; Laura guessed correctly at the spare wheel and I was off without delay. Alex couldn't believe such rotten luck; he and Laura had a good-hearted way of winding each other up.

Some 15km later, at 9.30 p.m., we made roadside camp. Meeting up with the media boys, I looked like I had had a tough day's cyclocross – a dirt-splattered face, some dried blood on my cut lip – but I looked very relieved to be there.

Helmut and Johnny were having lots of hassle with data uploading – not to mention their mountain of back-up, editing and sending data – so their end-of-day routine went long into the night. This was a real concern. The increased number of people on the road also made these end-of-day routines more drawn out. As far as I could tell, the Russians were enjoying and committed to the journey, but it wasn't in their nature to work quickly. Stopping meant standing around for a chat and smoke.

But thirty-five minutes later I was asleep, after having a recovery pump on my left arm, food and a shower. This was getting slick.

A big relief to be back on target – that was a 247-mile day – considering I have had my arm in strapping all day, I have strapping on my back, and the bruising is coming out across the palm of my hand. Yeah it was really painful today, not helped by seriously rough roads this morning. It has got better this afternoon. It has been incredible horizons, just vast, it goes on and on and on, these two- to three-mile descents then two to three miles back up the other side. Then you are swooping down again, it's just incredible. Didn't think I would make mileage at lunchtime, but pulled it out the bag by the end of it.

Day 11

Today we are making our way up to Perm, which marks the start of the Ural mountains; shortly after that we will cross into Asia. Spirits are high, a lot less fatigued in the crew than I thought we would be.

The morning's diary-cam was done by David as I was late getting on to
the bike at 4.05, and today it did seem that the Russian drivers were settling in better and understanding that their driving needed to improve.
There had been a lot of coaching from Alex in particular, things like
not passing me too closely, how to track alongside for handovers, and
generally driving smoothly. This wasn't easy when we had almost no
words in common; it was all about communicating using hand signals
and body language. One of them, young Dimi, designed and printed
big yellow stickers proclaiming 'Warning: Cyclist Ahead' (in Russian
of course!) for the back of each vehicle. David had planned this back in
Scotland, but there were issues with making them so it had to be done
from scratch in Russia.

It was a beautiful morning, with the sun rising over misty fields.
And it was all pretty smooth and an uneventful day for the crew. Sadly,
my luck with the wind had to change some time, and after ten days of
tail or sidewinds, a headwind built from early on and made progress
very tough. The graveyard shift through until 8 a.m. was fine, and normally after my ten-minute power nap and a bowl of porridge the
second shift was the easiest of the day, but this time I fought the sleep-
ies badly through the late morning. Perhaps I was so used to that sense
of flow with the conditions; this was my first time fighting for every
mile, and those conditions don't allow you to switch off at all.

From the moment we had entered Russia the landscapes had been
bigger, but since Moscow it was now more open, with wide roads and a
generous hard shoulder, the farms, woods and shelterbelts reminiscent
of eastern Canada. The road in the afternoon rose and fell in very steady
gradients, a mile or two up, a mile or two down, up, down and so on. It
was not varied, it was not steep, but it was a battle into the wind.

I remained impassive, plugging on, trying to decide how I felt. It is
so easy to get into a downwards spiral of negativity on the bike when
conditions are against you. 'It is what it is' is the only pragmatic
response, and finding a wry smile even if you don't feel it, committing
to put the same time in. However, today was one of the first days when
I kept a close eye on my power, not because I was trying to do more,
but because into the hills and wind it is very easy to do too much then
pay for it later. The magic number was 200 watts; doing more would

be very easy, but if I did for hours on end I would pay for it the next day, and risk marginally pushing into the red. I kept having to remind myself that cycling around the world was really a task in not injuring myself. Tap it out, keep the cadence high, play the long game.

Having to work harder, I felt the effort not so much in my muscles as in the contact points, especially my feet, particularly on the right side. A small increase in power to the pedals soon starts to feel like riding on hot coals.

The conditions calmed almost completely in the evening so it was a stunning final few hours, just like the day had started – an expanse of clear sky, a deep serenity. This unexpected finale made all the difference, and from having accepted a loss we all but cracked the 240 miles.

We parked on a track heading into a forest. At just gone 10 p.m. I stepped outside to finish brushing my teeth and to pee. Using my head torch, I walked further down the track, only thirty metres or so but far enough to give my legs a few steps, which they felt so unaccustomed to. I could see some other head torches, I could hear it was the Russians, and I could smell a strong waft of dope. It was unmistakable. I stopped and flashed my head torch straight at them. There was a quick rustle of moving feet in the undergrowth, but the voices stopped. I knew I had to deal with this myself, let them know that they were busted. I barked quietly, so as not to alert the rest of the crew: 'Hey, no!' I didn't know what else to say that they would understand. There was some more rustling as they hurried deeper into the trees.

Walking slowly back to the RVs, my mind was in overdrive, having been ready for sleep a few minutes earlier. My instinct was that if I went straight to David this would be dealt with swiftly and by the letter of the law (and contract): the drivers would be sent home and there was no way that this would not have an impact on the race. I just hoped that I had scared the shit out of them enough to stop it happening again. I don't have any issue with cannabis in people's own time, but for the 80 Days drink and drugs were absolutely banned. We couldn't have drivers under the influence. They were sleep-deprived enough.

I got back into the RV, chatted briefly with Laura, not mentioning my encounter, then tried to fall asleep. But my mind was still switched on, wondering if I had made the right call.

Just over the 240 miles. It was an absolute battle – first day properly into the headwinds. I'm not loving Russia for the trucks and traffic – I have been in a bit of a darker place today because of the conditions. It was also about 3,000m climbing today. But on the bright side, eleven days in and very much on target.

Day 12

Beautiful day, looks like a dry one, and once that mist rises I am sure it is going to be another hot one. Yesterday was seriously hot at times. We are heading for the most northerly point on leg 1 by the time I get to the city of Perm.

I felt surprisingly well rested after my five hours' sleep, and it was relatively easy to get going with a short focus on warming up then riding through the dawn. There was something fun about cycling in dense fog – the illusion of a tiny world, of pedalling gently along as if inside a ping-pong ball. In those early hours very few vehicles passed, but when they did they appeared in and out of my vision and in and out of earshot quickly, leaving me wrapped in a comforting blanket of cloud which my front light could barely penetrate. It is always coldest just before dawn, and as the clouds dispersed and the road rose and fell I raced through stretches of cold air, then warm, the stillness localizing pockets of different temperatures. It was eerily quiet. And then the sun burnt off this magical scene to leave a bluebird of a day.

It was such relaxed riding on much quieter roads, so Alex jumped on the spare bike for a few hours after first break and we chatted away. There had been way too much heavy truck traffic in recent days to allow this. Alex was never allowed to ride in front of me, so I could gain an advantage by sitting on his wheel, but the moral support was appreciated. I did, though, have a conversation with the media boys about this. I understood that it was more interesting to film two people than me on my own, but whenever Alex joined me the drone would go up and the cameras rolled, which made it look like I had support riders every day, or at least a lot of the time, which definitely wasn't the case. I had now been on the bike for nearly 200 hours since Paris and had been accompanied for maybe twelve of them, so I wanted the filming not to look disproportional.

The Guinness World Record rules clearly state that you cannot draft another cyclist or vehicle, that the challenger must remain a minimum distance of five bicycle lengths away, but Una in Scotland, Trent Key and Manni Ferreira in Cape Town (managing director and production manager respectively at MoonSport) and the boys on the road were getting confused about what did and did not qualify as drafting. Una was calling out a couple of shots in the weekly edit which, because they were taken from the back of the Media Vehicle, and because it wasn't clear that they were shot on a long lens, made it look like I was drafting the MV. And because the weekly edits were only a few minutes long, a single shot that lasted a few seconds, be it cycling with Alex or riding an unclear distance behind the MV, could easily be misconstrued for what was happening all the time. I wanted to avoid the public or press getting the impression that I was riding with the aid of a support rider or vehicle.

Manni and Johnny's final opinion was that *any* shot taken from in front of me would look like drafting and they were rightly worried that this would negate my record attempt. I had to explain that standing in front of me on the road as I cycled past was not drafting and filming on a long lens from the vehicle also posed no advantage to me. In practical terms I probably had to be within a metre of the vehicles to gain any advantage. But bless them for being so cautious. If this hadn't been clarified we risked having eighty days' filming of my backside as I cycled away from them in every shot!

By midday it was the hottest it had been since Paris, and over lunch break we set up the massage table in the shade to work on my right calf and quad, trying to address the build-up of tension from such asymmetric cycling. I tried eating as I was being massaged but it was too painful and I couldn't help but cry out pitifully. It was comically sore, embarrassing really – I could tell Laura was using the lightest touch. She assured me that many of her Olympians had been real screamers, that I wasn't too bad. These necessary torture sessions had been met with concerned looks from the crew to start with, but by now were just an accepted part of the routine.

Add to this the fact that I was chewing mainly on the right-hand side of my mouth to avoid the still tender teeth after the crash, and my left elbow remained heavily strapped. I'd grown used to the dull ache in the arm, or spasm of pain if I jolted it over a bump, but still couldn't override my body's natural tendency to protect this. It seemed crazy that I was risking a repetitive strain injury by cycling lopsided. But it is amazing how the body reacts and copes with discomfort.

The roads got busier in the afternoon as we passed the most northerly point on leg 1 near the town of Izhevsk. Keeping my wits about me on the busy ring-road was a concern, and we were trying all sorts of tricks and tweaks to the nutrition plan to avoid this daily afternoon slump in focus and average speed. On the plus side, the tailwind was back, especially as my route turned southeast, and we cruised on incident-free right through the evening.

In the Follow Vehicle, Laura and Alex were continuing to monitor the amount of sleep that everyone was getting. In the past three days Helmut had been spending more time in the FV, ready to cover action but able to get a few short catnaps. The next priority was Johnny, who was doing most of the editing, so getting even less sleep at night. While Johnny was sure he couldn't sleep during the day, when Laura did convince him to come to the FV, he immediately passed out for an hour and a half. David was the next on their priority list. He was sleeping around four hours a night with no daytime naps and this was not sustainable. I understood the strain he was under as he felt that he couldn't leave the Russians, but we needed David to stay sharp.

Simple tasks that would merit no description on a more relaxed road-trip became quite an ordeal – for example, how each vehicle's water tanks were refilled, something which needed doing every few days. It was the job of the MV to scope forward to find a source, which wasn't easy as fuel stations normally didn't have taps, and this location would then be reported back to the FV. When I reached this point, there would be a quick handover of spare wheels and parts for the MV to take over in support as the FV ducked out for water. It sounds simple, but conveying the need for urgency was difficult.

As well as topping out at our most northerly point, it was also the biggest climbing day so far and compounded the previous day's efforts.

My feet were screaming, especially into the final four-hour stint. The pain was hard to deal with, but I was trying not to curl my toes, or adjust my foot angle, as I knew this would make my foot lose its fluidity in rotation, causing tendon issues across the foot arch and in my Achilles. Like running flat-footed, the impact would be far greater if the foot became rigid, not to mention the loss of power transfer to the pedals.

Your feet are always going to hurt with this many hours in the saddle, but I had made a very basic error, and the scale of this problem was now becoming apparent. The custom-made insoles that I had had made fitted perfectly and were of a material with some give. The plan was to ride a new pair of insoles every 2,000 miles, so I had nine replica sets made. But none of these was identical to the first, either in shape or material, and I hadn't tested them. So while my original insoles were now wearing thinner and thinner, none of the replacements was usable.

At 9.20 p.m. I came across David and the Russians in a garage car park, cooking dinner. The FV team were expecting me to roll on for another ten minutes, but I called it a day. I felt pretty broken, and another ten minutes' sleep felt like a just reward after a day of ridgeline after ridgeline, up and over, again and again, for nearly 250 miles.

A burly, ruddy-faced man in a denim jacket wandered over as I got off the bike. He looked like a nuisance and I was concerned this wasn't a safe spot. But David had more experience of Russia, and after a brief conflab, translated by Hishgue, we settled the 700-ruble fee (about £10) per vehicle for overnight parking and were now under this man's watch. This didn't instil me with any newfound confidence in security, but at least he would leave us be. The lorry park was perhaps half the size of a football pitch and with plenty of overnight customers, so there was heavy demand for two shanty-style long-drop toilets, the sort with a makeshift wooden frame over a simple hole in the ground. It was a stinking cesspit, an unpleasant exercise in how long you could hold your breath.

It's been a biggy, 250 miles, and well over 3,000m climbing. Even though we are going through the Ural mountains tomorrow it should be a lot less climbing. After that it drops to less than 500m climbing a

day. Cleats really hurting, so very much looking forward to getting
past the Urals.

Day 13

This is the sorest I have felt in the morning, with quite a tension headache from this neck position. Yesterday was a huge day by all accounts,
today should be less. First thing is just about getting up and off, use the
first half hour to ease into the bike, everything hurts. I am really looking forward to some flatter lands in three or four days' time. All my
contact points hurt – hands and feet especially . . . My seat is fine; saddle sores aren't too bad. Let's go!

At 3.50 a.m. I looked haggard, and felt battered. The hangover from a
big day is always tougher to deal with than the day itself.

Overall, we were now a good 60 miles up on target. After twelve
massive days from Paris we had put four hours' ride time in the bank –
which didn't seem much, an average of 245 miles a day so far. It had
seemed utterly mental, the longest twelve days of my life, and we were
only just into the black. I felt I was drowning in this intimidating
thought, of having to repeat what I had done since Paris another six
times before the finish. I then buried these feelings and got focused on
the road in front of me, which was already completely lit, although the
sun had yet to appear over the horizon. Heading southeast from this
point, I was expecting the days to gradually shorten.

Ten years ago I had crossed into Asia a long way to the west of my
current longitude, across the Bosphorus in Istanbul, a natural and
definitive border between Europe and the east. Now I was in a vast forest
in the middle of Russia when I came across a rather strange monument
at the roadside. It was a pillar of what looked like red granite, the height
of a lorry, with a metal obelisk shape on top and a disc around it – part
Eiffel Tower, part rings of Saturn. This monument, marking the transition from one continent to another, was on the far side of a four-lane
highway, so not a scenic spot to stop or a place that evoked a sense of
ceremony.

There were a few data and tracking problems which, while mundane, were a constant concern for the crew, trying to make sure every mile was logged in multiple ways. A few times it was a simple PICNIC (problem in chair and not in computer) – either my forgetting to switch on the Garmin or forgetting to put the Trident GPS tracker back in my jersey after lunch, when it needed charging. But this morning it simply wasn't pinging to the satellites and after a few hours we switched units, as we were carrying three. The daily rains had killed our first tracker and more care was taken from then on to waterproof the others. It was the job of the crew to check the website to ensure the tracking was working, but with the busy early-morning routines this wasn't always happening, and it was Una who often reported back if there was a break in the online tracking. That morning Alex was busy filming some videos for the leg 2 and 3 mechanics for information on their daily routines, so was distracted.

Not even two weeks in, Una was already legendary on the team for seemingly never switching off. Back at Base Camp in Scotland, now five hours behind challenge time, she was up and communicating with the teams as we set out at 4 a.m. every day and remained in touch throughout our nineteen hours of being awake and on the go. It was brilliant support for the crew, who also felt under a close watch!

I had spotted Hajaa, the Mongolian MV Prado driver, making quite a few trips into the long grass as I spun by, and flagged this with Laura. Sure enough, before first break she admitted to having a bad stomach and diarrhoea so was immediately quarantined and reminded about health and non-contamination protocol. It was tough love for the crew, and I felt sorry for her cooped up, feeling so unwell. But there was no stopping. Johnny and Helmut, who had been in the MV, were closely monitored and kept away from the FV for the next twenty-four hours, with David driving for the rest of the day.

Soon after the non-event of crossing into Asia we had a dental rendezvous at a petrol station on the E22 just west of the town of Yekaterinburg. Jonathan Lamont, my Irish friend from Sudan, had contacted Mark Rakestraw at the British Embassy, who introduced us to Matt Osbourne, Deputy Consul-General at their office in Yekaterinburg, because that was on my route. Glass ionomer resin is not on your average shopping list, but we needed to rebuild my tooth as quickly as possible – it was becoming quite sensitive to cold and heat and needed protecting. Una was relaying what was needed from the dentist, Burjor Langdana, and Natalia Pietra, a Russian lady from Matt's office, somehow found it, for the modest sum of £50.

David had gone ahead to make sure the handover was a quick hello and photo, but no further delay. Matt was waiting, looking every part the diplomat in his suit, with his translator and driver by their black embassy car. I hadn't seen anything so smart and British since the Reform Club, although he did lose the tie for this occasion! Matt had read *The Man Who Cycled the World*, had ridden from Land's End to John O'Groats, and was absolutely delighted to be involved. A quick natter, a photo, and we were off. We barely lost any time – a slick operation all round.

The actual operation was meant to happen that night, or so Laura thought. But I was keen to get this broken tooth protected, not least so it would stop grating the now ragged inside of my lip.

On a very busy ring-road south of Yekaterinburg we came upon a crash and the road was blocked to vehicles, so I loaded up with spare inner tubes, little cans of CO_2 (a faster solution than having to carry a bicycle pump), energy bars and water – the normal supplies whenever I got separated from the FV – and rode on. It was a very hot afternoon, with a lot of traffic and constantly changing views around me in the industrial suburbs, in contrast to the monotonous mega-miles of previous days.

In the FV Laura made the most of the traffic jam to practise making teeth out of the resin, seeing how quickly it set, testing the right quantities of powder and epoxy (resin), and chatting to camera: 'Unfortunately Alex won't let me practise on him, so I used a mould instead and made a couple of tooth shapes (in case I accidentally knocked out Mark's!). I'm glad I practised with it first, because it took a few goes to figure out how to work the paste and see how quickly it set. I thought we would be doing it this evening at the end of the day, but Mark's keen to get it done in his next break, so no time like the present, we decided to crack on with it.'

We managed to regroup before the end of the third shift and we were doing well for mileage, so at a fly-infested roadside parking lot, with a thunderstorm brewing, Laura got ready to perform the dental surgery. I quickly had some food while the final prep took place and as I ate the heavens opened, rain bouncing off the roof of the RV with loud bangs of thunder closing in overhead. It was wonderfully snug inside, and there was a sense of excitement about the imminent op.

Alex was acting dental nurse and sat at the head of the bed, holding my head still as I lay there, mouth wide open. First, Laura took a nail file to the bottom edge of the tooth, buffing off the jagged enamel. It wasn't a pleasant sensation, but it didn't hurt. While most of the front enamel had chipped off, the nerve wasn't exposed or sore to pressure, only hot or cold liquids. Laura used her phone light to inspect the now smoother tooth before carrying on. In the five days since the crash, this canine and the tooth behind it had returned to their proper position, after having been jammed upwards into the gum. While still a bit loose, they were firming up quickly.

When mixing the resin in the food prep and sink area of the RV, Laura had to work quickly, as it set in a few minutes. And if you ever find yourself in a similar situation, here are the key steps after having filed down the tooth to take off the sharp edges:

- Rinse the mouth with warm salt water
- Dry the tooth
- Apply Anhydrin to prepare the tooth to optimize adherence of the resin
- Mix the powder 3:1 to the liquid, which takes thirty seconds to turn into a thick/dry consistency like chewing gum
- Apply to the tooth and continuously mould over two minutes to provide a smooth edge
- Leave for two minutes to set
- Apply layer of Vaseline
- Rinse with warm salt water
- Remain on a soft diet for the remainder of the day

It went very well. So well that I fell fast asleep, snoring gently despite having a wide-open mouth, Johnny snapping away, Helmut filming,

Alex holding my lip out of the way and Laura sculpting my new tooth. It took two attempts, two layers of dentine, before Laura was happy with the shape and finish.

I woke up to a group of amused faces peering down at me, Laura looking quite relieved and pleased. 'Right, let's go,' I said, and started pulling my shoes back on, pausing only for Johnny to take a few photos of Laura's handiwork. Meanwhile, Alex jumped outside, cleaned the chain down, checked the bike, and had it standing by the roadside as I stepped out.

We had stopped for just thirty-five minutes.

The final stint was under broody skies but the storm had passed and the roads were starting to dry. We parked up in a sandy lay-by, and the mood was buoyant. An extraordinary team effort, and it was lights out by 10.10 – a solid day.

Made it across Europe in twelve and a half days and we are now in Asia. A huge milestone. Today was a 243-mile day which included 2.5km of climbing. But these roads – I have passed one touring cyclist in the whole of Russia and I can see why. Certainly the roads that I am on are not for your average cyclist, they are absolutely brutal. You need a mountain bike on many of them. The team can see me for 2km with my rear light, but often can't be close by. If they sit directly behind me then we create a problem with undertaking drivers, pulling on to the dirt sections at the side of the road and flying up my inside. The buffeting from heavy trucks passing too close is also unpleasant, but not quite so reckless.

Day 14

Just gone 3.30 a.m. local time, about 4 a.m. challenge time, and a beautiful start to the day. I like it at this time as the roads are nice and quiet. Day 14 was the end of Around Britain, and I have to say mentally and physically I am in much better shape now than I was then – so good news. Sure it feels like I have been in the tumble-dryer though! There was quite a bit of rain in the night, but it has cleared now. The bike has taken a huge amount of abuse without issue, riding these 28mm

> Panaracers which soak up so much of the tough road surface, and road
> joins. The only puncture since Paris has been glass, and you can't fault
> that. The bike is certainly fast, I just need to keep the engine going!

I was so focused on getting started, the normal routine, that I didn't
notice anything out of the ordinary. The deep sand meant that I
wheeled the bike to the roadside with Alex and I was off. It took a bit
longer than usual for the FV to catch up, and I did look back a few
times, but there it was. Half an hour in it was time for my breakfast
smoothie on the bike, which they handed out of the window as I rolled
along. In my early-morning daze I still didn't spot the issue.

Laura was driving.

At 4 a.m. David was up with Laura and Alex, but the Russian
drivers were not ready. Whether they were still asleep, or just not ready,
it wasn't clear – I was focused on getting started, paying no attention
to what others were doing. But this moment had been coming. The
Russians had been told on numerous occasions to be ready on time,
but they were having to be chased. When I left, the race started and I
needed support. So Laura and Alex took the only available option.

Laura was uninsured and according to the contract with the vehicle company and the drivers wasn't allowed to drive – none of the
British crew were. But Laura and Alex were alone in the FV for about
an hour and twenty minutes, albeit on almost completely empty roads
at that time in the morning. This was partly because of the Russians
sleeping in, but also in their rush to catch up they got the second RV
bogged down in the sand and it had to be towed out.

When we regrouped, and I was made aware of the situation, David
was very angry and targeted this at Laura. She was told that she had
'technically stolen' the vehicle and when she defended herself by saying that in the same circumstances she would do the same again, David
responded by telling her that if she did, she would be sent home. I only
learnt about this falling-out after the event and it goes without saying
that no one was going to be sent home, least of all my performance
manager. But it was an unfortunate incident as it soured relationships
and trust. Everyone pulled themselves together and got on professionally afterwards, but it was a turning point that was difficult to come

back from. The bottom line was that it was wheels rolling at 4 a.m. every morning, not 4.05 or later, and the team leader had to take responsibility for the crew being up and ready. The silver lining was that I was pretty certain the Russians wouldn't sleep in again.

I plodded through the very quiet Saturday morning dawn shift oblivious to all of this, trying to stay alert on the bike. David, driving the MV, captured fantastic tracking footage into the morning sun with Helmut – which was the upside of Hajaa being ill and quarantined, as she could be an erratic driver. Johnny and Helmut had been going mad trying to get her to drive at slow, steady speeds for filming but her emergency braking followed by enthusiastic acceleration made this comically impossible. I had often been halfway through chatting to camera when the Prado would lurch forward for no obvious reason and accelerate out of sight. When traffic did need to pass, the protocol was to accelerate gently forward, indicate, pull into the side, letting both the traffic and me past, then catch up steadily. Hajaa was really trying, but we had missed some important landscapes and pieces to camera.

After first break we made better miles with a gentle tailwind on improving roads, thanks to the infrastructure around Tyumen, the oil capital of Russia. Zooming out on the map we could see we were now about halfway across the breadth of Kazakhstan, which lay not far to our south, and Kazakh trucks were a common sight on the roads. Tyumen was one of the first settlements in Siberia and had boomed since the creation of the Trans-Siberian Railway, but my only impression of it was hundreds of sixties-style concrete tower blocks. The sprawling outskirts looked like fields of termite mounds – a very industrial and uniform place to call home. I enjoyed the fast and busy ride though, staggered by the views and reminded once again of how little I knew about Russia. Who knew there were so many people in Siberia?

Ice cream and filming with the crew at lunchtime seemed to go a long way to lift the tension of the morning and Alex joined me for a stint in the afternoon, perhaps needing to blow off some steam. The roads quietened and straightened out and were now flat as a pancake, beside endless wheat fields. We capitalized with a shorter afternoon break and the predictable conditions meant that I could dictate the finish from about 40km out. Despite riding by time, I really wanted to crack the magic 400km again. At 9.25 p.m. and 401km we stopped, putting another 15km in the bank.

A big bowl of stew appeared that the Russians had made – which Laura secretly threw away, careful not to offend them. We didn't need more fall-outs. The crew had been told a number of times that I couldn't eat processed meat, nothing artificial, yet it was only those with a performance sport background who really understood and remembered this. It wasn't the first or last time I resorted to an expedition boil-in-a bag meal. The big bonus for the end of the day was a warm shower. It seemed ridiculous that we had made it this far and not figured out how easy the RV shower was – the assumption was that it used too much water and would take too much time, so we had skipped it. Every evening I was used to stripping in the small RV shower room and washing with a flask of hot water, a basin and a face cloth. But a proper shower was a revelation after thousands of miles with a wet flannel.

> It's been a dry day, one of my first days in Russia when it hasn't rained at all. And being Saturday, there were a lot less trucks, I felt a lot safer on the road – I actually quite enjoyed it. It was a beautiful finish. It is getting quite cool; just as the sun sets, there is this mist lying over the valley floor.

Day 15

> Start of day 15 and it's cooler this morning, 12°C, lovely mist hanging over the fields. Sunday, so hopefully nice and quiet again. I managed to get a shower last night, first time in two weeks! So I am feeling a bit fresher this morning. Big day ahead I am sure, more flatlands. Couple more days of the flatlands.

What a well-oiled machine – the Russian driver was just about ready as I pulled away at 4 a.m. exactly. I was layered up for a much cooler morning shift. The easy roads, lack of navigation issues and the steadily increasing experience of the Russians as well as the core team made for fairly slick progress. When I say easy roads, I mean for our vehicles – not for me, given the trucks, which were back in earnest despite it being Sunday. With no hard shoulder there were a few very close passes, and nothing I could do but flinch. The road surface was also generally poor: lumpy, cracked and potholed. Each day was ending with a soot- and grit-blackened face and kit. It wasn't matching up to my expectations of riding into the wilderness.

The afternoon rolled on with more long, flattish roads and wide horizons of buckwheat and woodlands. A brief rainstorm before third break passed in half an hour, and the final four-hour session was a run-in to the city of Omsk.

I was then astonished to overtake a couple of touring cyclists, a Russian couple who knew about the 80 Days and waved madly as I sped by. I was so in the zone and flying along it didn't occur to me to slow and be sociable until afterwards, and then I kicked myself for being rude, but the media crew did stop and film an interview with them.

Omsk was a major milestone, the second largest city east of the Ural mountains in Russia, with over a million residents. The first junction into Omsk was gridlocked so in case I got lost on my own Alex handed me a card with the name of the next big city on the route written on it in Russian – НОВОСИБИРСК. It just became known as 'Hobo', and given it was 560km away, that was possibly a precaution too far!

It was the young driver Dimitri's birthday, so I signed a crew T-shirt for him and we all sang 'Happy Birthday' and tucked into cake. And the next day he appeared in a pair of the crew's Rudy Project sunglasses. The mood in camp could hardly have been better.

End of day 15, and perfect timing – a beautiful red sunset and we have just made it around the town of Omsk. I wasn't meant to make it this far but it has been another cracking day distance wise, 406km, so it is good to crack the 250 miles again. Nice to make it around the city, that's a big old place, don't need to do that in the morning. Over the last three days the local time has changed by three hours, so that is the last 750 miles' riding – so it shows our plan to lose fifteen minutes a day is really working. We haven't really noticed it and it also means we are really optimizing daylight: I am not having to ride in the dark at all, which makes such a difference. Plan has come together there. This is the point on our journey where we have the most crew on the road – we have Russian drivers, we have some Mongolian drivers as well and they can't drive more than eight-hour shifts, and we have three vehicles, so the team is quite bulked up at the moment. Still got Alex and David and Laura and the guys from MoonSport who are doing all the fabulous photos and filming, but we also have all the local contingent, and this travelling circus is making good progress.

11

Never-ending Russia

Day 16

It's just before 4 a.m. local time . . . no, that is challenge time – I keep
making that mistake as I am the only person on the team who is looking at both times. Everyone else just living in challenge time. Yeah, I'm
a bit sore when I wake up in the morning, obviously! Just need to not
think about it too much, and get on the road, and half an hour in most
of those aches and pains have eased off. Quite a lot of bruising is coming out of my thumb and my hand where I landed on it last week – it's
amazing it takes so long for the bruising to come out. I have what
should be the elevation for each day – they aren't always accurate – but
day 16 looks like the flattest day on leg 1. So quite excited by not climbing up hills today. Right, let's go, I have four minutes to go . . .

Helmut and Johnny always waited respectfully until Laura gave them
the nod that they could come into the RV and film. We were trying to
mix up the start- and end-of-day video diaries in terms of location, but
with such a rigid routine there were limited ways and places we could
do so. These were immediately pinged back to the team in South Africa
for editing then uploading to Facebook and YouTube. The predictability of this twice-daily content, as well as the GPS dot updating every
fifteen minutes, was by now growing an impressive global following.
The original brief was to make these video diaries very short, ideally
around thirty to forty-five seconds. But I just couldn't speak that
quickly and concisely so soon after waking at 3.30 a.m., and typically

quite a lot had happened by eighteen hours later, so Johnny had given up asking me to say it again, keeping it short. After another three-minute ramble I would look at Johnny, ask 'Is that short enough?', and he would just laugh. I was just creating more work for him.

The poor media boys looked shattered every morning, Johnny in his black hoody, Helmut having to work even before his first cigarette of the day. But they were stoically supportive, very selfless and completely committed. Typically for these early-morning pieces Helmut would be filming and Johnny holding an LDC panel lamp in my face, a bright white spotlight which woke me up a bit more. Many of these morning videos filmed inside the RV featured a turquoise spork, which for me was just an efficient way to shovel in breakfast – but I didn't realize how ridiculous this salad-server-size ladle looked onscreen, and how it was becoming 'a thing', a distraction from what I was actually saying, and often commented on!

It was a pleasant 18°C with no wind at all. This far north I was pretty much not having to do any night-riding at all with the benefits of our challenge time. After a gentle climb away from Omsk for 10km or so it was flattish, as advertised – about 578m of climbing in 240 miles if the research was correct. Indeed, we had very straight, flat roads all day.

During the morning the wind did pick up, against me, so I was conscious of needing to slow myself rather than push harder into it, especially as I could see that the road would turn south, when the wind would be more over my left shoulder. I needed to be careful as I had still not been riding normally since the crash. While protecting my left elbow, my right knee, neck and most of all my right foot were constantly sore.

Laura summarized my state of mind in her notes: 'Mark is definitely on that brink where if he is cruising, steady state, he is fine – but as soon as he gets a headwind, like this morning, and then he gets a pounding with the roads – that's when it takes it out of him, and he really struggles.'

The main change in the day was the road, which went from tar to concrete in the afternoon. These large concrete slabs with tar-filled cracks every five metres produced a metronome of jolts every few seconds. Passing vehicles made a 'de-dunk, de-dunk, de-dunk' noise as their front then back wheels clattered over this corrugated surface.

On the bike it was a real pain in the neck, which was already very sore. Sitting upright holding the bars and brake hoods was very painful on my bruised hands, so being down in the aero position felt better, but put the neck at a more acute angle for the bumps. We discussed improvements on the move, firstly to drop the tyre pressure to 75psi on the back and 70psi on the front, very soft for a road bike but a bit more forgiving, plus the 28mm tyres could take this without pinch puncturing. The other option was to raise the aerobars a bit, but on checking the travelling garage we realized we didn't have the bolts to swap the 20mm risers for the 30mm, so David was on bolt-finding duty once we reached Novosibirsk the next day.

In the late afternoon I was filming when I unexpectedly came back on to tar, and the sense of relief was huge:

> It was meant to be the flattest day of stage 1, so was looking forward to fast miles, but in actual fact it has been one of the toughest days so far. I had a cracking headwind all morning and this afternoon came on to concrete roads. Little lips and gaps you are dropping off every second when you already have sore feet and backside and hands, that constant vibration, banging, mile after mile, hour after hour, is making it very painful today. My biggest worry, to be honest, is running myself into the ground, getting an injury or niggle, which means I ride the next couple of months in pain and I just can't cover the distances. So I am still in the mindset of 'I need to protect myself, I need to ride sensibly'. Russia has been tough miles for sure. I have to play the long game, forfeit the miles; in the long run I won't regret it. Oh . . . is this back on to tarmac? Fantastic! Tarmac! I had resigned myself to concrete bloody roads for the rest of the day. Smooth rolling, I'll take that.

Day 17

> I feel better this morning – I had an extra half hour's sleep, five and a half hours! To think it took six days to get across Europe, we have now been in Russia for over ten, with a week still to go – it's a big old place. Another big milestone today – Novosibirsk – which means New

Siberia. Hoping I can stay more in the zone today; yesterday was an absolute battle. Let's go . . .

It was another day on straight, flat roads, and thankfully slab concrete was less frequent. It was a landscape dotted with swamp pools, birch woods, wheatfields, and in parts just gravel. It was also hot and sunny, and there was an added incentive to keep going: the monstrous flies, clegs and mosquitoes. This was more what I imagined the west Siberian plateau to be like, almost uninhabited, although that didn't stop this being a heavily used trunk road.

A headwind came and went all day, seeming to swirl around. Endless straights, endless miles. The distances were so vast we seemed to be creeping towards Novosibirsk. As a back-up to digital mapping we had a paper map for leg 1a, which we had raced across at such an impressive pace, but our paper map for leg 1b was to a very different scale, and it was quite depressing to look at how insignificant 240 miles really was. Alex likened us to John Cleese as Sir Lancelot endlessly 'rushing' Swamp Castle in *Monty Python and the Holy Grail*.

I spent the day consciously trying to find a better mindset. Yesterday had been the first day I felt a bit overwhelmed, a bit down about things. When you are hurting it is really hard to think your way through some of these big days. But I ended up getting very close to 240 miles, which was a miracle. Today I was just trying to keep my focus really short as there was not much out there to distract me. Never-ending wilderness. The next city 100km ahead, the last city 500km behind me – that's a lot of space. I was just trying to tap out the miles and stay in the right headspace.

After an unchanging ten hours we reached the much talked-about junction near Novosibirsk – we had all been forewarned that it would be poorly signposted (and obviously in Russian) and so easy to miss after hundreds of kilometres without a junction – and skirted north of the city, leaving David and the team to head in to resupply. The change in terrain was immediate, back to steady rolling roads as it had been after Moscow, but also back to concrete.

As she watched me from the FV, Laura had noticed that my right leg was kicking out and I reported back that my posterior knee pain was getting pretty unbearable. Alex and Laura had a closer look at my cleats on each pair of shoes and discovered a noticeable divot in the carbon sole of each right shoe. They spent a couple of hours looking into my foot position and then fabricated a lateral 1.5mm wedge out of ultra-thin plastic for under the outside of the cleat, to stop my leg kicking out. This was a calculated gamble, as I have never ridden with a wedge, and changing the geometry of my leg angle was risky considering it was rotating about 85,000 times a day. But with an impending injury to my right knee, something had to be done. The right pedal had been pretty chewed on its outside edge as a result of compensating rightwards, so Alex replaced the pedal and cleats. Like the hamstring injury on Around Britain, it is these slow, creeping issues and injuries that are hardest to spot, especially when you are generally sore all over.

Alex chimed in on the video diary: 'You are looking much flatter and smoother on the rotation. Immediately, as soon as we looked at you after the changes, out of the window we could see – he is fixed – you were just kinking off to the right with your heel before . . .'

Given the headwinds and foot issues, I was pragmatic about finishing the day at 228 miles. We had so far covered 4,147 miles, at an average of 244 miles a day. Una reported back that the Guinness World Record for most miles cycled in a month was just 4,011 miles by Janet Davison in 2015, so if all went to plan I would blow that to pieces with around 7,100 miles. It was a fun fact to chew over with the team while I ate dinner and got treatment, well aware that many cyclists have done more than 4,011 miles in a month, but the record just hadn't been claimed. Even at 7,100 miles, I suspected perhaps one or two people had ridden more. But it was definitely a world record we planned to sweep up en route to the circumnavigation, so at the end of day 17 we toasted our milk chocolate to that!

I was straight into the FV as usual, while Alex got busy cleaning and checking the bike outside. My end-of-day routine was stripping and washing in the shower cubicle as quickly as possible, while Laura went over to the MV to get dinner. Washing was still normally a thermos flask of boiling water poured into the basin and cooled down with cold, before a lather with the cloth. When we were carrying enough water I used the shower, but if this was the case I would normally eat first to allow the water time to heat up. Every evening was subtly different, within the same strict timeline. I would then smother my backside and between my legs, which had a pretty raw sweat rash, with Sudocrem and also pawpaw cream. After that I would tuck into a big plate of dinner, a solid dose of fat, proteins and carbs, followed by a pudding to satisfy my sweet tooth – a treat I looked forward to at the end of every day – and normally a peppermint tea. Using the big pneumatic leg pump, the RPX Recovery Pump, like a sumo suit for my legs meant I could get treatment while eating.

End of day 17 and I will take that. Just the second day since Paris that we haven't nailed the 240 – but I had a headwind all day, so there was a time that I thought we would lose a lot more than that. Quite a change of scenery: I made it past Novosibirsk, and it was just flat, flat, flat, just marshes. Just done about 600km flat and straight – now we are into big rolling hills, and into the woodlands. Laura or Alex noticed that there was rub on the carbon on the sole – well that shouldn't happen, the pedal shouldn't be making direct contact with the shoe, which made me think that something was worn out that we hadn't checked, so we have changed the pedals and changed the cleats. In that last four-hour set the discomfort has gone from behind my knee. And my foot is not as sore. I was thinking 'Is this an injury?' and then suddenly you change something as simple as that. That is a sign of the miles – going through a set of pedals in seventeen days!

Day 18

We are camped surrounded by marshes, so it's mozzy land here, lots of bugs in this part of Siberia. I was quite looking forward to the flatlands and they've ended up being some of the toughest days so far. It just shows the biggest differential to speed is not terrain, it is wind by far – so I don't really care about being back into the terrain, as long as I don't have a headwind. And it looks a bit more interesting. There is no wind at all at this time in the morning, it tends to pick up as the day goes on. There are no big towns ahead, no big milestones.

The muggy and overcast start soon turned into steady rain as I climbed away from the roadside camp. It remained busy, over rolling terrain, and wet until after Kemerovo, which was the first city since Moscow that we couldn't bypass – so we used the Bluetooth headset for the team to navigate me through the centre of town. We had one helmet set up with this earpiece, battery and transmitter, and I was getting deft at being able to change this over on the move. But there was quite a lot of uncertainty about the route, causing us to stop and lose time. The internet was very patchy in these remote parts, which revealed the limitation of our mapping and navigation options. Our paper maps were too large-scale to get us through busy places like this, and we were reliant on the Russian satnav system, which was lucky, but not part of the plan.

To inject some unintended daily humour into the team we had Sasha, the boss of the Russian drivers, a man of around forty, bald with a beard. He was a lot more smiley than the others and spoke better English, so was the perfect leader. Like everyone, he found the long hours in the vehicles tough, but he had a novel coping mechanism: he used every break to do the most elaborate stretches. Sasha tended to wear tight T-shirts and very short shorts – a strong eighties look. I had first spotted these roadside routines in the forests west of Moscow and was mesmerized. They became a talking point and cheered us up on those endless Russian roads. The whirling arms, the deep lunges, and what can only be described as retro dance moves. While this wonderful routine was performed unashamedly, it still felt rude to stare, although it was hard not to. I would often be sitting in the RV, quickly working through a meal or treatment, and would spot him entertaining the passing trucks with these antics. I tried to encourage Johnny to film them, certain they would go viral on YouTube.

Having learnt lessons from Kemerovo, the team gathered together for prep before the next hurdle, Mariansk; but this was overkill which reflected the guilt at messing up earlier in the day, as our three vehicles passed straight through this small town. It had a distinctly Wild West look, with clapboard shack-like houses, but quaint, and we were past it without losing any time.

Oddly, the one 'friendly' encounter I didn't mention on my end-of-day video diary, as I didn't want to advertise it while I was still in the area, was with two young lads who pulled alongside, wound down the window of their old battered black saloon, and waved a handgun. They didn't exactly point it at me, the driver just looked across as his passenger waggled the weapon in the boastful manner of 'look what I have got'. Soon after, Alex joined me for a short stint and we chatted this over, and I decided there was nothing to worry about, it was just youthful bragging.

An absolute battle, 236 miles, far hillier than I expected it to be. We set out this morning and it was heavy rain for the first three hours – not the easiest way to warm up; soon dried out and ended up being a beautiful day through much quieter roads. There has been a really noticeable change, even the houses – feels like we are going into the wilderness, and a poorer part of Russia. I thought no one would know who I was but today there were lots of toots and waves – a guy slowed down, took a selfie while he drove, and a guy pulled alongside, shouted 'Mark' and shoved me a protein bar, a muesli bar – so I am in the middle of the wilderness here, and somehow people have heard about the 80 Days. There was a lot of friendly camaraderie.

Day 19

It is the start of day 19 and it has been raining all night, we woke up to rain, but it's dry right now. I'm very sore this morning – yesterday took a lot out of me, so a bit of a battle this morning. I'll let Laura say a few things . . .

I trailed off, unable to focus on the filming while sorting out my tracker and gloves, sore and agitated to get going. There was something comforting about being alone with your own grumpiness on the bike, the discomfort of those first miles, which were more bearable than the interaction with the team and camera. Just let me suffer alone and I'll be fine in a bit.

Laura did a better job of summarizing the moment: 'We are just teetering on that edge and we have about nine days to go in this leg – even getting half an hour's extra sleep made all the difference, so we could do with a nice little tailwind again and get him to finish just a bit earlier one day. I think that would make the world of difference, it would just keep him ticking along. As soon as he gets a day of hills or extra headwind, you can see it takes a lot more out of him.'

We had had many conversations back in Scotland about the heat of midsummer in Russia, and did some sessions in the climate chamber getting adapted to temperatures in the mid-thirties. But for all the hours Alex and the team had spent sorting tools and kit, the one thing none of us ever thought about was a crud catcher for rain and wet roads. Having constantly wet shorts was a catalyst for the dreaded saddle sores. And so Alex cut a 1.5-litre water bottle in half, cobbled together a makeshift mudguard and ziptied it on to the underside of the saddle. Tying a piece of plastic to my dream bike looked sacrilegious, but I was very grateful.

It rained hard all morning and the team did their best on the comms and with food and hot drinks to keep my spirits up. I was cheered up most by Alex's kind attempt at making me a hot choc while on the move. This was a balancing act of pouring hot milk into the powder, lid on, shake – bang! They had an impressive hot chocolate explosion inside the RV, and a lengthy clean-up process.

Meanwhile the media boys were loving the conditions. Big terrain or broken roads is quite hard to capture faithfully on camera, but bucketing rain is pretty obvious, so they spent long periods tracking alongside using the osmo, a camera with a stabilizing gyro, to capture the full glory, including in slow motion, of the fun we were having. The roads were much better through gentle rolling wooded land-scapes, with a light tailwind, so once I'd accepted the conditions I was happily warmed up and in the flow of a good mileage day.

Coming into the town of Achinsk a back puncture was swapped like an F1 pit stop and the team morale was high, feeling the momen-tum of a good morning. At the end of eight hours' riding, planning to stop for lunch, we came through a very heavy rainstorm, so rather than step into the RV like a drowned rat I opted to delay and dry off a bit, plus try and get ahead of the storm so I wouldn't have to ride through it again. For this I was rewarded with more strong tailwinds off the back of the storm for the next hour which chased me up a long drag of a hill. Laura wasn't delighted to be meddling with her nutritional and rest plans but I was determined to make miles in the lee of the storm so we powered on into the afternoon.

Nearing the city of Krasnoyarsk, we were faced again with the conundrum of going through the middle or around the ring-road, and there was more frustration that this hadn't been researched in enough detail. As I looked down on the city in the valley, the ring-road, with three big ridgelines over 25km, felt like the wrong choice. Perhaps direct would have been faster, and kinder on the legs, even with junctions and traffic lights. But ring-road it was, and into the evening I rode across a vast bridge over the Yenisei river and up Karaulnaya Hill to a rolling plateau of pine and birch.

The mood in camp remained high, a long way literally and emotionally from the start of the day. We were a quarter of the way through the World attempt in nineteen days! This called for a group photo and a quick chat with the team. The sun was setting and it was a stunning evening now the storms had passed. And most of all it was wonderful to pause, just for five minutes, and say hello to my team. Every day started with me emerging from the RV and setting off after a quick chat to camera, and every day ended in the same fashion, because every moment counted. The only people I was in regular contact with were Laura, Alex and David – yet there was this team of eight people across three vehicles working tirelessly on my behalf whom I never spoke to. I could see in this rare moment together that they were enjoying the race, but were all tired, really being pushed.

It's the end of day 19 and a big milestone, because this is officially a quarter of the way around the World. It was a big day, just shy of 400km, so about 248 miles. And it's so nice to stop and say hello to my Russian crew – to acknowledge them and say thank you. I realize I am grumpy and tired most of the time – I'll go back to that now!

Day 20

It's much lighter this morning and we are a bit higher up, so it's about 5°C cooler, perhaps also because of the clear skies. I'm feeling OK, all things considered. Looks like I will have a bit of a favourable wind again today, which we will try and make the most of – the next big milestone is to get out of Russia.

Laura's notes managed to convey how we both felt a quarter of the way around the World. The 'warm-up' was over, and my body was now well adjusted to the sixteen-hour days and lack of sleep. It was now a case of being utterly consistent and spotting issues fast. I'll hand over to her here.

'Apart from general body and muscle fatigue after a hard day on the bike, if Mark gets any issues which could develop into an injury, then it's usually due to there being a change in something external which is the root cause. When he actually shows signs of an injury, we need to look at the key contact points between the body and the bike; i.e. front set-up for his aerobars, saddle position and pelvis, feet insoles and shoe set-up, clothing, and see if anything has changed from his norm. Since the accident his normal mechanics have been thrown out and that has had a knock-on effect, causing some secondary issues to manage.

'So, current issues being treated:

'Right knee – Posterior knee pain on extension of the knee, related to a neural mechanical interface. Possibly triggered by altered mechanics, due to right foot pain. As I watch Mark ride, I can see that the right foot is held in supination so the inside of the foot is pulled upwards and most of the pressure is transferring down through the outside of the foot. Had a look at the cleats and pedals and there was significant lateral wear just on the right side, so Alex changed both the pedals and cleats to new sets. Interestingly you most probably wouldn't think to change out your pedals within five years if you are a normal day-to-day cyclist, but these have done over 4,000 miles in seventeen days! We have also adjusted the cleat angle to bring the shoe into a more neutral float position, as Mark had reported he felt he was always needing to push his heel outward against the float. Immediately cycling with the new set-up alleviated his pain, so no matter how much treatment you do to address neural dynamics or whatever you think the pain generator is, addressing the source/cause of the injury has to be the priority and easiest gain.

'Right foot – Due to not being able to weight-bear fully through the left arm, this meant a transfer of increased load going through the right side. The right foot under the balls of the toes developed pressure bruising so required additional gel padding and strapping to offload. Mark also made adjustments with ensuring his pedal stroke was smoother and I made adjustments to his insoles to provide more support through the midfoot and cushion under the toes. Although all this helped, the biggest gain was from the cleat/pedal change. Bilaterally he gets burning in his feet on a day of big climbing, so he is now wearing his full compression socks rather than guards to reduce blood pooling in the feet.

'Shins and calves – Secondary to above, with Mark making small adjustments to try and offload the foot every time he pedals; often means he compensates with gripping of the toes and holding his ankle stiff in to plantar flexion [toes down]. Soft tissue release and acupuncture through the tibia anterior [front of the shin's muscle], as well as the plantar fascia [sole of the foot], tibia posterior and FHL [big toe flexor] and soleus [deep under the Achilles/calf muscle], has helped to ease this tension. The insole adjustment also works to support under the foot to make it feel more comfortable and allow the foot to relax.

'Neck – Upper occipitals and right side C2/3 (likely due to being jammed from impacting the road during incident). By working on his thoracic mobility and postural taping of his scapulas [shoulder blades], this helps to offload higher up in the neck. He has also received local treatment such as acupuncture, soft tissue release and joint mobilization to gap the joints that are irritated.

'Hips – It becomes obvious towards the end of the day that Mark's hips tighten up and he doesn't get full range so starts to compensate with rotation in the back or the hips drifting out into external rotation. At this level of volume, if the hips were to go without treatment, it could easily lead to a secondary injury in the lower back or knees due to poor alignment and inefficient pedalling.

'Apart from these things to manage alongside his left elbow and the dentistry work from the accident, Mark is holding up well and the above niggles being addressed are nothing to be concerned about. Early awareness of tightness and niggles is good to flag, so that they don't develop into more of an issue. Preventative work also helps to keep Mark efficient by maintaining range and power, and it keeps him in less pain. Basically it's these small percentage gains that help the miles tick away.'

Despite this incredible detail and depth of experience, Laura summarized her job as perhaps 10 per cent being a physio and about 90 per cent being 'mum' – sorting kit, sorting food, checking I cleaned my teeth!

On the food front, there was a routine for the main meals from 3.40 a.m. until 10 p.m., both liquid meals on the bike and solid meals off the bike, but Laura was also using food treats to pick me up psychologically, although sugar and caffeine were carefully rationed. I have such a sweet tooth that the treats cupboard in the RV was well guarded, and Laura would ration out my sweets each session. They tried lots of options, including some weird Russian concoctions, but I always craved my favourite Werther's Original. The stash of Cocoloco custom-made cookies and slabs of chocolate (of all flavours) was also under close watch. Left to my own devices, like most of us when over-tired, I had no self-control and would have worked through the lot in a couple of days. David had bought a box of Ferrero Rocher the day before to celebrate the quarter-way but had then forgotten them in the RV, and like scavenging dogs Alex and I were all over these before the boss (Laura) could lock them in the cupboard.

So I was on strict sugar rations, albeit still needing 9,000kcal of food a day, but Laura (and Alex) had fun with some brilliant creations for when the going got tough. They would be watching me closely, looking for when my head started to drop, or my cadence slowed, and then jump out from the roadside bearing, for example, a layer of wafer biscuit (the size of a Ryvita) smothered in Nutella, with sliced banana, then peanut butter, another wafer, Nutella, banana, peanut butter and wafer – a triple-decker and a welcome wee pick-me-up! I started rating these on a scale of 1 to 10 – as a scale of difficulty for eating on the bike. This triple-decker was a fairly safe 3: plenty to hold on to, but with the risk of sliding between the layers. However, the banana, cut lengthways as a banana split, plated skin-side down and smothered in peanut butter and Nutella with a spine of chocolate drops sticking out, was a more challenging 8 and had to wait for a particularly smooth section of road.

The rain began soon after the start, which was a chore, and I settled into a fairly dull day of rainstorms and forested hills. Inside the RV, the usual routine was for Laura to do the first smoothie and then have a wee snooze around 5.30 or 6 a.m. for half an hour. Alex would do the next bit of food at 6.30 then hopefully have a wee snooze himself, around 7. On days like today though when we were approaching tricky sections – getting around the town of Kansk – sleeps were forgotten about. The Russians were coming into their own navigating these small towns using the Russian version of Google Maps, called Yantex, and we had more trust now in their understanding of which route would be best for the bike.

Climbing again, away from Kansk in a big river valley, it was more rain showers and lots of spray on the road, with uninteresting miles until the town of Tayshet. Keen to avoid the issues of the day before, Alex did some research and could see it would involve a couple of hundred metres' more climbing to bypass the town. But the Yantex was in the other vehicle, and getting it back was not as simple as it might sound, given the very patchy phone reception. So when I reached an important junction, David was standing by the roadside looking exasperated, saying he didn't know what was going on. Alex ran out from the FV, shouted at me to carry on, grabbed the Yantex and we raced on, saying they would talk about it later. David's tendency was to want to talk about issues as they happened, but there was no time for that, the race never stopped. So I was left on the bike thinking there were cracks in the teamwork. I heard later that Alex had proposed the detour which David had initially agreed to, then, within a minute, he called back to counter this – to stick to Plan A, as the support team were busy doing different tasks and had an expectation of the plan. David didn't doubt that missing the hill would be good for cycling, but he made the call that it would stretch the support team in different ways for minimal gain. During the call David felt that Alex had hung up on him.

We took the faster route and that was all that mattered. The technical issue was a very patchy mobile phone signal. The team dynamic issue was about roles and responsibilities. Yes, Alex was overstepping his role as mechanic, but I could see why, as this level of detailed route-setting and analysis wasn't happening from the vehicles that were scouting ahead. Meanwhile Laura was trying to protect me from being aware of all this, to keep me in a positive mindset, which is why debriefs needed to happen at a time when they weren't a distraction. The race was in front of us, not behind us, and issues only needed discussing if there was anything to learn from them, otherwise they should just be forgotten, water under the bridge.

Once back on the P-255, our planned route, David returned to pick up two of the Russians who had been abandoned at the initial junction. I later heard that Sasha, who was David's direct report over the other drivers, had been very angry at this loss of face in front of the team and threw a slap at one of his colleagues. I'll never know the truth of how serious this was as I was miles down the road.

'This is a day I wish I could forget,' I commented to Alex as I came to a stop at 9.30 p.m. Heavy rainstorms, big climbs, feeling flat after yesterday's excitement, then issues within the team. This combination led to an inevitable end-of-day discussion about needing to reduce stress levels and sit back and let the legs do the work, confident in the bigger picture taking care of itself, but it was tricky with so much at stake, with such punishment to endure each day.

Thankfully the tension between Alex and David was resolved swiftly at evening camp, which was a seemingly quiet spot away from the road, up and over the embankment of the Trans-Siberian railway track. Trains clattered past throughout the night, but I didn't mind; it was an atmospheric soundscape.

It's the end of day 20 at 241 miles, so a good day, in that sense. But a funny old day. The local time is 10.30 p.m. I have finished through that low mist as the evening cools down, plus we are quite high here. Today has been another 2,500m climb with rolling hills. But the story of the day was rain, rain, rain. It started dry but massive, massive rain today, so quite nice for it to clear for last couple of hours. Following a train track into this evening has been beautiful. But it was head down and wet most of the day. Good to hit mileage on a day like today, as it was miserable.

Day 21

We are a full three weeks in today and it's a thick fog this morning. Relatively high here, rolling roads into the forest, which is meant to continue – never-ending Russia. Not a huge amount to report, feeling pretty battered at this time in the morning. But keen to crack on.

Gradually the morning cleared and gave way to a calm, much warmer day – the welcome aftermath of the storm – and a decision-free, fast-rolling first few stints for the team. My 8 a.m. routine was now set and it was one I so looked forward to: pulling in, handing over my bike, stepping inside the RV and just collapsing on the bed. Ten minutes, that was the plan.

I never set an alarm, and the team were under strict instructions to work away from the RV and keep as quiet as possible. At ten minutes, Laura would knock on the door and I was normally already up, eating porridge and enjoying a coffee. My eight-minute naps were often joked about, how ridiculous eight minutes is for a sleep. But they worked wonders, completely reset my thinking for the day. And the silly mind trick at 4 a.m. was that I only had a four-hour ride before getting a sleep. Then it was a twelve-hour ride, as opposed to getting on the bike at 4 a.m. and trying to focus on a sixteen-hour ride. Just a daft mind game to help me think my way through each day.

The road deteriorated to a hundred kilometres of old pitted tar and then a stretch of compacted mud that looked like a long-overdue section for repair. Road signs had suggested it might happen, but there was no machinery in sight. If this got wet, like yesterday, the clearance between the 28mm tyre and the frame wouldn't be sufficient, the wheel would immediately clog up and I would grind to a halt. This had been a big problem when I was racing through Ethiopia on the Cairo to Cape Town race. So the spare bike was set up with 23mm tyres in case the roads stayed bad and the heavens opened. The 23s would be a lot less comfortable, but we were carrying them for exactly this reason, to get through any dirt road sections that turned muddy.

After eight hours we stopped for second break on the outskirts of Tulun, a small town built on timber and coal production. From here it was 240 miles to Irkutsk, the main city in the region (or *oblast*) I was in. I was riding by time, but it was still hard not to get obsessed by the 240 and multiples thereof. The roads had returned to being pretty perfect with a wide shoulder – steady and easy miles, in an unaccustomed heat.

Spirits were high and there was good craic with the team as Laura made me groan and yelp on the massage table. I even asked Alex to remove his water-bottle mudguard, as it was such an aesthetic sore on the bike. Within five minutes of wheeling out after lunch, having plastered on suncream, the clouds rolled in, the air cooled and the rain beckoned. Within ten minutes a tropical-style deluge had begun – odd at a latitude of 52° north. Pretty much the whole four-hour stint, through little villages and open farmland, was punctuated by strong cloudbursts.

We were a week from the end of leg 1, if all went to plan, and conversations were already being focused on what flight we could make out of Beijing. The crux point for this would come a few days earlier, at the Mongolia–China border, which was not open twenty-four hours. So if I timed my arrival badly, late in the afternoon, then I could say goodbye to the last and first shift of the day – immediately losing the best part of eight hours' ride time. Considering it had taken three weeks to build up a four-hour buffer on the target, losing eight hours was huge, even if we did have a twelve-hour contingency for each leg of the route. It all showed how easy it was to lose time, how hard it was to hit and maintain the long-term average.

Third break was a rushed fifteen minutes. There was a lot of chat about what lay ahead, the miles to the border with Mongolia, how we would get across, and starting to pad out detail for transport and timing options for Beijing. This added a new level of intensity and purpose. Russia had been feeling a bit timeless: endless days of miles without a real sense of progress. There was now a sense of moving from this groundhog day existence to a very tight countdown. In reality nothing had changed, but there was suddenly light at the end of a rather dark tunnel.

It's the end of day 21 and once again I didn't think I would hit mileage today – not that I am chasing mileage, I am trying to ride to time, but of course I always have an eye on that magic number, that 240, and I have just pipped it, with 241 miles. We will be out of here in three days. Russia has been such a monster – today started off cracking, beautiful, couldn't be better, and then the heavens opened and it was diabolical, soaked through. And then it ended beautifully – I mean, Russia has thrown everything at us and it has gone on for ever. Hopefully the cultural change in Mongolia will give us a lift.

Day 22

It's a nice start again. Looking around it has obviously rained quite a bit, but it's clear now – hard to tell, these are such long days and it has rained pretty much every day in Russia in the afternoon. I am expecting more big rolling hills. Irkutsk by lunchtime then Lake Baikal, finishing up on the shore. It looks like two much bigger climbs this afternoon. Very much heading southeast now towards Mongolia.

It was now darker in the mornings, and I enjoyed the cocoon-like feeling of setting out in a pool of light, being shrouded in first light, then welcoming the sun coming over the horizon. That was always a short period of time when I could think about the world around me, watch the light change, enjoy the pace of change in temperature. As the day wore on I would lose track of the sun and spend long periods not particularly tuned into the world around me, but for sunrise I was always in the moment, quietly observing the world waking up. When sunrise happened behind a shroud of cloud or rain, it was always a bit disappointing; the day slowly came into greyscale rather than vivid colour, and without the same sense of theatre.

Regardless of the conditions, I always rode with lights on all day, with a flashing back light and a solid front light, which was switched to flashing once it was light. On the odd occasion my front light was set to flashing in the half-light of the start, the blinking would drive me demented. It was mesmerizing, and the poor support team reported the same torture, watching a blinking red light for sixteen hours a day.

The first 100 miles passed easily, following the Angara river, and the crew made a decision to slightly re-route through Angarsk, to stay in the flatlands of the valley and try to bring our road miles in line with our planned miles. After three weeks we were now 67 miles up on the 240-miles-a-day average, but only 15 miles ahead of where we expected to be on the map. And so our overnight stops were only about an hour out from the plotted locations and it looked like leg 1 would end up being slightly further than we expected, mainly because of being re-routed on to smaller roads through parts of Europe and all the ring-roads we had taken through Russia.

After crossing the Irkutsk river, I turned southwest for the first time since Paris. It was alarming to see the Garmin 1000 on my bike indicating a westerly tack – the wrong way around the world – but for the next stretch, skirting round Lake Baikal and then south to the Mongolian border, there was no other possible route, and I had flagged this with Guinness World Records. You aren't allowed to cycle the same degrees of longitude twice, except when the road you are on leaves you no option.

I also left the wide valley floor, the water system that flows into the Yenisei river to find the Arctic Ocean thousands of miles to the northwest, and the next four hours were by far the most beautiful parts of Russia we had seen – long switchbacks, alpine riding which on fresh legs would have been just perfect. As things were, I struggled, and my legs protested a lot, having to hold closer to 250 watts for long periods just to creep uphill. The road was also very busy with trucks and for the first time motorbikes, which I sensed was a sign of the touristic nature of the area we were coming into. In the RV it was trickier driving, with the very low speed and the need to be constantly aware of trucks and traffic, but it worked out well in terms of shift patterns as they had Aleksei, the most natural and confident of the Russian drivers.

The reward was sweet: a blissful, fast and very long descent to the town of Kultuk on the shores of Lake Baikal, with Helmut desperately trying to keep up and get tracking footage. The road turned east and followed the southern shore of the lake, but I should have guessed it wouldn't be flat – it's a common false assumption about coastlines and lakesides. The film crew had been talking about the iconic landmark of Lake Baikal, the world's deepest lake, and how we would film it, but the road never really revealed its scale and beauty as we were kept in a corridor of trees, through small towns and over short, sharp hills, getting only occasional glimpses of the water. We had all been looking forward to this natural wonder, but the afternoon quickly went from the anticipation of an enthusiastic filming and sightseeing foray to a tragedy.

At around 7 p.m. the FV was ahead of me, leapfrogging sections then waiting for me to catch up due to the nature of the hilly, twisty roads and the volume of traffic. Coming over the brow of a steep forested hill, on a right-hand bend, they were met with the sight of two smashed cars in the road, the aftermath of a very recent head-on collision. Laura and Alex quickly ran to the scene, where they found a man in his fifties grieving over his wife (we assumed), who had been hurled through the windscreen. We had talked quite a lot about the lack of seat-belt use in Russia and also the fact that there were both left- and right-hand-drive cars on the road; this accident seemed to be a combination of these issues, plus an attempt at overtaking near the brow of a hill.

When I caught up I stopped, but Alex ran over to the FV, handed me some food and a puncture kit and told me to carry on, saying there was nothing I could do. I hesitated, but he was right, and rather than be another spectator I wheeled on slowly, sobered by what I had seen, unable to think about anything else.

Laura, meanwhile, was straight in there to check the victim's vital signs. There was still a weak pulse but no breathing. Alex retrieved the big medical kit and TempusPro at the same time as Johnny and Helmut caught up in the Prado, so they took spare wheels and headed on to catch up with me on the bike. Two ambulances soon arrived on the scene but Laura was in control: as she could no longer find a pulse, she was looking to intubate, attaching defibrillator pads to the lady's chest. But she died in those moments.

There was nothing else Laura could do and they swiftly packed up the medical kit as they got thanks from bewildered onlookers. The husband was inconsolable. Alex told me he sensed there was guilt, as well as anguish, at being the overtaking driver. The paramedics started to clear the scene and cover the body.

It was a very intense moment for Laura and Alex, and back in the RV there was understandable shock and a few tears. By the time David caught up, we had all regrouped. As an ex-policeman, David had a lot of experience of trauma scenes and was able to offer good advice and counselling.

There was more camaraderie than normal in camp. An air of disbelief and pragmatism at the same time. Thoughts of everything before the last few hours were forgotten. I could see how affected Alex and Laura were and yet how professional and calm they remained. I wished they had time to go for a long walk and have a cry, breathe some fresh air, think it all through and find some peace. But instead it was lights out, alarms set and race on.

I wanted to have Laura and Alex in my end-of-day video diary, but Alex was obviously uncomfortable with my summarizing the day without having seen what had happened. So events got explained with the cameras rolling, and it was hard to pull together my thoughts and to know what to say.

> It's been a massive day, a tough day on many fronts – but before I get to that . . . I wasn't really aware of it, because I carried on, but a few hours back, we were one of the first on the scene of a serious car crash, which these guys stopped and helped at and unfortunately it involved a fatality. A real reminder of safety on the road and never an easy thing to see. In terms of the ride, it has been much tougher than I expected – I have managed 231 miles, so amazing considering after lunch I knew I had some big climbs, but they were much tougher than I expected, they just went on and on. My legs feel absolutely stripped. It's been a tough day on many fronts. Well done to these guys for trying to help out.

Day 23

> The sky ahead is painted in reds and oranges and yellows, absolutely beautiful. I like this time of day as I have the roads to myself. Hopefully a bit of a recovery after yesterday which was a mammoth 3,750m – then at the end of today my route is going to cut up and over the hills towards the Mongolian border.

Despite following the lake all morning, again we never actually got to the shoreline. I was wrapped in a warm jacket from the start, with the world's largest freshwater cooler to my left. All things are relative; it was still 11°C and I would soon be in the winter of the southern hemisphere. But there is something about getting on the bike in the dark after five hours' sleep that means the body feels chilly, or maybe it simply craves being snug and going back to sleep. It's definitely always a conscious effort to warm up mentally and physically.

After three hours and enjoying the warmth of the early-morning sun I headed further east, away from Lake Baikal. Not just had I left the woodlands and sharper terrain and moved back into farmland, but the world around me looked different. Rather than neat fences and fields of crops this was now open grassland. Within a day's bike ride the people I saw along the roadside had also changed, their faces more Asian, less European, wider, darker. It was the first noticeable change in ethnicity for a few weeks. And it was amazing to see it happen so quickly, as if Lake Baikal was a geographical and cultural border.

Aleksei now had a stinking cold and was quarantined, keeping himself in the front seat of the FV at Laura's request, and everyone was very conscientious about not cross-contaminating. Everyone kept away from me; when I stopped, conversations happened at a distance. It was necessary but odd.

The major turn happened early in the afternoon, as we skirted to the west of the town of Ulan-Ude, now in eastern Siberia. The town straddles the Uda river, which I followed upstream, although the gradient was very shallow. We were now exactly 3,500 miles east of Moscow, which to put into context is further than Vancouver to Miami, a complete diagonal across North America – and we were still nowhere near the east coast of Russia. In fact, this was as far east as I would get in Russia, as my compass once again turned alarmingly westwards towards the Mongolian border. Even though I knew it would happen, it was still unsettling and felt like wasted miles, as every effort for the last 360 hours of cycling had been about furious easterly progress.

Climbing gently through open lush grasslands, we had our first sights of the steppe, of Mongol *ger*s and the nomadic lifestyle of the herdsmen. David was quick to correct my calling these habitations 'yurts'; the word 'yurt' derives from Turkic languages, whereas *ger* is Mongolian. It was exciting; the whole team (perhaps with the exception of the Russian drivers) couldn't wait to be out of Russia. I was charging along, partly on a gentle tailwind but also full of anticipation until third break after twelve hours, around 5.30 p.m. After just fifteen minutes off the bike I was keen to eke out every mile on these great roads and leave us within striking distance of the border for the morning. But within a kilometre we hit roadworks, the perfect roads were gone, and I gingerly picked my route through lightly compacted dirt roads. By the time these were cleared, the evening conditions were much calmer and the difference to my speed was around 5km/h, significant when losing over 20km in the final four-hour block of the day.

For the final few hours Alex came for a spin, which I'm sure did the world of good to ward off his threatening cold and clear his head after the events of the past twenty-four hours. The road slowly turned south by the time we reached Lake Gusinoye, basking in a golden late-evening sun. The terrain looked less fertile here and the greens were now mixed with more sandy soils and scrub. Trees were more scarce and stunted; the pines and dense forests of yesterday had disappeared.

There were a few fairly challenging drags from Lake Gusinoye, but the reward was utterly glorious after we reached the split of the Selenge river and we absolutely flew the final hour. Alex turned to me and said, 'You are going to do this!' I laughed, and said, 'Yes.' He carried on, 'After Around Britain I had concerns about your physical resilience for the 80 Days, then after the hectic nav out of Europe and the lack of sleep I was also worried about the team letting you down somehow, but now I am genuinely confident you are going to do it. You're in the zone and the team has proved itself. I'd place a bet that you're going to make it in eighty days!' I laughed again. I had felt this same trepidation from most people around me before the start, but it was the first time anyone had said out loud to me that they had thought the 80 Days was over-ambitious.

The wide valley around us grew dark very slowly, the road was deserted – we could ride across the complete width of it – and I absolutely loved the anticipation of change, the relief of completing another chapter, and the sheer joy of riding my bike in such a beautiful place. This felt a million miles from the heavy trucks and rains we had grown to expect. Spotting the RV at the roadside, all ready for us to stop and make camp, I gestured that we were carrying on. Laura, standing there in the dark, just laughed, unsurprised though perhaps slightly exasperated at our exuberance. But there was no way I was finishing even a minute before 9.30. Every mile closer to the border felt like a triumph.

I beamed at the camera as we called it a day in a gravel lane off the A340, in the middle of nowhere, preoccupied with saving the ride on my watch and cycle computer.

I'm a bit paranoid about losing data! We are close to the Mongolian border now. Bang on 240 miles today, which is a relief, and those last 20km were a beautiful descent. It is unbelievable how the landscape has changed. Climbing up from the lakeside still looked utterly Russian, suddenly turned the corner and into this weird dogleg south to the border, and it's open, barren, almost no trees, with herdsmen in the fields. Absolutely amazing. Quite excited by what lies ahead.

12

One Steppe at a Time

Day 24

Look how happy David is, as we are getting to Mongolia. It's a big morning, day 24, and I have a gentle tailwind. It's darker than other days. As we travel south, each day starts in a completely different way – it is much milder this morning, and it is just 100km from here to crossing the Mongolian border. A country I have been really looking forward to getting to – and I am not just saying that as David is here! Nice to get a change from straight roads and trucks of Russia. Based on the original plan, we are about 40 to 50 miles up on that. And it should be three and a bit days through Mongolia, with much more gradual hills than around Lake Baikal.

It was completely dark as I stepped out of the RV at 3.50 a.m. (challenge time). It was now David's turn to be beaming from ear to ear; I couldn't muster those expressions so early. Because for David, Mongolia was his second home, a country he knew very well, and his relief was palpable. Russia and China had always been the big unknowns and bureaucratic battles during the planning phase and, despite being used to wilderness expeditions, this first taste of a mission which was purely about performance and ultra endurance had been an incredibly complex job for him, so all credit to him for juggling the biggest team we would have on the entire race.

I'm guessing that the Russians don't massively value the Kyakhta–Altanbulag border with Mongolia. It was a single lane in each direction and after the refuge of tarmac for a few smooth miles to warm up I was flying down a hill only thinking about the crossing when the tar ran out. Quickly braking, I rolled carefully on to the dusty, dry gravel and my speed was halved for the next few hours. The bike coped admirably, but my body protested at the constant jolting. My neck was sore but bearable most of the time, but that knot of muscle joining my neck to my shoulder blade, tasked with holding my head up, felt like a little ball of flame as my arms jolted for mile after mile, my head like a bobblehead toy. After many miles we passed some graders and bulldozers, evidence that this was a huge stretch of construction and not just a dirt road. Most of all it was just slow going, and very sore on my damaged left elbow – perhaps a fitting final furlong before we could escape Russia.

Back on to old tar, the road left the open ground and entered an area of woodland, rising slowly, and I expected to come across the first checkpoints over each horizon. There was a low rumbling noise, which I assumed was earth-moving equipment on the road ahead. Then out from the scrub to the left lumbered a tank, kicking up a cloud of dust.

There were more of them, lots more. Here the deep tracks of the military road converged and ran alongside the main road, so I was soon climbing to the din of unsilenced diesel engines belching plumes of smoke every time they accelerated. The dirt road had huge dips, either intentionally or naturally, and would have been impossible for any normal vehicle, but the tanks lurched from peak to trough without issue, although it looked like a pretty miserable ride.

When climbing, the tanks were marginally faster than me, but as the road started to flatten out I outpaced them, so over the coming miles we jostled for the lead. At times the tanks were less than ten metres away, and most had soldiers sitting on top, wearing helmets and goggles, all completely caked with the dry sandy soil.

Some waved, and I waved back. But I wanted to keep a low profile, not cause any delays in this military zone. I didn't relay this to my team, assuming it was common sense. But Alex and the media boys had more confidence, signalling to the soldiers about their cameras. They obviously got back some reassurance about this because the next I knew they were alongside tracking me, filming the tanks in the background. Some of the young recruits might have thought this was fun, but it made me nervous. It only needed one senior officer to take exception and stop us. So close to the border and in such a remote place, we really didn't need to be drawing undue attention to ourselves. But nothing happened; we got to a point where the tanks crossed the road, dropped down the right-hand side, and then disappeared off into the trees.

This was a very different scene to the pine forests of Russia; these were open woodlands of larch in this forest steppe, a cool, humid ecosystem known as the Siberian taiga, which would give way to more birch and aspen further south, before the trees would all but disappear as the steppe gave way to the Gobi Desert.

Soon after leaving the tanks I came across a checkpoint, a large lay-by with a small hut and a group of police stopping cars at random. Hishgue, our Russian-speaking Mongolian fixer, was on hand to translate and smooth our way. She often wore a long dress, but today had on a silver jacket and fashionable three-quarter-length trousers, and as always big sunglasses – not exactly the attire you might expect for a gruelling expedition. I was uncertain if her presence would expedite my progress or draw further attention to us. My instinct is always to keep a low profile, but with the size of the crew and vehicles we weren't travelling like I was used to on previous trips. Cycling around the world the first time, and the length of the Americas, I kept the BBC tag well hidden; I was always just the solo touring cyclist. Once border officials start asking questions, it is hard to get them to stop. But this was different, and I needed to trust the experience of David to get me through as efficiently as possible.

My passport was taken away, and the younger policemen left with me seemed interested in looking at the bike and then taking photos of us together on their phones. David and Hishgue came back within minutes and there were a few more conversations before I was waved on. We had passed the first hurdle.

Reaching the border proper at 8.10 a.m., it was immediately clear that we were in for a longer stop with some more officious Russians. There was nothing I could do, so I climbed into the FV for a longer snooze than usual, as it was first break anyway. We weren't allowed to cycle the few hundred metres of no-man's land between the Russian and Mongolian sides and the customs officials went through the vehicles pretty carefully. I tried to sleep on as they came into the RV and looked in cupboards above and around me. David then threw my bike on the roof rack of the Prado and I joined Hajaa and the media boys for the short drive across.

Laura, Alex, Dimitri and Hishgue were meant to catch up soon after in the RV, but in a bit of a shock it turned out that Alex's visa had run out on 24 July, the day before. In the end it was only a few hours' delay for them, but during the process it felt like they could be there for a lot longer. Laura and Dimitri had to wait with the RV while Alex was hauled in front of a number of stony-faced officials barking in Russian to each other, with Hishgue trying to explain, begging, keeping the peace and translating for Alex. Lots of questions and paperwork ended in Alex being taken at breakneck speed in the back of a police car to an ATM twenty minutes away to take out 3,500 rubles (about £45) for the extra day's visa. With forms finally stamped, at last everyone was free to go. Alex felt terrible for the team, and particularly Laura, who never wanted to be away from supporting me, but she remained positive and pragmatic, using the time to catch up on admin. Alex's final diary entry was perhaps clouded by this visa issue: 'So eventually got out of bloody Russia. The land of rain, rubbish roads, trucks and mosquitoes.' My feelings were only marginally more positive: there had certainly been a few incredible moments, but in general, what an epic slog.

The FV had set off for the border at daybreak, to make sure a vehicle was waiting on the far side. Once I was back on my bike and through the passport and customs check on the Mongolian side, I thought I was free to go. But another fifty metres on, through heavy metal gates, I was stopped at a final checkpoint. The soldier asked in broken English if I was travelling with a group. I had to answer yes but knew this would mean having to wait. I could see David another hundred metres down the road, a bear of a man, all smiles and ready to welcome me into Mongolia.

The soldier signalled for me to cycle back up to the customs building, but I shook my head, dismounting and pushing my bike over to
the side, signalling that I would wait. He looked displeased but was
also distracted by a few other vehicles that he waved through. I was
concerned that if I returned to the customs house I would be lumped
in with the visa issues and not allowed to carry on until this was
resolved. I had slipped the net this far, so played the waiting game,
hoping the soldier would eventually let me go. It helped that David
was within eyesight, waving enthusiastically at me, which I pointed
out to the soldier. After about ten minutes, with no movement from
up the hill and obviously no further instruction over the radio, he
waved me on without a glance. I didn't need any further encourage-
ment and rode into Mongolia.

David, a cloth tied around his head for protection on what was
going to be a warm day, was excited to get going and to show me his
adopted country. He wasn't the only one reinvigorated by the border.
We had nearly a three-hour head start on the rest of the team. As soon
as they were allowed across, they transferred med, food and wheels
from the RV into the Prado in order to catch up as quickly as possible.
Hajaa, who had driven nervously in Russia, perhaps relieved to be on
home soil took to the wheel with complete abandon, much to the
shock of Laura and Alex.

They caught up around 2.30 p.m. and we called a break straight
away. As soon as we stopped I broke down, sobbing at the roadside. I
couldn't explain it. I felt so sore and broken. After taking my bike from
me, Alex set up the massage table which I sat on while I ate, pulling
myself together. David, the media boys, the Russians and the Mongolians kept a respectful distance, not knowing how to deal with this
unexpected moment, or perhaps assuming it was for Laura to look
after me. Alex and Laura worked around me but didn't say much, just
letting me have a bit of time. It was the first time I could ever remember
cracking up on an expedition, aside from after an accident, like smashing my teeth. After a while I felt better, and I encouraged them to get
the media boys involved: there was no point in them running away any
time I was struggling. As much as I don't enjoy being filmed at my lowest ebb – who would? – it was an important part of the story and I had

Left: Lunchtime roadside treatment.

Above: Waiting for the Mongolia–China border to open.

Below: Reaching Badaling, at the Great Wall of China, after twenty-eight days.

Above and right: Vast horizons heading into the Nullarbor Plain across the Great Australian Bight.

Above and right: The aftermath of the crash near Melbourne.

Above: Snapped crank – that's a first!

Above: Ed Pratt, en route to becoming the first person to ride a unicycle around the world.

Left: Helmut and Johnny – the team behind the cameras.

Below: Reaching 9,000 miles, half way around the world. With Fleur, Tim, Claire, Tony and Ry.

Right: The tired team grabbing power naps whenever possible.

Above and below: My giant spork – perfect for shovelling back over 8,000kcal a day.

Left and above: Past midnight: a 280-mile day and the finish of Australia in Brisbane.

Above: Trying to eat lunch while Laura works on my painful neck and limbs.

Below: Chatting with supporters who have driven out to find me.

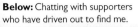

Above: Menzies Aviation working hard to get nearly 400kg of kit and my team through the airports fast.

Left: The freezing graveyard shift, climbing over the Southern Alps, NZ.

Right: Riding the lush west coast of NZ over the Haast Pass.

Left: Relief and exhaustion at reaching the Picton Ferry to the North Island.

Right: Hail storm into Auckland, having ridden the North Island of New Zealand on less than four hours sleep.

Above: The Alaska Range as I start stage 3 from Anchorage.

Above: The construction roads of the Yukon Territory.

Above: Little tricks – brushing my teeth to stay alert.

Below: The roads to ourselves in the wilderness of the north.

enough awareness to know this was just such a moment. It's easy to film and share the adventure when all is going well, when the sun is shining. But that is never the whole story.

It was a big emotional low, I was feeling sore, broken and exhausted – but perhaps this was also an escape for the relief, the long-pent-up anxiety over getting out of Russia.

Across the border the road kinked due west for a short while to the small town of Suhbaatar, into the prevailing wind. These border towns contained spaced-out single-storey buildings, home-made houses with tin roofs painted red and sometimes green, surrounded by solid wooden fences, presumably to keep out the dust storms. The roads had no line markings for long stretches, so merged seamlessly into the landscape. I was soon introduced to the sheer emptiness of Mongolia, the least densely populated country in the world. It was challenging terrain, big rolling roads, a few degrees too steep to cruise over; long grinds uphill followed by cruisy descents, then repeat. Those first hours were utterly beautiful, but pretty rough.

The silver lining to my tearful breakdown was that I felt so much better afterwards. The fog had lifted from my mind and a steely resolve had returned. I was renewed.

It rained for a while after lunch, but it was warm rain and I was feeling surprisingly positive and defiant as we reached the town of Darhan. The Mongolian Cycling Federation had put out the word and David knew there would be quite a bit of roadside support in the towns we passed. Sure enough there were about eight cyclists waiting for me, and word came back from David to Laura a few miles before we reached them. Concerned about my fragile state of mind, Laura asked David to discourage these cyclists from joining me, and Alex gave me this update as we rode into town. I felt pretty awkward, especially when I spotted them up ahead, standing with their bikes, ready to ride, but with David and Hishgue kindly asking them just to wave from the roadside. I waved back as cheerily as I could, but felt rude. These guys had made the effort to come out and support me and I didn't want to stop them riding a few miles with me. But at the same time I did not want to overrule the team. I was so grateful for their concern about me, for protecting me.

Before I had left Darhan, three of these cyclists caught up with me anyway, which abated my guilt slightly. None of them spoke any English, so it was an enthusiastic conversation of thumbs up and pointing at each other's bikes. One gent, dressed in red lycra, which looked like retro styling but was in fact just very old, wore brown leather brogues and a soft cycling cap with no helmet. He looked older than he probably was, after a lifetime of frugal living in the outdoors, but imparted a wonderful sense of resilience, of enjoying life. He smiled broadly at me through yellowed, irregular teeth. While the man with the brogues mainly cycled alongside me, the other two made a point of racing past me, stopping by the roadside, then racing past me again. David had explained to me the importance of physical prowess in Mongolia, how wrestling was still a part of the culture, especially in nomadic society. So, while we weren't about to wrestle, I sensed these younger lads felt the need to beat 'the champ', as David put it, to show their worth. Then again, this had happened quite a bit on Around Britain as well, so maybe it's just human nature, the competitive spirit.

For the rest of the afternoon the road traced an insignificant line over small ranges and through vast valleys. It was easy to feel lost and very small in this landscape. I passed the odd small village of *gers*, typically no more than five of these round shelters, in cleared areas of the low scrub. They seemed close by, but with nothing else in the middle or foreground they were probably a lot further away than they looked. There was the odd herd of scrawny sheep, more the build of a goat, with herdsmen riding bareback, wearing thick jackets and baseball caps. One herd, a few hundred strong, crossed the road in front of me, and I slowed to let them pass. It was amazing to witness this simple, pretty much unchanged way of life in this utter wilderness.

It was never going to be a big day with the slow start and border crossing, but my spirits rose as the evening wore on and I pushed well into the dark, gone 9.30 p.m., until my Garmin told me I'd ticked off 200 miles. There was something about that arbitrary milestone that I didn't want to fall short of. But to think, most of the advantage of twenty-three days' cycling had been lost in a single border crossing. Going back to the original plan – seventy-five days of riding, three days of flights and two days of contingency – I was now back bang on target, with the leg's twelve-hour contingency to play with if I was to make the flight from Beijing that had been booked long before the start in Paris. There was a lot of discussion about whether I could make an earlier flight, but without some massive days and a bit more luck that wasn't going to happen.

We made camp on a flat section of gravel just off the road.

I am in Mongolia, and it has been a massively tough day. It's hard to remember all that has happened – I have covered only 200 miles and it was a real push to do that. The first 50 or so miles to the border was a lot of construction roads, broken roads, and I lost a ton of time – it was like mountain biking. Body-jarring, unbelievably painful across those roads. Then I lost just over two hours on the border – and you can never make that time back. Into Mongolia and there is massive change, wide-open vistas, it's just beautiful, stunning – and a lot less busy. Quite broken roads, not construction roads, but by the time I stopped I was feeling incredibly sore – I don't mind admitting, I cracked up at lunchtime! The combination of frustration and pain – I don't know how it comes across online, but there is a lot of suffering on the bike. I am definitely going to new depths. So frustrating to have lost 40 miles – I have worked for the last twenty-four days to build that, and there it goes in a oner, with a border crossing. But it is what it is – we put everything into today. But at least we are into Mongolia . . . so let's count the successes.

Day 25

It's just coming up to four in the morning challenge time, and I'm in Mongolia. There are quite a lot of conversations about timings ahead. The challenge is that the Chinese border is not a twenty-four-hour crossing, it closes at 6 or 6.30 in the evening and opens at 8 a.m., so even if I had got across the Russian border in no time at all yesterday, and absolutely flown, it would have been a massive challenge to get there by 6 p.m. tomorrow evening – and that didn't happen. I can hopefully complete Mongolia today and tomorrow, climbing up, up and up to the

top of the plateau today and then hopefully levelling off and dropping
down to the Gobi Desert to the border. Right . . . we have three minutes till we need to ride. Let's go.

Heading south since Lake Baikal, the days were shortening quickly and
the first hour was now properly in the dark. After first light at 5 a.m. I
enjoyed a creeping golden dawn on a carpet of green rolling hills across
the Mongolian steppe. There are very few roads in Mongolia, and of
the 50,000km total, 10,000km is tarred but the rest is gravel and dirt.
I had heard that mining companies, creating a lot of the country's
wealth from its natural resources, had given Mongolia a great network
of trunk roads, but maybe this was old news, or the incredibly harsh
winters had quickly warped them, because they were rough riding.
Still, the sheer beauty made sure this was all forgiven. Each false summit revealed another picture-postcard horizon as I worked my way up
to 1,700m altitude, past the capital of Ulaanbaatar.

I guess Mongolia is one of the only countries I have visited that is
exactly what I'd imagined and hoped it would be. Unspoilt. And
rather than in pockets, like the national parks of Europe and North
America, the entire country seemed to be untouched. I realize that is
not the case, thanks to the aforementioned mining and the fairly polluted capital which I would soon reach, but for the most part I was
lost in the world around me, drinking in sights of wild horses grazing
on the hills, the shadows of clouds racing across desolate valleys, or a
motorbike kicking up a tail of dust in a straight line as it sped to some
remote *ger*.

Ulaanbaatar, which translates as 'red hero' – a reminder of its
Soviet past – sits in a wide basin and is home to around 40 per cent of
Mongolia's three million people, meaning that the rest of the country
is pretty much empty. To put that into context, the USA is about six
times bigger than Mongolia but with well over a hundred times the
population.

I took first break slightly early before freewheeling into Ulaanbaatar. As I raced downhill I zipped past a cyclist, who quickly turned
and made chase. Antonio Garygou, a Frenchman, was on a cyclocross set-up – a smart choice for Mongolia. An English teacher whose

partner worked for the French Embassy, he had been following my progress on GCN, and apart from being great company he was also a very helpful guide, taking us through the busy little capital.

Because Mongolians are traditionally nomadic people, there was no city here a hundred years ago, just a community. But since 1990 and the onset of democracy and a market economy the city had doubled in size and was now fringed by large districts of *gers*, although rarely fashioned from animal hides now; instead felt, tarpaulin or canvas are favoured. And rather than homes that could be built in a few hours and carried on the backs of camels or yaks, these were permanent, on wooden bases. But they still burnt coal fires, and in temperatures that can dip to minus 40°C this causes serious winter pollution.

On a sunny day in late July we had a fairly clear view of the cityscape, and by the time we were through the industrial outskirts and stopped at the first traffic lights we were a group of seven bike riders. Three young racer whippets and the head of the Mongolian Cycling Federation had joined us, alongside Alex on the spare bike, wearing the Bluetooth headset to communicate with the FV, to help navigate the city. The teenagers didn't speak a word of English and were kitted out with impressive bikes, clothing and equipment. I could imagine that road cycling at this level was unaffordable for many Mongolians. Their boss was a heavier-set man on a hybrid bike who spoke pretty good English and chatted as we made our way into the city, talking about his squad, most of whom were racing in China at that point. His issue, inevitably, was securing enough funding to develop a squad of talented riders. I could see that these young guns were fast, although they were skin and bone, so probably didn't have endurance in their legs yet.

Antoine recommended we turn south before the centre and ride the 'Mountain Road', which David had mentioned as an option the night before but Alex had reckoned against on the basis of its name. But it turned out to be a good call, and we turned 90° off the main drag that would continue to stop-start down Peace Avenue, the boulevard through the heart of the city. Soon the traffic thinned, and we crossed a bridge over the Tuul Gol river before turning left and following its south bank along the Sky Resort road, skirting the base of the

mountains. We passed a museum, a university, an ornate public garden and a number of holiday resorts – this was another side to
Mongolia, a side which I guess has mainly emerged in the past few
decades. The FV followed, but by this time the other RV and Prado
were tackling the city centre. It was a very easy route and good fun,
passing the miles, enjoying the company. The Mongolians turned
back on the outskirts but Antoine stuck with us for another 20K
across some jarring concrete roads, which he assured me would disappear as soon as we met the main road coming back out of the city.

Before this junction we diverged from the river and started to climb,
and over the next hour gradually ascended a number of false summits
to the highest point on leg 1 at around 1,800m. We were now heading
southeast, with the Gobi Desert a couple of hundred miles ahead, the
Chinese border about 400. I could feel the gentle nudge of the northerly wind even as I climbed, and I was excited, hopeful we would be
cruising from here on in. There certainly had to be a lot of downhill.

We stopped for lunch just over the summit next to some prayer
flags, back in parched grasslands that covered a vast vista. There was
a sense of anticipation, of momentum. Oh, the difference twenty-four
hours can make! Not that we had let go of the idea of reaching the
Chinese border before it closed the following evening, but the pressure was off, and the next 400 miles, in a day and a half, would be a
recovery ride if this tailwind kept up.

It did. The steadiest of descents saw me drop just 700m over the
next 300km, which I managed easily by 9.30 p.m. We flew like I have
never flown before on a bike, for so long, with so little effort. The tailwind howled along at about 20mph, which meant that I did the first
8km from lunch at 40km/h without turning a single pedal. I was
simply bowling along, beaming from ear to ear, sitting upright with
my arms lightly balanced on the elbow rests of the tri-bars, a veritable
spinnaker in the wind.

In mid-afternoon I encouraged Laura to jump on the spare bike for
the first time – if you were going to experience a few miles of a cycle
around the world, this was about as good as it got. So Alex slammed
the seat-post down and Laura jumped on, borrowing some of my kit.
It didn't matter that she had trainers on my cleat pedals, it didn't

matter that it was a 60cm frame, as it was really just a case of holding on! She enjoyed an hour cruising along. The hills had disappeared into the distance and we were now on a plateau, the vista broken only by a train track which ran parallel to the road. The trains were also vast; I lost count of the carriages, but they did their best to span the horizon. This was just perfect. I only wished Mongolia and this empty wilderness could have lasted for seventeen days, and not Russia.

Third break was fairly brief – none of us wanted to step off this conveyor belt – but I had already covered 312km and needed to eat and get some treatment. Needless to say, the evening was sickeningly perfect, hours when I wished time would stand still, as the grasslands slowly gave way to sand, and the occasional herds of goats and strings of horses were joined by the first sightings of camels, the starkness of the day giving way to the softer shades and shadows of the evening.

We ended on a tally of 425km, 264 miles. The wind was dying off into the night and there was no sense in going nuts as the following day was curtailed by the Chinese border. Even with this unbelievable afternoon's progress there was no way we could complete Mongolia before the border shut.

Unfortunately David had been feeling burnt out, with a cracking headache and grogginess for the past twenty-four hours, so he was kept away from the FV. We were now used to this protocol and I hammered the First Defence nasal spray and kept my distance; discussion about the logistics of the Chinese border crossing could wait.

But before that, there was more reason to celebrate such a cracking day – we were now a third of the way around the World route, just over 6,000 miles at a pace of 241.5 miles a day average. To think that when I rode almost exactly that distance from Cairo to Cape Town I took that world record from 59 days down to 41 days. I got here in twenty-five days! David had asked Hishgue to make a Mongolian banner for me, with calligraphy showing my name and a proverb about mental strength.

Laura's diary captured the mood within the crew, a relief that mirrored mine: 'It still surprises me that although Mark is cycling for four hours at a time, you'd think there was a ton of time to get things done, but those four hours soon get swallowed up with his fuelling and fluid management, plus simple tasks such as washing, cleaning, playing "mum" (although never will be as good as Una!). Everything seems to take an age and multi-tasking definitely goes out the window when you are both sleep-deprived and have limited resources! Once we crossed into Mongolia I will admit that I felt a big sense of relief. Russia surprised me with some amazing vast landscapes that I hadn't envisaged seeing, but I'm not going to miss the constant feeling of my heart in my mouth as I watched big artic lorries overtaking Mark at over 70mph into oncoming traffic. Also Lake Baikal that we were looking forward to seeing will now always be tainted with experiencing a fatal car crash and no amount of trauma training can prepare you for trying all your best to save someone that passes away in front of you.

'However, Mongolia is a beautiful country to cross into and such a contrast to be in a calming landscape with quiet roads, albeit bumpy conditions for Mark.'

That was some day. It all comes together – 6,000 miles, bang on target. Go back to the original sum, seventy-five days' riding, three days' flights. I couldn't be in a more different mood to yesterday.

Day 26

I am riding for the Mongolia/Chinese border – the sun is not up yet, but there is the first hint of light due east. It is beautiful. The grasslands have given way to the scrub and sand as we reach the Gobi Desert. I think it is unlikely I am going to make the border by the time it shuts – that would have been a bit of a miracle – which means we will have forced rest tonight. Maybe I will get eight hours' sleep! But this still keeps us on schedule – just uses a big chunk of our contingency. But stick to the positives, at this rate I can still finish leg 1 on exactly the time I said I would. It looks like another dry, hot day ahead.

An hour into the day, Helmut filmed the morning video diary out of the side door, tracking alongside on ideal, empty roads. It was calm and beautiful in the desert under the stars and a new moon when we had got away, sharp at 3.59 a.m., too fast for the media boys and their morning videos, but in fact it was a perfect morning to film later on the road. Overnight my back tyre had a very slow puncture, which Alex changed before the start, and then again another forty-five minutes into the day, caused by more glass. After sunrise a slow but helpful tailwind returned, and while I cruised fairly effortlessly, the crew had a big job of packing up the vehicles. From the border, the Russians would be making the 6,500km return drive to Moscow and we would be met across the border by a new team of Chinese drivers.

A couple of teenagers joined me for a few hours in the middle of the day and worked admirably to keep up on their mountain bikes. But thanks to the flatlands and tailwind they managed, and although we had no language in common, I enjoyed their company. I did wonder what their return trip would be like – they carried a bottle each and no food – but they knew what they were doing, on good bikes. One wore cycle mitts, a cycle jersey, tracksuit trousers, Converse trainers and a baseball cap; the other had clipped-in mountain bike shoes, mountain bike shorts and a tracksuit jacket but no helmet. I enjoyed their obvious enthusiasm and only wished I could ask them a few questions. It was hot going in the middle of the desert, but the wind meant I didn't have to cycle hard and any sweat was wicked away.

It was a cruisy day on perfect roads until the final miles to Dzamin-Uud, the border town, where the road simply ran out. I came around a roundabout and a concrete roadblock diverted us on to a sand road, but while there was evidence of roadworks, it was hard to tell where the old road had been. Looking on Google Maps, it didn't look like this road had ever been connected, which was very odd. The sand was completely impossible to cycle on and I set off on foot, pushing the bike where it was more compacted, dragging it where the sand was soft. I did try to cycle a few sections with a bit of gravel and grip, but after falling off a few times I gave up and carried on pushing. With a few new locals keeping me company, having more luck on their mountain bikes, I trudged through the sand and back to tar. These were just local lads who had spotted me and were enjoying the novelty, and the riding selfies, showing me they could cycle with no hands. One wore a tight white T-shirt and baseball cap on backwards, another a heavy silver chain and big sunglasses – a hip-hop-inspired look. I couldn't bottle my frustration that the media boys didn't jump on this; when they finally caught up I bellowed, 'You've got to film this shit when it happens!'

I was now only about 5km from the Chinese border, around a ring-road, but looking back I could see that the FV wasn't moving. After waiting for a while there was still no sign of movement, so I left the bike propped against a bank and set off through the sand, which was hard enough to walk through in cycling shoes let alone drive a very heavy RV. Sasha had managed to get it well and truly stuck, axle-deep in the soft sand. Everyone was getting stuck in, digging out the wheels with their hands, using the floor mats for grip, but there was no way it was coming out by itself. The Prado was brought up, but we weren't carrying a tow rope, which was a schoolboy error. So, using a few linked kryptonite bike lock chains, we set about towing it out. It still took all of us pushing, me on the passenger door, to get the RV unstuck. It was an unexpected final challenge to finish Mongolia, which I sensed that the crew quite enjoyed. It had been an easy day, and the time pressure was off – the border was already shut for the day – so getting stuck in and playing in the sand wasn't the end of the world.

I am always cautious about camping or stopping close to international borders, but the locals seemed very relaxed and reassured us that we could park up in a dirt area within a stone's throw of the closed gates, next to some railway sidings.

There was, again, a mood of relief, and I had photos taken with the Russian drivers, thanking them all for the past fortnight of hard work. They had come a long way, literally, and despite the cultural gulf and a few issues along the way, I could see that they had tried hard, and it was a seriously rough schedule. I doubt anything in their life would have prepared them for the last fortnight and they had struggled but ultimately coped. I'm sure they were very, very relieved to see the back of me, but I could also see they cared about the success of the race.

We set up the massage table behind the FV to get some privacy from the local lads, who hung around all evening, and made the most of more time for treatment. David had raced ahead during the afternoon and already managed to meet the Chinese crew, crossing with quite a bit of kit to save us time the following morning. In theory we only had what we really needed. In reality that was still a lot of stuff. And the Russians did well out of it, going home with a lot of food and kit that we weren't using. There was no point taking it into China and then having to throw it away. Everyone also made the most of the showers in the RVs, using the last of the water, knowing we would be in much more cramped vehicles on the other side.

Here are Alex's notes, reflecting on nearly four weeks of being cooped up in support:

'In the van there have been few days when nothing at all happened to punctuate the day, be it simply a puncture or a nav issue or whatever, and this has kept life interesting. The pace was not excessively hectic, but there is always the underlying sense of being ready for action if anything happens to Mark, or he needs something. This is keeping us focused, and we relished the infrequent hour or two of calm to relax. We haven't been at all bored at any point.

'In the cramped, jiggling space of the van everything (making wraps, mostly!) takes longer than you'd anticipate, and I think Laura and I have enjoyed and are comfortable with that sense of everything in its place (from rowing and bike touring). She and I have become very intuitive through Asia, which has made things much more enjoyable than they might have been. There is also this subconscious sense of being involved with something amazing, and as the days have progressed it has been becoming increasingly clear that Mark can genuinely pull this completely outrageous feat off. Mark's determination, focus and willpower is a massive privilege to witness.

'We are an odd wee slick-functioning bubble, generally without much reference to location, but in the occasional quiet moments we could look out the window and remember we were in the centre of Russia or Mongolia, many miles from Paris, and the scale of the world would pop back into view. The experience has been absolutely unrepeatable and a fantastic honour to be involved with.'

At the end of day 26 and that is the Chinese border. And it is closed. So we are stopped before sundown. And these local cyclists helped us through the last few miles. Amazing rolling roads through the Gobi Desert – just camels, a train track alongside me, the biggest horizons you will ever see in your life, just vast. But then for the last section, the road disappears in the sand – so our RV got stuck in the sand; a team effort to get it out. The plan from here is, get across the border tomorrow morning, then I have got two days to make my flight. Obviously I won't make a 240 day tomorrow, as that border doesn't open until 8 a.m., and there are 406 miles to cycle in China. It's doable, but we are racing for a flight now, once across.

Day 27

We are waiting for the border to open. That was the biggest night's sleep since Paris, eight hours, which is incredible. But we are right next to a trainline and these guys blare their horns all night. But still feel better for a few more hours' kip. It's strange to get up when it is light. And it'll be a massive relief to get across this border, and then I need to get at least 200 miles today and then try and get to the airport tomorrow. It's a big target for the next couple of days.

I woke when it was already light and lay there, listening to Laura moving around the galley kitchen, boiling water, pouring cereal, the morning routine. Except it wasn't 3.30 a.m. (our time), it was 6 a.m. local time, and I just lay there, dozing, enjoying the sensation, relishing not having to immediately force myself to get up and get going.

Hishgue marched us all around to the warehouse beside the railway to find a toilet, but the lady there wouldn't let us in, which I don't blame her for. But there was a heated conversation in Mongolian while we watched on, like a class of school kids wanting in for a wee-wee! The area was all very open, with nowhere to hide from the border guards and the bustle of the road and railway, so we scattered into this military suburbia to find our own hidey-hole.

On a bench by the railway sidings Helmut filmed our start of day. I looked shattered. The darkness of 4 a.m. is great at hiding the details of your complexion, but under the scrutiny of the sun across the Gobi Desert I looked, for want of a better description, hung over.

At 7.15 a people-carrier arrived from the border, just as the crew finished packing up the Russian vehicles. There was a very long queue of vehicles already parked up, waiting to get across. But thanks to David's hard work we were ushered through first by a local fixer, tasked with getting all the kit from the Russian vehicles to the Chinese, as neither could cross the border.

I set out on the bike, with Alex riding alongside me. There were a few hundred metres between this first barrier and the main gate. Once we'd stopped, I propped the bike against a chain between two bollards, wandered over to a dilapidated building and sat on a bench, out of the sun, waiting for something to happen. After fifteen minutes a soldier approached and we were instructed that for the next section to the customs house, a no-man's land of no more than 500m, I would not be allowed to cycle or even to wheel the bike – just like coming into Mongolia. There was no obvious reason for this, it was just the rules. No one else was allowed across yet, we were still first in line, so it would have taken me a minute to pedal, but instead it took much longer. Everyone and everything was packed to the gunnels into a people-carrier, with no roof rack or space inside for the bike, so Alex in the front seat and Johnny in the back had to hold on to the bike at arm's length through the open windows, which was precarious.

The Chinese customs building was from a different epoch: modern, large and air-conditioned. While our fixer's vehicle could drive around this building without checks, every item of kit needed to pass through an airport-style scanner. This was quite a task, a massive hand-relay, and I wasn't sure why we couldn't do a vehicle check like at every other border. This was a box-ticking exercise, I thought: not one of the guards was watching the scanner screens. We then had to queue up for the passport check, which was tricky with a mountain of kit, and once through that, everything was loaded back into the same vehicle to drive a further 500m to clear the border area, where David was meeting us at the roadside with the Chinese crew. I said a very brief hello, waved at the new crew, then got straight on to the bike. It was 9.30 a.m. – a very fast crossing considering the process and amount of kit.

I was completely fixated on reaching Badaling, the end of leg 1 – there was no way after everything we had been through that I was going to slip behind schedule in these final miles. I had been ahead of the mileage all the way since Paris and the only reason I was now chasing time was because of these last two border crossings. Time on the bike, average miles, had been bang on target. But I had lost just shy of twelve hours across these two borders, the equivalent of about 180 miles' riding. In order to get on the midnight flight out of Beijing airport to Perth, via Singapore, I'd need to break the back of those miles today. Riding late had to happen, and after eight hours' sleep and a 9.30 a.m. start I was raring to go.

The reason for finishing at Badaling was that if I rode another 40 or so miles all the way to Beijing airport I would be further east than Perth airport in Australia. It is important not to cross the same lines of longitude twice, except where unavoidable through turns in the road. The reason Phil Mestecky, my researcher, had come up with the idea of Badaling was that it was at the Great Wall of China, an iconic landmark. The Arc de Triomphe and the Great Wall were perfect markers to start and end leg 1. However, so focused was I on each day's ride I had honestly forgotten that Badaling was at the Great Wall. So as we raced into China the crew were speculating about whether we could simply finish somewhere else. We had done 60 miles further than planned in leg 1, so why not stop short and take the stress out of making this flight? It was Una who jumped in and reminded me that we were heading to the Great Wall of China, which had been agreed as our stage finish with Guinness World Records, so there was no other option. Somehow, the Great Wall of China had never been mentioned to Laura and Alex. It was always referred to as Badaling, so they only made the connection when they parked next to it! Around the same time as they began thinking, 'Where's Mark?'

The Follow Vehicle was now a King Cab pick-up, the back of which had been converted into a camper-van, with a small cooking area and a sleeping area above the cab itself. Laura was stuck in the cabin with a mountain of bags and boxes while Alex explained follow-driving techniques through an interpreter. The roads were pretty quiet to start with and a dual carriageway lent plenty of space to pick up speed pretty quickly.

The juxtaposition was startling, in part seeing Chinese wealth on the back of Mongolian trade, but mostly in the change in infrastructure – big roads, modern buildings. Everything here, like the contrasting customs houses, looked a few decades newer.

Erenhot was a much bigger border town, with major corporate buildings, and I enjoyed that sense of excitement that always comes with pedalling into a new country, the contrast and new sights that come with having crossed an arbitrary line. Back into the desert, I passed a huge field of solar panels on my right and was surrounded by wind turbines casting their long turning shadows across the sands. Then, placed just as randomly, I came across life-size dinosaur statues, for miles. This region may be called Inner Mongolia, but it felt a very long way from the country of Mongolia in terms of prosperity, urbanization and population. No amount of artwork or infrastructure would make me prefer this over the vast, unspoilt emptiness of Mongolia, but I was soon lost in the world around me, excited to be in China, not knowing that this was the honeymoon period, the calm flatlands, which would not last for long.

A gentle headwind grew into the early afternoon until my speed dropped to less than 20km/h. On a day when I was riding to distance and not time, this immediately meant I would be riding an extra two or three hours to go the same distance. And it got pretty nasty – perhaps yin for yesterday's yang, to cadge the locals' philosophy.

It was torrid riding and I had a cracking headache, so I worked away to rehydrate and shake this off. I felt agitated and needed to settle down, focus; the next thirty-six hours would define the success of leg 1. We took a very quick first break after four hours and I reiterated my concern about Johnny and Helmut, that they were missing this story about our race for the flight. Alex went off to try to galvanize them over the importance of this. They seemed to be just filming shots of me cycling, lots of big landscapes, another day on the road, with no sense of urgency or narrative around the culmination of the past four weeks. The past few days had been proof, if proof was needed, that getting ahead of schedule took weeks of consistent effort, and this hard-earned advantage could be lost so easily. It would take another continent to build up the sort of buffer we had just lost.

The perfect road also got too perfect, developing from a fast dual carriageway into a too-fast motorway that wasn't safe to ride on, and we guessed that it wasn't legal either. The old road ran parallel to it, so I jumped the barrier, scooted across the lanes of oncoming traffic and pedalled back down a service road, gesturing that the FV would have to find its own route. I was now on a small road that soon left the desert floor and climbed up into grasslands and woodlands. I missed the expanses of the Gobi Desert, which had come and gone much quicker than I had expected. I love deserts and desert riding – the Baluchi Desert in Pakistan on my first world circumnavigation, the Atacama in Chile on my Americas adventure, the Sahara, the Outback ... each of those had taken the best part of a week, so it felt unsatisfactory to have flown across the legendary Gobi in less than a day.

Into the evening, after third break, at Alex's insistence a radio mic was put on me, and Alex jumped on a bike with the hand-held camera on a gimbal to get smooth shots. Neither Helmut nor Johnny had the ability to cycle and film at the same time, and filming from the bike we got some lovely shots and I was able to explain our mission to ride into the night. If I had been completely focused on performance, this filming shouldn't have mattered, but in truth it did: I am passionate about sharing the journey and I was so frustrated at not being able to film it like I was used to when on my own.

It was a tricky shot, holding the camera at arm's length into the wind, but when Alex returned to the vehicle, Helmut and Johnny were delighted. It was a breakthrough. We needed to do more shots like this, footage that was in the moment rather than reflecting on what happened at the end of the day. Then I messed it all up. I forgot that I was still wearing a microphone, and when Alex returned we rode along speaking candidly about how pissed off I was, how I thought Helmut and Johnny were lovely guys but lacked a directorial instinct, that they were missing important stories. Meanwhile, Helmut and Johnny were a few hundred metres behind in the vehicle, listening. Alex returned to the van a short while later to be met by Johnny who was understandably offish and cold. It would have been a difficult conversation to stomach after nearly four weeks of living and breathing the race. I was kept in the dark about this until later on. I was aware of the tension within the team but assumed it was just focus and the tough conditions.

As the day turned to night, I was making painfully slow miles in the hills while the wind created a soundtrack to my ride, blasting the branches of the trees at the roadside and around my helmet and visor so I couldn't even hear the engine of the FV. There was a lack of electrical power inside it, so keeping lights, phones, the tracker and external batteries charged was their practical issue. More amusingly, Laura and Alex had tried to swap places for a while in the afternoon, but Alex couldn't cope with the claustrophobic heat box, and soon emerged wide-eyed, running around the roadside like a caged animal. He wasn't made to go back in there again!

Alex swapped vehicles on the late shift to smooth things over with Johnny, who was understandably frustrated and anxious, feeling like he was not performing well enough for me while getting huge pressure from MoonSport in South Africa and Una in Scotland. Johnny was throwing his heart and soul into the project, there was no doubting his commitment, but underneath the tattoos, piercings and hard-man appearance was a very sensitive guy who seemed to me at times to be intimidated by the situation he found himself in. And the truth is I didn't have any quality time with him, certainly no time when there wasn't also a camera in my face.

Laura explained some of this to me as we raced to Badaling, suggesting that we should grab a coffee at the airport or ask Johnny to cycle a few miles when we got to Oz. I was embarrassed by my lack of professionalism and being so openly critical. But I was also in the 'just get on with it' camp, lacking sympathy. I wasn't about to dish out compliments and warm hugs just to make people feel better about themselves. The team had to look to themselves and each other if reassurance was needed. I also felt that the crew should be able to take critical feedback and adapt, quickly. I was so blinkered by performance and the road ahead that I had very little empathy or time to consider people's feelings. I wasn't out to upset people and was sorry that I had, but my tolerance for anything that distracted me was non-existent. I was being hard on my team, but I was being harder on myself. I couldn't be this blinkered and also compassionate at the same time.

We carried on until midnight, me in this personal rage which helped fuel my battle with the wuthering conditions, for a disappointing but nonetheless impressive 300K. It was just enough to keep us in contention for the flight. If those conditions continued, it would be a massive time-trial to Badaling, then a race by car to Beijing with at least three hours spare to check in.

The young Chinese drivers and translator looked completely dazed as they stepped out of the vehicle; they had obviously underestimated what they had signed up for and thought we were mad. Laura and I topped and tailed in the tiny berth above the cab, and everyone else had to sleep on the grass verge outside. Alex slept with my bike, next to the van, and David, Johnny and Helmut encircled the spare bike. They were asleep by 1 a.m.

Where are we? We are in China. It's midnight. China has not been kind to us so far, massive headwind, the biggest battle I have had so far since Paris. I thought I would have a nice cruise into the finish, but far from it, I've absolutely battled. It's a nice gradual climb up to 1,500m, and you wouldn't really notice it as it's so gradual, but that was incredible conditions. I was down at 15/16km/h for the final hours. It took two hours to cross the border this morning, which was fair enough, and I started riding at 9.30ish. The 190 miles took till midnight, which is crazy – but I had to do that, as there's no other way I would catch this flight tomorrow. It will still be a battle, but hopefully that wind will die in the night. Tomorrow is a new day. Three-and-a-half-hour sleep. Please say thanks to the Chinese crew as that was a big shift for them.

Day 28

After three hours' kip we were up and off, without even bothering to film the morning video diary. Ahead lay a daunting final day. We had about 350km to Badaling and from there it was 60km to the airport. Working back from my midnight flight, we would have to be at the airport around 9 p.m., which meant leaving Badaling by 8 p.m. At normal speeds I could expect to arrive there between 5 and 6 p.m. But if the conditions stayed against me, that could easily be a few hours later.

The poor Chinese drivers looked battered, like this was the toughest shift of their lives. I had always been concerned about how much control we would have over these foreign drivers, but at the end of the day we weren't allowed to drive ourselves in China, this service had to be provided by government-accredited tour operators. This wasn't your average tourist trip, though. We all worried that if they started calling the shots, there would not be a lot we could do about it. If they'd refused to drive at 4 a.m. after three hours' sleep, perhaps they would have been within their rights. This scenario certainly hadn't been what was sold to them during the set-up period. And our translator was a young lad, perhaps in his early twenties, a likeable and trendy chap in his tight white T-shirt and black baseball cap, not someone who oozed presence, so I worried he wouldn't have the respect of the drivers. Luckily they all seemed suitably overawed by the always smiling and physically impressive David Scott. I sensed they simply thought I was a lunatic.

The graveyard shift was once again into a southeasterly, but it was noticeably weaker than the night before. In the dark I was still focusing on the positives, that the road had to descend from over 1,400m to less than 600m, and also after the first four hours it would turn east at Ulanqab, at which time I'd hopefully pick up an advantage.

Dawn found me pedalling down vast four-lane highways, all but deserted, through a landscape of concrete buildings, cranes and construction. I wasn't in a city yet there were buildings in every direction. Some of the towns did cause some delays – heading into the centre of Zhangjiakou rather than skirting it – but we barely stopped after four and eight hours, so by early afternoon there was a sense of relief among the crew that we had done enough. We would make the flight.

I had been following the Yanghe river, which empties into the Guanting Reservoir, downstream. Having left the industrial parts of Inner Mongolia behind, I was now in the heart of Hebei Province. Beijing is one of the most water-scarce cities in the world, to the point that the Chinese have debated the merits of moving the capital south, away from sandstorms and droughts. This Guanting Reservoir, a touristy waterfront with rocky cliffs and the foothills of mountains rearing up to my left, was the first attempt to store water for the city.

The hinterland of hardwood forests which I was now pedalling through also afforded me brief glimpses of Haitou mountain and the Songshang nature reserve. Less welcome was a whole series of police checkpoints, which I was luckily waved through in a matter of seconds, but the RVs were not, so I was left alone for a long shift without spares or supplies. On any other day this would have been merely a tad frustrating, but today, if I punctured, we didn't have an hour or two to wait around. I could sense in the messaging Laura's frustration at these checkpoints, each time dropping further behind me. I pinged my location half a dozen times before they caught up, and I was very relieved indeed to be able to focus on the final few hours with the vehicles all together.

As you come close to Badaling at the Great Wall of China, there is a small roundabout and the main road carries straight on through a tunnel with a 'no cycling' sign. Therefore I didn't think twice about taking my only available option, a smaller road off to the left, also signposted Badaling. These final 5km were gradually uphill on a busy little road of tourist traffic, and I basked in the utter relief of making it. Grabbing my phone, I filmed a short clip, not realizing that this would be our only end-of-leg footage.

I'm cycling the last km to Badaling and the Great Wall of China – this is the end of leg 1. The sun is setting behind me, it's ten past seven at night, about 6,675 miles from Paris, in twenty-eight days – I think that's 238 miles a day average. And what a finale through China. My greatest hope was to stay on target for leg 1, but I was willing to accept with all the logistics and tricky border crossings and unknowns that I might be chasing time, I might be chasing time heading into leg 2. But to be bang on target, exciting. I think my support team are stuck in traffic somewhere behind me, so it's just a nice moment to stop and appreciate – we are a long way from Paris! Thanks for all the support everyone.

I pedalled up to where the road ran out. On the left was an imposing, ornate gateway to the Great Wall, and straight ahead was a pedestrian precinct with coffee shops and tourist tat. The juxtaposition of ancient and modern was inevitable but jarring. I stopped and dismounted amid the mingling tourists, waving off some immediate offers for a taxi, and soaked in the moment. It was a shame the crew weren't there, but I expected them to appear any moment.

I called home, tweeted the end of leg 1 and sent back the video message I had shot on the bike. Then I sat on the kerb and waited.

By this time it was getting dark, and a message came through that the crew were waiting at the finish point. It still didn't occur to me that they would have driven through the tunnel I couldn't cycle through, so we spent the next twenty minutes trying to figure out where everyone was. It turned out Alex and Laura had been busy packing up for the flight, and hadn't spotted the driver taking the 'no cycling' tunnel. They were also in Badaling, at another section of the Great Wall only a few kilometres away as the crow flies, but in the mountains and traffic this was a forty-five-minute backtrack. I worked out that I could carry on through the pedestrian precinct, past all the shops and up a steep hill, through a walled section of track and find them. But by the time I did it was gone 8 p.m. and everyone was pretty stressed.

After such an epic first leg it was a massive anti-climax not to celebrate the finish with my team. Arriving in the dark, we grabbed some witness signatures from nearby tourists, took a quick photo, and threw the bike into the back of the van, racing off for the airport. This all took about five minutes.

The drive was a bit crazy. To start with I lay on the bed above the King Cab plastered in dirt and feeling sore, with mixed emotions – the high of finishing and then the faff of losing nearly an hour trying to find my crew. I was now feeling deflated and exhausted, and I was still really annoyed. I had to shake this off; we should still make the flight, so no harm done.

Laura offered up a paper cup of orange and strawberry juice as a toast to the end of leg 1. And we talked through the ridiculous last hour, as I tracked our progress on my phone towards Beijing airport, hoping we wouldn't hit traffic.

Alex had the tough job of taking my bike to bits and getting ready for the flight while in the back of a fast-moving van. Bracing the bench and table with his knees, he deftly took the wheels off, the derailleur and the handlebars and stowed them carefully. Laura and I kept out of the way, making final packing arrangements.

A man called Alex Tan met us as we pulled up at the airport and set about sorting our eighteen bags and nearly 400kg of kit. Menzies Aviation don't operate out of Beijing so they had pulled favours with Singapore Airlines to make sure we were looked after. Without this it's very unlikely we would have made the flight with just a few hours to spare. Our lithium batteries were flagged at the security scanners so I nearly lost all my bike lights, but having a man on the inside – David Liepins of Menzies, based in Scotland – helped get all our kit through, better still with a waiving of all the excess luggage charges. This was the only omission I know of in our budget, but over the course of the eight flights I would take it could have cost us tens of thousands of pounds.

Even Laura, used to travelling with Olympic and World Championship teams with full priority passes, had never experienced such a slick, expedited transition. I was left with the media boys at the check-in desks, filming 'Where's Shelley?' for *Blue Peter* and saying my goodbyes to David, Alex and the Chinese crew. David and Alex would have a few nights in Beijing before flying back to the UK. While always professional, I sensed they would both benefit from a bit of time to decompress together before returning to their families. They had not always agreed but had both invested so much in the past month. And I had a lot to thank them for. We had cleared leg 1 bang on target. I tried to bury the disappointment of having lost the advantage we had built up because in Australia, with better and quieter roads, I had every opportunity to start building a small buffer again.

Alex Tan had arranged for us all to get lounge access and showers, and this was all the chat among the crew – nobody had washed properly since Russia. But by the time we were through passport control and security we had literally five minutes until last call for boarding. We all dashed to the showers, and it felt very odd for my legs to be walking so quickly. There was only one male shower which I dived into, and someone was in the female bathrooms, so the media boys and Laura got on the flight a tad stinky. But Alex assured us the plane wouldn't go without us.

On the plane, I turned left and Laura and the media boys turned right, which I felt very awkward about. But the logic was solid and agreement unanimous – I needed a bed to sleep in so that I could get some recovery before racing out of Perth. Still, if the budget had been what it should have been . . . everyone deserved this brief luxury.

For unknown reasons we sat on the runway a long time, and I dozed intermittently, hoping to stay awake for meal service. I woke up as the plane accelerated, and it was surreal to look out of the window as the night lights of Beijing dwindled beneath us after take-off. The next I knew, I was being woken up in Singapore.

Laura and the media boys were completely focused as I met them off the plane, whereas I was oblivious to the fact that our delay on the tarmac in Beijing had left us with just twenty minutes until our gate closed for the connecting flight to Perth. Singapore airport is vast and there seemed no way we could make it. Unbeknown to us, all was in hand, as just inside the terminal a young Singapore Airlines rep met us with a buggy and whisked us across the airport. I was still very sleepy, not properly aware of this race, just thinking it was nice to be given a lift. Laura's reaction of relief told me that there was more at stake here than saving our legs.

Just over five hours later we touched down in Perth, by which time I had eaten well and received treatment from Laura – much to the bemusement of the rest of business class. I was in my kit, too, once again at odds with my fellow, non-lycra-clad passengers.

Part Three

Perth to Auckland

Tony Humphreys – team leader

Laura Penhaul – performance manager

Claire Guthrie – physiotherapist; in charge of performance from Adelaide to Brisbane

Ry McGrath – mechanic, driver

Tim Spiteri – driver, general support

Fleur Royds – driver, cook, general support

Johnny Swanepoel and Helmut Scherz – filmcrew

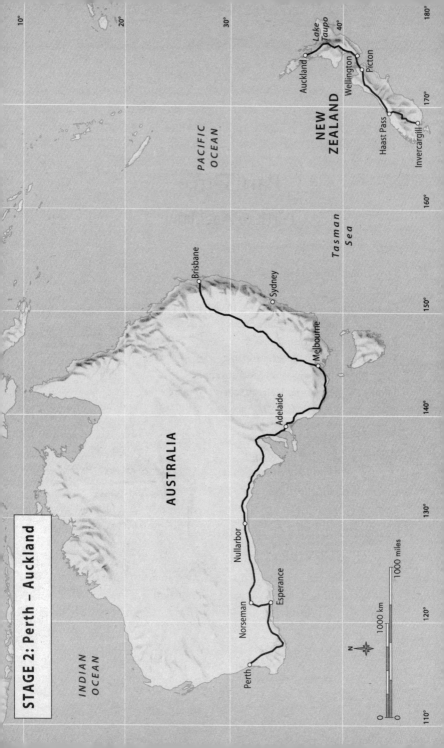

STAGE 2: Perth – Auckland

13

Ribbons of Tar

Day 29

Leg 2. Already.

While Russia had seemed never-ending, and individual days lasted for ever, now the last twenty-eight days seemed to have flashed by. Perceptions of pace had certainly been accelerated by crossing Mongolia and China in such haste. Leg 1 had always been my greatest concern, for two main reasons: my chances of picking up a repetitive strain injury in the first weeks, and the security and bureaucratic unknowns of Russia and China. We just didn't know if bureaucracy would put a brake on progress. All things considered, we had got through without delay. David had spent a huge amount of time and put in a lot of effort getting approvals. In fact we hadn't been stopped once by the police, so was all this work creating solutions for problems that didn't actually exist, or was it the reason we had made such smooth progress? I'm certainly glad that this homework was done, that we had the red carpet laid out ahead of us. Although Russia's idea of a red carpet is rather potholed and polluted!

From wheels touching down on the runway in Perth through to clipping in and riding out of the airport was thirty-five minutes exactly. I was first off the plane. Richard Bonner from Menzies Aviation was waiting on the air bridge and we quick-marched along the tunnel, which made my legs protest. They felt tight and very unaccustomed to walking, not least after ten hours' flying. The passport desk had been forewarned, and I was welcomed by an officer enthusiastically telling me about his cycling adventures. But the conversation was left unfinished as I was hurried through as soon as my passport was stamped.

A cardboard sign with GOOD LUCK MARK, a wee stick drawing of a bicycle and a massive Union Jack were the first things I saw as I came through arrivals. Then I spotted my crew, all kitted out in their fluorescent yellow T-shirts, filming with GoPros and phones, alongside a motley gathering of expat well-wishers. The crew had been here for nearly a week training and setting up the vehicles for Australia. Everyone was so excited and I felt a tad overwhelmed. On the plane I had completely switched off. I hadn't even thought about what lay ahead, or how my team would be feeling. Of course they were fresh and raring to go!

Menzies had obviously been instructed to get me through as fast as possible, and they did that in record time, while I was the one who was a bit more laid back, just relieved to be there. My mindset for weeks had been to make that flight from Beijing, then on the flight to try to use the time to recover. I now had to reboot and refocus for another massive target – the 3,000-plus miles to Brisbane. The sense of urgency from those around me definitely helped me get back in the zone.

I had managed a shave and looked a whole lot fresher. Having considered keeping the beard for the whole 80 Days, I decided that a clean face was a small psychological trick to restart each leg. If not fresh-legged, I was refocused on a new continent.

Posing for photos with sponsors, team members and well-wishers took less than five minutes. In fact we needed that time, for the one bit of kit that was missing from my hand luggage was my Mavic cycling shoes, so I was ready to ride out in a pair of trainers if Laura didn't somehow get to the hold bags and retrieve them. She managed this, incredibly, but it took a while longer for all the kit, especially the camera equipment, to clear customs, and I was well down the road by the time they caught up. Apart from the relief to be in Australia, the greatest joy for Laura, Johnny and Helmut was finally to get a shower, which they reported on with the delight of a kid in a candy shop. Only a shower-in-a-can had made them fit for travel!

At 1.20 p.m. local time I pedalled slowly out of the car park outside

Perth airport, following directions on a note that Tony Humphreys, the leg 2 team leader, had handwritten. A couple of turns and then I would be on Route 30, the Albany Highway, for the rest of the day. I appreciated the fact that day one of Australia was a half day: I wasn't in the mood for sixteen hours. Instead I had eight hours to warm up the legs and get back in the zone. And those first miles, stopping regularly at traffic lights and cruising on smooth roads with a westerly wind, were perfect. I could just spin the legs, remind myself to cycle on the left, and enjoy the novelty of everything around me. The suburbs of Perth were the most familiar views I had seen for a month yet I was now on the other side of the world. I enjoyed the experience, in a fresh and excited way.

I was riding one of the spare bikes. The plan was to build up my main bike as soon as possible and switch back. The only way we knew the difference between the bikes was the top caps – the main bike was red, the spares were blue and black. So while Alex was flying back to the UK with the black bike, which would then be sent to Anchorage ready for my flying start to leg 3, I was now riding the blue bike, which Tony had flown out from the UK. Even though it was exactly the same bike, it felt so different, without the best part of 7,000 miles to bed in bearings and gears. Though the red bike was being maintained with a new chain every eight days and new tyres about every ten days, the difference was like going from a pair of well-worn leather shoes to a brand-new set, rigid and ready to impress, day one off the shelf. There was nothing wrong with it, but it felt odd, and I was quite looking forward to getting the red bike back.

The afternoon saw me pedalling on empty roads through dense woodland, thick white lines adorning a ribbon of tar into the emptiness of Western Australia. The road gently undulated but never enough to get me out of the saddle, and I enjoyed the gentle warm-up. By 6 p.m. it was dark, and I layered up quickly. I hoped it would be like a Spanish winter training camp, although without the snows of Calpe, and that I would avoid the worst of winter until New Zealand, which I fully expected to be gritty. But as soon as the sun dropped the temperature did too, quickly, and I was left for the final shift in the pool of my headlight lost in my own thoughts, no longer able to see much around me. A couple of joeys graced the edge of my beam before hopping back into the darkness, reminding me where I was.

I have to say, this hasn't sunk in yet. It all feels a little bit weird. I've done 198km (about 120 miles), but I have spent the last couple of hours saying to myself, I am in Australia, I am in Australia. Just thinking, the day before yesterday I woke up in Mongolia, fought the fight of all fights into a headwind, slept for three hours, and then yesterday rode to the Great Wall of China. And then right at the end of the day, literally rode till dark. We didn't even have time to do some of the filming we wanted to do at the end of leg 1; we were straight in the vans and go, go, go, racing to the airport. Got on a midnight flight, which was then delayed, slept for five hours, woke up in Singapore, we were raced through the airport – huge thanks to the guys at Singapore Airlines as we wouldn't have made that flight otherwise – jumped on the next flight which was at final call, and arrived in Perth. Alex has gone home – he'll join us again in leg 4, up through Europe; also David Scott, a huge thank you for leading us through leg 1. I'm used to living life at a fairly quick pace, but the last three days has just been a bit weird. It feels like a bit of a dream.

Day 30

I've been on the bike a couple of hours already and the first sign of daylight is creeping into the east – it's going to be a beautiful sunrise. So there is going to be a good five to six hours of night-riding, which is going to take some getting used to. I am cutting southeast here down to Albany. The bike is feeling great, no issues during the flight, and I feel strong.

My piece to camera as I stepped out of the RV was so incoherent that we ended up re-filming it on the bike. I had started with a waterproof jacket and a thin PrimaLoft jacket – a comfort blanket against the dark and chill of the night. A few hours later I was riding with just a fluorescent vest over my jersey, thin arm-warmers and a buff.

There is nothing like riding through every sunrise and every sunset to give you that sense of a journey. With the prospect of nigh on 1,000 miles every four days, I was certainly excited but intimidated about tackling Australia again. A decade earlier they had been my toughest and most painful miles, with unseasonal conditions across the Outback. The southern hemisphere, in my experience, has winds that are far more consistent and ferocious, perhaps because of the lack of landmass to break them up. The two biggest battles I have faced, for thousands of miles each time, are the Australian Outback and the Patagonian pampas of Argentina. Other parts of the world can get turbulent, but rarely for such prolonged periods and vast distances. Whereas leg 1 had been entirely different to my route a decade before – Paris to Beijing, rather than Paris to Calcutta – this Australia leg was pretty much identical. So it was a pedal down memory lane, albeit at over twice the pace, and not having to sleep rough with huntsman spiders in my tent.

I could have gone due east from Perth but I needed to make up miles for the 18,000 total, while not going back on myself. If I took the direct route across Australia and North America I would finish over 1,000 miles short. And I always wanted to make the miles in the most credible way, without looking like I was doing massive north to south loops. Following the south coast of Australia fitted this agenda, but did mean I wasn't heading due east initially. I was certainly looking forward to leaving behind the weather systems from the Indian Ocean. That first afternoon riding out of Perth had been in a high, a calm honeymoon period giving me time to build a positive relationship with Australia, but she was not forecast to stay in such a good mood for long.

So Tony Humphreys, Laura's land-based expedition manager on her Coxless Crew Pacific row, was now team leader, the new David. As one of the last recruits, he had had a busy few months making arrangements from the other side of the world. More used to sailing and rowing expeditions, what he lacked in terms of David's big character he made up for in quiet confidence. I was also confident that there would be a better dialogue between logistics and performance. As everything was aimed at making the bike go faster, in theory we had little else to worry about in leg 2, where navigation was now much easier and roads were better. All the concerns that David had rightly been working on during leg 1 were lessened, so we could purely focus on performance. Plus Tony and Laura knew and trusted each other.

Claire Guthrie was physio. The plan was for Laura to take time off between Adelaide and Brisbane, so Claire was with us from Perth to shadow Laura and then take over as performance manager for about a week in the east of Australia. Claire had been recommended by Sarah Perry, the organizer of Tour de Force, where amateur cyclists get to cycle the route of the Tour de France a few days before the pros. While not with the same life experience as Laura, Claire came with bags of enthusiasm and was a keen cyclist. We had trialled a number of physios during Around Britain and my choice was purely down to attitude, not ability. I trusted they all had the ability to be a great physio, but I liked the unnatural amount of excitement that Claire had at 3.30 in the morning. Perhaps there was also a subliminal bias given that she was Scottish!

Ry McGrath was my new mechanic, and had heard about the opportunity through his local bike shop in Melbourne, owned by a man called Pete, who was himself asked if he wanted the job but as he had his new business to focus on said instead he knew someone who could do it – and that was Ry. This was serendipity, because Ry, a Welshman, had come to my talk in Durham after my first World cycle – the same event where I met Mike Hall. During the Q&A, Ry had said that if I ever needed crew he would love to join one of my expeditions. I had long forgotten this exchange, but what a fantastic coincidence, and I could immediately tell how invested in the project he was, both in terms of attitude and aptitude. As Ry put it, 'Lo and behold, nearly ten years later it has worked out. I am not riding, but I am spannering, and I can't complain, it's pretty good!'

I would never have thought you could improve on Alex's mechanic skills until I worked with Ry. Alex is a lifelong professional bike rider who knows a huge amount about bikes. Ry is a professional bike mechanic, with all the qualifications and experience that brings. For me, the layman who knows surprisingly little about bikes, they were both super geeks, but the difference was clear as I watched Ry work.

The all-important drivers and all-round grafters were Tim Spiteri and Fleur Royds, friends and fellow policemen from Melbourne, recruited by Leven Brown. It was reassuring to have some Aussies onboard, locals who knew the lie of the land. Tim and Fleur were also passionate adventure athletes, so had jumped at the opportunity to take leave from their day jobs and road-trip across Australia.

However, an unforeseen challenge was that it immediately became evident that having a couple of coppers onboard meant we wouldn't be allowed to cut any corners. Within a few hours of leaving Perth I was told to stop using my mobile phone when waiting at traffic lights, and Ry wasn't allowed to start building the red bike in the back of the RV. Everyone needed to be seated and buckled up at all times. Remembering the kamikaze ride to Beijing airport, this law-abiding attitude wasn't something we could argue with but it would immediately cause issues if the crew couldn't prepare food for me unless the vehicles were stationary. It hadn't even occurred to me that we were taking risks going through leg 1; there had been regular discussions about when it was safe to move around in the vehicles and when it wasn't. But in Australia it was clear that there was no way Tim was ever going to switch off from being a policeman. You couldn't fault him in theory, but in the vast wilderness the practicality was wearing for my performance team, who struggled to support me the way they had been used to.

The Albany Highway is about 250 miles long and draws pretty much a straight line southeast between Western Australia's capital city and its oldest settlement. A single carriageway for the most part, it cuts through the Wheatbelt and then Great Southern, two of the nine regions of Western Australia. But 'Wheatbelt' is misleading – there was the odd patch of wheat, canola and barley, but for the most part I pedalled a gently undulating tree-lined path past roadhouses, settlements and crossroads with names that harked back to people and practices from yesteryear: Coalfields Road, Muir Highway, Mount Barker. It was enjoyable being back in a part of the planet I could relate to – still interesting, but less otherworldly than Russia. By lunchtime we reached Albany, just as the weather turned and the heavens opened.

Every single morning I had woken up, had a swig of water then put a saliva swab underneath my tongue for a few minutes. Interestingly, that day my cortisol levels (the stress hormone) were the lowest they had been since leaving Paris. It had certainly felt like a physical and emotional relief finally to get through leg 1, now here was the scientific evidence for that. And regardless of the growing storm, I had a very happy-go-lucky attitude as I donned my rain gear and headed out for a torrential afternoon shift along the south coast of Western Australia.

There was also another world record up for grabs – the month record. Amanda Coker of Americaland and Steve Abraham of Englandshire have ridden more than 7,000 miles in a month, both having taken on the nutty Tommy Godwin year record of just over 75,000 miles. The great Tommy allegedly rode 8,583 miles in a month in July 1939, although this was never verified. The official female Guinness World Record for the month, Janet Davison's, still stands at 4,011 miles and I was happy to set the male record for the first time simply as a benchmark for people to try to beat, as opposed to thinking I was actually the person who had cycled the furthest in a month. I also knew that there was no way I would beat this distance in the next month, or any given month period between now and the finish in Paris, as those periods would all be broken up by more flights.

It's the end of day 30 and it's been a big day in many senses. The first full day in Oz: 405km today, so 252 miles! I do feel a little bit sheepish, if that's the right word, as I am pretty sure a few people have cycled further, but they haven't claimed the Guinness World Record for the most miles cycled in a month. It's about 7,050 miles to here from Paris.

Day 31

It's about ten to four, and as you can hear, there has been heavy rain overnight. It rained a lot yesterday and it's still raining. It's quite hard to get up and out at this time in the morning when it's genuinely cold out there and just chucking it down. The forecast is good the next couple of days, in terms of wind direction, which is really all that matters.

It's hard to be as motivated on the bike when it is wet, but at least the
bike will be moving fast. The body is feeling OK. I'm always feeling a
bit battered at this time, after five hours' sleep, but once you get up and
out . . . It's best just to try not to think about it too much.

Ry had put the lighter-weight Panaracer tyres on as the roads were
much better in Australia, and I was on the 12×25 block as there
weren't really any hills to write home about. But by mid-morning we
made another unexpected change to the bike set-up as the conditions
did not live up to my optimistic early-morning video diary. I was
making painfully slow progress along the coast as that promising
wind had swung to being bang onshore, occasionally on to my front
right, and it was howling, consistently over 25 knots and then gusting.
It was hard to hold on to the bike, let alone speed up, so we swapped
out the front wheel, using a shallower 32mm rather than 47mm rim,
which was catching the wind like a spinnaker.

I pedalled out of the Great Southern and into the Goldfields-
Esperance region, with the Southern Ocean showing me her full might
(when I turned north I would be losing the coast for a day, finding it
again along the Great Australian Bight near Nullarbor). From the
start, near a community at Jerramungup, it was tough going. What
hurt, other than my legs from the big effort, was my neck, from constantly bracing into a side wind. I spent the day leaning to the right,
which over sixteen hours takes quite a toll. The torrential rain did
lighten as the day wore on but it was much colder than I had hoped
Australia would be. In that intensity of rain nothing seemed to keep
my feet and hands dry so I was resigned to just keeping my core dry.
But my injured fingers from Around Britain quickly swelled around
the joints. We got through a pile of talc powder and tried riding with
latex medical gloves underneath layers of cycling gloves with Gore-
Tex mountaineering mitts over the top. But after hours and hours of
rain nothing stayed dry and my hands were like shrivelled prunes,
with joints that looked arthritic.

The small tourist town of Esperance marked my turning point
north for a dogleg to an even smaller community at Norseman, where
I would turn right again and rejoin the direct route east you would

take from Perth across the Outback. The area is wide arable land, but also very sandy, so at least the rain stopped me getting sandblasted.

On days like that I lived in my own world even more than usual. I didn't listen to music or audiobooks; I wouldn't have heard anything over that wind anyway. There was less communication with the Follow Vehicle, I was just left in my own head for long hours, not looking around, not glancing back. Even a nod or a second of eye contact with the team breaks that trance, that long stare you get from hour after hour in shit conditions. But that hardening or zoning out, the immunity to cold and discomfort, is necessary in order to get through. If you were too 'present' in conditions like that you would probably give up. You would certainly start feeling sorry for yourself. You need the ability to go into idiot mode, to smile at the absurdity of your own situation, to allow time to pass without your constant attention. The wild conditions definitely made my world close in: it was just the road in front of me, and I felt detached.

The night-ride was a blast, a recovery ride north, and we finished at Salmon Gums. If you are thinking it's odd to name a town 'fish lips', let me tell you that the name derives from a type of eucalyptus tree that is ubiquitous to the area.

End of day 31, and a bit of a battle. Made it 239 miles, one mile short – I'll take that! Heading along the south coast to Esperance there was a massive sidewind, which at points was coming front right. What an absolute battle. I stopped and peed at one point and I think it landed two fields away. Pretty fierce. It was a very hard-fought day and I am pretty sore. Five hours' sleep and let's re-run the fun. Hopefully we can avoid more days like today, as those conditions take a huge amount out of me.

Day 32

Start of day 32 and I am five minutes late starting this morning. I am pretty sore after yesterday, so it took me a bit longer to get up and going. I've got to be a bit sharper in the mornings. Being late means that I have to add on time at the end of the day. I'm not going to start not riding the sixteen hours a day, because over time that would have a massive impact on mileage. Also it is taking a bit longer to get up and ready in the southern hemisphere because I have so much more clobber to put on. It's about 5°C now. It'll be good to finish the southwest corner of Australia and head into the middle bit.

The Eyre Highway, 1,041 miles from Norseman to Port Augusta, includes the longest straight road in the country at 91.1 miles between the roadhouses of Ballandonia and Caiguna. In the western parts there are several emergency airstrips where the road widens out for the Royal Flying Doctor Service. You come across huge yellow signs saying R.F.D.S. EMERGENCY AIRSTRIP followed by black and white stripes, like piano keys, painted on the road, with a turnaround bay for small aircraft, and then a long stretch where the bush has been cleared on either side of the road. Between signs telling you to watch out for landing planes and 50m-long road trains, it's a road with very little traffic but some very strange vehicles, all of which have been stocked up for a major crossing. It's seventeen hours' driving and one of those wonderful roads of the world. There is no going to the shops, no turning off at any point; everyone is committed to the same adventure of getting across this vast expanse. The only supply points along the way exist exclusively to sustain travellers and are placed strategically so you can drive without having to carry extra fuel. The Atacama Desert in northern Chile is similar, and I just love these ribbons of tar through true wilderness.

I turned right at the BP garage at Norseman and headed into this expanse without a backwards glance. A decade ago I had stopped for a long while, with a great deal more trepidation. I had eaten the feast of a man who didn't know when he would find his next meal, chatted to an enthusiastic Irishman working in the garage, and tied on six large bottles of water to the top of my pannier bags, ready to face the heat of the Outback. My memories of the forests that followed are of being plagued by swarms of horseflies, attracted to the black of my lycra shorts. I couldn't cycle faster than these dreaded vampires could fly, and it was an apt welcome to a part of the world where a lot of things slither, crawl and swarm.

This time I was going to run that long gauntlet in winter and I had an RV behind me, so the adventure was far less wildman and naive, although it would almost definitely hurt a hell of a lot more this time.

Nullarbor means 'Plain with no Trees', but the Outback has many landscapes, and those first hours were through beautiful forests, home to most eucalyptus trees on the planet. Having already met the salmon gum, here I was pedalling past a sparse woodland of blackbutt and gimlet trees, stunted and hardy specimens holding on to life and creating habitat in this arid expanse. Inland, the Fraser Range rises to towering granite hills, but the highway only rose and fell gently in their wake.

It was a dry day and much calmer, but I dearly paid the price for battling so hard the day before. Considering the improved conditions I should have gone much quicker, but until lunchtime progress was painfully slow, simply because I was so weak and sore on the bike. Still, riding into the Outback was certainly a psychological lift – the illusion of better progress as I headed east again.

Another psychological boost, which I hadn't bargained on, was the reaction to the One Month world record. A quick check online told me that the comments in the press and social media were very positive. More importantly, despite the tough conditions over the past forty-eight hours the One Month milestone seemed to have given the crew a new spring in their step. I wasn't flippant about the achievement, bearing in mind my reservation about the fact that people have ridden further, but I always knew we would do it if we were en route for the 80 Days, so the One Month was never an important target for me personally; however, for the team I could see that it was a tangible milestone, the first major recognition of all their hard work and commitment. Just as it had for Alex in Mongolia, I wondered if for others the penny was now dropping that we could actually do this.

But as I pedalled along, I wondered how many of the crew had given our chances proper thought, or whether they just believed me because I said it was possible. Or perhaps the cause for the team's increased morale was something else – the settling of nerves and a newfound commitment to leg 2 after the stresses of leg 1. It was hard to tell – I had so little interaction despite them following me all day long. But I did often sit on the bike wondering how my crew were feeling, cooped up, following my blinking red light for four four-hour blocks. A glorious team effort, but a brutal routine none the less.

I was looking forward to the famous 90 Mile Straight but should have clocked a lot sooner that I would arrive well after dark to stand underneath the massive brown sign saying AUSTRALIA'S LONGEST ROAD. Even in the daytime it doesn't look like a straight road as it is constantly dipping, but between this late shift and the following graveyard shift I rode its entire length in the dark. A decade ago it had taken over a week to get here from Perth.

It's the end of day 32, and it has been a tough one: 376km, so only 234 miles – a bit disappointed. We woke up and it was 5°C, but as often happens it got colder through dawn, and I just couldn't get going properly. I felt rock bottom that first set. I guess my batteries were low. Yesterday took a lot out of me with that sidewind. My right hip flexor and the right-hand side of my neck, from bracing into this, were all pretty painful. So until lunch I felt pretty awful and my speed suffered. Thankfully I have been much faster this afternoon. To only lose six miles on a day when I felt so weak, it's been a good day, but it's been pretty hard-fought.

Day 33

Start of day 33 and we are just a couple of minutes late starting out this morning – need to get the discipline back into this morning start. I have a bit of a pressure point, a sore on my left Achilles, right at the junction where it meets the foot at the bottom. We think this is reacting from a slight compression from my overshoes, so we will have to watch that. With the overshoe stretched, any extra fold in the bottom of my tights or my socks over the long hours causes a small amount of pressure on the tendon that can grow into a serious issue – like the hamstring injury from over-compression during Around Britain. So we have just strapped it this morning, to protect and support. The aim is to make it close to the South Australia border by end of today.

Other than the rudimentary test of standing on the scales every morning, the saliva samples were the best way of knowing my levels of immunity. Anecdotally it was pretty clear when I was struggling, run down, but science was a useful back-up. Laura was working with Jo Dunbar, a physiologist back in the UK, taking samples every day, analysing them once a week and reporting her findings to Jo. The following is beyond me, but I'll include it for the docs and science buffs. The data showed my salivary IGA (immunoglobulin A), amoles and cortisol levels, so a mixture of protein levels and stress hormone. The assumption was that there would be a trend over time, a drop-off in immune profile, as you would expect in any ultra endurance event. As you could see my immunity drop-off, it was even more important to educate and remind the team to be extra careful with germs and hygiene.

I passed a number of small roadhouses all day, that is all. Road signs became the main landmarks: BEWARE UNFENCED ROAD NEXT 150KM (even though it was unfenced long before the sign and long after this warning elapsed); a diamond-shaped yellow warning sign for kangaroos; and a silhouette of a bear – which must have meant wombats although I never saw one – with a rectangular yellow sign underneath displaying an arbitrary distance, like '52KM'. About 52km down the road I would cycle past another one.

There was no more woodland but it also wasn't yet the true desert, which started a bit further inland. Still benefiting from the coastal morning dew and occasional rain, the roadside was thick scrub, with the odd gangly tree.

What bliss – I rode on a gentle conveyor belt, an encouraging westerly wind. There wasn't a single piece of geography, natural or man-made, to punctuate the day, and I tapped along at 25km/h, playing I-Spy for kangaroos.

End of day 33 and we had a very cold start, it was 3°C. Never expected Australia to be this cold! But the middle few shifts I flew as I had a tailwind, so made up great miles, and then the last shift into the night again, and I was just left to spin it out. Covered a relatively easy 401km, just under 250 miles, which is good and makes up for some lost miles yesterday. Just passed the odd roadhouse today and the odd roadkill kangaroo, which stinks, especially when it is windy – the smell follows you after you have passed it. Some live kangaroos as well, which was sweet. It's quite nice, as I can vividly remember this section of the route.

Day 34

It's just gone four o'clock in the morning and somewhere ahead in the darkness is the state boundary, so that is the next milestone. Big sea cliffs off to my right somewhere. I remember camping on the edge ten years ago and then waking up with my tent on my face because the high winds had blown it down. I've got a nice little tailwind again this morning which is great. Because it has been so cold the last couple of mornings I thought I would do things differently this morning: I am wearing shoes that are half a size bigger with thicker socks on, and these long gauntlet lobster-claw mitts with hand-warmers inside, just to keep my fingers and toes warm. I guess after five hours' sleep I'm struggling to wake up and the last thing my body wants to do is warm up as well, especially when going along at this gentle pace. I'm not about to do intervals just to warm up. So trying to feel a bit more snug. Sorry you can't see my sponsors under all these jackets – so thank you Artemis, LDC, Cardtronics, Visit Scotland, Menzies Aviation, KOGA, Pana-racer . . . but I am opting for warmth!

The media boys had caught up with me as I was zipping along with sand and scrub just visible in the darkness of the roadside. I had managed a few snatched conversations with Johnny since Perth, cleared the air a bit after the build-up of tensions in Mongolia and China.

I was well aware that the UK audience was now enjoying my early-morning videos as they went to bed and my late-evening videos as they woke up. Nicci had stopped showing Harriet, my eldest, the morning videos because she felt 'Daddy looked a bit scary' after limited sleep. But the global audience was growing through sharing the footage with Global Cycling Network, and I would become aware of the anticipation as I reached the more inhabited parts of Australia (not to mention New Zealand and North America). While I had pretty much been left on my own since Paris, apart from a few supporters in Mongolia and the welcome party in Perth, from the messages relayed by Una and Nicci I knew that a huge number of people were getting in touch and commenting on seeing me along the route. There was a sense that after I got out of the Outback the dynamics on the road might change, perhaps back to something like Around Britain, although hopefully not quite so busy.

I threw my arm up to beckon the FV to come alongside. Ry was in the passenger seat so I relayed the problem.

'Something's not right with my left pedal, it feels wobbly.'

I'd had these pedals since day 17, so maybe it was just worn. It felt like it wasn't flat; it fell away from my foot as I applied pressure. I thought it could be the pedal body or the bearings, or even the cleats on my shoes.

'No problem,' Ry responded, 'we'll pull in ahead and switch them over.'

As I pulled over next to the waiting RV on the verge, I tried to clip out but the crank just snapped. I was left with the pedal and half of the crank arm attached to the bottom of my shoe, the stump still attached to the chainset.

I laughed, Ry looked bemused, and the rest of the team took a minute to understand what had happened. How do you break your crank? It should be the thickest, strongest piece of solid metal on the bike!

Ry jumped into action, stripping the left crank from the spare bike and swapping it over in a matter of minutes. 'Do the interviewing afterwards,' I called back to the crew as I grabbed some suncream. 'Let's go, go, go.' I was pleased they were on this and filming, but stopping Ry working and asking him questions could happen once I was down the road. 'Whatever makes the bike go faster . . .' I said, repeating Laura's mantra – every action had to prioritize bike speed.

After the small hamlet of Eucla, both RVs got stopped at the state border for an inspection but I was waved through and they caught me up without issue. After crossing into South Australia, we reached the part of the highway where the Nullarbor National Park meets the Southern Ocean along many miles of staggering sea cliffs up to 200 feet tall. This is the Great Australian Bight – 'bight' simply meaning a bend in a coastline (although I wonder how many tourists misspell it and assume it relates to sharks!). Here the landmass drops without warning to the roaring waves far below, where the tectonic plate that carries Antarctica broke off about fifty million years ago. The scale of this geography is mind-blowing to experience. Equally you could drive through thinking it's the most featureless landscape imaginable, as from the road you aren't aware of those cliffs just a few hundred metres off to the side – only dirt tracks lead to this spectacle. So for the very first time I told the Follow Vehicle to go and do some sightseeing, 'You might never be here again,' I shouted through the window once they had drawn alongside. 'You have to go and see the edge of Australia. I'll be fine, just catch up soon!' The crew looked surprised but delighted, and turned off.

Barrelling along, without the sound of a vehicle behind me, I then became aware of the buzz of the drone overhead. I took one hand off the bars and gave it a massive wave, freewheeling at over 40km/h. It was utterly glorious – a sunny, early spring day on the Nullarbor Plain, effortlessly eating up the miles. I was always impressed with the drone and Helmut's skill in piloting it so close to me and over such a range. But even he underestimated the strength of the wind this time and overcooked the flight. When he stopped filming and started flying it back to where he was standing at the roadside a few kilometres back, the little machine, well within its normal range, struggled, unable to punch through the wind, went into auto-pilot and crashed. There was a flurry of activity and concern on my watch (WhatsApp) as the crew raced to try and find the downed drone. Luckily its GPS was still transmitting and it had landed without damage. Best of all, Helmut was delighted with the shots, so it was all worth it.

By mid-afternoon I reached Yalata roadhouse and the whole team were back together, spirits high, relishing this conveyor belt across the middle of Australia.

I've been off the bike about fifteen minutes, I've had a wash and I am sitting here doing recovery pump, which is these pneumatic compression sleeves on each leg using a small electric machine. This is my wee bed in the back of the RV, with the spare bike. It's been a cracking day across the Outback – covered 421km, so about 262 miles. Really good tailwind, one of my best days so far. Sore neck from being on the tri-bars all day, but apart from that pretty good. But I broke my crank. Never in my life have I broken my crank. Just sheared the metal off. Today was also a good day because we clocked over 8,000 miles. I'm here with my hot-water bottle and a big plate of pasta. I'll be asleep in about twenty minutes for another five hours' sleep to do it all again!

Day 35

Start of day 35 and I slept all right, so feel OK. Ten years ago today I set out from Paris to cycle around the world the last time. A lot has happened to that record since – to think when I set out in 2007 the Guinness World Record for the fastest circumnavigation by bicycle was touring style, solo and unsupported and stood at 276 days! And I eventually went around the world in 194 days and 17 hours, so I was riding about 100 miles a day. So amazing to think what has happened in terms of my adventures and also the circumnavigation WR. I am going to look out for a British cyclist who is trying to become the first to ride a unicycle around the world. Apparently he is doing about 80km a day, so I will catch him at some point today.

This was Ed Pratt, a twenty-one-year-old from Somerset who had set out at the age of nineteen to cycle around the world on one wheel. At the start he'd hoped it would take two years, but here he was two and a half years later, halfway through his circumnavigation. Ed had dropped me an email long before my departure. His route had already taken him across Europe and central then southeast Asia, and as I set out from Paris he'd set out from Perth, so our paths were due to cross almost exactly halfway across Australia.

I simply love the Britishness and eccentricity of this ambition, and what an education straight after high school! I can't think of a better way of learning about yourself. Here are Ed's own words about why he chose a unicycle: 'Most of the appeal of the world ride comes from the fact that nobody has ever done it. People do it on bikes all the time, so what's to stop anyone attempting this feat on a unicycle? I'm also keen to meet new people and I've found that the unicycle, through the interest it creates, is a great way to do this. It also offers a great physical challenge, but also complete mental focus, because you know if you don't see a pothole or bump in the road, you're coming off! When you're unicycling, you're unicycling, that's it, and I love that.'

I took the road around the edge of Ceduna, so nearly missed Ed. He had taken a few days off as his saddle had broken – an even bigger problem on a unicycle than on a normal bike as it's a big banana-shaped thing that you need to balance. Ed had bodged a repair and tried to pedal out to meet me, but I was too fast and already gone. On his way back he passed my Media Vehicle, who picked him up and brought him out to meet me down the road. By this time I had reached first break, jumped into the FV and was having my ten-minute power nap.

I emerged, feeling a bit groggy, to be met by the most unusual sight: a tall, very thin Englishman wearing a thick green hoody and fluorescent vest and a red cycling helmet with a home-made floppy brim taken from a safari hat. The bright green steed he was holding was much bigger than I expected, a 29-inch wheel, much as you would find on big mountain bikes, as opposed to the teeny wheels of the circus unicycle. What was more impressive was the amount of kit: two blue canvas panniers were carefully packed above the wheel but below the saddle, and in front of this was a smaller red bag for bits and bobs; if that wasn't enough, a roll-down dry bag was bungeed on top, alongside three drink bottles. The handlebars projected out front like a time-trial bike, although it would be impossible both to sit upright and get an aero-efficient position – I guess these horns for handlebars were simply more comfortable.

Intriguingly the wheel also had a heavy-duty disc brake on it; however, the idea of pulling this brake seemed pretty crazy as by stopping your only wheel, which was the point of balance, you would be immediately catapulted forward into the road. My only point of reference is having ridden a penny farthing, where you are also directly pedalling the axle, and even then your best form of braking is simply to slow your feet, resist the rotation. Uphills are torturous, downhills downright dangerous. On a unicycle you have the same challenges as a penny farthing but with even less stability.

We set off at a very leisurely pace and chatted. I was acutely aware when I was freewheeling downhill that he was still madly pedalling, like a hamster on a runaway wheel. I applaud Ed's tenacity and sense of adventure, but after about twenty minutes I had to pick it up a bit, so with a fist pump (mostly for fear of unbalancing him) I raced on. What a wonderful pace to see the world at. And if you haven't see Ed's YouTube clips, you are missing out.

From Ceduna I was cutting inland to Port Augusta rather than round the Eyre Peninsula. Near Wirrulla the roads were oddly painted with red tar down the middle and grey tar down each edge, and with the cracking wind and empty roads it felt like I had my own racetrack. It was smooth rolling as I left the Outback and started to pass parched grazing and then the first fields of crops. The Eyre Highway became the Tod Highway in the small wheatbelt town of Kyancutta, which looks like a ghost town with no shops or accommodation besides a petrol station. As I passed, the wind kicked up a sandstorm, adding to the air of tumbleweed and a better yesteryear. It blew clouds of grit across the road so I pulled my buff high to my nose, glad for my visor.

The reaction online about the snapped crank was hilarious. The GCN cycling audience were making particular noise, using their #wattagebazooka. The event certainly gave me credit for strength that I simply didn't have! I was happy to claim the glory for breaking an unbreakable part, but the truth was I couldn't have cranked out 1,000 watts even if I had wanted to. If you looked closely at the break you could see concentric rings on one side, a fatiguing in the metal that had happened over a long time. At 90rpm since Paris I had probably done around three million pedal strokes and this low-intensity, high-volume strain had done it.

It was a Dura Ace STAGES Power crank that I had snapped, and the priority was to get a replacement, for two reasons: one, I was now riding without power data, and two, so that the spare bike was rideable. It wasn't a spare part that we carried.

Cracking day mileage wise – 420km, 261 miles. Amazing tailwinds again. We have very much come out of the Outback now and into farmland and inhabited Australia. Kind of a shame to finish in the rain as it was a glorious day. Met Ed Pratt – spent two and a half years getting to this point! It took me thirty-five days! But very cool to hear his story. I am officially over halfway across Australia, which is cool. Claire is getting ready to take over from Laura in the next few days. It has been quite ridiculous since Perth, I have been utterly spoilt. I had a moment earlier when I had to laugh, realizing how different this was to ten years ago when I was completely on my own. I had two people putting suncream on my legs as I had a racing stop! But there are a couple of things we need to sort out in terms of performance. In the afternoons today and yesterday I have been struggling to keep food down. I am on about 8,500 to 9,000kcal a day and I have been a bit sick, a bit of reflux. So we need to try some different food types. And now I am on the flatlands and so on the tri-bars a lot longer I'm having issues with my neck and the pain from that position. But all round a good day, second day of 420-odd kilometres. But feeling a bit battered – you can see how bruised my hands are – so there is just time for a quick recovery, quick shower and then bed.

Day 36

It's 3.44 a.m., just doing my shoes up. The usual morning ritual: the alarm goes off just before 3.30, it takes another ten minutes to get ready because of all the winter weather clobber. The forecast today is pretty much rain all day but starting in the dry. So I am wearing the shoes that are half a size bigger with waterproof socks. Here is my morning concoction of pills: we have multivitamins, probiotics (to keep my tummy happy), omega 3 oil, some echinacea and arnica, some omeprazole to try and settle the reflux, and a couple of paracetamol, to manage multiple aches and pains. The plan is to be on the bike at four, but as we are working in challenge time we are now half an hour behind local time. We have been moving back time by ten minutes a day across Australia, to keep up with the time zone changes, compared to moving by fifteen minutes a day through leg 1.

The early darkness shift was just me and my music. Since my iPod had broken in week one, my sister Heather had sent another one out to

Australia. However, in the rains of Western Australia this also died despite efforts to waterproof it. I didn't often listen to anything during the dayshifts as I needed to be more alert to traffic on the road, although in the middle of Oz I could zone out for long gaps. The road trains were the only real menace: you could hear them coming from a long way off, and it was worth hugging the hard shoulder. Even when they pulled out, their sheer volume and speed meant that their draught would suck you into the road and you could easily crash.

The new iPod was packed with spoken-word recordings – podcasts and ebooks – so I was still nicking the crew's music for the graveyard shifts. I just needed a soundtrack to get me through those first hours. They were such cold, dark, lonely hours, and I wasn't thinking much, so music filled that space with a bit of warmth. I had barely spoken to Fleur; in fact on one of my lunch breaks I had to ask her to come across from the Media Vehicle and chat as I ate, otherwise I was worried I would go across Australia without getting to know her. It was Fleur's iPod that became my soundtrack through Oz, although as Fleur is a Kiwi it was headlined by Crowded House, followed by a solid dose of Elton John and backed up by some dubious country and western music.

Until Port Augusta, the end of my four-day easterly tack, it stayed dry and fast. As I cut across the bridge over the estuary, with small boats anchored in a line downstream, the Princes Highway started to cut south and I stepped off the conveyor belt. The Outback had been bliss, a perfect run; it couldn't have been more different to a decade ago, when they had been my toughest miles. There was only one thing in common: it was just as windy; the question was whether it was with you or against you. I can't imagine a day in the Outback without wind.

Shortly afterwards, as I pedalled past a sign saying WELCOME TO WAKEFIELD, I looked over to a big farm of wind turbines on the hillside, beyond which was a narrow peninsula and the Spencer Gulf. The coastal weather those turbines were built to catch was brewing visibly, a heavy skyline which I pedalled into with a wry smile and a real sense of 'here goes . . .'.

We made it to 60km short of Adelaide. It was a fast morning heading slightly northeast, then cut down towards Adelaide and got absolutely battered, and it has been such a slow afternoon. The last few days, in the final four hours the wind has died down, whereas today it did the opposite: a big storm blew in and it was absolutely wild. I was struggling to see the road at times, the rain was absolutely lashing down. I haven't had conditions like that before now. But then it cleared, and the moon came out, and the last hour was just beautiful. I have freezing feet and I've just taken my rain gear off. I really struggled this morning getting going, just feeling wiped out. I don't know why I was more tired this morning, just couldn't get going. But then a good storm wakes you up. We are coming up to the halfway point, 9,000 miles, so maybe not a surprise I have a couple of days where I'm a bit switched off and struggling mentally. Today is the first day I have had to take a Pro Plus on the bike, just to stay alert. So yes, a real battle, but success: we made 240, and at points in that storm I didn't expect that. Right . . . I need to get inside and warm up.

Day 37

It has calmed down in the night. That was quite a storm at the end of yesterday. It's a beautiful start, much milder, it's about 10°C. Another big milestone ahead when we get through Adelaide. The good news is once I get past Adelaide and I'm cutting up towards Brisbane things can get a bit warmer. I hope! I still live in fear of New Zealand. If the weather is colder there it's going to be tough because Australia has been colder than expected. Laura is dropping out today for a week and Claire is going to be looking after me.

Ry had put the 28 cassette back on in preparation for the Adelaide Hills and changed the chain again, as well as new tyres. He had also widened the tri-bars to try to ease the tension through my shoulders, back and neck. The last four days of flatlands had been very fast and efficient, but I was suffering from bad tension headaches and a restricted range of movement.

Four weeks on from my crash near Moscow, Laura was still work-ing on my left elbow whenever there was time. It was now a dull ache that I was very used to, and the roads were constantly smooth, so none of the jarring moments that had punctuated Russia and Mongo-lia. I wasn't riding with it strapped up all the time any more, and on balance my neck was now more painful, which distracted me from the elbow. At the time of the crash we had spoken about the possibility of my having a fracture, and if I did, what that would mean long-term, and the consequences. While Laura was the physio, it was my deci-sion to carry on without diagnosis – I had not felt unsafe to ride and could weight-bear. The issue now was my very restricted range, fur-ther confirming that I most likely had a fracture in either my radial head or the bottom of the humerus.

Apart from that, now a week into Australia and nearing the overall halfway point, it was very evident that my level of fatigue was pretty strong. While conditions had been favourable, I was struggling more, especially in the early and late shifts. Laura and Claire were in closer comms and using all their tricks to keep me alert. It was tempting for me just to binge on sugar and caffeine, my natural go-tos when tired, but they wanted me to avoid the mental (and physical) highs and lows that this caused, so tried to distract me by giving me my toothbrush to clean my teeth while I rode, or putting a cold wet flannel on my neck and face. Furthermore, they were obviously working hard to be more aware of my condition, checking up on me more often. It must have been constantly exhausting in the FV. They needed to be think-ing two steps ahead, making sure they didn't ask me questions, just giving me instructions, and if they did need to ask questions to keep them very simple so that there were no more demands placed on me. This may sound ridiculous, but anything more compli-cated than a yes/no question left me feeling confused; even then I often had to ask them to repeat the question. It was much easier if they did the thinking for me. All I had the focus to do was get on the bike and ride.

A physical symptom of this fatigue was the reflux, so there were also a lot of conversations between Ruth McKean, my nutritionist back in Scotland, and Laura about creating variation in my food and drinks. As the day went on I was vomiting food back on to the road, so eating was a chore. A struggle with nutrition obviously then creates a knock-on effect in terms of levels of fatigue. The increased darkness and much colder temperatures in the morning and evening were also probably affecting factors.

Because Laura knew me so well by now she could tell as soon as I woke up if I just wasn't switched on and I could see that she was nervous about stepping out of the team, having to trust someone else to have this level of intuition. Although I could see how well she got on with Claire, Laura's were big boots to fill. But as the accumulating fatigue caught up with me, it was all the more reason for Laura to hit refresh for herself, so that from New Zealand onwards she was at least brighter than the rest of us. So we waved her off in the dark of the morning, and Claire was now in charge.

Challenge time had worked flawlessly for everyone until this point. But Laura was the first to leave 'the bubble' in the middle of a leg. She checked in for her flight, sat back at the departure gate and relaxed for the first time in a long time – only to watch her plane pull back off the stand and head for the runway. 'I'm living in my own made-up time zone' must have been a novel excuse as Laura tried to explain herself at the customer service desk.

Laura had been clear that there needed to be a gradual transition in the role – she described it like changing the driver of the car while moving. Claire had been awesome in getting stuck in straight away and taking on board a ton of information, all the processes and routines plus the quirks of how to get the best out of me when I was in different mood states. I knew that Laura had often asked Nicci for her opinion when I was in a very dark or particularly difficult place mentally. As Laura had said, the physiotherapy delivery probably took up about 10 per cent of the performance manager role; the rest was nutritional or medical, and 60 per cent playing 'mum', which included nagging everyone about every detail of timing. I needed my performance manager to crack the whip so I didn't have to, to think constantly for me and try to be one step ahead all the time so that all I had to worry about was pedalling. To take just one element, the weather, this meant ensuring I put on a jacket before it rained, changed the visor if it wasn't sunny, got thicker gloves as the sun went down, put on suncream as the sun came up, and so on. None of it was rocket science, but as the bike rider it was amazing to experience this often unspoken relationship, to have that level of trust in someone who was constantly thinking about your performance. On the flip side, Laura had already pre-warned Nicci that unfortunately she'd have another toddler in the family when I got back!

What helped Laura step out was knowing that Tony was in charge. She had trusted him with her life during their Pacific row and knew what a conscientious leader he was. Tim and Fleur were also working incredibly hard and had been crucial in a nearly seamless transition from leg 1 to 2. There was, however, an underlying friction between them and Tony. Tim was definitely the stronger character, and while a diligent worker, he wasn't a fan of Tony's quiet leadership style. I was aware of a difficult dynamic developing, but I could also see how hard Tony was working to keep any team issues from me. It all came down to professional boundaries, which are so important to keep, especially when living on top of each other on expedition.

On the northern outskirts of Adelaide I cut east around downtown before leaving the suburb of Burnside and starting on my biggest climb across Australia. Greenhill Road sounds quite quaint, but it's a lung-busting 20km up through the Adelaide Hills. It was also absolutely stunning: looking over to my right the cityscape got better and better as I climbed through the mist of the early morning.

Shortly after starting the climb I lost the plot when I realized the media boys had gone into Adelaide together to buy a spare part, even though this was one of the most beautiful and interesting landscapes on the leg, not to mention the physical challenge of it. It only takes one person to go to the shops, and we had discussed the significance of these climbs at the start of the day.

Trying to refocus on my job, I got back into the gentle rhythm of the steep climb – that dull ache in the quads and calves, sitting back in the saddle, gently resting my hands on the flats of the bars, keeping my upper body as neutral as possible, soaked, sweat stinging my eyes. The only downside of a visor was that it steamed up when I got hot and there wasn't enough airflow. As I gently fixated my gaze on the next corner and worked my bike upwards, the overhanging trees dripped on to the road, giving the impression it was still raining. It was a glorious route, making the previous day's sandstorms seem otherworldly. I was soon in lush rolling farmland with small fields and neat, expensive homesteads – more a picture of the Cotswolds than the Australia we all imagine.

We rendezvoused with the full crew near the top. There was the usual 'no worries, let's just get on with it' and we promptly took a few wrong turns, immediately spotted them, and probably only lost fifteen minutes in the process. But I could tell that nerves were jangled. Laura was gone, the media boys were on the ropes again, and we needed to settle into a new team dynamic.

While we'd stopped very briefly to hand over some food, as the roads were now too narrow and windy for the FV to drive alongside, a car pulled up and a lady came running over.

'It's Shonnie!'

I had stayed with Shonnie and her family in Adelaide a decade ago. I didn't even know she knew I was cycling across Oz again. It was great to see her and she suffered a very sweaty hug, handed me some home-made goodies and took a quick photo before I raced on. I wished I'd had more than sixty seconds to stop and chat.

Within a mile I passed a cyclist who immediately turned and fell in alongside. Steve had been tracking me since Paris, and for the glorious long descent out of the Adelaide Hills I enjoyed my first two-wheeled company on the bike in Australia. It felt very strange to have a conversation outside of my team about things other than food, the route, weather and sleep. We talked about his family, we talked about the area, its culture and politics. It was the most normal everyday chat between strangers on their bikes, yet for me, having been deprived of thinking or talking about anything apart from myself for thirty-seven days, it was an odd mental change in gear. I enjoyed it for a few hours, but when he eventually turned I struggled to concentrate; my mind was drawn to my discomfort, having lost its focus on the targets ahead. I was so used to breaking up the route and day ahead into chunks so that I always had waypoints, be they places or just blocks of time to focus on. But after engaging in a few hours of enjoyable small talk I was now left with no idea of what the next waypoint was. I was just riding my bike, without the sense of purpose I was used to.

Having got back in the zone, got the blinkers back on, I reached the flatlands and we then turned right off the main A8 at Tailem Bend and on to smaller roads to reach the coast. It was only then that I realized how helpful the onshore wind had been. Tacking into it, following the marshlands around Lake Alexandrina, I punched through weakly for a few hours at less than 15km/h. I was losing about 7 miles every hour; over the rest of the day that would mean losing over 50 miles on a day when I was already behind schedule owing to the Adelaide Hills. I relayed this to the team, but Tony was already ahead of me, realizing this was a crucial moment in the ride – I couldn't throw away these miles. After I'd fought my way to the small coastal town of Meningie, he re-routed me 90°, back inland, not worrying about the about-turn, just focused on making faster miles. It worked, but those four hours had taken a lot out of me. Into the late shift I was racing back along the A8, then getting close to the border of the state of Victoria.

Towards the end of the day, the FV pulled alongside and Claire called over, suggesting we finish a little bit earlier than 9.30, like we had done in the past few days. 'No way,' I called back – not on a day when we were short on miles. Concerned with my reflux and fatigue levels, we had been happy to call it a day ten or fifteen minutes early on those days when I was flying with a tailwind. Psychologically, when I was averaging over 260 miles a day I could deal with losing a few minutes' ride time for the extra sleep. Logically, stopping earlier today, a much tougher day physically, made even more sense, but psychologically I couldn't deal with that as I wasn't hitting the average mileage target.

A while later they pulled alongside again and Claire said, 'I think you should think about stopping a bit earlier – just thinking of your battered body.'

'No.'

It took an age to manage that reply, but the team got the message pretty clearly.

Battered body, battered body, battered body – those words rattled around my determined, demented mind for the next hour. I felt alone.

This was hard enough without my team pulling on my reins. I knew how much pain I was in; I didn't need to be told fourteen hours into a day. Poor Claire, she had taken over on a very tough day, and I was obviously very fragile. I wouldn't like to be looking after me when I get into a hole.

Late in the evening I reached Nicci on the phone – early in the morning in the UK – and talked this through. I could hear in her careful responses that she understood my position, but this upset feeling, which seemed so massive in my little world, was really nothing, just my tired mind digging in and overreacting.

I had a chat with Claire about this when I ate dinner, but I could see she was a bit worried. I just didn't have the capacity to deal with any action or communication that was a brake on progress. My tolerance was non-existent, and I could tell this was making me difficult to work with. I wouldn't compromise.

It's been a tough old day, the head has been all over the place. But we made it past Adelaide early doors and had a big old climb through the Adelaide Hills at first light, coming up through the cloud – it was absolutely stunning, but up, up, up. Thought I would make my average speed with the descent, which was fast to begin with going east, but then as we cut pretty much due south to get to the coast I got absolutely battered. With that really strong crosswind coming in off the ocean, we altered the route and initially headed back inland, which gave me quite a push, as the wind was right behind me; and then we are heading south again now, but being further inland there is much less wind. It has died almost entirely now. So I have done 225 miles – lost fifteen on an ideal day. But considering the Adelaide Hills and that battering, we will call it a success, but that takes a lot out of you. We are getting dangerously close to halfway – and that will hopefully be tomorrow's excitement!

14

A Sense of Perspective

Day 38

I'm pretty sore this morning. I slept all right I guess but I woke up thinking it was the middle of the night and nipped outside for a pee and discovered it was the morning, which is quite disappointing. I say the morning – it was 3.30 a.m. Tough day yesterday, it took a lot out of me, I am hurting. The weather forecast is for the wind to die down a wee bit and if all goes to plan we are aiming for a Sunday/Monday finish to Australia then off to New Zealand. That still worries me because I keep thinking it will be colder down there. In leg 1 I couldn't wait to get here for smoother roads, and now I am here, I keep thinking about getting back to the northern hemisphere where it is warmer! Right, must get off and on to the bike because it hurts first thing in the morning. I think the team are doing well but I think everyone is feeling the miles now. Right at the end of today or early tomorrow morning we will officially be halfway around the World. But my view on this trip is so micro, it's so focused on the next horizon, that halfway doesn't feel that big in itself. It's everyone else who keeps talking about halfway; I am just focused on the next four-hour block.

It was Tuesday, so about six days left in Oz. Despite the concerns over fatigue, and day 37's poor miles, the fast miles across the Outback had put us in a strong position, nearly a quarter of a day up on schedule. Ahead lay the biggest logistical bundle: within a week we'd have to fly from Brisbane to Invercargill, via Christchurch, cycle the length of

New Zealand (factoring in the Picton Ferry between the South and North Islands), then embark on the big transit from Auckland to Anchorage, probably via San Francisco, possibly Hawaii. Una, Mike, Jo, Tony and the dedicated team at Menzies led by David Liepins were doing a lot of contingency planning, depending on how fast I could complete Australia, and a lot of sweet-talking and deal-making with airlines to try and get us through as fast as possible. Yes, 240 was the magic daily number, and we were pretty obsessed with riding sixteen hours a day, letting the distance take care of itself, but once that flight out of Brisbane was set we would be riding by distance alone and it made sense to set a bit of a stretch target, something which kept me ahead of the block programme.

If we were clever, by making an earlier flight that had a quicker check-in time, or shorter layover, we would make back the equivalent of eight hours or half a day's riding. As we always knew in theory but really only understood now after thirty-seven hard days on the road, it took weeks of consistent riding and a bit of luck to make half a day up on the schedule, so if we could 'cheat' that same amount through not having to hang around airports as much I would 'happily' bury myself for a few days to make that up. Doing, say, an extra five hours on the bike over the next six days would pay dividends and put me eight hours ahead. But Una, Laura and Claire were always erring on the side of caution, thinking I was already on the edge of unsustainable. I, however, felt it was all a mental game: I could knowingly put myself into the red for a number of days as long as I could get recovery on the flight and try to reset my focus for the next country.

It was back to beautiful, fairly gentle and more interesting countryside riding into Victoria. Best of all, it was warm – I was down to my jersey in the middle of the day. Quite a few more people came out and rode sections with me, which was fine, but took some getting used to. They were all just excited to find us and simply wanted to join in. There were no delays, no issues, everyone was very respectful. However, with so many requests coming in to my team on social media and online, I recorded a video message about this at lunch stop.

'People are in touch every day asking for details of the route ahead. People are more than welcome to stand on the roadside and support, or to join on the bike, but I am not allowed to draft. And keep in mind I might not be the best company, depending on my headspace! We are not giving out any more route details than are on the website as we don't want to let people down – like yesterday, when we changed the route because of the winds. The best we can say is what's on the website, that is our planned route, and then just follow the tracker and come out and join me. My team on the road and in the UK are completely focused on my performance and so we are not going down the route of making arrangements with people to meet at certain times. But you are welcome to join me for a few miles.'

I pushed the last session very late, watching the digital miles tick over on the cycle computer. I normally didn't leave it on that screen – it wasn't psychologically helpful, for example, to be looking at 200km when you needed to reach nearly 400km each day. But now I had a specific number before we could all stop. Once I'd reached it, we pulled into a wide lay-by and I called everyone out of the RVs for a team celebration. This hadn't felt important at all until I was within a few hours of it, but now we were here it was a huge, fantastic relief, and one worth celebrating.

Well, that is 9,000 miles! And halfway around the World!

The team cheered loudly, and it was a wonderful moment to stop, look around and see what it meant to them. This was tough for everyone; I could see their toil and commitment. But it did feel a bit odd to be surrounded by a team I didn't really know. None of the core team was here, no Laura, Mike, Alex or Una. These guys were all fantastic, but I didn't feel I knew them. It was no disrespect to them, they were giving their all. I loved the bloody, heartfelt relief of reaching halfway but, being selfish, I just missed having someone there who I was close to. To be honest, the hug that meant the most was with good old Johnny. We had been through it all together, thick and thin. He shared exactly how big this moment was.

End of day 38, so it took about thirty-seven days and eighteen hours since leaving Paris. Reaching 9,000 miles within a couple of hours of where we planned is awesome. It is dangerous to start multiplying that by two for many reasons, not least because we have got six flights in the second half. Halfway, it's just another day on the bike, and I need to prioritize recovery as we actually rode a little bit late to make it to half-way, rather than getting there at 4.30/5 a.m. tomorrow morning. So a huge thank you to all the teams through legs 1 and 2, these guys around me, the guys holding the cameras, Helmut and Johnny; and I would like to give a big shout out to somebody who hasn't even been men-tioned yet but is running Base Camp, and that is Una, my mum, who has always been at the heart of these expeditions. So thanks to every-one back in the UK who keep the wheels rolling, and while I can't see it all as I am busy pedalling, I am certainly aware of all the amazing support online. Today, and this evening in particular, coming through some of these towns in Victoria, we had loads of well-wishers – I don't know how the word is getting out but it's just incredible. We are half-way around the World – thank you everyone!

Day 39

I definitely feel more tired this morning – only four and a half hours' sleep and I really feel the difference when I get less than five hours' recovery. Looking ahead now at the second half of the World, which is exciting. This morning I am heading for Melbourne where a couple of local cyclists are joining me, and a few journalists. Damian, a chap who I met ten years ago when he was going for the world record for cycling across Australia, is joining me for a few miles, which is cool.

It was a beautiful start to the day, a cracking dawn, and I counted down the signs towards Melbourne. The body took a bit longer to wake up, and I pedalled along in the dark shaking and bobbing my head, going 'la-la-la-la-la' out loud and all sorts of other nonsense to kick-start my hard drive. But it was pleasant to be less cold; far from warm, but certainly a good few degrees better than in the west.

It was reassuring to know that Damian would be helping with getting through Melbourne, which I remembered as a tricky city to navigate.

Una had been trying to track him down for ages using old phone numbers and emails, even asking a local cycle club, who said they couldn't help because of confidentiality. Mum was getting nowhere, but then Damian, obviously following online, sent an email to Muckle Media, my PR company, when I was already in Australia, offering his help. It is amazing how many people from a decade before were still watching from afar and getting back in touch.

Mid-morning, Fleur and Tim were going to be dropped off at Melbourne airport; they would be flying out to New Zealand to get the new vehicles set up and everything ready for when we landed in Invercargill. They would also be taking the spare bike to be built so that it was ready to ride, which meant I wouldn't have a back-up from now until Brisbane, and it would just be Tony, Claire, Johnny and Helmut from today until the flight – the smallest crew at any stage of the 80 Days.

After first break – the normal power nap, a bowl of raisin, banana and honey-infused porridge, plus a strong coffee – the road soon widened to a dual carriageway. Being early in the day it was pretty deserted and the FV sat in the slow lane behind me with its hazards on. It did cross my mind that this might be frowned upon, but when a police car came by and slowed down to see what we were doing, its occupants just gave us a wave and carried on.

The FV pulled up alongside me for a moment of communication with Fleur, who was driving. There was a wide hard shoulder so I was staying off the road. It was easy spinning, pretty flat, visibility was 100 per cent, and we were going around 30km/h. We finished discussing a turning up ahead so Fleur slowly let me pull ahead, as we had done many times before. Then suddenly—

Thud!

It took a split second to register what had happened. As the FV slowed down next to me, I glanced back to see a car, a small grey hatchback, embedded into its rear.

It hadn't been a loud smash, more of a hollow, deep thump. There had been no screeching of tyres, no protesting wheels on tarmac. There was just a thud.

I braked, heart racing, propped the bike against the crash-barrier and raced to the side of the car. I had been very close, maybe five metres from the point of impact, and was at the passenger door within seconds. All I could hear were the words 'My baby!'

I could see an infant in its baby seat, not moving. I can't describe the sickening feeling. Claire appeared at my shoulder just as the driver made it out of the car. Both airbags had gone off but the front of the car was barely visible, it was so meshed with the back of the RV, the storage area and my bed.

A lorry pulled alongside and stopped. The driver immediately leant out of his window, offering a safety knife, those special ones for cutting seat-belts. I opened the back door and Claire cut the baby seat from its tethers and very gently lifted it out. I wasn't really aware of what else was going on; every focus was on the baby. As Claire carried the seat towards the grass verge, tilted gently backwards, the baby let out a cry. He was alive.

The mum was hysterical, pacing further down the road, trying to make a phone call. Fleur, Ry and Helmut – who was with us to film me meeting Damian – were out of the FV by now, Fleur taking charge of the scene, making sure traffic was stopped and getting everyone away from the vehicles. Ry looked very dazed and had a big lump on his forehead. Helmut was straight into action, but I immediately told him not to film the baby.

For fifty metres back down the road there was a trail of all our stuff: bike tools, spare parts, and a lot of my clothes and bedding. Nicci had made up a blanket with lots of pictures of Willa and Harriet on it. It was the first thing I saw.

Once the boy started crying, he didn't stop. Every instinct was to scoop him up and give him a cuddle, but Claire was firm that he had to stay in his baby seat in case of a neck or spinal injury, and rested it on the ground so he couldn't sit up or move too much. There were some bumps on his face, but it was hard to tell through the tears. I stayed with them a minute, then went over to see how Ry was. The mum was still on her phone and I could hear the call was to a family member, saying she had had a crash and to come immediately.

I put my arm around Ry; he was very shaken. In fact, Claire and

Fleur had almost identical lumps on their heads where they'd smashed into the windscreen. But Ry's was definitively the worst.

The police and ambulance were on the scene incredibly quickly as we were close to the outskirts of Melbourne, and the police had passed us just minutes before. By the time they arrived the mum was looking after her son but also still juggling phone calls. She was obviously in shock and looked completely lost about what to do. I put an arm over her shoulder, trying to calm her. She was very young, maybe around twenty; her baby could only have been a year old.

The police started to sweep up our kit and I picked up my blanket and some of my clothes then walked twenty metres down the road and perched on the crash-barrier, watching the scene of carnage. They were starting to let more traffic pass, although it would take a while to move the motorhome and car, which were both completely written off.

Next, Tony, Tim and Johnny turned up in the Media Vehicle; they had raced ahead to meet Damian. By then I had taken myself down a small farm track and was sitting on a bench. I was shaking visibly now that the adrenalin of the moment had passed. The little boy. I couldn't bear the thought. Nothing is worth a life. A little baby. Willa was the same age as that boy. I tried not to think about it.

After a good chat with Tony, I moved into the other camper-van and tried to shut my eyes, but obviously couldn't sleep. There was also nothing I could do to help, so I just lay there, overthinking.

Eventually, Ry appeared at the door with my bike, now with the spares bag clipped under the saddle. Tony gave me instructions, and I was sent on my way. As I slowly pedalled past the scene, the FV was being clipped on to the long winch of a tow truck, while Claire and Johnny desperately tried to empty out all the kit.

I carried on alone. We had been stopped about two hours, but there was no urgency in my effort. I didn't care where I was. Everything that had been going through my head for the first five hours on the bike had been replaced with the crash and the what-ifs. The biggest what-if was that poor kid. He was going to be fine, I already knew that, but I couldn't shake those first few moments seeing him unconscious. The second what-if was had I been on the other side of that white line, riding in the road rather than on the hard shoulder: considering the driver hadn't seen an RV in front of her, I doubt she would have seen a cyclist. Speculation is a dangerous game, but I saw her getting out of the car with her phone in her hand. And there were no skid marks. If that had been me in the road and not the RV, I'd be dead. And if that slow-moving vehicle had been something like a tractor, it would have been game over for her and her beautiful boy. It was sickening, and I had little motivation to focus on the ride. I just spun my legs, riding gently for the first while. And well done to Claire, she had been brilliant. What a calm and professional manner, focusing on what is important while other people are losing their heads. I thought about Ry and hoped he didn't have whiplash.

For the first miles skirting Geelong, when the A1, the Princes Highway, became the M1 and not permissible for cyclists, I turned on to beautiful country lanes, the Devon and then the Barrabool Road, and I carefully followed the map on my phone, having no idea how long I would be riding without support.

Twack – there was a clatter on my helmet. It didn't hurt, but I got a huge fright and a bit of a jolt. I was cycling along in the middle of farmland and couldn't figure out what could have fallen on my head.

A few minutes later it happened again, and I looked up in time to see a magpie getting ready to dive-bomb again. I was obviously near its nest, and for the next half an hour I ran a gauntlet of the black-and-white kamikaze birds. Twack, twack, twack – they were very accurate and I braced myself each time, glad they were targeting my helmet and not my shoulders or back.

The magpies are a good metaphor for how a subset of the Melbourne population acts towards cyclists. The greater Melbourne area is about 100 miles across, if you take in Geelong and the towns around Port Phillip Bay. I remembered it being difficult from a decade ago. My experience of the greater area is not positive, from both 2007 and 2017, and it's a well-known issue. Of course, for the past ten days across Australia I had experienced none of this as I was in the wilderness; such antagonism only really happens where vehicles and bicycles share busy roads. I'm not going to give too much space or fuel to this issue, or use the local derogatory terms, but enough to say that these human 'magpies' made navigating the outskirts unpleasant. I was nervous whenever cars passed very close to me and tried to ignore the angry taunts. Maybe I was more nervous because of the morning's shunt, more emotional and affected by their shouting than normal.

Before I reached Melbourne itself I was caught up by a red saloon, driven by Damian, who had gone back to the crash and picked up Claire and Ry, plus a pile of spares. Meanwhile, Tony was off trying to get the media boys a new vehicle (because the old one was now the new Follow Vehicle), sort out the paperwork for the crashed motorhome, and still get Tim and Fleur to the airport in time. Alongside all this was a pile of kit to be sorted.

To work through the grid systems of Melbourne involved a series of north and east tacks, and a lot of traffic lights. The easterly tacks were faster, but northerly was straight into the wind. All in all it was slow progress, but I was very pragmatic about that fact. During the graveyard shift I had been focused on what it would take to reach Brisbane, breaking down the miles and the days, setting myself up for a big finish to Australia. All that advantage seemed now to have been lost but I was just grateful still to be riding. The race could easily have been over.

Pedalling north between a section of stop lights, a motorbike passed, its driver wearing a saltire flag like a superhero's cape, emblazoned with GOOD LUCK MARK messages. I was immediately cheered – whoever it was had done a great job tracking me down in the labyrinth of suburbs.

She let me catch up and then drove skilfully alongside, chatting away. Unbelievably, it was Jenny Reynolds, a girl from the year below me at Dundee High School, whom I hadn't seen for over fifteen years and whom I had barely known at school, apart from being in the orchestra with her. It was a great effort and the perfect moment to pop up with a Scottish welcome, to reminisce about home.

I called a stop for lunch at the turning on to Boundary Road and it wasn't quite the usual optimized nutrition: a foot-long Subway, bottle of Coke, packet of crisps and some cookies. I felt I needed to explain to Damian and Jenny that this wasn't typically how I was fuelling myself Around the World in 80 Days.

Jenny turned back and Damian carried on acting as FV. As we

skirted south of Melbourne airport, the road broke free of the grid system as it negotiated some steep gullies and hills. I had entirely forgotten that Alee Denham had been set up to ride with me. A well-known blogger for his site Cycling About, Alee had been contacted by KOGA to do an article about my bike. I met him at the bottom of one of these gullies late in the afternoon, just as Tony, Helmut and Johnny managed to find us with a new, much smaller vehicle which would now be the Media Vehicle. It would be tight sleeping arrangements for the final push through Oz.

So I was not in the right frame of mind for an in-depth interview as the fresh-legged Alee started alongside me up the steep brae. I really just wanted to be left alone and to get this day finished and forgotten. I wasn't rude, but I also didn't make any effort at polite small talk. Alee seemed to understand the lie of the land; it had been an all-round shit day and he was popping up in the final few hours of daylight for a cheery chat.

Since we now had two support vehicles back on the road, I gave Damian a heartfelt thank you and he disappeared homewards. But an hour later he rocked up again, this time on his bike, lights on, ready for the late shift. What an absolute gent. Oddly, he rode a time-trial frame but with flat handlebars, the same set-up with which he had tried to break the Perth to Sydney record. The conditions had not been kind and he hadn't managed it on that occasion, but it had launched his charity, Hope Builders, which is still going strong.

It was a long, gradual climb away from nearly sea level at the ring-road around Melbourne to the Old Sydney Highway, which is designated a C-road. As the light faded we climbed up and up, commenting on how quickly you leave the busy suburbs behind. Then the tarmac ran out. Without warning, the narrow road became a well-compacted gravel track. No wonder no cars had passed in ages. Alee soon turned back, but Damian battled on alongside me as we gingerly picked a route through the dirt and stones, as the day turned into night. This was hopeless. Damian assured me that he had ridden the Hume Freeway, which we were running parallel to. I could see the line of headlights a good way below us off in the valley to the right. After miles of this slow going I reached a junction, and as soon as the FV caught up I signalled that we were turning off.

There was a good deal of confusion in the support vehicles – this gravel road had surprised everyone – but the consensus was that cycling the Hume Freeway was not allowed. But it was late in the evening and I would take that risk rather than continue at 6mph on dirt. Cutting east, we came straight back on to tarmac and off the ridgeline, a cracking descent as I thought 'Well I am not cycling back up that!' At the valley floor we reached an underpass and followed the slip road on to the highway. There were no signs about not cycling and we now had a similar set-up to the road we had crashed on, a dual carriageway with generous hard shoulder. Damian soldiered on well into the night, reassured by the fact that he would have a descent and a tailwind back into the city. Regardless, it was a fine effort, and despite me not being very chatty, I really appreciated the camaraderie.

I was in a tired and sober mood when we finished at 9.30 p.m. After such cracking progress across Australia, a moment like that morning's crash could have ruined everything, ended a life even. It had me questioning once again whether we were risking too much. I hated seeing my crew injured on account of supporting me. This was professional, this was worthwhile, but at the end of the day this was sport, and sport should be about having fun and creating positive memories. I reassured myself that I was also in safe hands, and that accidents will happen when you are in harm's way. But I still struggled to shake the what-ifs and some of the angry exchanges of the day. All in all, I just wanted to get away from Melbourne – which I am sure, like everywhere, has a warm heart if you know where to look for it.

It's been one of the most difficult days on the whole ride. It really makes me pause and think. A huge thanks to Damian for being support for most of the day, after thinking he would be riding. And he came back out and rode in the dark with me this evening. Top guy. I've now turned north, and as soon as I did I'm clattering into a headwind. That is the forecast for tomorrow as well. So slow going, big rolling climbs coming out of Melbourne. The sum total of today is that I have lost a ton of time, lost about 50 miles today, so probably lost all of the advantage I built up for the whole of Australia. But it is fine, because it could have been a lot worse: that was a very serious incident this morning. Well done to the team, not just on the scene but then for sorting everything out afterwards.

Day 40

It's ten to four, day 40, and I think there are a few headaches in the team this morning after yesterday's crash. I have just been outside, and the winds are already up. I was hoping the first set of the day, the 4–8 a.m., would be calm but not so, and that's the forecast for the day, going into a strong headwind. Quite a lot of climbing today as well, so all in all just getting ready for a bit of a battle. It's fine, I have got to keep playing the long game. It could be four days' cycling from here to Brisbane, but with that headwind there is absolutely no point gunning it because your gains from that are minimal; you can't go that much faster into a big headwind, you have to keep tapping it out and be consistent, efficient around breaks, minimize time off the bike. My feeling is there is going to be plenty of time when I get back to North America, where it's going to be light, it's going to be summer, warm, and hopefully there is not going to be such mental wind to make up miles. If you think, yesterday it was the equivalent of losing a four-hour block in terms of miles – that is seriously hard to make up. The priority at the moment is to keep riding sensibly and not beat myself up. Get to New Zealand in good shape mentally and physically. Overall, I am just relieved the team are OK this morning.

Everyone was in a subdued mood after the trauma of day 39, and this was accentuated by the slowness of our progress and the blandness of the scenery as we left Victoria behind and began to make headway into New South Wales. The towns of Shepparton and Jerilderie were some of the only punctuation points amid the endless farmlands. It was as a consequence an uneventful day's riding, flat cycling albeit into those sapping headwinds, but a huge tonic for my scrambled mind.

Day 40 out of eighty, that feels significant, and I no longer have to wear all my winter gear, because I have been going north, north, north all day, so I have left Victoria and I am up in New South Wales now. Amazing how much warmer it is. I've made just over 210 miles, which on most days I would be disappointed about, but I knew from the forecast that today was going to be a big battle into the headwinds. The last thing I told myself last night was that today was going to be absolutely brutal, so I woke up expecting that, programming that. So actually I am pleasantly surprised to have made 210, as opposed to being disappointed that I have not made 240. It was pretty boring, just flat, flat, flat, flat farmland. My Garmin was saying it was a 19km/h headwind most of the day, so it is just grinding it out. Yeah, it's funny, I stayed in a good mental state because I was actually expecting it to be tougher than it was, so oddly I am celebrating 210. But it does put into pretty sharp focus what I have to do to get to Brisbane in time. I was hoping to get there in the next three days but will have to speak to Tony and the team and see what is now possible. It very much depends on what the weather allows us to do. Yeah, all round a punishing day, when there are no downhills and it is constantly into the weather. The soles of my feet are bruised and swollen. A shame I broke my crank, because I have no idea what power I was putting out today. A tough day, but a good day.

Day 41

Start of day 41 and I am still trying to fight a cough a wee bit. The winds seem to have died down a lot in the night, so yesterday's battle is hopefully behind us. It's certainly a lot warmer which is great. And I know Tony's been looking at what's possible in terms of distances and roads ahead, so what's it looking like?

Tony relayed that we had to do an extra 40 miles over the next three days, Friday to Sunday, on top of my 240 a day, which was not as bad as I thought. The nagging headwind was also forecast to drop down completely and be replaced by predominantly a tailwind.

The original block programme had us flying out, including the contingency, later on the Monday. Before Adelaide I had been speculating about a Sunday evening flight, but the crash had lost us nearly 50 miles and yesterday was another loss of 30 miles on target. A 253-mile average for the next three days seemed very punchy on the back of 190- and 210-mile days, but it was all still possible. Riding harder was out of the question; it would simply be a case of riding longer, sleeping less. Going into the red, knowing I would get brief recovery on the flight to New Zealand.

I was following the 650 miles of the Newell Highway across New South Wales, fairly flat with the odd bend, a wide, sparsely tree-lined highway with light traffic and short on good views or entertainment. It was a commute of a day, and by lunchtime I was due west of Sydney on the other side of the Blue Mountains. Through the towns of Forbes and then Parkes and for most of the more sociable hours, 10 a.m. until 5 p.m., I had local riders with me, some doing long stints and therefore getting past the formalities and settling into a decent mileage. Considering the lack of anything of interest, the company was welcome, and after the excitement and battle of recent days a boring day's riding punctuated by enthusiastic Aussies on their bikes was fine by me – until I was left alone again after the town of Parkes, when I really crashed mentally.

Skirting the Goobang National Park, the terrain got a bit more interesting and I bullied myself not to stop. It felt like I had zero motivation to keep riding, and it was scary when I lost that purpose, because for long hours I hadn't been thinking ahead. It took time to build a mental construct that made the targets of the day more important than the discomfort and fatigue I was feeling. I had loved the company, but now at seven, eight, nine o'clock at night I battled with the comparative loneliness, reflecting on whether it would just be simpler to stay alone rather than have a brief respite which left me unfocused afterwards.

It's ten o'clock, a bit of a later finish at the end of day 41, and I was putting a lot of pressure on myself today as I had to get a good mileage in to keep hopes alive for making a Monday morning flight. Today started well, and the first couple of sets this morning were relatively fast, because of a gentle tailwind and being relatively flat. This afternoon the winds dropped off, but it has become really rolling and we have stopped very near the town of Dubbo. I've done 245 miles today, which means there are about 520 miles to do in the next forty-eight hours, which is possible, but it's going to be a big, big finish to Australia. I hit the mental doldrums in the last four hours there. Mentally and physically just hit rock bottom. Sometimes I don't cope as well as others.

Day 42

I feel pretty sore this morning. It's much colder out there. I thought it was going to get consistently warmer as we headed north towards Brisbane, but it's such a clear night. I am back wearing larger shoes, thicker socks and overshoes and in toe- and glove-warmers. The pressure is on for the next couple of days. But I'm trying not to think about it right now. I just need to get on the bike and ride that first four-hour set, warm up and get woken up. But I am going to have to get a solid day in today to give myself a chance of then getting to Brisbane by the end of tomorrow. Whatever happens, tomorrow will end up being a much longer day. I'll probably end up riding a normal sixteen-hour day tomorrow, and then keep going for another four-hour set, finishing in the middle of the night for an early-morning flight down to New Zealand. That is the idea, but right now that's just a bit intimidating, so just need to get on the bike and make today count. I think it's meant to flatten out a bit. If I could get some good rolling averages for the first couple of sets this morning, that would be a huge help.

As I entered the Orana region, about 50 miles into the day, the gently rolling farmlands started to climb consistently into the Warrumbungle mountain range. Apart from having a fabulous name, this was also the highest point of my ride across Australia. The road was taxing for heavy legs, although it was never steep, but I was at least rewarded with the first scenery of real interest since the Adelaide Hills. It had been such a clear, frosty start at minus 1°C, but had now cracked into an 18°C bluebird of a day, with cloudless skies and breathtaking views across lush pastures – a pleasant break from the tinderbox monotony of the flatlands. It was gorgeous.

After descending through Coonabarabran and across the Castlereagh river there was a brief climb back up before I was on average descending again very gradually for the next 150 miles. When we stopped in the Pilliga Nature Reserve for lunch there was a general sense of relief, of having cracked it. It was such a beautiful day, spirits were high, everyone felt like Brisbane was just around the corner and the troubles of the crash and the headwinds were behind us.

I also realized this could be one of our last chances to get iconic 'sponsors' photos in this part of the world. We weren't doing well on that front. At the Great Wall of China we had arrived at nightfall without enough time, and at the 90 Mile Straight we had once again been foiled by arriving at night, so apart from airport photos there were slim pickings for branded sponsor photos. But here was the perfect vast, empty Australian road, disappearing off for a kilometre behind me, red baked earth and the clearest of sunny skies. I stood there in the middle of the road with my bike propped behind me, holding each banner at arm's length, as the team ran on and off the road to swap them over. It was fun, a brief moment when I saw everyone working together and laughing. It took less than ten minutes yet felt like a massive distraction and delay – this was the biggest compromise we had made for the schedule, outside of incidents, on leg 2.

Carrying on after some food and treatment, I expected the FV to be with me shortly. It wasn't, and twenty minutes later I punctured. I looked down at my back tyre, then back down the very long and empty road. For the first time that I could remember I just waited, getting more and more annoyed by the minute.

Fifteen minutes went past, then a car came over the horizon, but I quickly realized this distant blob was not a white motorhome. The car came to a stop and a man dressed in normal trousers but with a cycle jersey and cap on jumped out with a camera. He introduced himself as Stephen Jones and said he had come out from near Sydney to find me – well over five hours' driving. I shook his hand and quickly explained that I had a puncture and was waiting for my crew. He nodded, as if that was a normal situation. Inside I was fuming: this wasn't normal at all. Of all the days to be sitting at the roadside, twiddling my thumbs . . . today was a day when every moment counted.

Stephen explained that he had followed all my adventures and was planning his own world cycle, starting in 2021; he gave me a business card with his details on them. He was not of an athletic build but obviously a die-hard enthusiast, and I applauded his efforts to find me and take on the world himself. But after a few brief pleasantries I cut to the chase and asked him to drive back down the road and find my crew. Poor Stephen looked a bit perplexed at my request, but he kindly spun around and headed southwards to find the crew. Ten minutes later they returned together, and Stephen grabbed a quick photo, but it must have been a very awkward dynamic to witness as the crew very sheepishly changed my wheel and got me back on the road.

I had lost less than half an hour but I was furious, and Claire and Ry knew it. I'd just stood there limply in the sunshine at the roadside and faffed away 10 miles' progress. Getting them on the comms, I blasted Claire for not supporting me, asking what had happened. It seemed that the media boys, on a roll from the sponsors' photos, had asked everyone to stay back and do some interviews. But it wasn't their fault, it was the job of Tony and Claire to constantly think where I was. It was unacceptable for both vehicles to be in the same place, having an extended lunch and filming session, while I carried on unsupported. One vehicle always needed to be with me, especially on such a crucial day. They had dropped the ball, and because I was counting every moment I simply couldn't understand such a lackadaisical attitude. Maybe Claire wasn't confident enough to speak up in the group, so I asked Tony, back in the Media Vehicle, to get on the phone. Claire had obviously had time to forewarn him about my rage, as he had been oblivious to my puncture and delay. He immediately apologized and I trusted from his tone that this would never happen again.

The afternoon and late shift continued through dense forest and I made strong progress towards the Queensland border, which I hoped to reach by daybreak on my final morning. On days like this, when I had switched from riding by hours to riding by miles, I simply clocked off 100km per shift. In one sense, watching kilometres made the hours go past quicker, but it was hard not to obsess over average speed, doing multiples of current speed, so as the day went on my finishing time narrowed down from a three-hour window to an hour, and then as I rode past normal finishing time I counted down every kilometre. I did think about doing an even longer shift: it seemed risky leaving so much for the final day. But this penultimate day in Australia was about doing as much as possible, without overcooking it for the final push.

Just over 400K, and it certainly wasn't a natural or easy day to get 250 miles. Ridden till 10.45 p.m., so over an extra hour, and those last few hours really hurt. There have been a lot of conversations today about whether I can still make this Monday morning flight. I've left myself with about 285 miles to cycle tomorrow. And so I'll get four hours' sleep, then attempt to do that. If I can do it, it'll put us half a day ahead of schedule. There is no point in hurting myself, but it might just be possible. A half-day in the bank, that is massive, absolutely massive, so without doing anything crazy, let's see. I'm just going to think of tomorrow as a normal day, and then when we finish the 240 miles just have another break, then get back on the bike and ride till, I guess, the middle of the night.

Day 43

Less sleep last night! I'm feeling OK considering. Today is hopefully the end of Australia. It's cold again out there and I think it is pretty flat for the first four hours into Queensland. Then I have got a bit of climbing for the second set. The road is going to turn easterly. And then we drop off at some point, down to Brisbane itself. There is not much help from the wind at the moment, so I just hope I can get a good rolling speed, so I am not riding too late. If all goes well I'll get on that flight at 9 a.m. tomorrow morning to Christchurch and then on to Invercargill. Arriving at the bottom of the South Island around 5 p.m. tomorrow means I can still get a set on the bike tomorrow evening. That's the plan. Because if I get the evening flight, there is obviously half a day lost. That is what we are gunning for, but at this time of the day I just need to get up and on to the bike.

My voice sounded rough and broken when I asked Johnny if it was day 43, but by late morning I was into Queensland, the road was starting to turn east towards Brisbane, and I'd clocked off another big milestone – 10,000 miles since Paris, in forty-two days and seven hours. It was a beautiful day again, but with amazing contrasts. It dropped to minus 2°C as I came through dawn, then it was utterly clear so that the moonlight lit the fields and cast shadows under the trees. This bitter cold was far more bearable than the wet of Western Australia, and by 10 a.m. the temperature was once again climbing into the teens. It was like a winter's ride in Mallorca with scenery that could also have been Spanish.

It was Sunday 13 August, and my daughter Harriet's fourth birthday. The day had also been chosen for a much bigger birthday rendezvous, for my father-in-law's seventieth – friends and family on my wife's side were together for a celebration at the Kitchin, the family restaurant in Edinburgh. I pedalled along, recording a video message to send back, feeling a very long way from home. I knew that Harriet was struggling a bit with my long absence, and even though she knew in theory that 'Daddy was cycling around the world', it was hard to know what she really understood by that. Two and a half months away is an eternity in the life of a little girl. I was managing to speak to her once or twice a week, although Nicci was much better at sending little WhatsApp messages to me every day, which really kept me going. Every evening I would look forward to these as I got some treatment and scoffed another thousand calories. It was a brief moment of refuge and family before lights out and sleep. But if I had to be missing these big birthdays and celebrations back home, then I was glad to be distracted by my biggest mileage target since leaving Paris.

More and more riders joined me as I left the rural farmlands and headed for the coast. It was a long and very gradual climb, over about 100 miles, to the big town of Toowoomba, by which time I had quite a peloton. From there the road just drops, in the most jaw-dropping fashion, off the Toowoomba Range by about 500m to the valley below and then remains fast along the final 60 miles – a highway to the major town of Ipswich, the first suburbs of Brisbane, from where bicycles are once again diverted on to smaller roads.

I had some real characters with me: a young fine furniture maker who had lived in Scotland, used to half a year at a time working on what sounded like the world's most expensive tables; there was a young lad in his late teens, accompanied by a friend, who hoped to make it as a pro bike rider but who was coming back from time off after over-training. There was a group of veterans, mates who had ridden together for decades and whose easy banter I immediately enjoyed; they had the experience to know that they were there to support me, it wasn't for me to entertain them. All in all it felt like a veritable victory lap, and I took my final break at the summit in Toowoomba, where most of the riders, by now a group of about twelve, decided to turn back rather than have to climb back up the range in the dark.

The descent saw the teenagers hurtling ahead with the abandon of youth and familiarity, me following hot on the brakes, not trusting my tired arms, legs and more importantly mind to react quickly to anything untoward. I was happy when the gradient dropped back below 10° and I was able to reap the rewards of my climbing and feel the encouraging draught of a tailwind towards the coast. Eventually these lads peeled off as well, to be met by their enthusiastic parents, waving beside their cars in a petrol station. For an hour I was left alone, but I knew that ahead somewhere was Adam Scott, my guide into the finish.

Adam was a friend of a friend of a friend; it was a very weak link ten years ago which I could barely remember now. But back then he had been a keen triathlete, and a decade on he had been following my progress online and had got back in touch to volunteer his services to see me through the busy suburbs. He had long since stopped being a triathlete, and this was going to be a rather antisocial shift late into the night, but I remembered Adam as having boundless energy and looked forward to his company for the final miles.

Adam met us, with his brother-in-law in the car, with an offering of some dark chocolate Tim Tams, my Australian biscuit of choice. This got our assault on Brisbane off to a great start as we followed a laby-rinth of cycle tracks and backroads, the clock ticking past ten and then eleven o'clock. The roads were pretty quiet, and it's always more inter-esting cycling into a city after dark – the yellow glow and deep shadows of a sleeping suburb, blocks of industry then housing and then a green-belt, a section along a dimly lit park with kangaroos and wallabies grazing on the verges, completely unbothered by us pedalling by. Adam was worried about slowing me down, thinking I would be going race pace, but I was heading for nineteen hours in the saddle and 280 miles so I was very happy to sit up and relish those final miles.

Australia was a winter ride, so I should have expected it to be windy and at times wet, but on balance, despite some very gritty conditions, I had got across faster than planned. It had taken much less than half the time compared to a decade before, so while certain shifts had dragged on for what seemed like weeks, it now felt like a very fast fortnight since I had ridden out of Perth. And those final few days, starting in the bitter cold but growing into perfect conditions, had been my favourite days of riding since Mongolia.

I pedalled slowly through the dimly lit Anzac Park, with the dark hillside of the Botanic Gardens behind the freeway to my left, then back into the streets of downtown, on to Sylvan Road and the rugby pitches of Toowong Memorial Park, where I had been told the RVs could park overnight. I then spotted the team at the far end of the road, across the traffic lights, all lined up and waving madly on the banks of the Brisbane river that flowed black and silent to the Pacific a short way downstream.

Laura was excited to be back and had enjoyed her time off with friends on the east coast. For Claire, it was the end of her responsibility; she was exhausted but had done brilliantly. What a tough job, especially the crash, but in a strange way it had been the making of her on the trip. I'd sensed that she was worried about 'dropping the ball' and messing up, and she hadn't been particularly strong or decisive in the period between Adelaide and Melbourne. But, forced to step up at the crash, she had been a different person since: more confident, more of a leader, and less nervous around me. With the exception of my being left stranded with a puncture the day before, the team had worked efficiently under a lot of pressure throughout the week that Laura had been away.

We took photos and filled out the witness book before bundling into the Media Vehicle for the short drive to Adam's house. It was very odd to be in the front seat of a vehicle driving through the streets of Brisbane at 1 a.m. The crew had a big job to sort all the kit, but I was getting a bed at Adam's. I was very saddle-sore and it was painful to peel my lycra off for a proper shower, which hurt and soothed in equal doses. After relishing a huge bowl of cereal, I carried on the midnight feasting in bed with chocolate and cakes, before finally setting my alarm for 6 a.m.

So that is the end of Oz at half past midnight! What a day. I was here ten years ago and it's a pretty cool place to finish on the waterfront, with the bright lights of Brisbane twinkling in the background. Today has been a big day – 451km . . . that's a lot of miles. But it has also been an amazing day. Twenty hours and twenty minutes since I set out this morning with nearly 3,000m of climbing. But I have been joined by so many people this afternoon, and that definitely helped time fly by. Fourteen and a half days since leaving Perth, which is a great feeling . . . and I have made the flight. So now I will get on a plane to New Zealand and crack on with leg 2 half a day ahead of schedule. So that makes the last three days a good fight, a worthwhile fight. It basically means for every extra hour I have had to ride into the night these last days, we get two hours in the bank. That is the way it should work out, which is a great feeling. But for now I need to sleep!

15

Land of the Long White Cloud

Day 44

After about four hours' sleep we are at the airport and the team from Menzies Aviation are pulling out all the stops to sort out all this kit, to get us on to that flight as quickly as possible. My team were up most of the night, they had an hour or two's sleep at most. We have a flight to Christchurch, a two-hour layover, then we land in Invercargill around 5 p.m. So I should get three and a half hours on the bike this evening, then straight into another night's sleep, which is what I need, because I feel pretty battered after the last three to four days of pushing to the end of Oz. But it has been worth it, puts us half a day ahead of schedule. Although a better way of thinking about it is not that we are ahead of the riding schedule, simply that we haven't used any of the contingency this time.

Adam's wife and kids were up and ready to see me off as we set out for the airport. I felt like I had a killer hangover – dehydrated, heavy eyes, aching. But I did my best to have a normal moment with the family, despite it feeling like an out-of-body experience. My voice sounded husky and I was dressed oddly. This was because all my non-cycling clothes had been left on the crashed motorhome, so Laura, on the last day of her holidays, had been sent to buy me 'travel clothes' with the remote help of Nicci. The result was some pretty tight cream chinos, a long-sleeved grey T-shirt and some cheap deck shoes. It wasn't the look I was gunning for, but she had done well in the circumstances, and on a tight budget! To be fair, she had offered to buy some expensive trainers but I had shot this down, saying it would be a waste, in the hope we would still get back all the kit from the motorhome.

We touched down in Christchurch after a three-and-a-half-hour flight during which I slept pretty solidly. I looked out of the window as we taxied in, and despite it being half past two (a result of jumping forward two hours in time) it was pretty dark outside and bucketing with rain. The cloud base was so low that I was filled with dread for what New Zealand would be like. Australia had been far colder than I had expected, and I was now dropping from 26° south to 46° south – halfway to the South Pole!

There was quite a bit to be sorted out in terms of kit and crew, especially for Johnny. Travelling on a South African passport, it always took him longer to get through. But we were met off the plane by a big chap from Menzies called Simon Hinman, who immediately took charge and delegated some of his team to look after the film crew. Johnny always looked like the dishevelled teenager in the group, even though he was in his forties, thanks to his hoody and beanie hats, plus I suspect he slept less than anyone, so he looked cross-eyed with tiredness as he walked off the plane. Simon told me that he had an office cleared with a sofa ready for me; there was no lounge access here, but we would have complete peace to recoup.

'Where is the food?' I asked.

'What do you need?' Simon replied, happy to oblige.

'Lots.'

He led me straight to the restaurants, and by the time the crew cleared passport control, sorted out the kit and were brought to me, I was halfway through a meal of the biggest burger they made with chips, a bottle of Coke and a couple of chocolate muffins. It was glorious to eat normal, unhealthy food and not just vast quantities of wraps, pasta, liquid meals and other very well-crafted sports fuel. I closed my eyes and relished the mouthfuls of decadence. Casual onlookers must have thought I had just been afforded my first meal in days.

The ninety-minute hop to Invercargill, right on the south coast, was stunning, coming in low over the tapestry of flat fields of the Southland Plains and the wide meanders of the Oreti river glinting in the late afternoon sun. It was clear and dry, to my huge relief. While I had set out on my previous trans-New Zealand cycle from Dunedin (which translates as 'Old Edinburgh'), this time I was much further south, but the Scottish heritage could still be found in many of Invercargill's streets being named after rivers – Dee, Forth, Tyne, Esk, Don, Ness, Spey, and the one that I grew up on the banks of, the Tay.

Invercargill airport has an end-of-the-world feeling about it, like Ushuaia in Tierra del Fuego, a remote outpost with a single runway and a big shed, despite servicing a reasonably sized city. There was only time to eat a bit more before I emerged to a wonderful local welcome. The last thing I felt like doing was cycling; after so much sleeping and eating I felt somewhat less 'hung over' but definitely less athletic. I had been off my bike since half past midnight and it was now 6 p.m. New Zealand time. Our accounting for time zones through Australia had worked pretty well at ten minutes' change per day but in New Zealand we didn't need to do a thing; we could live in the local time zone as it didn't change for the thousand miles to Auckland.

Tim and Fleur were rested and ready to roll with the spare bike made up and two RVs well stocked. Fleur was particularly pleased to be home as she hadn't lived in New Zealand for years and had used her few days' recovery to catch up with family. I sensed that Tim had not taken the crash in Melbourne in a matter-of-fact manner, so it had been a good thing that they were both immediately off to New Zealand.

A young Scottish lad called James, a metal worker by trade, was ready to ride with me. He had been down in Invercargill for a year but was making grand plans to cycle home to Scotland over a year, maybe two, through Asia. Dressed in baggy shorts and a thin jacket, he led me from the airport on the west side of the city to the reassuringly named North Road, through the suburbs of Invercargill. Such was the windswept bleakness of the scene it could easily have been the Western Isles of Scotland, and James seemed completely at home.

After we said our goodbyes I spun my legs, feeling pretty lethargic but loving the novelty of being in a new country. I also felt like I had got away with it – my fear of landing in the south of New Zealand in the clutches of midwinter seemed unfounded. This was bleak but thoroughly pleasant, certainly no colder and a lot calmer than a lot of Australia. It helped that these first miles were flat as a pancake and almost completely in the dark, so I had reduced awareness of my surroundings, except for the lushness of the grass on the verges compared to the parched scrub and dirt in Oz.

After eating dinner I went outside and found Ry working away in the light of his head torch, building up the red bike, in sub-zero conditions. We were parked in a farm lane with an audience of cattle looking over the fence out of the darkness. But despite the deep mud and muck, the smells were frozen in, and long blades of grass were already painted white with frost. Ry was laughing at the absurd conditions for 'spannering', as he called it, with the metal tools freezing to his flesh, the oil thicker and the batteries of the lights draining in a matter of hours. This was proper winter riding. But at least if it rained in these temperatures, it would fall as snow. Ry managed to fix on the new Stages Power Meter, which had been sent out to Melbourne, so I could at least keep an eye on power again.

I've done an epic 50 miles! But then again I didn't land till nearly 6 p.m. Setting out at sunset, it has been cold but beautiful. And a nice 50-miler to warm up the legs and get going again. I wanted to do a full four-hour set, but Laura pointed out that in the past three days' riding I have done about 780 miles and scraped four hours a night sleep, so prioritizing recovery tonight rather than pushing it late again.

Day 45

It is chilly! The plan over the next three days is to get the South Island done with much bigger climbing today and tomorrow, to try to get to the crossing at the end of the following day. It's a three-and-a-half-hour boat crossing to Wellington, which would really keep me on schedule with this advantage I have built up. But some pretty punchy climbing today and tomorrow to focus on first. Some tough conditions ahead, but it is good to be in NZ.

I set out wearing my thickest down jacket, a mountaineering Haglofs, a veritable sleeping bag, plus hand- and feet-warmers under three layers of gloves, a hat underneath my helmet and my buff pulled up over my nose. However, when I stepped out I was amazed to find that it was 4°C. I was in a sea of very heavy fog, in the pitch darkness, which my Exposure headlight did little to penetrate, so for that first hour I was pedalling inside a ping-pong ball, following the Oreti river as it meandered its lazy path across the flatlands to the town of Lumsden.

From there, where the river diverts in from the west, the road carries on northwards. The South Island of New Zealand is oblong in shape but lies at a 45° angle, so my route north, the Kingston-Garston Highway, headed straight for the west coast. I started to climb up to Lake Wakatipu and was glad for the effort. Cycling through the fog had soaked my jacket and gloves and the temperatures plummeted well below freezing. Despite being caked in a thin layer of ice I was snug and quite happy, except for very cold fingers. No number of hand-warmers or glove combinations seemed to fix the painful swelling.

The graveyard shift was all in the dark, and after stepping into the Follow Vehicle at 8 a.m. for ten minutes' kip and some warming porridge it was still dark when I continued on my way. The first slivers of dawn were creeping into the horizon, though, suggesting a glorious clear day in the Southern Alps.

I could tell that the team were absolutely loving this area, around the Devil's Staircase – alpine views over the glacial lake as I pedalled into the region of Otago, snow-capped mountains on either side – as every time I looked they were out of the vehicles taking photos. This in itself was great, I was glad for them, but I was having an internal battle, struggling to refocus on the next big target, and seeing their relaxed enjoyment made me feel even more alone and distant. Australia had required such huge focus, especially towards the end, that I was finding it difficult to shelve that and pick a new massive milestone. I could feel the lethargy of letting go mentally, the relief of having hit a target, then I had to battle with the knowledge that I needed now to do it all again. It felt like there was an inner voice saying, 'I did what you asked me to do, and now you are asking for the same again?' I was just grumpy, in a big mental slump for most of the day, fighting my demons.

I was also acutely aware of how beautiful this country was. Many cars passing me had skis on their roofs, and as I cycled past the Remarkables Ski Resort I wistfully imagined taking time off for a ski. Growing up, skiing had been my main sport; I was an instructor at the age of sixteen, but hadn't skied for two years now in case of injury.

The cheerier my team got, the grumpier I felt, which was unkind of me, and I tried not to make this obvious. I just felt very alone with my mental and physical pain, while they were all acting like this was suddenly a holiday. Only Laura sensed my struggle and was sensitive to it.

The Media Vehicle was sent back into Queenstown to stock up on more hand-warmers and supplies as we cut east, following Route 6 through the stunning Kawarau Gorge and then north again towards Wanaka. Historically an area of gold mining, this is now the home of bungee-jumping, whitewater rafting and other adrenalin sports. Starting now to shake off my depression, I appreciated the sheer rugged beauty of it.

My options through the South Island were dictated by it being winter and by the devastating earthquake that hit Christchurch and its surroundings in February 2011. The very flat route that I took up the east coast in 2007 was across the Canterbury Plains and then on the Kaikoura to Blenheim road, a sliver of tar hugging the steep hillsides, sea cliffs and shoreline. But this remained shut after the landslides which followed the tremor, so I had to go over one of the three high passes of the Southern Alps – Arthur's Pass, the Lewis Pass or the Haast Pass – to reach the west coast. The middle option, Arthur's Pass, was shorter but higher so we risked getting stuck in the snow. If we made it all the way to Christchurch and then followed the Island Hills road over the Lewis Pass, it would be a clear east-to-west section, which would break the GWR rules. So I was aiming for the Haast Pass. This route had been tarmacked only just over twenty years ago in order to link up the sparsely populated west of the island. In fact there are no communities at all in the 50 miles between Makarora, near the summit, and the village of Haast itself on the coast. It is a no-man's land of dense beech forests between the two rivers from which these villages take their names.

I reached the top of the pass late in the afternoon, just as it got dark. Very few cars had passed since the turn-off to Wanaka, and I skirted the shores of Lake Hawea and Lake Wanaka in the growing darkness, before a final push uphill. It was never steep but had added close to 3,000m of climbing. The good news was that I had also climbed out of my self-pitying and was relishing the excitement of the pass – it certainly beat another day through Australia's often feature-less landscapes. I had been consistent on the bike all day, tight with breaks, and was now preparing to cycle late – but knew this wouldn't be enough to reach 240 miles, given the terrain.

I paused at the top and put my warm down jacket back on for what I knew would be a very cold and dark descent. It did not disappoint, cold fingers gripping my brakes excitedly as I soon shook off the Fol-low Vehicle and got into the flow of the sweeping switchbacks. I was reassured that the road was wet and not icy, but the amount of loose gravel on the corners did make me nervous and slow down more than usual. It would have been very easy and costly to crash in these condi-tions. But I teetered on that edge of flow and control, thrilled at the speed, lost in the tunnel of my headlight. What a glorious alpine des-cent to do in the dark; with pretty much no one passing in either direction, I had the racetrack to myself. Eventually it started to flat-ten out and my forearms were pumped from the braking, so I let the bike freewheel, bringing my hands from the drops to the tops and shaking out the tension.

On and on into the night . . . there was nothing at the roadside out-side the dense corridor of trees, and the road kinked slightly west for a long while (which always upset me!). In the darkness my senses were much more tuned in and I heard a major waterfall off to my right, and the zing of my tyres on the wet road. Eventually, following the Haast river downstream, I reached the village and turned right to follow the west coast. By the time the RVs had caught up we pushed it late to make up precious miles, knowing how tough the schedule would be to reach the Picton Ferry, but also because it was very difficult in the dense forest to find anywhere to pull in and stop for the night. We made a couple of attempts and wasted a bit of time before settling on a lay-by that was so wet we then had difficulty getting the FV back out of it, its wheels skidding in the thick mud. This was a very soggy world, a huge contrast to the frozen wonderland on the other side of the pass.

I've ridden till just gone 10 p.m. and done just shy of 225 miles. It's been quite a tough day. Maybe it was a bit of a hangover from Australia, physically and mentally in the doldrums a bit. I think we maybe got the fuelling strategy slightly wrong as well. Just trying to get my head and body into gear with the new country, and it wasn't exactly a recovery ride with that climbing. We want to catch the very last ferry, the 6.45 p.m., the day after tomorrow. And we have to be there an hour before the check-in, but that could be a vehicle, not necessarily me on the bike. If we don't get that ferry, the next ferry is 8 a.m. the following morning, so we would lose the fourth session of the day, the morning session waiting and then the second session being still on the ferry. So we would lose certainly three-quarters of a day's riding, about 180 miles, if we don't catch that ferry. That would potentially undo the advantage that we have built through the big finish in Australia, so it is all to play for. It's gone 10 p.m., tomorrow is more big climbing so time for some recovery.

Day 46

It's early doors and it's a very different world here on the west coast. I can hear the waves, the ocean, and it's very wet. It's all ferns and almost jungle compared to yesterday when it was much colder and drier. This route is slightly further in terms of distance than the other routes through the South Island, but that doesn't matter as I need the miles, I need it to all add up to 18,000 miles, so this isn't about taking the most direct route, it's about taking the route with least resistance. Today is important. I kind of wish we were doing some more normal sixteen-hour days, not having to push it as much after that big end to Australia, but getting to the North Island in time is kind of crucial, as we could lose a ton of time if we get the ferry crossing wrong. If I can get on that

ferry at the end of tomorrow, then I can really start to look forward to
the weekend, flying out in good time, and that will be my longest recovery of the whole trip, up to North America, via San Francisco. I can get
some proper sleep. Rather than arriving in Alaska with a lot of work
still to be done to keep under eighty days.

Despite following the coast, there was nothing flat about the first eight
hours, hugging the foothills of the national park that is home to
Mount Cook, New Zealand's highest peak. Past Fox Glacier and
Whataroa, the road was constantly short, sharp climbs until it reached
the wider plains north of Hokitika. In this very sparsely populated
corner of the country there was almost no phone signal and the houses
were mainly small, ramshackle and looked damp. Moss even grew on
the edges of the tarmac where car tracks didn't pass. Telegraph poles
were wooden on one side and green with lichen on the other. Into the
afternoon I picked up speed across the flatlands, but the smirr of the
morning turned to a more constant rain which gradually intensified.

A few locals joined me along the flatlands, and then a school-
teacher, originally from Scotland, met me on the road out from
Greymouth and ended up riding a very gritty late shift in the wind
and rain. All kudos to him for sticking it out, and by the time he asked
me at 9.30 p.m. what time it was, he was aghast, couldn't believe how
far he had come, that he now had to ride the return journey alone,
which would get him home around midnight in time for school the
next morning. We stocked him up with some bars and fresh water
bottles and wished him good luck for his return leg. I cracked on
alone for over an hour, but when I stopped I wondered how much further he still had to get home, as I smugly got into the warm FV and
stripped off my soaking cold kit.

It really had turned for the worse and we had made some tough
miles as the road cut inland with mountains on both sides. The weather was barrelling through the valley, and the forecast was for it to
get much worse, which I accepted with a wry smile as I scanned some
social media messages, watched a few videos of the kids and lay down.
This brief moment, between saying goodnight to Laura and falling
asleep, had to be my favourite of the day. A moment when all I was

racing towards was sleep. And it was a wonderful moment of calm, reflecting on another crazy day, not yet having to worry about the next. I had been so wet, and it was so late, that Tony filmed the end-of-day video diary.

A really big day today for Mark, pushing really hard. We have a ferry to try and catch tomorrow afternoon and if we do get it, that's a massive saving in time. So he's ridden until 10.45 p.m. and covered just shy of 230 miles, after getting going at 4 a.m. I need to sit down now and crunch the figures. But we still have a lot to do tomorrow, including some good climbing in the morning. Hopefully there will be a long descent in the afternoon to catch the ferry in time. But certainly it's not a done deal yet and the weather tomorrow is not looking great. Probably quite a strong cross- and headwind . . . but fingers crossed.

Day 47

Slept deeply, but only for just over four hours, so woke a couple of times hearing the rain in the night. Laura has looked at the weather charts and there is a big storm coming this morning. You can feel the wind moving the motorhome. And it is right on the nose, so looks like 25 to 30 knots of headwind and then gusting, while obviously pouring with rain. So I have quite a target today to get to the ferry, but I am just going to have to be sensible, because there is no point in beating myself up into that. I am just going to have to get out there and see what it is like and ride sensibly. I would be gutted to miss that ferry, but equally, I have got to think of the big picture. No point in giving myself an injury or getting ill in it. I'll just get out in it and see. I think by mid-morning the wind is meant to come around slightly. But I think it is going to be pretty miserable either way.

I was already wet after stepping out for a minute to pee as I sat on the edge of the bed in my massive down jacket and tried to collect my thoughts for the camera. You could hear a real crackle in my voice; I looked haggard, my eyes were heavy, and I felt utterly resigned to a hellish morning. Every instinct said to stay inside, go back to bed. The storm was battering the motorhome. It made no sense to step into the dark, the high winds and rain. All that lay out there was misery. Bracing myself, I popped a Werther's Original in my mouth, pulled my jacket over my mitts and headed out.

Holding on to the bike on the roadside, I was already getting battered by the wind. Mounting and riding off seemed futile in those conditions. And yet I tried to settle into a rhythm. Those first few hours were the toughest of the entire ride so far; the conditions in any other situation would be deemed unrideable. The wind howled, causing a constant din in my helmet, I came across lots of major branches down across the road, and on a couple of occasions a gust came through that blew me to a complete stop, forcing me into a track stand. It was very dangerous on the bike, not to mention the freezing cold. There was nothing I could do for my hands and feet, which were soon numb, and I knew I would pay for the damage being done to my left hand. But I plodded on. Throughout that ridiculous early-morning shift I was only thinking about keeping my bike upright and moving forward.

At a couple of points I thought seriously about stopping. It wasn't that I couldn't bear to keep suffering in those conditions, but I calculated that there was simply no way I would make the ferry crossing point by half past six. And if I wasn't making that ferry, what was the point in fighting this crazy fight? That was my rationale for giving up. Why risk injury and illness riding through this incredible storm when it was to no avail? I would be waiting for the ferry tomorrow morning anyway. It was five, six then seven o'clock in the morning, still pitch black, still hammering with rain, but despite every instinct saying 'Stop, you can't make the ferry at this snail's pace!', I couldn't. If I stopped, I was giving up on everything we had built since Melbourne. So instead I just said 'Give it ten more minutes' and hoped the winds would ease.

After the first ten minutes it was no better, but it was no worse, so I gave it another ten minutes. Inside the FV Laura was equally worried, ready to pull the pin, but wanting it to come from me, not her. If I had said it was crazy, that we were risking too much and I should stop, she would have immediately agreed. But, as stubborn as me, she hung on in the hope that conditions would improve.

I barely got off the bike for nine hours straight, only stopping quickly to change some wet gear. I didn't stop for morning break, I just carried on in the vain hope I could still make the ferry simply by not stopping all day.

Daybreak came very slowly and late, but the storm did seem less menacing when I could see the trees that I'd only heard in those early hours being whipped by the winds, their branches straining and sometimes breaking.

The weather was coming from the north, so the stint from Reefton to Inangahua was the slowest. From there I was into a more winding and hillier route following the Buller river upstream through a much narrower valley, with the high peaks of Rocky Tor and Sphinx on either side.

Near the top of the watershed I reached the Marlborough region. Here I left Route 6, which I had been following since Invercargill but which now headed to Nelson, and turned on to Route 63. I had been climbing steadily since daybreak and although the storm had abated, my speed had stayed tempered by the climbing and regular roadworks, with gravel sections and stop signs to let traffic through in only one direction at any time, which could mean a delay of up to ten minutes.

Despite all this, I sensed hope – in spirit and by name, as I came across Hope Saddle at just over 2,000 feet. I knew I was in for a very long descent and was now heading pretty much due east, following the Wairau river for the next 60 miles downstream. I was continuing to do multiples of my speeds, and reasoned that if I sped up a little bit and didn't stop at all, I could still make it to the ferry.

A couple of gents in their fifties came alongside in their sports car and cheered loudly. The passenger bellowed that they were ready to come and ride with me, but that the conditions were too awful. We laughed – that was a good call. I had not been in the mood for company, but now that the sun was starting to dry things out and my wheels were turning without a constant battle, my mood was soaring. I felt like I had really battled and won. There was now just the matter of finishing the job and reaching that elusive ferry. These chaps were beside themselves with excitement and their enthusiasm was infectious. In such a remote and, in my experience, wild part of New Zealand, I was simply impressed that they had road-tripped to find me. They kept stopping and taking photos, and wildly cheering. It did me a world of good.

The Wairau Valley widened as I followed the river downstream, and now the wind, which had been battering from the north, swung in behind me from the west and I absolutely flew. It was effortless, unrecognizable from the morning, and I rode along beaming in the utter relief of redoing my sums, knowing that I was now going to take three or four hours off my earlier estimates since my speed had gone from less than 20km/h to over 40km/h. I was so wired to getting to Picton that lunch was a rushed affair, mainly to put on dry kit. I was sore but I was feeling defiant and was now loving it. Rarely can I remember a day of two more contrasting halves – this was now an easy cruise.

Firing along the now flat valley floor, surrounded by the vineyards that the Marlborough region is famous for, I was joined by a man on a serious-looking racing set-up, an S-Works frame with deep section TT wheels and aerobars. He introduced himself as Craig Harper, a local joiner, who happened to hold the world record for cycling the length of New Zealand – 4 days and 9 hours. It was a pleasure to ride with Craig, who had taken on the 'Ride of the Long White Cloud' in February so was still in fighting shape, already dreaming of bigger records. It was a pleasure to share the road with someone who understood the mindset. I wasn't having to answer all the usual questions about how you keep going, what hurts, and the other FAQs – here was someone who got it, and we could spend the time talking about more important things, like the wine of the region and the crazy weather.

Reaching the outskirts of Blenheim, it was a sharp left on to Route 1 for the final miles up and over to Picton, and as Craig had warned me this steep-sided valley funnelled the wind against us. But it was a feeble sting in the tail; I was already buoyant after having turned our fortunes around. Not having given up during that graveyard shift was the toughest decision on the ride, or it had certainly felt like it in the moment. Climbing up past the rural airstrip at Koromiko was the final landmark before a sweeping descent to the ferry terminal. I was in a triumphant mood.

In fact we had an hour to kill before the ferry, so after turning the Garmins off at the terminal I swung the bike around, waved goodbye to Craig who was riding back to Blenheim, and set the team the task of finding a decent restaurant. Here was a very rare opportunity for everyone to sit down and have a meal. We crowded into a busy bar and ordered steaks all round. I was not a relaxed customer, worried we would miss the ferry, and a few messages were sent to the chef, who obviously wasn't used to working to our kind of schedule; but when a table full of food was in front of us, it was a wonderful moment to sit back and look around at my team, to see their enthusiasm, feel the camaraderie, be a part of the laughs. I lived alone on the bike yet there was this amazing ecosystem around me, living and breathing and creating this journey for me.

I spoke to Tim and Fleur in particular, with whom I had had only very brief conversations since Perth, and thanked them for their hard work getting ahead to NZ. And to Johnny, who I sensed was finding this whole whirlwind the hardest thing he had ever done, but he was hanging in there. Tony was cool and calm as always, although I could see under the surface he was dealing with some tricky team dynamics while doing everything he could to keep the details from me. His focus was keeping my life as simple as possible, and while he didn't give away much emotion, I could see how relieved he was to make the ferry – he loved the marginal gains and data around how to save time on planes and boats.

Onboard, we gathered on the passenger deck. I had been allowed to cycle on to the ferry, but then my bike was locked safely away in the FV. While the crew set up camp for the nearly four hours until we reached Wellington, Laura took me off to a cabin that had been booked for me. I had grabbed a quick shower on the FV so as soon as I was left alone I fell on to the bed and passed out.

Having set my phone alarm for 10.30 p.m., I was very disorientated to wake up in a ship's cabin with Laura banging on my door. Making my way wobbly-legged down to the car deck, I was handed my bike to cycle off the ferry. I must have looked the antithesis of the pro rider, utterly haggard. I certainly wasn't prepared for a welcome party as I pedalled up the ramp and into the ferry terminal. About eight people were waving me ashore and a couple of them were on their bikes and ready to ride.

'Hello!' I managed, bleakly. 'Thanks for coming out so late.'

'No problem.' There were numerous excited responses, then, 'Are you happy for us to ride with you?'

'Ha! It's eleven and I'll be riding at four a.m. Sorry guys, but you are welcome to join me in the morning.'

I carried on around the terminal building as everyone else was trying to disembark behind us. By this time I'd lost track of the welcome party and felt bad for not having made more time for them. But I must have looked an absolute state in my trackie trousers, down jacket, no socks and crocs. 'That guy is cycling around the world?' would have been my response to meeting me in the middle of the night in Wellington.

We parked up within a stone's throw of the terminal, once we had found a place where the police wouldn't move us on, and I went back to sleep for another few luxurious hours.

South Island done! So today has been a ridiculous day, setting out in a storm. It was ridiculous conditions. It was the first time in the ride where I thought 'this is just silly'. I thought at this speed, in a storm like this, there is just no way I am going to make the ferry. So if I am not going to make the ferry until tomorrow, I might as well sit out the storm. I stopped with the team after nine hours: I rode straight through those first nine hours and they said exactly the same thing, they were sitting in the vehicle saying 'this is just silly'. But I persevered, we got through it, and I just can't believe how we have made up time.

Day 48

I'm in Wellington, and what a massive relief to make the ferry last night. Over six hours' sleep, and I do feel better for it, although my throat does not feel great. From here it is about 650km to Auckland and so about 400 miles, and I am hoping to make a flight tomorrow evening, Saturday. But I also have just over 11,000 feet of climbing today. The first 100 miles look pretty flat, and then it's up. So I am not going to get much help from the weather. It is dry, but I am still going to have that headwind against me. It is a big target, but if I can make today and tomorrow count then I am on my longest recovery on the whole trip. That is all I am thinking about at the moment. This last ten days have just felt a bit relentless. It was always pushing, pushing, pushing, but within a predictable routine until Melbourne, but since then we have been riding pretty much by distance rather than time, and so it has all been pushed up a gear. These big targets – make a flight to New Zealand, make the ferry, and now make a flight to America – are all coming back to back. But if I can do it, I'll be the best part of a day ahead of schedule, which is hopefully worth the fight.

The flags were fluttering aggressively above the ferry terminal as I cycled out. Wellington is known as the windiest city in the world, so this shouldn't have been surprising, but it was added kudos that yesterday's storm had made the front page of the *New Zealand Herald*: 'Many flights in and out of the capital are grounded as gales with gusts of more than 100km/h continue to hammer the city. Power was earlier out to properties and firefighters were busy securing roofs, trampolines and signs in downtown Wellington blown loose in the fury of this morning's gales. Rain is now starting to add to the weather misery as the area braces for a deluge this afternoon.' In a city of high winds, that hooley stood out as something special.

There are some very steep roads leading out from the waterfront, especially as Route 1 cuts up and over the peninsula from Wellington Harbour towards the Tasman Sea, and my legs protested angrily even as I looked forward to some flatter miles up the west coast. Our early-morning task was to mark the antipodal point for Guinness World Records, as I was now on the opposite side of the planet to Madrid. My GPS tracks would do the trick, but further evidence was needed, and there wasn't anyone to ask at 4 or 5 a.m., so the media boys scouted the roads ahead, looking for any signage or landmark (remember, it was dark) that would prove exactly where I was, and when.

After a few hours I reached the State Highway as it hugged the water's edge and could hear the waves crashing ashore off to my left. But I was pretty focused as there were a lot of trucks and Friday-morning traffic heading north, so I stayed on the hard shoulder at first. It was wet, and when I then steered gently back towards the edge of the road from the hard shoulder, I rode on to a new thin seal of tarmac. This layer was very black and shiny with rain, and being still under the veil of darkness I couldn't tell how deep the lip was between the old and new.

I went down fast. My front wheel skidded out as it mounted this shallow lip and I slid with arms outreached across the road. It was a sort of comedy dive, and while the blacker-than-black tar had caused me to crash, it was very smooth to fall on. I jumped up in fright, aware that I was sprawled across the lane of a busy highway, and dragged the bike to the verge. The FV was right behind me and stopped quickly. I had lost some skin, but there was nothing major to worry about. Laura gave me a thorough check-over, cleaning the grit out of my open sores with chlorhexidine and applying some absorbent antiseptic wound dressing to stop the weeping or bleeding bits sticking to my lycra. The bike was also all right, apart from a few scuffs, and the new rear mech hanger, which had been bent inwards.

I was back on the road within fifteen minutes and kicking myself for the incident. My hip hurt a bit from the impact, but I felt fine. It was more of a fright, like all crashes because they happen so quickly, and on top of that I was in that slightly dazed early-morning state. Both this tumble and the one back in Russia had happened at about the same time of day, in the dark and on wet roads. You could blame the conditions, but I was also aware that I was not at my cleverest at 5.30 a.m. Staying sharp was tough during that graveyard shift, rather than just dropping into autopilot and pedalling for dawn.

Bulls is a small town 100 miles north of Wellington with a sense of humour. Most signs, including the police station (CONSTA'BULL), pun on its bovine name – NEW ZEALAND GETS ITS MILK FROM BULLS and so on. This had been a day's ride from Wellington a decade ago, and I had enjoyed its hospitality, but this time I reached it after a bruising morning, knowing that from here on was climbing. I followed the Rangitikei river upstream for an age before reaching Waiouru, denoted by a big tank on the roadside, and the National Army Museum, which looks like a giant blackened warehouse given some camouflage. I was now above the tree-line, and after the military camp and a parched-looking golf course it was back into the wilderness of a vast military training zone.

The road continued to climb gradually through the afternoon and I settled into a good rhythm, resigned to the fact that it was going to be a very long shift. I couldn't put anything more on to tomorrow; if I was to make the flight, I had to ride 400km today. On any average day that was just an extra hour's riding, but today was like that final day in Australia all over again – a late shift that would take me well past midnight. Except this time I didn't break it up as 4×4 plus an extra shift, I simply pushed on and took a break every 100km, which made for four five-hour shifts.

The road topped out on a section called the Desert Road, which is as breathtaking as it is bleak. This is the Rangipo Desert and is part of the North Island Volcanic Plateau, with views over the three active peaks of Mount Tongariro, Ngauruhoe and Ruapehu to the west of the Kaimanawa Range – still a vast distance away but looking snowy and inhospitable as I pedalled the final hour of daylight, cresting out at well over 1,000m. The winds were easing off into the evening and I had a very long, fast descent to Lake Taupo, shrouded by dense freezing fog which came from nowhere and made it very cold and a bit more nerve-racking than it would otherwise have been.

We stopped briefly for some food at the petrol station at Rangipo, where some local riders found me. I had been alone all day but didn't mind the company into the dark late shift. One chap was particularly interesting, a local prison guard who definitely used his bike to get away from people as opposed to being sociable. I sensed that his day job was psychologically tough, and I respected that he didn't need to chat, just wanted to come out and enjoy some miles with me. Some others were the opposite, rabbiting away enthusiastically about the fact that I 'must' come back and take on the 'epic' Lake Taupo Cycle Challenge, where 7,000 participants ride a 100-mile circuit of the lake. It did sound fantastic, genuinely, but I wasn't really in the mood and neither did I have the energy to sound enthusiastic about a sportive as I was seventeen hours into just one day of my own ride!

Lake Taupo, even at night-time in the winter, looked like a wonderful playground for both tourists and locals, but the east shore had a few punchy climbs before I reached the town of Taupo itself at the head of the lake and started following the valley uphill again. It was a punishing way to finish a 400km day, but I crested out and free-wheeled the final miles. It was gone midnight when I called it a day.

Done . . . 400km, about 250 miles, and that was a massive fight. For the first part of the day we had a stiff headwind, but it was absolutely beau-tiful once it got light, but seriously punchy at over 3,000m of climbing. I'll get about three hours' sleep, maybe slightly more, back on the road before 4 a.m. And it should be a downhill start!

Day 49

3.51 a.m. and wet weather gear is going on, as that is the forecast. It's just under 150 miles to Auckland airport. I'm feeling a bit ropey, but very motivated to cover that distance by 4–5 p.m. this afternoon. My flight is about 7.30 p.m. It doesn't matter how tough today is, tonight I will be sleeping a full night on a plane and it's my longest single recov-ery on the entire 18,000 miles, which is definitely cause for celebration. We clocked over 11,000 miles yesterday. And right now I am still up at 600m and so today has to be on average down. Although if yesterday is anything to go by, there will be quite a lot of ups on our way down! Time check, seven minutes to go, let's do this.

I rode out alone, but not for long. In the darkness I came across a chap called Andrew on his bike; he had driven across the North Island the night before to find me, and slept in the back of his car at the side of the road nearby. Despite the forecast it stayed dry and I was com-pletely distracted from the big countdown to Auckland. Soon after daybreak a few other cyclists joined us, including Bob, who commit-ted to doing his biggest ride ever by joining me all the way to Auckland airport. And so the morning turned into a very sociable affair – a father and daughter joined for an hour, some other young racers for a longer stint, and while I often rode at the front, feeling like the Pied Piper, I was never alone. I was grateful for their local expertise when navigating the town of Hamilton, then again in the busy outskirts of Auckland – the airport lies to the south of the city centre but still through miles of hilly suburbs.

The sting in the tail was two-fold. First the final climb, 200 vertical metres up and over a ridge. I wouldn't have realized how slow I was if it wasn't for my fellow riders trying to stick with me but simply not being able to ride that slowly uphill! My legs were dead, and I spun the granny gear, resigned to taking as long as it would take, ignoring any reassessments that my new buddies might be making about my elite status. There was simply nothing left in my legs; they were going through the motions, but with feeble power.

Relieved when it was over and enjoying the run into the city that followed, I was joined by quite a few more riders and we numbered between seven and ten for those final miles. They included a friend of my Arctic rowing buddy Billy Gammon. Billy had lived in Auckland before rowing the Indian Ocean, and here was Tom Wigram, his mate, a well-built chap dressed confidently in all-white Skoda-decaled lycra. It takes a man with extreme body confidence to wear white lycra. Especially when it then starts lashing it down!

What rotten luck – for the final twenty minutes, the heavens opened. But rather than a smattering of rain, this downpour started quickly and built in an inescapable crescendo to become the heaviest hail-storm I have experienced. Weak as a kitten, I was already dressed in full leggings, plenty of layers and my fluorescent waterproof jacket, and was just bemused by the sudden assault. My new friend, whose lycra shorts and short-sleeved jersey had now turned shockingly transparent, might as well have turned up to a paintball fight wearing just his underwear. The ice balls bounced off my helmet and visor in a din, and even through my leggings these little bullets stung. Some of the less well-dressed cyclists looked skelped and reddened by the incredible pelting. It was comically violent, and through the absurdity of the storm everyone found the funny side and we put our heads down and cracked on for the refuge of the airport. Of course, before we got there, and as quickly as it had started, the storm passed and we were left reminiscing about what a fitting send-off to New Zealand that had been.

We made it to Auckland airport, and now I would get to go back to the summer. There was a cheer from the group of cyclists around me.

Simon Hinman was waiting outside international departures, with a team from Menzies Aviation. He had flown up especially and was prepped for another slick transit. I wasn't much help to anyone. I was freezing cold, and after chatting with the well-wishers and bike riders, taking photos and doing the sponsors' banners, I stood around for a few minutes until Laura took charge and bundled me into the FV to get changed and warmed up. By the time I came out ten minutes later the team had both RVs unloaded, the bags were being checked by the Menzies team, and Ry, Fleur, Tim and Tony were stripping the decals. I padded over to Ry, Tim and Fleur to say a heartfelt thank you and for a pathetic few minutes of conversation, considering their commitment over the past three weeks, before being whisked off through the airport.

To my great regret and embarrassment, however – and I realized this as soon as I was through security – I didn't speak to Tony, the main man, who had held together leg 2 so brilliantly, especially the insane race from Melbourne to Brisbane then the length of New Zealand. He had orchestrated these transits perfectly, making a whopping day on target, and I forgot he wasn't coming with us. I didn't say thanks. I tried to make amends with a WhatsApp, but that seemed rather poor. There was no excuse, despite my fatigue and stupor, not to remember Tony. He did a superb job at keeping everyone focused on what mattered most – keeping me on the bike and making it go as fast as possible.

New Zealand in slightly less than five days was not quite Craig Harper's world record but not far off, and on the back of forty-four days' racing and through some seriously challenging winter weather I was proud of that effort. Despite all that NZ had thrown at me, it had to rate as one of the most beautiful countries so far, again only pipped by Mongolia. I felt shattered and bruised from my eyeballs to my toenails as I slumped into the lounge seats, but utterly content.

Now . . . food . . .

Because I have really pushed it through the end of Oz and up NZ, I've made a day on schedule. I now have a day in hand, a full day ahead of the block programme, which means twelve hours ahead in terms of ride time, plus having not used the twelve-hour contingency for leg 2. What an amazing buffer to have. I thought if anything I would make time in the final third – Alaska, Canada, plus mainland US – but to be a day up at this point is really best-case scenario. But I have really dug deep in this last week. I've been suffering on the bike and I have not slept nearly enough, so I am on an absolute high to get here, but I need to get some recovery. It's awesome – I have had a peloton of riders today, so many people have come and joined me for sections. The support along the roadside is phenomenal. To be on the other side of the world and given such a welcome is pretty mind-blowing. Especially considering the current around-the-world record holder is Andrew Nicholson, a New Zealander!

Part Four

Anchorage to Halifax

Mike Griffiths – team leader
Laura Penhaul – performance manager
Jo Craig – cook, driver, general support
Nick Charlton – mechanic, driver
Johnny Swanepoel and Helmut Scherz – filmcrew

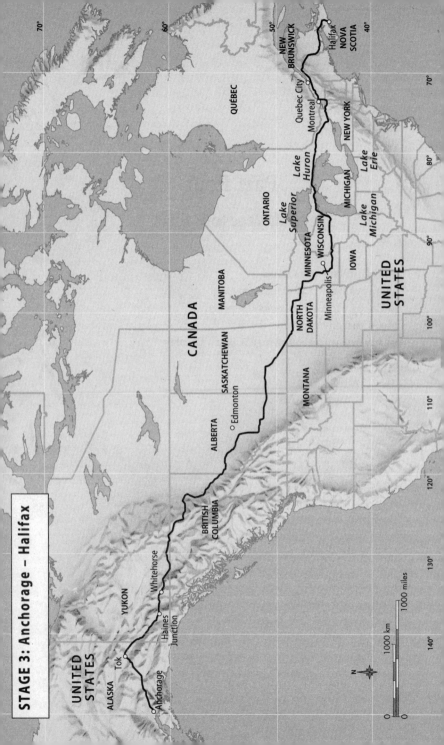

STAGE 3: Anchorage – Halifax

16

The Rocky Road

It's day 50 and I am not on my bike, which is quite a relief. We are sitting in San Francisco airport in the lounge being utterly looked after. The guys at Menzies Aviation have pulled out all the stops at all the airports to get us through as fast as possible. We all had a pretty decent flight from New Zealand up to here and I slept about six hours, freshened up, had a shave, and from here it is a five-hour flight up to Anchorage, and my priority is to not sleep on that flight because I will land at night and I will want to get a few more hours' kip, then get on the bike at four o'clock tomorrow morning and ride. Straight into the start of leg 3 which is in the diary for about twenty-two, twenty-three days to get across North America. It is another big, big stint and I am going to try and stay awake so I am straight into the time zone.

And therein lay the Phileas Fogg blunder. I knew it, we had studied it, and yet we all still made the same mistake. I had got on a plane at the end of day 49, flown for twelve hours, woken up and therefore thought it was now day 50.

Wrong – it was still day 49. I had crossed the International Date Line. It made theoretical sense, but experiencing it felt utterly weird. Because time was our obsession, because we had lived every hour so precisely, accounting for travelling east so meticulously, living in our own time zone for most of the way, it felt impossible that this was anything other than what it counted up to be – day 50.

Tired minds are not good at this sort of thinking. And it took another few days before everyone agreed what day we were on. Days 0 to 48 and 50 to the end were all a little bit shorter than twenty-four hours, and to compensate, day 49 was two days long, or very nearly, if that makes any sense at all. We left New Zealand on the evening of Saturday 19 August (day 49 of the ride), and now, in San Francisco, it was still Saturday 19 August. All you really need to care about is that the people in Paris experienced 80 Days as a continuum – it was only we who were 'time travelling' – so as long as I got back to Paris within eighty calendar days, that was all that counted. It is a dangerous game to add up the days as you experience them, like Fogg and I did – you will experience the illusion of an extra day and it is a very convincing one and hard to shake off.

After landing in San Francisco I had been met by an American Airlines delegate whose job it was to look after VIPs. I was whisked off the plane, taken straight to the front of the immigration queue and on to the lounge, as he indiscreetly name-dropped all the celebrities he had looked after. I must have looked (I certainly felt) more like a student with a hangover than travelling royalty. I asked for some reassurance that my team would be afforded the same welcome then, making the most of the buffet, waited for them all to catch up.

Before long I found out that I'd joined the elite category of athletes who could 'happily' cycle 400km but can't walk up a flight of stairs. I was asked by the team at Menzies if I could pop up to the terminal level for a few photos. No problem. But I should have taken the lift. My legs simply wouldn't move – it was the most peculiar feeling, as if I didn't have hamstrings any more. I could just about lift my foot on to the next step, but transferring weight did nothing except hurt a lot. I pulled myself up the handrail, in an unconvincing show of athleticism to my concerned-looking hosts.

Back in the lounge, the media boys wanted to make the most of having me in a place I couldn't race off from – there hadn't been time since the day before Paris for a sit-down interview. Then it was off to the gate, and the next flight north to Alaska.

Coming out of Anchorage airport I nipped off and bought a big tray of the most unhealthy cinnamon doughnuts I could find at Krispy

Kreme and presented them to Laura and the media boys. Welcome to America! That sugar hit should counter the jet-lag.

I felt a tad spoiled swanning off from business class and straight into an airport hotel room while the media boys had slummed it in economy and then were back in the motorhome. Simon from Menzies in Auckland had managed to get Laura upgraded to business too, which Johnny and Helmut took in good spirits. She certainly deserved it, but they all did, and I wished we had the budget to fly everyone with the luxury of a bed. I was sore enough after seventeen hours' flying and would have been broken with an economy seat. Cycling 11,000 miles in forty-nine days did come with some perks.

I ordered room service while Mike Griffiths sorted out my kit and Laura did some treatment. Sitting cross-legged in bed with a plate of cheesy dough balls, a massive plate of spaghetti, and a wedge of cheesecake, I was in heaven. A bedtime picnic feast. It was a thrill to be back in America.

This is the end of day 50 [I was wrong!] and I have arrived in Anchorage, Alaska. We have Mike here, who has been really at the heart of all the logistic planning for the entire World route – but over and above that, this is his stage as team leader. We now have got a stripped-down team. We obviously needed a few more people on leg 2 because we had people jumping ahead to New Zealand and getting other vehicles set up. Apparently, our new motorhomes are super-sized, as you would expect – so we are going to live in comfort! I feel relatively good, but it was really hard not to sleep on that second flight from San Fran, to minimize jet-lag. It is 9.30 p.m. at night so I want to go straight into a normal night sleep, five hours, and be on the bike at four in the morning.

Day 50

Start of day 51 [wrong again!] and this is Alaska. I feel OK, all things considered. From here we will spend a couple of days heading through Alaska down the AlCan Highway which is familiar to me because it was part of my route when I rode Alaska to Tierra del Fuego. Then we eventually head south of the Great Lakes into mainland US, and then back up to Canada and fly out of Halifax. It's exciting to be here and I need to get my head into gear again because I've had a full twenty-four hours off the bike. I feel refreshed, but I also feel sore if that makes sense, because the body has started to go into recovery. We have the new team: Mike Griffiths, team leader, from Leadership Challenges, we've got Jo Craig from Leadership Challenges, and Nick Charlton the mechanic. Right, let's do this!

I was awake before the alarm, lying there in the dark, thinking about what lay ahead. I had cycled this first 1,000 miles or so through to northern British Columbia before and was eager to get stuck into it, but also quite happy at 3 a.m. to take fifteen minutes to pause, just lie there and let thoughts about the day ahead wash over me. Leg 3. Back into summer, the last major continental crossing.

Aargh . . . here goes. I got up slowly and applied chamois cream to the seat of my shorts – an oddly satisfying pre-ride ritual. Pulling up my leggings, then shorts, I clipped on my heart-rate monitor, put on my vest base-layer, thwacked the bib straps over each shoulder and stood up. Shit. I was stiff. My fingers didn't want to bend, let alone my legs, and my lower back was a dull ache. Turning my neck slowly from side to side, I couldn't get my chin anywhere near my shoulder: it had a complete range of about 90°. Sinking my index fingers and middle fingers into the base of my skull, I tried to ease off those pressure points that were small lumps of angry muscle.

Laura knocked on my door and I was happy to be disturbed midway through this morning ritual. In the motorhome, on any other day, it was all a bit more rushed and public, so I was now spurred back into action, throwing my sleeves, jersey and jackets on and heading back to airport arrivals – the official start point.

Laura had mentioned she was excited to have a dog mascot, which I didn't understand until I saw the side of the motorhome, which had a life-sized retriever decaled on the door, as if it was hanging its head out of the window. It certainly added a friendly welcome to my home for the next three weeks. In fact the motorhomes were plastered in designs – landscapes of America. They were indeed very spacious, something which would make the next three weeks a bit more comfortable, especially as we now had less crew.

It was very cool to have a send-off party from the airport. Three local riders pitched up and were ready to show me the best roads out of Anchorage, so thanks Nick and David and the other chap, whose name I didn't catch. David sported an impressive beard and was an amateur racer, whereas Nick, with a fine goatee, was a hardier soul, kitted out with a large saddle-bag for adventure riding and used to bigger distances. When the others turned back after an hour, and even when the heavens opened and we'd settled into a morning of steady 'Scottish' rain, Nick stuck with me all the way to Palmer, where he would loop back on smaller roads for a century.

There was a lot to adjust to. I was back on the right-hand side of the road, distances were in miles, and everything here made New Zealand look like toy-town. This also meant a generous hard shoulder for most of the time, and while our motorhomes were the biggest we had on the World, they were dinky compared to the average. The average holiday-maker in the Alaskan summer is driving what looks like a rock band's tour bus, typically towing a four-wheel-drive vehicle, a couple of bikes on the back. These were ubiquitous, and they were simply huge – hotels on wheels. The 'snowbirds' migrate north and south each year and make up most of the sparse traffic on these roads.

Anchorage is a fairly generic American city built on a grid system and home to every major chain store you will find in the US. But outside Anchorage is the real Alaska, which is a truly unique and wonderful wilderness. Mike and Jo had flown in the week before and driven one of the motorhomes back from Whitehorse in the Yukon, so they also knew what lay ahead, although driving a vehicle never gives you a true impression of the terrain and road quality as experienced from the saddle. But they did report incredible wilderness – everything I had loved about these northern expanses from the Americas expedition.

All you really need to know about the road east of Anchorage is that it is absolutely beautiful, initially following the Glenn Highway along the Matanuska river, past a huge glacier tumbling through the forest to the valley floor. For most of the morning the rain and then

low cloud cover kept the mountains shrouded. But as the afternoon
wore on it lifted and revealed a skyline of imposing snowy peaks. I
was inspired to ride towards but happy to know that I would skirt
around these Wrangell Mountains. To the north, they merge with the
eastern edges of the Alaska Range, which forms a wide arc around
Anchorage, all the way to the start of the Aleutian Peninsula. So close
to the Pacific, these mountains and their glaciers are Arctic in nature,
maritime in weather, which is what makes them so wild. The crown-
ing glory is Denali (formerly known as Mount McKinley), which I
wouldn't see from the Glenn Highway. On my last trip to Alaska I had
cycled due north to the small dead-end town of Talkeetna and spent
three weeks climbing North America's highest peak before getting on
my bike to head south.

So in truth, those first miles out of Anchorage were new to me, but
by mid-morning I was back on familiar roads. What was unexpected
was a sequence of hand-drawn signs, randomly tied to crash-barriers
and underneath official road signs. I spotted one, then another, every
hour or so. ALASKA IS WITH YOU #80 DAYS; #80 DAYS. EPIC RIDE. GO MARK.
Someone was obviously road-tripping ahead of us with a car full of
whiteboards and a thick marker pen!

It had to be uphill from the coastline at Anchorage, but I had forgotten by how much. Eight years ago I had been travelling touring
style at a leisurely pace of 80 miles a day, plus this stage was the gentle
recovery ride off the back of a tough mountaineering trip. The graveyard shift was sociable and flat, although it soon got very wet as we
followed the estuary of the Knik river, gaining speed and rapids as I
worked my way upstream. The road kicked up more in the last shift,
after turning left at the T-junction at Glennallen, following the Tok
Cut-Off highway, skirting the impressive high peaks I had been riding
towards all afternoon, and following the white waters of the Copper
river upstream. We called it a day at the small hamlet of Gakona.

It's the end of the first day in Alaska and it is still light! It's nice to ride
in the light again. Quite a tough day with over 3,000m of climbing.
Absolutely stunning, tumbling glaciers, mainly tree-lined, which I will
have to get used to. It is all trees down the AlCan Highway and I am

just loving being back in Alaska. Covered 235 miles, so to get that distance in on a big climbing day, first day back on the bike, is fantastic. I'm feeling great, feeling strong on the bike. Those nerves about getting back on the bike and worries about how I would feel have gone.

Day 51

Breakfast at ten to four, day 51 [got it now!] – we are heading for Tok Junction which is the only turn-off today. In fact the only turn-off for quite a few days. I have been travelling northeast to get to Tok Junction – from there you can go north to Fairbanks and the north of Alaska or you can go east for the start of the Alaska Canadian Highway which is really an amazing road, an epic road. At the end of yesterday there were quite a few sections of gravel road, construction roads, where they are fixing the winter damage. I think that is going to be the story going forward probably for the next few days. Quite a few people on social media are telling us that there are some pretty gravelly sections of road ahead – but that's OK, it's not too much slower. We had wolves last night around the camp. As I went to sleep Mike and Johnny saw a wolf walking through the trees nearby and then the guys said they could hear them later on, but I was fast asleep. Right, a big day ahead, aiming for the most northerly point and then into Canada.

I shouldn't have been surprised that this wasn't exactly the hot summer riding I had been dreaming of when in New Zealand. Tok Junction is 63° north, by far the most northerly point on our World route. Edinburgh is 56° north and is rarely sweltering in the third week in August. But after staying fully covered up on day one out of Anchorage, it was drier today and warm enough to lose the leggings and feel the freedom of spinning lightly.

Our new mechanic Nick had driven a motorcycle around the world in his youth and now lives in a remote community on the west coast of Scotland, running bicycle rentals and a small cycle shop. He certainly had the life experience to live rough for three weeks but he had joined the team late on, after others had been dropped after Around

Britain. So he was an untested team member, and in such a small team dynamic I just hoped he would work well with Laura, Mike and Jo. He was a very good mechanic so that was the technical bit covered, but he also needed to be a dedicated driver, navigator and all-round team player. There was no longer any extra capacity in the team – it was stripped to a minimum for leg 3 and everyone would be stretched.

Nick was certainly enthusiastic from the start, and I could see that he was utterly meticulous with the bike. But he was definitely quirky and, although quietly spoken, had strong opinions. These could all be positive traits, if they were indeed kept positive. Nick was the only person who in the build-up had called out the elephant in the room – do I still get paid if Mark doesn't make it as far as Alaska? That was reasonable and perhaps practical, but it was a little notch of concern about his priorities. This wasn't necessarily a negative, but it was a shame that we hit the ground running in Alaska with a team member who had been completely thrown in the deep end.

In his quirky way, Nick didn't wear team T-shirts and shorts but opted instead for his own dark blue mechanic's overalls, which he had bought online for a couple of quid each. The combination of this attire and his Einstein-like hair earned him the nickname 'the nutty professor' from the very start. He seemed to like being noticed for such eccentricities. For these first days he was just getting to grips with the routine, which everyone else already knew well. Even Jo, who had been a key player on Around Britain and had supported RAAM races many times, knew exactly what to do, playing mother hen, feeding and making sure everyone was looked after. Nick was more reserved, although I could tell from his reactions that he was paying close attention to everything that went on.

It was just shy of 100 miles to Tok Junction and the road was a series of big rollers on the valley through the eastern tongue of the Alaska Range. It was a bonus (although that wasn't how it felt at the time) to get the lion's share of the climbing out of the way in the morning. At the turning, the road then dipped further south all afternoon, and I came across the border long before I expected it, because I had forgotten that there was a gap of nearly 18 miles between the actual border, with the US border station, and the Canadian checkpoints near

Beaver Creek, the westernmost community in Canada. It's the biggest gap I know of across international borders, and it used to be much bigger. Until 1971, the US operated its border station back at Tok, nearly 90 miles shy of the border, which gives you an idea of how little happens in between these points.

Rolling out of the US, I needed to insist my passport was stamped so as not to have issues when I re-entered mainland US in North Dakota. Canadian customs was also a pretty open border, a single booth with just some temporary plastic crash-barriers stopping you driving around the side. I've been through fast-food drive-throughs with tighter traffic management and security.

Until recent years people lived in this no-man's land between the border and the customs, but now there is nothing, nobody, and the sleepy community of Beaver Creek boasts around a hundred residents, most of whom work for the Border Services Agency. I politely noted that they didn't work for the road authorities. The change into Canada was marked.

The lack of road markings for those first miles into Canada helped the road merge seamlessly into the vast landscape, giving the Yukon an even greater sense of wilderness. When you stare at road lines for sixteen hours a day, their absence is noticeable, and it makes the road seem unfinished, lacking punctuation marks. The Yukon therefore seemed a little less developed than its westerly neighbour. When the road markings did appear for sections, they were a solid white line down the sides and yellow dashes down the middle. There is something wonderfully North American about yellow road paint – you know where you are, even if there is no pick-up truck or gas station in sight. I must stop talking about road markings, but it was all I was musing about as I contemplated the scale of this ribbon of tar. The AlCan, all 1,387 miles of it, is one of those wonderful commutes, like the Nullarbor, where everyone is on an adventure. I would follow its entire length from here to Dawson Creek in British Columbia.

Actually, before I do stop talking about roads, let me just say that the change in road quality was also immediately obvious: the Americans go big on tar, light on gravel; the Canadians go big on gravel, light on tar. It was an abrasive mix, and I soon reached long sections of construction roads. This entire road is built on permafrost, so while this is a stable ice road in the winter, the thaw then cracks and crumbles the thin crust of tar, making the summer months a race to skim and re-lay long sections, back to the compacted gravel foundations. At lunchtime, Nick reported the effect of this on the bike. My tyres, which were due for a change in the coming days, had started to blister in patches, exposing sections of the webbing that protects the inner tube. Rather than wearing down evenly, the rubber was now thin; these friable, corrugated roads were causing the final layer to lift off in thumbnail-sized scabs. Not even the roads of Russia had been so hard-wearing.

I was left with these musings all afternoon as I climbed back up to nearly 800m and across the White river, with very little else to punctuate time. There was not a lot of wildlife, and I remembered this from my Americas ride – how the abundance of bears, deer, bison and birds started in northern British Columbia. However, in the afternoon, perched high on the pines and swooping low across the road, I did spot a few majestic bald eagles, their scalps and tails of white making them look like large golden eagles dipped in paint.

We had no problem finding a place to park up at the end of the day and for now I was enjoying the predictability of getting back to a routine 4×4-hour day, none of the riding to distance. Leg 3 was massive and I needed to get a chunk of it done before I could find the motivation to start sprinting for the east coast. The three big chapters of North America were the mountains and forests of the west, the prairies at the heart of the route, where I should be able to eat up the miles, and then the lakes and lesser hills of the east, when I could really start winding up for a big finish through Europe. That was how I had it broken up mentally – this first week was always meant to be the tough bit, down the AlCan Highway, across the Continental Divide and the Rocky Mountains, when I would average over 3,000m of climbing a day. I wasn't about to push that – sixteen hours a day was enough.

Good day's work – well done all! 245 miles, perfect, that averages out yesterday. End of day 51 and we are in Canada – another big milestone. The tarmac, the roads in the Yukon are notoriously rough. I remember that from last time. So we are going to drop the pressure in the tyres and put some more padding in the mitts and grin and bear, because the next days might be a bit uncomfortable. But it's been a beautiful day today, clear skies. It took a day and three-quarters to get from Anchorage to the Canadian border. From here we are heading southeast for a long way.

Day 52

Welcome to the wilds of the Yukon! I've just done about 8K and today we are aiming to make it through Whitehorse, the Yukon's capital town. I am going to get a bit more darkness for the morning and late shift as I head south.

I was already on the bike when the media boys caught up to film the morning video diary – we were now back to kilometres in Canada rather than the miles of America. The first shift took me through dawn and to the shores of Kluane Lake and the hamlet of Destruction Bay, where I had taken a memorable day off on my previous visit to meet the wonderfully nutty locals, drink beer, play guitar and talk about driving snowmobiles into the frozen lake in the middle of winter in order to find a ray of sunshine, because the houses lay in the shadow of the mountains for months. This time my return was less cheery, as we came across our first grizzly bear trotting along the verge. She was looking very agitated, and I passed quickly and carefully. The media boys stopped in the store and learnt that her cub had been hit by a truck a short while before and everyone was being advised to stay indoors.

Saddened, I pedalled on to some long sections of gravel construction road along the lakeside. There were a few short climbs on this section and that evening I was amused to find out that I had picked up a KOM (King of the Mountains) for one, simply called 'Alaska Highway Climb', with a climbing speed of 25km/h. There can't be many KOMs around the world that you can beat without trying with a heart rate of 108!

The AlCan followed the shape of the lake south and then east, from where it climbed back up over 1,000m on a few sections. This coincided with the weather closing in, and for a couple of hours it was very wet and windy, before I was rewarded with a cracking descent into the first proper town in Canada, Haines Junction (boasting over 500 locals), where the AlCan cut due east to Whitehorse.

I was in a funny place mentally. The emptiness and the reality of what lay ahead had me struggling for motivation. I could tell I was being quite serious all day, closing myself off from the team, just needing to focus.

Mike jumped on the spare bike for an hour once it had stopped raining. He was starting to get grumbles from Nick that I was being too protected, that no one was allowed near me. Nick felt, and Mike agreed, that Laura and I had this double act which meant that the rest of the crew were kept at a distance, that the crew needed more access time with me to feel connected with the race. Again, I felt more exasperated than understanding. 'Just get on with it' was my attitude. This working dynamic had functioned well for the entirety of legs 1 and 2, so why mess with the formula? I understood that on Mike's RAAM teams it was all about developing leadership through the experiences of the support teams – but this was different. Our core purpose was to get Around the World in 80 Days, full stop. The crew were there to make this happen. This was a professional, focused environment. Of course I cared that the crew were able to share in the glory of the race, but I just didn't have the capacity or patience to change my behaviour or mode of communication to look after them.

This was the extreme end of endurance racing – get on with it or get out. If I was hard on them, then I was harder on myself. It was the only way to keep enough focus while suffering this much. I felt that I was tough, but fair. I knew I was very direct, I didn't dress things up if something needed to be sorted, and I had no tolerance for slowness. But I felt that was all fair given our mission. There wasn't a spare moment in the day for idle banter. Lunch break was the only time when I could have any snatched conversation with the crew and this was during the ten minutes while I ate.

I was left on the bike feeling angry. I was already in a difficult place mentally with the scale of leg 3, what lay ahead, and now I was being asked for more camaraderie. 'For f***'s sake, toughen up' was my response as I punched the handlebars in frustration.

It was a particularly hard late shift from 5.30: I was physically hurting like hell and mentally in the dumps. There was a big descent shortly before Whitehorse but I was into the wind so it wasn't very fast and I was kept working on the flatlands as we skirted the town. The team gave me the option to stop short, but I couldn't face that after such a grotty day so pushed late to make it back into the wilds. We passed a sign for a parking bay 500m ahead and I signalled to stop there. I was done. The FV didn't see it and shot on. I waited for them to come back, but they didn't, so I carried on into the dark. We found a less suitable patch of gravel by a junction about ten minutes later. It shouldn't have been a big deal, but after 240 very tough miles in the saddle I was pretty grumpy. Another ten minutes was near my breaking point and I tried to shake myself, to stop stewing, to greet the crew with a smile.

It was not what I felt inside.

It's the end of day 52. Today I had some really tough shifts, some long shifts on the bike. I guess coming straight off the flight and into, rather than some nice easy recovery days, three big climbing days, today mentally was a bit in the doldrums.

Day 53

Start of day 53 and it is ten to four in the morning (challenge time). It was raining heavily overnight. It has stopped at the moment but there is a weather front coming in off the Pacific and so it is likely to be a wet day. Although it doesn't seem to be particularly heavy – steady rain as opposed to massive downpours. So I am on the AlCan Highway all day again with no turns – just heading southeast. I am hoping I can put yesterday into a box as mentally and physically it was really, really tough and I plan to see today as a new day and be in a slightly better frame of mind. Right . . . let's go.

The back of the 'Cruise America' motorhome was an arid rocky out-crop scene under turquoise skies, classically American but from much further south, perhaps Moab in Utah. It was certainly a pleasant summery view on a very overcast and rainy day. In both Europe and Oceania the team had fully decaled the European RVs with sponsors' logos, especially the FV, which was most often photographed and filmed with me, and the decals stood out well on the white vehicles. During leg 1b, through Russia, Mongolia and China, we had gone low-key, deciding that logos could draw undue attention to ourselves. Here, on leg 3, the ornate graphics already on the motorhomes meant it was difficult to make sponsors' logos visible. There was little we could do, but it was one of those daft details we hadn't thought of before Mike and Jo picked up the rental vehicles. Every day on the road cost thousands of pounds so sponsors deserved to be thanked and profiled.

My route took long diagonal tacks across mountain ridges, and between them I followed a series of lakes. In the middle of the day this meant riding the beautiful shoreline of Lake Teslin for over 100km, before dropping into northern British Columbia and then back up into the Yukon as the road followed the meandering path of least resistance, climbing up towards the Continental Divide. Some 300km into the day, this was a big ask for weary legs, but it did mean that I had a gradual descent to enjoy for the final shift into the dark, aiming for Watson Lake. As planned, I stayed much more positive, pragmatic and in the moment. It wasn't a bundle of fun, but I was definitely less fragile; the tough conditions weren't about to tip me into a fit of rage or depression this time. I think the team had had a bit of a parley as well, and everyone seemed on their game, a bit more upbeat. Or maybe that was just my perception as I was in a better place.

The Continental Divide, that watershed between west and east, the spine that runs the length of North America, is a psychological mile-stone, but it didn't actually mean that it was downhill from here to the prairies. There was still quite a bit of the Rocky Mountains to face. I spun past but didn't stop at any roadhouse. These infrequent dots of civilization acted as way-markers for the day's progress and for fleet-ing moments were a change in scenery. Signs such as NISUTLIN TRADING

POST, advertising 'Gas, Motel and Groceries', looked like they had been unchanged for generations. Perhaps only the road had been upgraded. And in an attempt to slow down the thousand-mile commute, each roadhouse had its own, rather unconvincing, full-size cut-out of a police car propped at the roadside.

The wildlife was once again the best company. I spotted some beavers swimming in a lake by their dam. The odd black bear grazed on the roadside, unbothered by my presence, and late on in the growing darkness a few coyotes sauntered on the road ahead of me. I spent a lot of that day playing 'Is that a rock or a bear?' This could be quite exciting, but more often a disappointment! I was then treated to a dramatic painted sunset; the afternoon had dried up but the remnant clouds reflected the setting sun.

It has been a much better day mentally. I managed to get back in the zone, which is a good thing – yesterday was an absolute battle. I've only done 370km which is about 230 miles, about ten miles short of perfect, but for about three-quarters of the day I had a headwind, nothing crazy but enough to hinder progress. Well over 3km of climbing again. Today was meant to be wet but the end of today was dry. One of the most beautiful days, a lot nicer than what I'd expected. So, yeah, to get to 370km on a day like today I am totally happy with it. Big days, these really are big days.

Day 54

Morning. Start of day 54. We are still quite high up here after having just come over the Continental Divide, so it's pretty nippy this morning. We've got some pretty cool views of the Northern Lights which I've never seen before so it's worth getting up at this time of the morning just for that. I am going to head due east to start with this morning, sort of dipping in and out of British Columbia and the Yukon, along the border there, and then the roads cut south properly into BC. The last day of the wilds; we will start to hit more towns and back to civilization tomorrow. Right, it's four o'clock . . . got to go.

Riding out under the ghostly green lights of the aurora made for a magical start. For once I wasn't wishing for dawn, quite happy to be alone on the road under the Northern Lights – what a magical sky to ride out under. It certainly set me up well for the day.

I had 1,000m of climbing in the first four hours which stripped the legs pretty well.

'We need some easier days,' I said to the crew during break.

'They are coming,' Laura reassured me.

'I know that we all know this,' I added, 'but especially in the morning shift when I am hurting and struggling, can we try and not do food hand-offs on hills? I can't eat while riding up hills. I know it shouldn't, but this just winds me up – it shows the disconnect between where I am in my head and where you guys are.'

The FV was constantly on the move, so as well as these snacks and treats, Laura had to prepare food that could be served very quickly when we stopped. A typical lunch might be pasta, pesto, some nuts, chicken and veg, so proteins, carbs and good fats, also some spinach for iron. And a chocolate milk and a coffee to get back on the bike, so I didn't slump after lunch. Dessert would be a fruit yoghurt and slice of toasted banana bread, giving me a 1,000kcal hit.

In the Media Vehicle, Jo's biggest task outside a lot of driving was fuelling the team. To keep this simple, she had decided on a six-day menu that was on rotation, and everything was one-pan meals that could be reheated in the evenings – chicken stroganoff and rice, spaghetti bolognese, chicken stew with potatoes, pearl barley and lentils, salmon and pesto pasta with beetroot and feta salad, Thai green chicken curry, and chicken stir fry. The lack of fresh vegetables and fruit in Alaska and the north of Canada meant using frozen and canned vegetables and root vegetables, which were easier to find and transport. Fresh, tasty and plenty of it was the aim.

#80 DAYS. GO MARK. A stick drawing of a winding road and the mountains.

This was the fifth day of these regular signs, all of them unique, and we had by now figured out the kind but elusive culprit. John Schnell had taken it upon himself to road-trip (so far) nearly 1,000 miles from Anchorage and we had no idea how long he would be with us.

He drove a grey four-wheel-drive towing a trailer with a roof box and bike. Often dressed in a camouflage jacket and baseball cap, John looked more like a hunter than a cycling enthusiast, and when I spotted him on the roadside he was normally armed with a long lens on his camera, or the remote control of his drone. I waved and shouted a few 'hellos' but he was never around when I took breaks. While I never got to speak to John, the media boys tracked him down, and then Mike, Laura and Nick found him. In fact, I was suffering from the pressure sores in my shoes, and they pitched up after lunch with a pair of flat pedals.

'Where did you get them?' I asked.

'Off John's bike! Try them for a bit with a pair of trainers, just to give your feet a change.'

'Ha-ha! Thank you, but I'm not cycling in trainers. Please give John his pedals back.'

Early in the afternoon I came around a corner and there was no need to guess if what I was looking at was a rock, from any distance. A lone, very large bison was grazing on the roadside, its oversized head and shoulders looking unbalanced on its spindly legs and hindquarters. Such amazing-looking animals. I slowed down and spun slowly past it. Further on there were about six more, a few lying down on the grass at the roadside, and I looked back nervously as Helmut and Johnny got out of the MV and crept towards them for a better shot. They looked placid enough, but I'd grown up on a farm and guessed they could be as flighty and unpredictable as cows, except wilder and bigger.

A bit further on I came across the main herd, and what a sight. I'm guessing there were around fifty bison all across the road and the wide banks of grass inside the tree-line. They were in no hurry, walking in the same direction I was heading. They were certainly an intimidating sight, but what really made me nervous was the number of calves. I spotted at least half a dozen that had been born that spring, huddling in behind their mothers. I definitely didn't want to get too close, so I signalled for the FV to come up closer, acting as a distraction and, if needed, a blocker.

We proceeded slowly, on a slight incline, but my heart rate soared with adrenalin rather than the effort. The bison were not for moving,

completely unfazed by the motorhome, and as we came within metres
of them I felt very small and vulnerable. Mike was driving while excitedly wielding the GoPro out of the window.

'You'll be all right, they won't do anything,' he said, smiling
confidently.

'That's easy for you to say,' I replied nervously. 'Hope you are all
comfy in there!'

The bison parted slowly but came within a metre of me as I pedalled gingerly across the width of the road to find a clear path, trying
not to spook them. Then, for no obvious reason, one started to canter,
and they all broke into a run. I tucked in front of the motorhome so as
not to be overtaken by those I had just passed. They ran up the banks
on the right side of the road, leaving it clear for cars coming in the
other direction.

I loved it. This was the reason I have always loved adventure cycling. You can plan trips to the nth degree but you'll never know what's
around the corner. And it's incredible how moments on the road can
alter your psychology: the thrill of that encounter left me pedalling
lightly for a few hours, feeling less pain, in a far better place. Nothing
had changed physiologically, it was just that riding through a massive
herd of bison had cheered me up.

This was needed as the day finished with a massive climb into the
Muncho Lake mountains, which was a big detail not to see coming.
In fact Mike had told me that the final set was pretty steady and following the river, so I was confused when I found myself climbing up,
up, up.

Comms were very patchy and had been since Anchorage, and while
Mike knew the route well as an overview, he was still relying on technology for mapping, and without data coverage we couldn't zoom in
and do detailed planning. I asked where the paper maps were – we
were meant to have a print-out of every day's plan, including topography. There were some red faces as the road kept going up and I was
facing by far the biggest climb of the entire trip, one that we knew
nothing about.

After an hour of climbing, I passed the MV parked at the roadside
with Jo standing outside. 'Look,' she shouted excitedly, 'a porcupine!'

My response was stony. I didn't need to say anything. She could tell this wasn't what I needed to hear at that moment. Bless her, Jo was doing an amazing job to keep the team happy and it wasn't her climbing this massive mountain, so how could she possibly be on the same page as me? But it didn't stop me having a sense-of-humour failure.

I climbed into the growing dark, eventually stopping in the wide summit lay-by to pull on overshoes, my down jacket and thicker gloves for what would be a cold descent. The reward was very steep and I clung on to the dropouts, feeling the annoyance flow away as I made up some miles. As the road flattened out back in the tree-line and followed the bends of a river, I asked the team to find a spot somewhere ahead. I was done in, and on such a twisty road there weren't so many places to pull off the road.

I asked Jo to pop into the RV when I was finished for the day. 'Sorry, Jo,' I began. 'I was in the hurt locker, and I wasn't very excited about the porcupine. You might have wondered about my reaction. I just wasn't in the same place as you at all.'

'I know, I saw the look on your face,' she said. 'It's OK. If I was doing what you were doing every day, I would be in the same place as well. Hopefully dinner will make up for it, put you in a good place.'

Credit to Mike as well, he was shouldering a huge amount of pressure and managing quite a difficult team dynamic. Also, he was so keen to get it right that I trusted him not to make the same mistake twice. He took a lot of pride in his work.

That was a tough old day in the end: 365km, just shy of 230 miles. It was going pretty well, in terms of mileage, until the last set in the last four hours when it just started going up and up. It's the upper end of the Rockies here and we ended up well over 1,100m. That was tough going, really tough going, leg-sapping stuff. I have been having some issues the entire trip with my custom insoles, there were some mistakes made with them, and the average climbing in the last five days has been over 3,000m a day, so the pain in my feet has been compounded by climbs and very tough going. For the last five days I have just been in a corridor of trees basically. It is beautiful but it is getting a little monotonous, so it will be good to get some recovery, get out of the hills, get out of the trees and find the flatlands. These flatlands are somewhere ahead but maybe another day or two of this to go though. Punishing stuff.

Day 55

Today we will be heading east to Fort Nelson and, good news, will be back into comms, which will help sort some navigation issues and conversations back to the UK. The last couple of days we have almost had no signal at all which has made it tricky for the media guys to do their job as well. It's good to see progress on a map because when you are in that tunnel of trees for a couple of days the sense of progress is limited.

Northern British Columbia does not disappoint. While the Yukon wins for sheer wilderness, that sense of being in pioneer country, BC wins for interest – the scenery changes with every horizon. My route started out gently along Toad river, which I reached in the darkness, and then cut up across the Racing river to climb to my highest point of leg 3 by the end of the morning at around 1,300m. Picking up the head of the Tetsa river, it was a long, undulating descent off the Rockies to the town of Fort Nelson at 200km, before the road cut due south and skirted the foothills all afternoon.

At the high point I watched an elk and her calf swimming across Summit Lake as I navigated around sheer rocky outcrops. The road-builders were hard at work again, and the dry gravel sent plumes of dust into the air that could be seen for miles. These sections of construction were slow-going, but I was in a much better frame of mind to deal with the day's challenges.

I had been suffering more from a dry, hacking cough, the kind that morphs into a fit once it starts. Ever since the pollution and dirt of the Russian roads I had been coughing quite a bit. While I was used to this, the added issue now was my reflux, which was getting gradually worse. It tended to be fairly settled in the mornings, but as the day went on, often triggered by the coughing, I was bringing food up and having to spit it on to the roadside. Apart from being an unpleasant sight for those following, there were practical concerns around my energy levels and calorie intake.

There had been almost no farmland or managed land of any description in the past thousand miles. Coming off the Rockies towards Fort Nelson, that started to change. In those final miles of wilderness Helmut put up the drone for its 196th flight of the trip – and it simply flew away. With none of the high winds or other adverse conditions that Helmut was used to compensating for, on a stretch of open scrub, it lost signal and disappeared. Johnny, Helmut and Jo stayed back for a few hours, bushwhacking their way through a pretty extensive roadside area, but to no avail. The drone was gone.

They had only lost that day's filming, which was a shame as it included that stunning section around Summit Lake, but the race was on to get back into signal and organize a replacement. Manni, the production manager, had been doing the lion's share of the work back in Cape Town. In the middle of this wild stretch, with very few towns, he managed to track down a replacement drone in an Aladdin's cave of a hardware store by calling loads of people in the middle of the night South Africa time. So we called this new drone Manni. The lost drone had been called Birdie.

The end of day 55 and it's been a good day at the office, much better than yesterday. Back up at 1,000m here. A big old climb at the end of the day. This morning started with two really punchy climbs so the last set yesterday and the first set today are pretty brutal. But it was a beautiful start coming up past these lakes. Based on the first set this morning I thought this was going to be a painful day. But I had a massive descent off the Rockies, came through Fort Nelson, and it has been a beautiful sunny day, and considering how sore I was yesterday it's amazing what sixteen hours on the bike can do to make you feel better. I feel a whole lot stronger. I have ridden slightly late today, not because I wanted to but because there was literally nowhere to pull off this road for the last 10km. Considering we have covered 230 miles and we have now come off the Rockies I am pretty happy with today.

17

An Ill Wind

Day 56

> I'm feeling a little worse this morning. It's amazing how just ten, fifteen minutes less sleep affects me – I can really feel the difference. We were perhaps a bit relaxed at the end of yesterday and I got less than five hours' sleep. Just trying to get up and going. I finished yesterday quite high, about a kilometre up, and today there is a bit more climbing to do and then a long and very gradual descent. It seems to have clouded over in the night, so it's now quite mild. Right, I have less than ten minutes to get on to the bike . . .

It would be another 3,000m of climbing, for the sixth day in a row, but there was enough about the day to suggest this was the end of the west and the start of the middle chapter, the long-anticipated prairies. My first sighting of this was on the outskirts of Fort St John, where I hit some flatlands and found myself pedalling alongside vast unfenced fields of corn being harvested with a fleet of combines. FORT ST JOHN, THE ENERGETIC CITY read the welcome slogan, and I hoped for some of its energy by osmosis.

It was a brief patch of what was to come, as between there and the end of the AlCan Highway at Dawson Creek, the road dropped into a canyon at Peace river for the last of the seriously leg-sapping climbs. It was tough going and I was down to walking pace, out of the saddle, rocking the bike slowly upwards as the sweat ran down my visor.

The AlCan continued to be much more difficult terrain than I had remembered and I was once again left laughing grimly at the punches it was throwing. Perhaps I was a tad complacent as I had ridden it before, but the challenge this time, at three times the distance each day, was both condensed and magnified. It had also been a mental rollercoaster and I was feeling fragile, unable to cope with setbacks as well as I had through legs 1 and 2. This was now Groundhog Day, where I had played all my mind tricks, thought all my thoughts. There was no great sense of progress or any end in sight.

Fifty-six days in, I was now well within a month of finishing, but it felt like I had been living this crazy routine for ever and was running out of new inspiration, new ways to think my way through each day. I could tell that Laura was getting concerned, watching me closely. I had also barely managed to speak with Nicci since Anchorage because of the lack of comms, so perhaps not having that daily conversation to take me outside our little bubble on the road also wasn't helping my mindset.

I had definitely dug deep through the end of Australia and New Zealand on the promise to myself that this leg would be easier and faster. I had been looking forward to that sense of building towards the finish. That certainly hadn't happened yet, and my focus had been kept very short by the climbs and tough roads of each day. But there was also an assumption that once we dropped on to the prairies I would be set for nearly a week of fast riding – a recovery mentally and physically – plus the flattest section of the entire 18,000-mile route so an opportunity to easily make up the lost miles.

Dawson Creek felt like the first major town I had cycled through since Anchorage, certainly my first stop-lights and traffic. Plus this now felt like the Midwest, a working town where everyone drives massive pick-ups and is involved in big farming, big mining, big forestry, rather than small family enterprises, sustaining and sustained by the passing trade.

WELCOME TO ALBERTA. WILD ROSE COUNTRY. It was exciting to head east out of BC and into Alberta, picking up the first sign for Grande Prairie, which sounded promising.

LIFE IS GOOD, with a bicycle drawn into the word using the OO as wheels! I kept thinking that John must surely have turned back, then

I would spot another of his home-made signs. What a superb effort –
a week of road-tripping with us and still I hadn't stopped long enough
even to say hello, but his signs and cheery waves from the roadside
were something I was now used to and looked forward to. I wondered
idly if he was coming all the way across Canada with us.

In the afternoon shift, now on Highway 43, I was on a three-lane
highway, the sort you find in Ireland where the middle lane is left
for traffic in either direction to play chicken and overtake. YIELD
CENTRE LANE TO OPPOSING TRAFFIC a sign read. I hugged the hard shoulder as there was now a lot more traffic than anywhere on the AlCan,
and long sections of roadworks.

The tricky dynamic in the FV was unfortunately with Nick, who was
doing a brilliant job on the bike but unfortunately didn't seem to me to
respect professional boundaries. He had an opinion on Mike's job and
especially on Laura's job. It's great to have input and collaboration
when asked for, but this was really starting to cause issues. Things came
to a head when Nick lost his temper and threw some things around.
Mike was forced to step in, and I could see the strain this was having on
Laura. But once again they worked wonders to keep this pressure from
me as much as possible.

It's been a massive day, but not in mileage as I have only covered 226
miles. A bit disappointing. I knew I was in for a good descent for the
first 100 miles but it turned out to be massive rollers all the way, so it
never really felt like a descent, and so the sum total is I have done
3,200m of climbing. The main issue today was the wind coming in from
the southwest, definitely a lot more than forecast, and that slowed me
down quite a lot, which easily accounts for losing at least 14 miles on
target. I am just trying to get my head around it because for the last
week we have lost nearly 60 miles. I flew in to start leg 3 a day up on
schedule and I have lost a quarter of a day already. It is meant to flatten
out now, it is meant to get easier, but when five days in a row you are
losing mileage it is psychologically quite tough. I was suffering on the
bike today and so a big thanks to the team. I am sure it is not a bundle
of laughs when I am in that zone as I am pretty quiet; I go completely
focused on just riding those miles and into the headwinds – any bike

rider will know what that feels like. I'm pretty sore, and the legs feel pretty stripped. Thanks, team, we are in Alberta, we have cleared British Columbia now.

Day 57

I slept really well. I was out in seconds! Obviously pretty sore after yesterday, which was quite a fight. The winds should be coming around today as they are forecast to and it is quite mild out there. Heading more easterly today rather than south/southeast, past Grande Prairie, which sounds flat. Then make up some of these lost miles! I hope to make up these miles but also get some recovery miles as Canada has been punishing.

Welcome to the prairies – in my first set I cracked 101km. What an incredible difference, compared to yesterday morning when I struggled to do 80km. I climbed 300m, so at that rate it would be about half the amount of climbing as any previous day, but best of all I didn't even notice it on such gradual rolling terrain. The wind was definitively with us, and to top this off, as soon as I had got out of BC and into Alberta it was equally beautiful but the road quality improved a lot, and the ubiquitous roadworks all but vanished. This was what I had been craving for the past week.

I had passed Grande Prairie by sunrise and the whole mood in camp lifted. There was a sense of momentum again, not having to fight all the time. The roads were very wide and open; small towns punctuated the skyline with grain silos. There was a sense of excitement, of recouping momentum.

John Schnell then made his final appearance, although I kept looking for his signs in hope. He left us with the same low profile he had appeared with, just a final few signs in the middle of nowhere attached to fence-posts or crash-barriers. And he never said goodbye, but then again I hadn't spoken to him, even once. It was later that I learnt his story.

In 2003, John had a severe cycling accident while training for a triathlon – a punctured lung, compression of the vertebrae in his neck, lots of broken bones, a long stint in hospital and surgery. Although he went on to make a full recovery, his bicycle languished in the garage. Earlier in 2017 he had taken it to the local bike shop for a service, and then . . . nothing. He couldn't bring himself to go for a ride. Thinking he might be traumatized at the thought of riding his old bike, he started research for a new one. In July he had stumbled on KOGA's website and read about the Artemis World Cycle. From Australia onwards John had been following progress several times a day, and he started planning how he could come out and find me. So as I finished New Zealand, John drove to where he thought he could intercept me – in the remote wilderness of Alaska! A road trip of 3,000 miles.

Sundays were wash days, and Jo had the crew's kit piled. Laura was often left with my cycle kit. This was quite the feat of camp life – hand-washing and wringing everything out with the help of Helmut, then turning the interior of the MV into a mobile washing line. Although mundane, these simple tasks filled every moment that was not spent driving.

I had to film the end-of-day video diary myself because the Media Vehicle had had a fatal collision with a deer that had jumped into the road. The motorhome bore some damage and the media boys looked a bit shaken, but Jo seemed stoic as always, a trait that I'm guessing came from her years in the navy.

Today has been an absolute joy – I have not said that in a while. Covered 250 miles so over 400K. It's not been flat, well over 2,000m of climbing, but over massive rolling landscapes through Alberta. It's been fast. I have had a gentle tailwind. If you were standing still you wouldn't say it was windy at all but once you are on the bike it makes all the difference. I have not really had a day like that since Australia where I just felt like I was being gently pushed along. It was exactly what I needed after the first week in leg 3 where it has just been so tough. Just a day where I could spin the legs and just pedal through 400K like that has been fantastic. I was joined by a local rider today, Ray, for a good stretch – thanks for that. And Nick the mechanic joined me into the dark for the end of the day. I am in a totally different mood, but still need to get good

Left: Cup cakes from Jo to celebrate 14,500 miles, three quarters of the way around the World.

Above: Riding out at 4 a.m. under the Northern Lights.

Right: Mike working hard to reroute me out of the headwinds.

Below: Relieved to have a support vehicle amid a huge herd of wood bison.

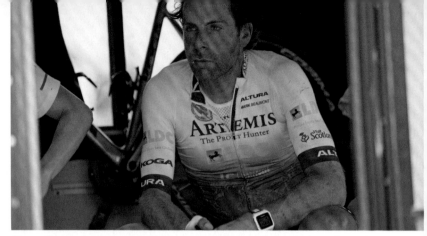

Above: Showing the signs of sleep deprivation and suffering after two months on the road.

Left: MARK EYES ON THE ROAD – a fan shows his support by streaking!

Below: A road hazard. Moving your house on the prairies.

Above: Mike, Jo, Nick and Helmut take a moment in the sunshine, while I get treatment.

Right: John Schnell, who road tripped for over 1,000 miles in support.

Below: Nick and Mike servicing the KOGA.

Left: Recovery pump and calories at the end of another sixteen-hour ride.

Right: Riding the final miles with Si Richardson from GCN, who had also cycled day 1 out of Paris.

Below: Welcome back to France in the torrential rain.

Above and below: Taking calories on the bike during stage 4 as I need every break to sleep.

Above and right: Final sunrise and an arms-length broadcast on *BBC Breakfast*.

Below: First sight of the Arc de Triomphe surrounded by a peloton of friends and fans.

Above: The finish line – a moment I'd visualized tens of thousands of times.

Below: In the media scrum and clutching the 'one month'
and 'fastest circumnavigation' Guinness World Records.

Left: Relief and celebrations with some of my incredible team – Helmut, Alex, Laura, Una, Tony, Mike, Jo and Johnny.

Right and below: Back with my family, Nicci, Harriet, Willa and Mum (aka Una).

Below: Over 18,000 miles in 78 days, 14 hours and 40 minutes.

recovery. Tomorrow still looks quite punchy with the hills, but then we are properly into the flatlands.

Day 58

Start of day 58 and I slept incredibly heavily last night, which I guess is a good thing but it's a bit more of a challenge to wake up and go. Today I am heading due south, skirting around Edmonton, and then the second half of the day I turn due east, Calgary off to my south. Feeling good, team is in good shape. I've just been sent the total distance so far, 13,120 miles.

I was on the evocatively named Cowboy Trail, but only patches of livestock farming remained, arable having taken over the majority of the land, so in such manicured pastures it was now hard to imagine a galloping cowboy.

The mood in camp was again buoyed by the long straight roads and easy rolling. Jo spent lunchtime ducking washing-lines of laundry while trying to cook spag bol, while I sat outside on the massage bed, enjoying an ice cream. In the ten minutes I had to chat with everyone most of the conversation, as you might expect, was about the battles we had just faced, and optimism about what lay ahead. Helmut, like any kid with a new toy, was busy setting up his drone and keen to get aerial footage of this vastly different landscape. Going into physio, I got some acupuncture needles in my neck and massage on my legs before falling asleep in the sunshine for ten minutes.

The day had started pretty fresh with a heavy mist that in first light sat like giant cobwebs across the cornfields. But dawn was a more convincing event now that I had left the weather systems of the mountains behind and I was into these cloudless horizons. Quite a few riders joined me through the morning as I zig-zagged what must have looked online like an odd route, across the North Saskatchewan river, then a 90° turn east for about 100 miles, before another turn south for the finish – giant steps across the countryside. During the morning this big commute south took me dangerously close to the mountains again as I climbed up through the village of Rocky Mountain House and other hilly-sounding places. By the time I topped out at over 1,000m, thankfully for the last time, I was very excited to turn east and on average enjoy a long descent for the rest of the day, although no 100-mile descent passes completely untaxed, in this case with both terrain and wind.

With so many more small towns now on the route a lot more cyclists joined in as the day went on, including an Irish couple who were cycling all the way to New Zealand. It was a pleasure to share a few miles with them, and I was in the right mindset to enjoy the company.

The end of day 58 and we have made it 240 miles – a huge success! It's been funny on the bike. There were times in the middle of the day when I didn't think I'd make the distance at all. I've pushed it a little bit late just to make 240 miles which is a big relief. And just going through the mental highs and lows of today was just weird. I am already having conversations with the team back at home in the UK and with people joining me on the road about the finish and what's going to happen in leg 4. That's messing with me a little bit because my focus still needs to remain incredibly short – the next four-hour block and what each day is about. But we are receiving amazing support along the route. I mean, I have not been to Alberta in my life, but I've had six people ride with me today and other people came out with home-made signs and, even better, home-made baking, on the roadside! So thank you to everyone. I live in this little bubble on the road with my amazing support crew but just to see people coming out and their enthusiasm is just phenomenal.

Day 59

For the first time since starting leg 3 there is less than 1,000m of climbing in the plan – which is great news! I am heading due east now, to places like Hanna and Kindersley, following the same road, crossing from Alberta into Saskatchewan: 140 miles from here I will reach the three-quarter-way mark for the World, which is a milestone that I have been looking forward to. I'm still up at about 900m here so hopefully it'll be a nice rolling start. Not even a whisper of a breeze this morning. Clear skies and it's 15°C, so a lot warmer as well – first time I have started without the leg-warmers.

The main punctuation mark of the day came early, just before coming on to Highway 9, when the road dropped unexpectedly into a deep forested canyon to the Red Deer river. Climbing back up into farmland, it was easy to count down progress to the state border as the regular side-roads were all named Range Road, starting at 285 and working downwards.

The big wooden sign for SASKATCHEWAN, NATURALLY came almost exactly as I clocked 13,500 miles. Stopping at third break, Jo jumped out of the Media Vehicle proudly offering a huge tray of blue cupcakes, twelve to be exact, each with a character from the message 3/4S! #80 DAYS. I was more impressed with Jo's ability to find personalized cupcakes out here in the middle of nowhere than with the achievement!

'Thanks, I'll need all of them . . . so find your own!'

Stopped on the verge by more vast fields of stubble, it was a welcome moment of camaraderie. They celebrated; I simply enjoyed the treat as I wasn't really thinking about the big picture in that moment. It had been a battle since dawn.

After that perfect still start, the headwind had picked up and there was nowhere to hide in these empty horizons. Three-quarters of the way around the World – a quarter was Russia, half was coming out of the Outback. If all went to plan, I'd get back to Paris in twenty or twenty-one days. But today I felt like I was riding with the brakes on.

During the afternoon I had a quick scan of social media – not something I often did – looking for some distraction from the conditions. The first Facebook message I saw was from a lady saying that she had brought her family out to the end of their road to wave and cheer me on. She was bitter as I hadn't even acknowledged them, which she took as arrogance, referencing how disappointed the children had been.

It wasn't a snub. I simply hadn't seen them. I always took every effort to acknowledge and thank everyone I saw, even when I was feeling in the dumps. It shouldn't have mattered, but because I was in such a dark place mentally, this criticism rattled around my head for hours; I just couldn't shake that horrid feeling after reading an angry fan message. Laura told me to bury it, move on, but I was not in a good place, and I took the message badly. I wasn't angry at the lady, but I did want to clear my name.

By the end of play at 9.30 p.m. I was wind-beaten and incredibly relieved to be able to pull slowly into the verge and stop. The team were even more attentive than usual, aware I was fragile.

I have done just 314km. Obviously a really short mileage – I've dropped over 40 miles, finishing shy of 200. I set out this morning with high hopes because it was calm. I was looking forward to my first flatland day, but as soon as the sun started to come up the wind picked up and I have had a really strong wind from the east all day. It was the sort of day that when I was pedalling downhill I was still riding at only 18/19km/h. Seriously slow; there is no recovery on a day like today. I could be disappointed, despondent, but it is what it is, it's the weather. The big blow is that I was so looking forward to getting to the flatlands thinking that I could make up those lost miles. However, I have got here and now realize there is a tough weather system that I could be facing for the next few days. After hoping it could be the fastest miles of the World, this could end up being the real crux of the 80 Days, trying not to lose too many miles over the prairies. I tried not to get too annoyed about it today. But a seriously tough day. The big milestone was that I am over three-quarters of the way around and I did that in about fifty-eight and three-quarter days. Only a quarter of the World to go from here!

Day 60

If anything, the wind has picked up in the night. It is very windy! I woke up a couple of times in the night with the sound of the wind on the motorhome. We are heading due east for the first 100km or so, then turning southeast. There might be a bit of rain this morning as well. It is going to be incredibly tough for sure. I just need to keep my focus incredibly short; there is no point thinking about what could happen further down the road. I guess it is damage limitation in terms of miles. We will just make progress while we can. I don't think there is anything in the forecast that says this storm will pass quickly, so I guess we are set for another very windy day. Day 60 – whoop whoop!

My sarcastic sign-off for the morning video diary set the tone – a wry smile as I set out to do slow battle for the next sixteen hours. I dropped into the small ring and spun the legs. Switching the Garmin 1000 on to the elevation page meant there was nothing to look at as the terrain was pretty flat, but it meant I wasn't constantly reminded of my speed. Don't try and fight it, just sit on the bike and do the miles. I flicked screens briefly to check my power. It was up slightly, over 200 watts, so I backed off even more, just accepting the pedestrian progress. I didn't want to push myself unwittingly into the red. Sipping coffee on the bike, then working my way through some toffees, I played every little trick to distract myself from how daunting the day ahead was.

The first 100 miles was due east, through the small towns of Rosetown and Outlook, descending gradually to the South Saskatchewan river, before then cutting south on to Highway 19. Many towns through the Midwest have given themselves bylines to their welcome signs – for example, WELCOME TO OUTLOOK – IRRIGATION CAPITAL OF SASKATCHEWAN, and other random claims to fame – which gave me a good sense of the local vibe as I continued with my slideshow of the world around me.

I was getting used to being passed by huge and unusual road haulage, including the world's biggest combine harvesters. None of them would fit on most of the world's roads, but here there was very little traffic and absolutely nothing along the very wide verges, so you could literally move a house by road. Which is what happened late in the morning. An old wooden two-storey house – a house on the prairie. This was no permanent caravan, or wooden shed, this was a big family house being driven down the road on a low-loader with more wheels than I could count. It took up the entire road and a lot more, but I could see it coming from a very long way off, not quite believing my eyes. This incredible sight gave the film crew something to get excited about; the rest of the day in this featureless landscape lacked interest. And it is difficult to film a story about the wind.

A cyclist called James joined me for a few hours in the morning but it was pretty hard to hold a conversation over the wind. I could tell this meant a great deal to him: he was so excited and had driven for a few hours to find us with his wife or girlfriend. He wasn't a particularly strong rider and struggled even more than me into the wind and after a few hours had to stop, saying it was just too much. He had battled well – these were truly wild conditions to ride in – and I tried not to be rude, but it made me realize I just needed to be left alone when it was like this. This felt unkind to James. I loved his enthusiasm and appreciated his avid support, but I had to be selfish to stay in the zone and get through this.

At lunchtime, we decided as a team to record a message for social media to this effect: 'I am amazed at the amount of support on the other side of the world. But days like today I need to zone out and focus, plus I am not allowed to draft, so if you want to support while it's pretty wild weather like this, please give me a shout from the roadside – brownies and cookies are always appreciated – but please understand I just need to be left to my own devices on a day like today, cause I need to stay in my own head, just to ride hard against this.'

The day didn't change in terms of conditions, but became kinder on the eyes as I left the cornfields and reached wilder countryside with lots of small ponds and some lakes, then acres of long grass that offered a very visual representation of the high winds.

A local joined us at breaktime and informed us, 'That damn prairie wind, it does this sometimes, but it's not normally from the east, it comes from the northwest.'

In the final shift, having ground my way through an unrelentingly slow day, I cut on to a smaller road, which soon ran out and I found myself on gravel. There was a scrambling of comms and research within the Follow Vehicle, with Mike suggesting this was just roadworks. It wasn't roadworks – you could see this road had never been tarred. But there were no options so I just ploughed on, 25km on dirt roads.

My end-of-day video diary felt as resigned as my start-of-day clip, but with a note of humour and relief. It had been a ridiculous day, but it was over.

> I don't know how to describe today – definitely one of my most brutal days on the bike so far. The winds . . . I remember riding winds like that down in Patagonia but I would be riding eight- to ten-hour days; today I rode sixteen hours. I have covered just shy of 300km, so it has been painfully slow. I know that earlier today there was a tweet and Facebook message put up by the team saying something along the lines of 'Mark is waiting it out', which was definitely the wrong phrase, as this sounds like I was waiting for the storm to pass. I have been out there all day and it just feels like I have had a hot hairdryer blowing against me all day. The forecast is similar tomorrow, so there is not a lot we can do. I guess the good news is that I arrived a day ahead of schedule to leg 3, but we are now eating into this advantage fast. It is tempting to ride on into the night and try to make up lost miles but there is little point until we have better conditions. This unfortunate setback will definitely mean that the final two to three weeks will be a lot punchier than any of us hoped – but we will worry about that when conditions change.

Day 61

> It's just before 4 a.m. Same wind as yesterday. It's not as strong but I'm not taking anything from that; first thing in the morning it could be anything, it's once the sun is up you know what the day is going to look like. It will be cool to get into the US today.

Stepping out at 3.50 a.m., I was met by the yapping of coyotes in the darkness and a team who looked tired but committed to the fight. Mike was busy explaining the route ahead as I made final checks.

'We are on big roads today, the 39 down to Estevan, then the American border at a place called Portal.'

'Looking ahead, can we check stuff like this?' I pointed at the smaller roads on the map.

'Yes, these are all good roads.'

'We don't want to end up on dirt roads like we did yesterday.'

'We'll go ahead and check.'

I knew I was giving Mike a hard time, but I couldn't face losing more miles on dirt roads; the weather conditions were tough enough.

I set out simply hoping to crack 200 miles and reach the US again. It was a modest ambition, but more realistic than anywhere close to 240. The small towns along the route were visible from miles off because of their tall grain towers, used as massive billboards for the community – 'Dog River', 'Moose Jaw' and other fascinating names. However, the visibility wasn't what it should have been. Despite the cloudless skies there was a haze in the air and a distinct smell of smoke. For hours I wondered what this was, until a local rider explained that smoke from massive forest fires just south of the border in North Dakota was being blown across Saskatchewan. The effect was eerie, another visual representation of the headwinds I was facing, and the air was acrid to breathe all day.

The strain was showing on the team. Everyone seemed very serious and I made a point of asking them how they were doing at the breaks.

This time off the bike was mainly used to treat my neck, which was taking a battering. It's easy to assume that it's the leg muscles that will hurt, but in reality, at this tempo of riding, the muscles just keep going if fuelled and hydrated. What gave us constant concern was the conditioning, the neck, the hands, the feet, and to a lesser extent the backside. It's amazing how the very acute pain in my neck from the first month on the road had settled as the body adapted to the time-trial position for such long hours. There was no longer any concern about my getting Shermer's Neck – the complete loss of neck muscle control and having to ride with a brace; however, whenever conditions changed like this, the pain in my neck became pretty acute. What seemed manageable in fair conditions suddenly became a real worry. I was also aware that the more depressed I felt on the bike, the more I felt pain, whereas with a better mindset I could think my way through it.

This should have been one of the biggest days of all as it was by far the flattest – 542m of elevation all day. But I had to bury that thought. I was doing well in real terms and that was all that mattered. With the same degree of tailwind it would have been a 280-plus day. Bury the thought . . .

My route southeast was locked into the grid system once again as I turned south past Estevan and made my way into the evening towards Portal, where Canadian Route 39 became US Route 52.

The Follow Vehicle jumped ahead through the border in case of delays and I approached the passport booth to be greeted by an athletic man my own age. It was a warm welcome back into the southern forty-eight states.

'Where and when did you enter?' he asked, flicking through my passport.

'Anchorage. I've been riding for twelve days.'

'Twelve days since Alaska! Hell, that's a long drive in that time.'

I was through pretty fast, delayed only by a few anecdotes on his part about adventure cycling. All the while he kept remarking on Alaska to North Dakota in twelve days. A bit of flattery in that moment went a long way. I appreciated the boost in confidence and the reassurance that it was all adding up.

I'm back in the US and finished riding through a massive thunder and lightning storm. I actually set out this morning with a storm on the horizon to my south and then all day the sky was hazy with wildfires in North Dakota. With this smoke, the whole sky tonight was an amazing orange colour, when the bolts of lightning flashed through it. Pretty amazing to see. I've had the same battle with these headwinds but I have made better progress as it has eased a little bit this afternoon. I have made it 210 miles, 337km. The sum total of leg 3 so far is that we started a day up on schedule, but I am now 15 miles up on schedule. I have lost 180 miles in the last twelve days. So that is massive; at no other point on the trip have I lost that number of miles. I have ridden on to ten o'clock because I can't assume my luck is going to change. I don't want to start feeling this is the sprint finish, but I do need to put my shoulder in a little bit, stretch the days beyond sixteen hours, because after nearly 14,000 miles I am not willing to give up on that advantage . . . I am not willing to give up the dream of 80 Days. This week has been the most different from what I expected – I had high hopes of the flatlands and then crossing into the US, that it would be fast. It's hard to not start questioning myself on the bike – am I weakening? The conditions are rough but is it also me fading a bit? That worries me.

Day 62

Mike has been doing a big job, an important job, trying to figure out what we can do in terms of this weather. The wind is coming from due south now, staying relatively strong today. I was really hoping I would get to the weekend and it would be a tailwind but that's not the case. We have looked at the option of continuing on a southeast tack as planned but we would continue to be into the weather all today. So instead we'll do a bit of a dogleg. A little bit south, so we will be into it to start with, and then due east, so the wind will be on my side for most of today. The forecast is to get a bit wet and then tomorrow the wind is meant to flip around entirely and come from the north, and at that point I will turn south and make up some miles. Because this section is cutting around the bottom of the Great Lakes, I am now in the US and I need to get a little bit further south before going east and then cutting northeast back into Canada. A lot of plotting and planning to make the most of a bad situation with the winds. Right, let's go.

Friday 1 September had a shaky start. The media boys were waiting outside as I stepped out of the RV and wobbled visibly, looking frail and withdrawn. Maybe half asleep is more accurate. The second day of July felt like a lifetime ago. This felt again like Groundhog Day, utterly never-ending. I had run out of new ways to think about each new day. I felt switched off, going robotically through the routine that I had now lived for two months.

It was slow for the first hour, but not full force, still pre-dawn. Better still, the wind was coming in from the front right so I started to hope – just a glimmer of hope – that this was swinging around already. Tacking left, eastwards – what a change, what an indescribable relief. Someone had just released my brakes. I effortlessly sped up by nearly

10km/h. It felt like I was riding a different bike. By late morning I had smashed out 200km on a magic carpet ride.

It was sensational, and after sixteen and a half hours' riding I called it a day at 270 miles (434km). The wind had blasted its path from the south through to the north as the day went on, helping me most of the way. I rode east through Langdon at 310km and then cut south until 390km, hitting the much bigger Highway 29.

What a turnaround, an absolutely amazing day. Considering I was really struggling to make 200 miles yesterday, to make 270 today is absolutely massive. The wind's not been perfectly with me all day, but it has been roughly in the right direction. I've been riding through never-ending flatlands, with only 700m of climbing all day. I have pushed it a little bit late again to make the miles. Putting a few more miles back in the bank is psychologically massive.

Day 63

Day 63, and I feel pretty rough this morning. But that is OK because yesterday was a 270-miler. The plan is to head southeast into Minnesota today, down towards Minneapolis, although I won't make it that far. It looks like the winds are still with me, which is good news. Just need to get the legs rolling, because I feel like a bear coming out of hibernation. Right, let's do it . . .

The jacket was off from the start. It was finally feeling like summer riding.

Mike's challenge continued to be to account for the weather while getting the mileage exactly right. I was a sailing boat, crossing a continent, trying to weave the most favourable path. It certainly felt like I had the spinnaker out now.

There were lots of conversations between Laura and Nicci, back in Scotland, about how to support me as I continued to withdraw into myself. Every time I called Nicci she already knew what was happening because Laura was in constant communication. I have no objectivity on how difficult I was to read, but I certainly felt pretty switched off emotionally. My tolerance for faff was zero, I was rigid in my thinking, unable to understand a difference of opinion, and I stewed on small issues for very long hours on the bike. Nicci was quietly understanding, always playing devil's advocate, but in a way that tried to help me move on. There was also a discussion about whether friends from upstate New York and Boston should come up to meet me to give me a lift, or even if Nicci should fly out. All options were being considered to try and lift me out of the pits. It's a very strange place to be, to have a flat mental battery, with the odd spark but ultimately dead.

Before lunch I got a call from Una as I pedalled. I knew there was a vast amount of work going on behind the scenes, figuring out transit options back to Europe, getting the kit to the RVs that were being driven out from London, and coordinating the press and sponsors. Almost all of this was kept from me; I was working on a need-to-know basis. But at the end of our call, Mum asked, 'Is it your understanding that day 80 is the Sunday or the Monday?'

My world closed in. How could this still be a conversation? We were working off a programme that had the 18,000 miles broken down to four-hour blocks. Time-zone issues had been discussed endlessly. We were closing in on the end of leg 3 and there was so little margin for error, yet I was being asked when the finish line was? I had no opinion on the matter; I trusted my team. Or I had trusted them.

I think that Mum immediately knew this had upset me and she said she would sort it out with Mike. The crux of the issue wasn't so much knowing when the finish line was, but the breakdown in communication between the road and Base Camp in the last week. Poor phone coverage was the excuse, but I was managing to make long calls back to the UK every day while cycling, so I didn't buy that.

I had a while on the bike to think this through – I just needed to ask Mike to call back and communicate clearly. This didn't happen.

I stepped into the RV and Laura handed me a plate of food, which I had no appetite for. 'Please ask Mike to pop in,' I said.

When he appeared at the door, I completely lost it. I tried to start calmly but ended up shaking with a rage I had never experienced before. Poor Mike, he got the brunt of all my stress, exhaustion and pent-up emotions breaking in a moment.

'How can we not know what we are aiming for? I'm out there obsessed on every hour and yet we don't know what day we need to finish?'

'I'll call Una and sort this out.'

As soon as the door closed, I broke down, sobbing uncontrollably. Laura put her hand on my shoulder, but didn't say anything. The door then opened and Helmut pointed his camera towards us.

'F*** off, just f*** off!'

I was shaking, the strangest feeling, adrenalin coursing through me to the point that it felt like my fingers had pins and needles. I have never in my life told someone to f*** off. I was completely out of my mind.

I pulled myself together over the next five minutes and asked Laura to go and get Helmut. She hesitated. 'Please,' I said.

He came to the door, and I apologized. The cool German – I don't think he was in the slightest bit insulted, instead was delighted to have captured such raw emotion on camera.

I couldn't eat, and certainly couldn't get a power nap. Laura was very supportive, quietly working around me, not addressing the issues, just worried how this was affecting me.

I called Mike back in and we had a more rational conversation. 'Mum said to me, "I just want to know if you are on the same page as Mike." That is when I lost it. I'm not on any page, I'm doing what I am told. If I am told to cycle this road, I will cycle this road. But to be told that there is uncertainty about the finishing line completely screws with my focus.'

A few minutes later, while I tried to pull myself together, Mike popped his head back in to say that a couple had just turned up to ride with me. It was the last thing I needed. I was an absolute state.

Laura caught up with them outside. 'Today is, um, a difficult day. He would hate to ever turn people down, and it's amazing you have come this far to support, so how's about pedalling out, saying hello, and then just making it a short trip if possible.'

The young couple looked a tad awkward but were very understanding, and it was a reason to pull myself together. We ended up riding for a while. The conversation distracted me.

When they left, I mentally crashed during the next four-hour set. Once the adrenalin went I was utterly exhausted – if it was possible to be flatter than before. What a storm about nothing; poor communication was the real issue. But for me on the bike, this level of uncertainty shattered the thin strands of focus I was clinging on to.

Another big day and it is just shy of ten o'clock. Obviously I've been going since four o'clock this morning – 270 miles, so 434km. I'm pretty sore from the 540 miles in the last two days but it goes some way to make up the miles that we lost across the prairies. I can't really think about making up those miles entirely because I lost so many in those four days of headwinds. I am rather thinking of it as putting a buffer back into the bank if those conditions happen again. If I get a fierce headwind anywhere else on the east coast or up through Europe then I have that margin of error built back in. To put 60 miles back into the schedule is great. This is going to make no sense for someone who is not watching the numbers the way we are. We are now in the state of Minnesota which has brought a real change in the last couple of hours. The wind has dropped almost entirely after having a tailwind all day and I have come out of the prairies and it is lakes and trees – a totally different feel about it. A big day, and I feel a bit fried.

18

Taking the Breaks

Today we will reach the most southerly point on leg 3, which is a good feeling. I don't know what it is like watching this from afar, but I definitely feel like we have been on the road a very long time since Anchorage. Today we will be going underneath Minneapolis, then cutting back up in a few days into Canada. It's pretty hard at this stage not to start thinking ahead, wishing you were another week down the road, so the trick is to try and keep the focus short, but of course there are so many conversations about what is coming next and ultimately the push towards the finish. I still feel like we are very much on target. I take huge confidence from coming 540 miles in the last two days. There is almost zero wind out there today, but once again it is pretty hard to tell pre-dawn: quite often the weather pattern for the day doesn't set in until the sun is up. But whatever happens, I don't think that is going to be a big player today. The second half of today is a lot hillier than anything we have done recently, a few spikes coming out of the Mississippi. Considering the last few days have been 500m to 700m climbing total, today is back up over 2,000m. Right, let's do it . . . go!

I might have been spinning easily, but I was on mental autopilot, not really acknowledging anything around me. I was in a bubble which felt like it was getting smaller and smaller. I was pedalling this routine that I knew so well, without having to force myself, but without much care either. I wasn't fixated on any goal, I was mentally drifting off.

This may sound like a state of Zen, but if that is Zen, I wouldn't wish it on anyone. I felt detached, and Laura was concerned about my level of cognition. When the team asked me simple yes/no questions, I struggled to answer. The cogs were turning very slowly indeed.

It was by far the hottest day we had had since Europe, over 30°C, and well into the fourth set of the day I reached the Mississippi river, the state boundary with Wisconsin.

For this final stint Mike joined me on the spare bike to clear the air. The fast-flowing river we were cycling alongside was a good metaphor for what we needed to do: move on. We didn't completely agree on what had gone wrong, but nothing that we disagreed on was important to the race ahead. It was all behind us, like the river flowing downstream.

It was an absolutely beautiful end to the day, crossing the Mississippi then following it southeast. Having left the agricultural flatlands, I was now in an area of extraordinary millionaires' homes – the affluent far reaches of Minneapolis.

It's the end of day 64 and we have made it into Wisconsin. Didn't have the massive tailwinds I had the last couple of days, but it wasn't against me, basically a sidewind for most of the day, so 245 miles. The fact that I have managed to make up so many miles in the last few days means I am only half a day down on schedule for the World, so about 108 miles. And keep in mind there are twelve hours of contingency per leg of the World to be factored on top. Today wasn't quite as punchy as I thought it was going to be, which is great, about 1,600m of climbing.

Day 65

Quarter to four in the morning, day 65, and what an amazing climate change. By far the warmest it has been and really humid as well. It sounds like a jungle out there with the crickets. I am pretty close to the Mississippi still and today I have a bit of a dogleg, heading across towards the shores of Lake Michigan, which I'll reach at some point tomorrow morning. That means I should be able to cross back into

Canada tomorrow. Feeling OK, but my mind is already starting to think 'if', and it is a big if. I don't want to get ahead of myself, but if we manage to keep doing solid 240-mile days then we could be within a fortnight of Paris now, which is exciting. I can start to get my head around that. Definitely counting down as opposed to counting up. Feels like a lot more than two months that I have been on the road, that is for sure! But for now, let's get going.

Midway through the day I would cross the Wisconsin river just south of Wausau. Back in my student days I did an internship in Boston for ten weeks at Liberty Mutual, a major US insurance company, and needed some paperwork sent down from the Wausau office. I spoke to Helen Sayles, one of the senior vice presidents, and remarkably Helen said that she was going to Wausau the following week and I could go with her. Certainly, I said, delighted to get a trip out of the office, not knowing that I would be on the company's private jet in order to photocopy and bring back a file of paperwork. That's the life I could be leading if I had stuck to finance . . . Anyway, flying into Wausau I remember looking down at this featureless expanse that I was now pedalling through.

I listened to podcasts pretty much every day and had now worked my way through every episode of *The Adam Buxton Podcast*, with his amusing rambles with the likes of Louis Theroux; more serious American series such as *Serial*, investigative journalism trying to unravel historical cases; then the even more serious and intellectually demanding *Reith Lectures* in their entirety. Best of all I had now listened to a few hundred *Desert Island Discs* – there was something compelling about hearing other people's stories, especially people I admire, how their lives are always more of a struggle, and therefore more interesting, than their fame would suggest. It gave me a point of reference for my own struggle. This ride too would soon be a simple headline, a series of soundbites, that would completely bely the emotion, complexity and commitment of the process.

That morning I started playing a podcast by John Rives, who has created a website all about pop cultural references to 4 a.m. John, a self-proclaimed expert on what he calls the 'worst possible hour', went from musical and poetry references to anecdotes about a time of day when nothing good ever happens. Apparently even Shakespeare referenced the negativity and bleakness of 4 a.m. in four of his plays. It made for amusing listening as I pedalled towards dawn.

I was looking forward to more flatlands in this area south of Wausau, once I had passed the hilly terrain of eastern Minnesota and western Wisconsin. In the growing dark we made it to the shores of Lake Michigan, just north of Green Bay, and cut north, once more out of the farmlands and into a strip of jaw-dropping real estate with private jetties, huge carports, and homes that are American castles. Each well-spaced property had generous gardens that were beautifully manicured, which made finding a place to park up for the night tricky. Coming into Green Bay West Shores Wildlife Area, we found a small patch of wilderness and ducked into the first side lane, hoping not to be asked to move on.

At 10.30 p.m., after I had stepped into the FV for bed, a guy called Michael De Mar pitched up and chatted with Mike and Nick, who was still servicing the bike. He was a lawyer from Chicago who had driven out four hours with the bike in his car to find us for an evening cycle, but it had got later than planned. Mike described it as 'an extremely emotional day' and asked if Michael, seeing as he had missed me this evening, wanted to ride in the morning. Michael said he couldn't, because of work, but then after watching my end-of-day video diary he decided to sleep in the back of his car and show up at 4 a.m.

End of day 65 and the facts are just over 400km, so 250 miles, so that was a good day. Today was one of the first days where I felt I was riding on complete autopilot. I was safe, but if you were to ask me to describe today I can't really remember it. I mean, I have ridden 250 miles and there were some quite big rollers, some cyclists joined me, but it was just a blur. I just felt like I was riding in neutral the whole day. I kept my speed and physically I absolutely managed it, but it is a really weird feeling when you do sixteen hours just not in the zone at all. Anyway, 250 miles, and tomorrow is a new day. I definitely need to take painkillers before that last set. That last set can get pretty sore towards the end.

Day 66

Laura is just strapping my feet underneath the contact point – they are pretty sore. This has been a big ongoing challenge. I have a pressure sore, a deep callus, underneath my right foot and the skin is just coming off under my left foot; underneath where the cleat is it's just falling to bits. We are putting 2nd Skin on the right foot to help displace the pressure, whereas on the left there is an area of broken skin so we have put Aquacel on this and then a dressing over the top to keep it in place. Today I am cutting through the lakes, Lake Michigan and Lake Superior. Slept well, just trying to get my head into gear. I don't want to spend another day completely zoned out like I was yesterday.

Mike had of course told Michael that I would be setting out at 4 a.m., which I was – challenge time. Local time was now 4.30 a.m. as we were once again living in our own time zone, losing ten minutes a day. So Michael was there for an extra half hour, being filmed by Johnny and Helmut, chatting with Nick.

'What about your work?' Nick was asking.

'Hopefully they won't miss me too much!'

A couple of freight trains clattered by on the Canadian National line, a few hundred metres away. Which just shows how tired we all were as this was the first time I had noticed it. I certainly hadn't been woken in the night.

I walked my bike to the roadside.

'Ready?' was all I could manage, in a hoarse voice.

'Sure, let's ride.'

We headed north under clear skies thanks to a nearly full and extraordinarily bright moon. I assumed it was a harvest moon, but was later told this was because Neptune was in perfect opposition to the moon and directly behind the sun, thus reflecting more light. It was extraordinary night-time theatre, the landscapes thrown into black-and-white vision. I could have ridden without my lights on.

An hour in, we were in the middle of rural farmland and the odd house we had passed was still in slumbering darkness when a jogger without any head torch lumbered silently past in the opposite direction.

'Was that a ghost?' Michael said.

'I guess we're not the only crazies out here in the middle of nowhere in the four o'clock hour,' I replied.

As dawn crept into the sky, I noticed a light breeze coming over my left shoulder, but I had lost track of which way the road was going.

'Which direction is that wind coming from?' I asked Michael. We had dropped into a comfortable silence for a while.

'West.'

'Fantastic! You'll have to excuse me, but I've become a bit obsessed with wind lately.'

I chatted about the allure and pressure of the 80 Days target. How in terms of the public following I had felt that if I fell behind in the first few weeks, the press and public would tune out because the 80 Days was out of reach. Michael told me he had been following since day 1 and had never had a shred of doubt about the 80 Days. In that early-morning shift, coming out of such a deep mental slump, it was an external point of view that did me a world of good. It took me out of my little bubble. Michael then told me about his 175-mile Ride-Across-Illinois-in-a-Day adventure that was inspired by my documentary *The Man Who Cycled the World*. Simply by taking me outside my own world and making me aware of the wider impact of these journeys, Michael helped me to climb into a much better mindset and find a new sense of purpose.

After a couple of hours, Michael turned back at Marinette, the last town in Wisconsin, before I crossed into the Upper Peninsula of Michigan.

I tell this story as it typifies so many people who joined me for an hour or two on the bike, all of whom had their own adventure stories, their own motivations; they had often road-tripped serious distances to find us and be a part of the race. While I often struggled to be Mr Sociable on the bike, I always appreciated their amazing efforts to support me.

The end of day 66 and bang on 240 miles. I have had to push a little bit late just to make the mileage. I guess it's about 9.50. And we are just shy of the Canadian border. When we woke up this morning we had a quick glance at the map and thought we might make it across the border, but not quite. I didn't have much help with the winds today and I had a couple of sections into it. But all in all I felt much better mentally today. However, it doesn't matter what headspace you are in during the day, hours 13/14/15 just hurt a lot on the bike. It's quite a tough finish and I am in quite a bit of pain.

Day 67

It is much chillier out there this morning – to think it was over 30°C a couple of days ago. It is now down in the lower single digits. I'll cross into Canada first thing this morning and follow the north shore of Lake Huron, so it'll be pretty flat for the morning. The wind is coming in from the northwest, so hopefully a bit more helpful than it was yesterday. Mike is working hard to make sure we hit exactly the mileage we need to now, as the closer we get to Halifax and flying out to leg 4, there is a smaller and smaller margin of error. The team are also starting to look at flight options out of Halifax, actually targeting a specific transfer. You can't fly direct so we will end up going via Toronto, or Heathrow, or Newark. But this is probably six days' riding from here. And if I was to guess I would say we will get a late evening flight out, but let's just see how the next few days go.

It was another of my morning videos inside the FV, sat on my bed, eating some granola and yoghurt. Glancing at social media comments later in the day, I saw that a good portion of them were not about my heavy eyes and swollen lips from the weather and fatigue, but the comedy spork, the salad-server-sized plastic piece of cutlery with which I efficiently ladled in the first portions of my daily 9,000kcal. The giant turquoise sporks were building quite the fanbase.

Coming through the border town of Sault Ste Marie, the pinch-point of the three Great Lakes, there were some unexpectedly punchy hill climbs and it was a bit of a stop-start affair before the iconic border itself, a near three-mile bridge, a heavy steel superstructure handling two separate roads. The heavy trucks made their presence felt as I raced this gauntlet, both in terms of the lack of road space and the gentle suspension of this seemingly unmovable structure. So I lost a bit of time, but it was a really quick border crossing – a glance at the passport and off.

The road turned south for a short while to reach the north shore of Lake Huron and then I absolutely flew east through the countryside of Ontario. I had to hit the 240 miles from here on in and if I could do it then I was six and a half days from Halifax.

The one aspect of the whole project which wasn't hitting target was the charity fundraising, for Orkidstudio. I was mentioning them about once a week in the video diaries, sometimes more, and they were promoted regularly on social media. James Mitchell and the team were hard at work building Sachibondu, a healthcare centre in northern Zambia, near the border with the Democratic Republic of Congo, and the only hospital facility for over 300 miles. They were sending back regular videos from the build, which I loved as you could see exactly how far they'd made their small budget go. But with the modest target of a thousand pounds for every day of the ride, we were now in the final fortnight of the race and had only raised £40K.

I was hugely grateful to everyone who had donated; a few people were donating a small amount every day of the ride, which was amazing. Plus the Artemis Charitable Foundation had just decided to add £10K to the pot, which was very generous. But it was still a long way shy of my dream. I simply hoped that if I completed the 80 Days then the press around the finish would be a catalyst for more donations. Laura was as always practical and focused, reminding me just to ride the bike, that the rest of the project would fall into place. There was nothing more I could do at this stage. But I pedalled along thinking that if everyone following the journey put in a pound, we would immediately smash the fundraising target by a distance. Fundraising, whether for the expedition or charity, is always hard miles.

Quite a few people came out and cheered from the roadside or rode short stints during the day, and there was a particularly vocal congregation in the town of Sudbury, well into the night shift. I'm guessing the local cycling club had got the word out as all through the town families and groups stood and cheered from the pavements, and a few cars rolled past, their occupants shouting support through the windows. It was quite hard to see what was going on in the dark but I waved back to everyone I spotted. One guy rode out of town with me and another stopped by the Media Vehicle to give us a big bag of fruit and some home-made cookies.

I've ridden late today – it's just gone ten o'clock at night. And I've not quite made the 240. The plan, which we really decided yesterday, is to start riding by mileage rather than by time. I am less than five miles short, so it is no big deal. But it's amazing how those little delays during the day all add up – I mean, first getting across the border into Canada and then there was a town to navigate and then a bit of a sidewind all day. Pretty rough roads, and then we just came through a big town and so the stop-start through traffic lights. It doesn't sound like a lot but when you are trying to hold 24km/h consistently for sixteen hours, it just gets impacted bit by bit. There was also a fair bit of climbing as well. It's also interesting that during the first shift of the day and the last shift of the day I feel absolutely fine; apart from the pains, I feel totally alert. But those middle shifts of the day I am really starting to feel the fatigue kicking in and that's a battle. I'm going to be back on the bike in five and a half hours so right now I had better get some sleep.

Day 68

It feels a wee bit milder out there this morning. I'm following the same road east, and there is not a huge amount to report as to where I will get to today. I am mainly heading towards Ottawa but I don't think I will get that far. It's quite a busy trunk road, without a shoulder, which wasn't the easiest with trucks yesterday, but the early shift should be quieter. Day 68, and it feels nice to count down towards getting the flight out of Halifax. OK, three minutes to go. Let's do a quick release move on the neck with Laura and then let's go.

Ever since New Zealand I had been fighting an upper respiratory infection, and in this early shift I again had a nasty hacking cough, which tended to bring on the reflux. It was once more a bit grim to be riding along in the dark, vomiting bits of breakfast on to the road.

The route we were taking was now somewhat different to the advertised one on the website, which was causing some confusion and a lot of comments from those trying to meet us en route. But the reason was simply because Mike was working hard to tweak the route to hit exactly 18,000 miles. There were lots of messages every day asking where to meet me, which road and at what time. Now, more than ever, the team needed to focus, so we just couldn't start making plans with the public. The vast majority of people understood this, but a few didn't and took umbrage.

One chap back in Wisconsin had even made the effort to come out and ride with me to relay the message about how rude I had been to put a video message online asking cyclists 'kindly' not to join me during those very windy days in the prairies. It was hard to know how to reply as we pedalled along side by side – had he really made the effort to come out and find me simply to complain about how at times I couldn't deal with company? The irony wasn't lost on me.

'It's a free road, we can come out and ride if we want,' he said.

'Yes, indeed.'

There was a long and I hope on his part awkward silence as we rode onwards, before he changed the subject.

I felt it was time to put out another message to the public, as there were too many personal messages by email and social media for my team to reply to individually: 'I'm really blown away by the level of support. The best way to find us is to follow the tracker each day; if I am coming close to where you are, feel free to come out and support, but please understand we can't make individual arrangements. There are also a lot of people already asking about the finish in Paris, and while my head is not quite there, the final roll-in, people are very welcome to join me from the Périphérique, the outskirts of Paris. If you can allow me to have the finishing line! I'm as social as I can be on the road, but understand that I am riding sixteen hours a day, so at times I am slightly in the zone . . . but thanks a lot everyone.'

Another concern and topic of debate was once again the weather. Hurricane Harvey had just torn through Texas, hence the battle I'd faced while in the northern states, and now Hurricane Irma was coming in fast from Puerto Rico and about to hit Florida hard. These Atlantic hurricanes had a tendency to track up the east coast with really bad secondary storms. It looked like I would reach Halifax just ahead of them, but imagine if we had plumped for the southern route across the US, like I had a decade before – I would have been stopped for days. The true cost of these storms could be counted in fatalities and millions of dollars, so I'm not equating my 'what if' in real terms, but it did cross my mind that we were lucky to be so far north. Lucky, because in all our planning, avoiding hurricanes had never been a factor.

It was a day of big rolling roads – not the safest trunk road with the trucks. And aside from other road users, I was starting to feel not very safe on the bike, not completely with it, so the priority was to get more sleep and recovery. There was now no period in the day when I was not battling to stay alert. I didn't normally take a sleep at lunchtime, but I was just having to switch off. I had to find a new mindset. I couldn't do another four or five days like this, trying to stay awake on the bike. I was now taking Pro Plus regularly throughout the day and growing more reliant than ever on sugar and caffeine to keep me alert. I was scraping the barrel and needed to get more recovery.

Here's Mike's log from day 68: 'So for the first time on leg 3, perhaps on the whole World, we had a bit of a scare. Normally Mark comes in at lunch break, and the crew are all waiting for him, ready to get all hands to the pump to get him off the bike to spin him around and get him moving again. Today he came in, not a single word, went straight to his bed, walked past all his food. This was unprecedented. And quite a shock for all of us, not quite knowing how to deal with this. However, he took his sleep and a bit of food. I joined him on the bike for a short period of time afterwards, really just to see where he was. We don't get much time to talk to Mark during the breaks. Laura has a lot of work to do with him, from massage to hydration, fuelling and change of clothes. For that first fifteen minutes on the bike I had very little conversation with Mark, he was in a really deep and dark place – but he was able to pull himself forward and continue the day and into evening in pretty good form, considering where he was from the morning.'

It's the end of day 68 and it has been quite a day: 392km, so a good bit over the 240 miles. Hopefully this is a bit of a turning point because the truth of the matter is that the last two to three days I have really been in a bit of a fog on the bike. It got to a point at lunchtime when I couldn't face riding on day after day after day, I felt unsafe on the bike, I felt like I was starting to not be sensible at all. So I came in at lunchtime and for the first time I just slept for twenty minutes; I didn't even look at the food, I just slept. This totally sorted me out and I have been in a completely different mindset this afternoon. I have felt much sharper and I've got that focus back. It also helped that it flattened out this afternoon and it stopped raining – it was an easier afternoon than it was morning. Highway 17 – it's not a road I would advise cycling on, it is very busy and not particularly cyclist-friendly.

Day 69

Start of day 69, and this is the busy bit of Canada. We are only 50 miles short of Ottawa here, cutting southeast to avoid the city so back on to the smaller roads, eventually coming around Montreal and then heading up towards Quebec City. Because there is a river between them, I'll be following that, so hopefully it will be a flattish afternoon. It was a bit of a late finish yesterday, I think it was about 10.45 before I hit the hay. Back on the bike at 4 a.m. but feeling better after that twenty-minute kip yesterday lunchtime. Hopefully that will set me up well. In the last four and a half days, through to Halifax, if I need to take a little bit more recovery than that, I will do – but I still have to hit the 240 each day. It's that sense of 'so near yet so far' at the moment. I don't feel like I can sprint to the finish yet.

Quite a few riders joined me, which I was kind of expecting, including one Cameron Fraser. With a name like that we had plenty of reminiscing to do about the homeland. However, more memorably, while

Cameron and I rode, another young man joined us for a stretch. He was a student with big dreams.

'I love cycling and want to graduate and just head off and explore the world,' he told us.

'Superb, do it, where do you fancy?'

'I was thinking of heading off to Alaska, maybe go as far south as California and then over to the east coast.'

He looked so excited, so I tried to respond with a note of humour, without sounding supercilious. 'You know that you have just described North America, not the world?'

'Ha, yes, but I couldn't afford to go abroad,' he said.

'You live in one of the most expensive parts of the world – get a ticket to Cairo or Istanbul or Santiago, in fact almost anywhere outside Europe and North America, and you'll have a cheaper trip, even if you take into account the cost of your flight. Plus, if you got to Alaska from here, it's cool, but it's not so different; the same for California or Florida – but for that same distance you can cross tens of countries, cultures and cuisines and it'll be the best thing you ever do. Just go, don't think too much about it.'

There was a pause, but he came back more excited than ever. I was relieved, not sure if I had squashed rather than amplified his dreams. A bit further down the road he fetched a cookie out of his back pocket and gave it to me before waving goodbye.

I wasn't in the mood for his cookie, especially as another rider had already met us with some home-baked biscuits that morning, so I handed it to Laura through the window of the RV and carried on.

A while later, chatting to Cameron, we saw ahead a black car which caught my eye. It was parked on the right-hand grass verge, but in the middle of nowhere. The trunk of the saloon, to use the local lingo, was popped up, and I could see a large white sign. I was quite used to seeing home-made GO MARK signs by now, so wasn't all that surprised, until I read: KEEP YOUR EYES ON THE ROAD MARK!

I was wondering why when a naked man jumped out from behind the car and ran down the road, shouting. I exaggerate – he was wearing his shoes, a woolly hat and doing a poor job of holding on to his modesty, flapping a scrap of cardboard over his midriff.

'Eyes on the road, buddy, eyes on the road!'

This certainly cheered everyone up. The oddest show of support yet, but that same enthusiastic student who had disappeared a few hours before on his bike had road-tripped forward, completely on his own, in order to streak. I would have assumed streaking normally belonged to the realms of nocturnal drinking dares but this was a very sober, solo mid-morning effort. Welcome to Canada!

'Does that often happen?' Cameron asked.

'No!'

Amusingly, this led to a conversation with Laura about how I wasn't allowed to eat the cookie he had given me. I questioned how being a streaker made your culinary gifts less trustworthy; was there a known correlation between public nudity and lacing baked products with drugs? I had eaten a huge number of gifted cookies and cakes across leg 3; which delicious home-cooked goodies we would receive from fans had been a daily focus. This was the first time Laura had said, 'You are not eating that, we don't know what's in it.' I wasn't going to argue further, but I enjoyed the ridiculousness of the situation. It put me in a good mood for a stint.

The cookie was disposed of humanely.

Later in the day my broken tooth fell out. The resin had held since day 13, to the point that I had pretty much forgotten about it. The gum was still sore to touch, up next to my nostril, way up at the top of the canine root, but the tooth itself had firmed up and Laura's DIY fix had held brilliantly. I assumed I had swallowed it, which was an odd thought, as the first I knew was when my tongue ran over the rough face of the tooth and I realized it had gone. It was amazing it had lasted this long, but it would definitely need fixing again before the end. Laura would need to practise her dentistry skills again.

The roads in Ontario are worse than their American neighbours but much better than those in Quebec, which are notoriously bad. I had been forewarned. I was in fact back within a stone's throw of the US border later in the day, this time New York State, and I was also already further north than Halifax. A straight line east would take me back into the US through Maine, but my plan was to remain in Canada as I needed the extra miles, looping north into New Brunswick and then back south to Nova Scotia. Following the Saint Lawrence river valley, I ducked on to much smaller roads to avoid the trunk roads that connect Montreal, Ottawa and Toronto. This was punishing riding and it remained hard to hold a high average speed, despite the flattish terrain. At lunchtime I had asked Nick to take some air out of my tyres to try and soften the ride.

At the end of day 69 we have made it about 389km, so just over the 240 miles. It's been pretty flat today with just over 1,000m of climbing. You can probably see the faint lights of Montreal in the background there. So we've gone from English-speaking into French-speaking Canada, and it's amazing to see that immediate transition into Quebec. All in all, quite a good day ... but I kind of wish on such a flat day that I could have gone faster and further – that would have boosted morale. Right, it's nearly ten o'clock so must get to sleep.

Day 70

At 3.45 a.m., Laura is about to put more dressing on my feet. Day 70! That feels like a milestone. I am not going to miss these 3.30 starts, they need to be experienced – pretty sore, getting up and rolling, just trying to stay in neutral until you're on the bike, don't think about it too much, just get the wheels rolling. Today is continuing to follow the river northeast, until it empties into the Gulf of Saint Lawrence, up past Quebec City. Then we can turn on to the last page of the road atlas, which is quite exciting! So, day 70, and I really hope to finish the World within ten days.

After eight hours on the bike I stopped and had to sleep again, really struggling to stay awake. On day 69 I had felt on a bit of a false high on the back of getting a bit of a lunchtime catnap the day before – I felt like I had flipped a switch. Unfortunately, today it had been switched off again, a big low, so a bit more sleep, just ten minutes, plus trying to fuel more on the bike.

It had been a bit of a frantic late morning, finding ourselves on a road that bikes weren't allowed on. We didn't turn on to any new roads, the same road simply evolved into a busier one without any signs. Mike was now having to work on the hoof to figure out the day ahead. As I passed the town of Trois Rivières on the opposite side of the river, a State Trooper pulled up behind me with lights flashing and sirens wailing.

Rather than go to me, the Trooper walked over to the motorhome, which had pulled up behind me. I stayed on my bike, twenty metres away, hoping that Jo would deal with the situation and that we would be waved on. I kept away, not wanting to get involved.

No such luck. Jo emerged on to the hard shoulder and walked over to me, explaining that I had to get into the motorhome. There was no option.

I pushed my bike over to the Trooper, who was young, maybe in his late twenties. I wasn't sure if this would make him easier or harder to sweet-talk. He certainly didn't crack a smile.

'How far is it to the next junction?' I asked.

'A few kilometres – but you can't ride here, you need to go in your vehicle.'

'If I get into the motorhome that would break the rules of this world record attempt. I understand I can't cycle here, and that is a genuine mistake, we aren't from here. Can you please do me a favour and just escort us to the next junction? I had no idea I wasn't allowed on this road.'

I tried to make this more of a statement than a question, to make it clear that while he had the authority, I wasn't about to get in the vehicle. With a nod, he turned and got back into his car.

'OK, let's go,' I beckoned to the team, and started riding fast.

I rode those next few kilometres like a time-trial. Stretched out on the tri-bars, hammering a much higher wattage, with the State Trooper sitting just behind, lights flashing. I didn't look back until I reached the turn-off, at which point he floored his powerful engine and shot off down the road – a bullish or at least youthful way of strutting off.

And that was that; I peeled on to the smaller roads and was left following the rural grid system on much tougher surfaces.

Incredibly, quite a few people still managed to find me on this alternative and more intricate route. One chap pitched up with his bagpipes to play on the roadside, which was amazing, a great morale boost. Sadly, no more streakers!

One other rider joined me for an impressive stint; I unkindly wrote him off at first as he was a big chap and looked pretty out of shape. Philippe, a true Québécois, spoke broken English but despite this started chatting as if we were well acquainted. It was obvious that he thought that I knew him, and it took a few minutes to figure out why. Nicci had been replying to all the messages left for me on Facebook and hadn't always been making it clear that it wasn't me personally replying. When I did see some of these conversations I wondered how people thought it could possibly be me writing while pedalling sixteen hours a day – but perhaps this practicality didn't occur to people who were just happy to get a reply.

Anyway, I soon figured out that 'I' had been sent Philippe's very personal life story in a conversation with Nicci, who he thought was me. I didn't know how to break it to him that it was my wife that knew all about him, and that he would have to start from the beginning if it was a story that he wanted me to know. He saw the funny side and told me how riding had turned his life around, perhaps saved it, and he was in the shape of his life, getting fitter by the day. He was certainly tough and on a mission. Across North America, I had been constantly reminded of how weary I was every time fresh-legged cyclists joined me and made the hills look effortless. Philippe was more at my level; riding at my pace, about 15mph, at least looked like it was taxing him.

I enjoyed his company because after sharing his story he allowed us to ride along in comfortable silence. I was not in the right headspace for small talk and got back to focusing on the numbers, aware of him tucked in behind me for the next four hours.

There had to be a change of plan. I was once again scraping the barrel, struggling on the bike, exhausted by the constant need to solve the mental and physical puzzle – so we decided to start using both morning and lunch breaks to sleep. My normal ten-minute power nap in the morning was now made a little bit longer, so I didn't have time to eat, but ate when I got back on the bike. I literally held a plastic bowl on my handlebars and had my porridge. We tried a Velcro and cable tie contraption that Alex had created for attaching the bowl in the space between the tri-bars, but on the clattering roads the first bowl of porridge was bounced out in seconds, all over the front end of the bike – a good visual representation of the sort of abuse my arms were taking constantly.

At lunchtime I got straight on to the massage table; Laura worked on my calves and despite the discomfort I just passed out. Using breaks for sleep and recovery was now a needs-must for safety on the road, and at least this routine meant that the breaks didn't roll over longer than planned – if that happened then I would end up not finishing till gone eleven o'clock and that obviously wasn't sustainable either.

It's 10.20 so I have had to ride late today to make it 236 miles, just shy of target. It's not been a big elevation day, about 1,000m of climbing; for that reason, like yesterday, I was hoping to go much further but the corrugated roads of Quebec got in the way. It's pretty tough riding and just the stop-start coming through some of these towns. I'm well north of Quebec City now and not a million miles from the right turn towards New Brunswick and Nova Scotia. Today the wind was coming in from the northwest all day and I was sort of going northeast all day so that wasn't exactly helpful either. But if that stays tomorrow, when I make the turn, it should be with me so hoping for more of the same. There is a real sense that I am heading back into the wilds now. So hopefully two and a half days from here and we are at the end of Canada.

Day 71

It's day 71, obviously just before four o'clock in the morning. Heading northeast to Rivière-du-Loup, a cool name – Wolf river – and from there cut a right angle and start heading southeast into New Brunswick, which is great – my final tack, finally heading towards Nova Scotia. Yeah, we will see what happens today. I know I am going to hit more hills when I hit New Brunswick.

By lunchtime I was just shy of the Quebec–New Brunswick border. Having followed the Saint Lawrence river since Montreal we had expected that to be flat and fast, but because of the wind and road conditions it certainly wasn't. In contrast, as soon as I left the water, turned inland and started to climb, I sped up massively. Up through the dense forests, it felt like we were back in the west on the AlCan; the road immediately improved and the wind was behind me. Every day was crucial, but there was now a sense of finale, that today and tomorrow would define the success of leg 3.

Crossing a new time zone into New Brunswick meant that our late finish at 10.40 p.m. challenge time was actually twenty to midnight local time. For these final days we needed to bite the bullet and jump from challenge time back into local time. Obviously, the point of challenge time was to avoid such jumps in time zones, but our teams hadn't worked out leg 3 as perfectly as legs 1 and 2, so we were left with this one-hour jump. I finished knowing that if I put in another consistent 240-mile day it would leave a final 100-mile roll-in for a Tuesday lunchtime flight back to Europe.

Outside of our little bubble on the road there was a huge amount of planning back in the UK in preparation for leg 4. The RVs needed to be delivered from London to Lisbon, and to help with this we called on two very different volunteers. Una first thought of Stewart Fairley, a long-haul truck driver who has supported my expeditions closely over the years. I had initially spotted his comments and support online, and we then met at many events over the years. I'm sure he wouldn't mind me saying that he used to be very out of shape, but that he credits following *The Man Who Cycled the World* with making a huge change to his life: he got himself into great shape, cycling, running and taking on many adventures of his own. I remember coming back from my nine-month expedition down the Americas in 2010 and Stewart pitching up at Edinburgh Airport to shake my hand and welcome me home. What a gentleman. And as a professional driver, he was the perfect candidate to pilot an RV out to Portugal.

For the second driver, Una asked Richard Curtis, who had got in touch in January 2017, again through social media, when I put that call out from the winter training camp in Spain about needing sponsors. As an avid bike rider and being between jobs, he was happy to help with the road trip. You couldn't imagine two more different characters now setting out to deliver the vehicles to Lisbon.

On the bike, I had a call with Derek Stuart from Artemis. I had spoken to Derek and Lindsay Whitelaw on a number of occasions on the way round, in quiet moments when time zones worked in our favour. A theme of our calls was the details of the finale, including most importantly a glass of fine red wine, which I spent a dispropor-tionate amount of time looking forward to. Derek assured me he had the perfect bottle in mind.

I also made several calls from the bike to Grampa. Throughout my adventure career I can think back to all the weird and wonderful places I have called Grampa, imagining him in his garden or old house in Warwickshire, excited and always enthusiastic to hear every detail. Our conversations were a barrage of questions on his part and I loved this interest and support. By the end I would normally manage to fit in 'And are you and Daphne well?' 'Yes, yes,' would come the quick reply, 'but thank you so much for updating me on your adven-tures.' He didn't realize how valuable those calls were for picking me up, keeping me going.

The people I heard from daily, outside the core team, were my cousin Catie in Switzerland and my big sister Heather. Quite often Catie and Heather would be chatting about everyday life and the fam-ily, but between them I don't think they missed a single day. Often these detailed messages would come in and I wouldn't catch up on them until the end of the day. I felt bad for not having time to reply, but their daily updates and support just kept coming and they meant a lot to me, especially in these sleep-deprived weeks.

Alex Glasgow, my mechanic from leg 1, was also getting ready to fly out to work with Stewart and Richard to get the vehicles sorted so we could hit the ground running. Even more importantly, Alex had been spending long hours online poring over the final 1,300 miles, try-ing to iron out the hills, rerouting along better roads, and getting lost in the detail so that some of the issues that we had in North America wouldn't happen during the sprint for the finish.

It's the end of day 71. It's been a very long day and I am well into New Brunswick, having done 403km, so 250 miles, and about 2,600m of climbing. I knew as soon as I turned away from the river that I would be going up, up, up, but in actual fact it was a faster day than yesterday, believe it or not. The roads were a lot better coming into New Brunswick, leaving Quebec behind, plus I had a gentle tailwind which was just enough to make a difference. And I have pushed late again. The clock is always ticking to get back to Paris! Nine days to go. It's very late and it's going to be I guess four and a half hours' sleep, then I need to do 250 miles tomorrow to make that flight from Halifax the following day.

Day 72

I have just started out. Less than four and a half hours' sleep, after 250 miles yesterday, so everything hurts quite a lot. But same routine – ha! – just trying to get up and think my way through this first set. It's dry this morning which is great, the wind is very gently helping me. Nick was working again on the bike last night. It's amazing how quickly you go through parts when you ride the best part of 1,000 miles every four days. So it was a new bottom bracket last night; today there is going to be a new chain and cassette, just getting ready for leg 4. The route ahead basically follows the river, but there is still a lot of terrain. It's a big day ahead, our last full day in North America.

The knock-on effect if I missed my flight to Lisbon, via Newark, New Jersey, was that I would land late morning in Europe, thereby losing half a day's riding. The planned flight would get me back on the bike by 9 a.m. – which still meant a massive five-day target to Paris. Reaching that 2 p.m. flight from Halifax was crucial.

Coming into the town of Fredericton, I was about to stop for first break when a car with a bike on the roof caught my attention, as the driver hollered loudly out of the window. Performing a U-turn in the road behind me, he then overtook, pulled on to the hard shoulder, grabbed his bike and pedalled after me, abandoning his car on the side of a busy two-lane bypass. When this excited cyclist caught up with me I suggested he go back for his car, that I was about to stop for morning break so he had time to re-park and join me.

As I grabbed my power nap I became aware of a loud voice outside – it was the cyclist being interviewed by Helmut. When I emerged, Laura forewarned me, asking if I wanted to be left alone. I said I'd be fine.

Pedalling away from the gas station where we had parked, we came to a roundabout to rejoin the main road. As I sorted myself out, checking that my bike computers were working, I was alarmed when the man yelled out: 'THIS IS MARK BEAUMONT – CYCLING AROUND THE WORLD!' He was absolutely screaming the words. I didn't know what to do. My reaction was to stare at the road, shy away from the embarrassment.

I let it slide and he settled in alongside me, talking at pace. I didn't need to respond – he was sustaining the conversation perfectly by himself. We then came up to some workmen on the road, and he was off again: 'AROUND THE WORLD IN EIGHTY DAYS – THIS MAN IS A HERO!'

I rested my hand on his shoulder. 'You don't need to do that. Thank you, but please don't.'

'OK,' he said, looking a bit taken aback. 'Why not?' Then he carried on, regaining his confidence. 'I forgot you British were so shy.'

'I'm not sure we are shy,' I told him, 'we just don't go around screaming at strangers.'

I said this jokingly, and he didn't seem put out at all.

'What do you do – what's your job?' I asked.

'I'm a pastor,' he replied. 'I run the church here.'

I looked down at his bike, and where keen roadies often have their name decaled on to their top tube, it said 'Pastor'. Probably my own age, he was the most excited and enthusiastic man you could imagine, completely at the other end of the spectrum to my current mindset. But the conversation was so boom, boom, boom, so over the top, that rather than piss me off it amused me hugely and cheered me up. There was no dimmer switch, no volume control; he remained on the pulpit for our entire ride, booming at me.

As we came to a long drag up, he mentioned that he would soon have to turn back. I was partly relieved, partly sad to see him go – he had certainly been the novelty act of the day. But before he went, he asked, 'Do you mind if I pray for you?'

I've been asked this half a dozen times over the years in various countries of the world, although never in the UK, and always by Christians. As I don't subscribe to any religion, it's always a strange situation. Ultimately, it feels like the prayer is being offered more for their own sake than mine, but equally it feels rude to decline. Besides, it wouldn't hurt.

We pedalled along as the pastor bellowed out his impromptu prayer for my travels. This was no Lord's Prayer, rather a few minutes of his imagination – rough phrasing but quite impressive and poetic.

'Amen,' he said when he'd finished.

There was a long silence.

'I didn't close my eyes, I'm afraid,' I joked.

He whipped his head around with a look of alarm. 'No, you weren't meant to close your eyes!'

Ah yes – sarcasm, still not universally understood.

And off he went, having cheered me up no end.

Later in the day I was joined by a Catholic minister for about twenty minutes. In contrast he knew nothing about me; he was just out on his bike for a ride, like he did every single day. This minister was in his sixties, quietly spoken and very humble. I also enjoyed his company, but for quite opposite reasons, mainly his calmness. Two men of the Church with very different ways of connecting with people.

Some 300km into the day I reached the town of Moncton, where the road started curving south again. After a very hilly graveyard shift on the small roads we had ducked back on to the major State Highway 2. The good news was that my speed had picked up massively; the bad news was that this more direct road meant that I would cut about 25 miles off my planned route, which would now need to be made up in Europe. But at this stage, faster miles and ensuring we made that flight were more important than beating myself up on the minor and very hilly roads to hit the exact mileage.

In the late shift a lot of riders joined in, and at one stage this became a concern. One chap joined me with no lights; some others rode down a slip road in the wrong direction to meet me. And there was a long section of roadworks that was tricky to navigate in the dark. With so much happening around me, I could tell Mike was worried. His concern, quite rightly, was my safety and performance – it was hard to chat to enthusiastic riders on this busy trunk road. The relief was knowing we had cracked it and I could relax a little, grateful for the local show of support.

OK, what time is it? About a quarter to midnight, so it is very late. And we are in Nova Scotia! What a funny old day. The first two-thirds were pretty horrible: the first section on tiny little roads which were slow, slow, slow, and then as soon as I got on to the main highway I thought that I would go fast, but just didn't have the conditions – I was going northeast for a long tract there, and the wind was coming against me. But as soon as we cut from New Brunswick into Nova Scotia and the road curved around southeast to begin with and then due south, I have just flown, and what a difference. You go from a day where you battle for 150 miles, and then you just cruise the final bit. I did 244 miles, and it is only about 70 miles from here to the airport. I guess I'll have about three and a half hours' sleep and then on the bike at 4, try to get to the airport about 10. It has been a tough three and a bit weeks in North America and I am sure these guys have a lot of kit to sort out as well, so less sleep for them!

Day 73

It's just shy of four o'clock, which means just over three hours' sleep, which is wonderful. How are you feeling, Laura?

'Bright and breezy, buddy!'

Course you are . . . I don't . . . no, I'm not going to say what I was going to say – feeling pretty rotten! I think there is one big pass, one big climb. I know the guys at Menzies Aviation are there waiting to get us through as quickly as possible. Looking forward to a proper shower and some sleep on that plane. The good news is that the guys are already in Lisbon, setting up at the moment, doing the shop, prepping the vehicles, making sure we can hit the ground running tomorrow. We will arrive breakfast time and just roll straight out through Portugal. Right, up and out, last push through North America.

Halifax airport is perched right at the top of a long climb. Of course it is – a fitting finale to leg 3! Even at that early hour a number of well-wishers pitched up to cheer me over those final miles and meet me at departures. The place seemed deserted, apart from the welcome party.

Nick had to return one of the RVs to Boston and Jo was on a later flight to Lisbon, via London. While having not seen a lot of her, she had been running around like a maniac, putting in long hours behind the wheel, doing all the errands, cooking and prep, and keeping us all going. The pressure but also relief was showing on Mike, not just in charge of leg 3 but also the big picture in terms of logistics – and there was pressure on him, in partnership with Una back in Scotland, to make sure the mileage worked out perfectly. But as we waved goodbye and cleared security it was Laura who suddenly beamed with happiness, sheer relief – she had suffered an incredibly difficult team dynamic throughout leg 3 and kept most of this from me. I didn't know whether she wanted to laugh or cry, probably both, but I was very sorry for the added pressure she had been put under to do her job. The details are between her and Nick, although Mike dealt with a lot of this strain as well.

All in all it was a ride from Alaska to be proud of, we had all absolutely battled.

That's us, end of leg 3, and we made really good time this morning. There was a decent climb, but with that wind I just absolutely flew. We didn't stop at all, and it is now about nine o'clock in the morning! 16,739 miles to here from Paris, so 1,300 miles to go up Europe. Just shy of 5,500 miles across North America, Canada and the US. I think we expected it to be happy summer riding, but the last week in particular, the compound effect of the sleep deprivation and the conditions, we have all been digging deep. A great team effort. I flew into North America with a day in the bank on our schedule – we have lost half a day on that, but we are still ahead of target, we are still on target to get Around the World in 80 Days, which is important! In terms of flights I now have about nineteen hours off the bike. Massive relief – sort myself out, get some recovery.

We had five luxurious hours until flying. The Menzies team had organized a room at the hotel adjoining the terminal building so that we could all rotate through the shower. Ideal, except the large smoked-glass panel in the bathroom gave those in the bedroom a distorted but pretty vivid view of the procedures. We knew each other well by now, but this was the next level, so we did our best to politely avert our eyes. I did better still, lying on the bed as Laura set about rebuilding my tooth again with the resin. Like the first time around back in Russia, I fell fast asleep. It was the blissful slumber of a man who didn't need to jump on his bike as soon as he woke up.

In Newark we had time on our side before the transatlantic hop. Steps were brought alongside the plane so everyone could be bussed back to the terminal. To our surprise, we were met as we stepped on to the tarmac by some suited and booted officials and ushered into two blacked-out Lincolns, big four-wheel-drives, and whisked off. Helmut and Johnny were particularly bowled over by the star treatment, which I was grateful for but too tired to get overly excited by. The chief executive of Menzies Aviation, Forsyth Black, had been in touch with each airport manager in the week before we arrived, saying 'Don't mess up!', and we had seen a friendly rivalry building up with each airport trying to outdo the last for speed and attention to detail.

'Excellence from Touchdown to Take-off' is the Menzies tagline and the crews were certainly having fun seeing who could lay on the plushest red carpet. I spoke to a number of them about this at different airports and they reflected that while they enjoyed their day-to-day jobs, there was a lot of routine – ground-handling is the sort of job where you only get noticed when you do something wrong. So they loved having the opportunity with the Artemis World Cycle to do something that showed what they were capable of, something high profile in the business – something they could show off about. In real terms it also made a massive difference to our speed and morale.

I had time for a shower and shave, as well as a team meal. Johnny and Helmut also had time to catch me for our longest interview since San Francisco. They looked shattered, but determined – everyone could now see the light at the end of this incredible tunnel.

We had always flippantly called leg 4 the 'sprint finish' because in comparison to the rest, certainly on the scale of a world map, it looked like a hop, skip and a jump. But I respected what lay ahead – further than Land's End to John O'Groats in less than five days, if all went to plan. Spain is the second most mountainous country in Europe; it's a punchy yet beautiful place to ride, and some of the roads I had taken in 2008 had been upgraded and were no longer permissible for cycling. After the hiccups through leg 1 with the Strava route, Alex's work in finding a route to thread the path of least resistance towards Paris would be crucial.

Part Five

Lisbon to Paris

Mike Griffiths – team leader
Laura Penhaul – performance manager
Alex Glasgow – mechanic, driver, navigator
Jo Craig – cook, driver, general support
Jonny Verman – additional photography into Paris
Paul Brown – media motorbike
Julie Cordier and her team – Paris outriders
Johnny Swanepoel and Helmut Scherz – filmcrew

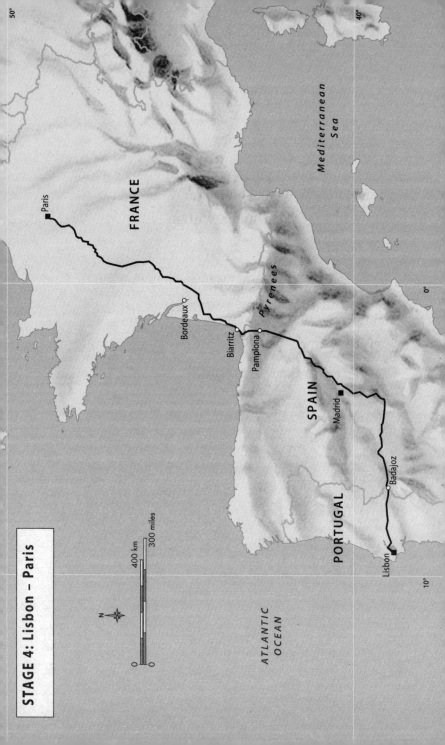

STAGE 4: Lisbon – Paris

19

The Sprint Finish

Day 74

> I'm back in Europe, which is a great feeling. Mentally I am well recov-
> ered after the flight and I slept as much as I could. Physically I am
> really sore. The body has started to go into recovery, so it will be good
> to get wheels rolling and get some miles in. I know that Spain is going
> to be punchy in terms of the terrain. No more flights, final push!

Stepping out of Lisbon Portela Airport felt like déjà vu. In February
2008 I had arrived here having flown in from Florida, picked up my
cardboard box off the carousel, stepped outside and rebuilt my bike,
completely alone. I remember feeling bad about abandoning the big
cardboard box, before clipping on my pannier bags and pedalling off.
I remember the call from Una, saying that the *Sun* newspaper had
been in touch asking if there was any way I could arrive in Paris on
the 14th rather than the 15th, and to carry a rose, so that they could
create a fun Valentine's Day story out of my circumnavigation world
record. I can see the funny side now, but at the time I was a tad indig-
nant. If I could have made it to Paris a day earlier I certainly would
have done, not for the want of a headline! But the sense was the same
this time round: I walked out of Lisbon arrivals with Paris very firmly
the talking point, the target, the excitement.

There is a joy in stepping off a plane in southern Europe that any
northern European can relate to. That glorious warmth, that promise
of a hot day at just gone 9 a.m. North America had rarely been a

summery experience and it was so exciting now to feel the warmth on
my bare arms and legs. The joy of no more flights was mixed in too – it
was a straight run from here. And there was also that welcome sense
of coming home: even though Portugal is a long way from Scotland in
every sense, it immediately felt more familiar and therefore safer.

There was a great welcome party of airport officials, some expats
and diplomats, including Kirsty Hayes, the British Ambassador to Portugal. Out of habit I went to offer her a fist pump, as our team rules
were to avoid shaking hands and the risk of spreading germs. Just in
time I realized and reverted to an old-fashioned handshake. Laura was
pedantic about germs, especially around flight time, and had a routine
involving alcohol gel, First Defence nasal spray and vitamins. Kirsty
said a few kind words of welcome, some photos were taken, and I was
soon ready to ride. I said a quick thank you to Stewart Fairley but had
no time for any real conversation before I was off, riding with Richard
Curtis, who would guide me through the first hours out of the city.

I wasn't allowed to cross the Tagus estuary straight out of Lisbon
on the busy A12 highway so I followed the city outskirts north on the
left bank of the river until I could find a smaller bridge. The cars
looked like toys, the roads dinky; the sights and smells were simply
wonderful – it was sheer joy to be back in Europe. Those first miles
were interrupted by traffic, but there was little feeling of urgency yet.
To be straight off the plane and racing would have been difficult, so I
was breaking myself in to leg 4 with a bit of company, some distraction
and an escape from the city. On the east bank of the Tagus I was
straight into countryside and Richard rode a few more miles with me
before turning back. His main role throughout the project had been
to be a critical friend on the filming, a point of contact if Una needed
any help with media-related questions. But in his own time Richard is
a keen roadie, and he certainly enjoyed the opportunity to share a few
sunny miles and set me on the road to Spain.

From here I would be climbing at an almost unnoticeable rate for
the rest of the day. The temperature also rose, and it was a blissful
honeymoon period. I rode through the small towns of Mora and Sou-
sel absolutely loving the surroundings – the arid farmlands, the fruit

orchards, the narrow road, the respectful drivers and the familiar crackle of cicadas.

Trevor Ward, a freelance cycling journalist who had ridden with me during training in Scotland on one of my favourite routes up Glen Lyon and Loch Tay, had flown out courtesy of Visit Scotland to ride for the next four hours. Trevor had been surprised and amused to be sent a health plan before he could join me so that he didn't pass on any infections. Our rambling chat was punctuated with a few media calls on the bike – a good warm-up for what was to come; I was already starting to answer questions about the finish, even though it felt a long way off, and having to reflect on a journey I was still on. He was sympathetic to the rigours of this routine, but the conversation took me to a different place, out of that short focus and performance mindset, trying to gain some perspective on the whole 80 Days, its successes and setbacks. I found our chat challenging but enjoyable, and realized that there was a hell of a lot of this to come, that our simple yet ridiculous routine on the road was about to be invaded by the world's press.

The high point of the day in terms of elevation came just before the border near the town of Elvas. I was now about 140 miles from Lisbon and picking up regular signs for 'Espanha'. The road cut under the Amoreira Aqueduct, a stunning 6km-long sixteenth-century water system for the fortified town, its four tiers of massive stone arches towering 40m above the road. It's hard not to be lost in the world around you when you are cycling through such historical places and I was kept in a state of blissful contentment, with that sense of fast, exciting progress that I had so missed in the larger countries.

The British Ambassador's aide road-tripped out with Jo, who was catching up, having landed five hours after us. I had to duck on to smaller roads as I crossed into Spain and skirted the town of Badajoz, the wide, arid plains of the borderlands making for a very fast rolling finish to the day through fields of olives, oranges and plums.

We parked in a wide gravel lay-by in an industrial area near some big trucks and storehouses. It wasn't perfect, but we didn't care; it would be a shortened sleep and then off at 4 a.m. as usual.

It's the end of day 74, and we have Alex back! We have got him back for more punishment and we also needed an injection of energy, and Alex brings that in abundance. It has been three-quarters of a normal day's riding, because we didn't land until gone 8 a.m. this morning and we have then jumped an hour forward into Spain. There was one big old climb, up 450m and then back down, making it 175 miles to here, so 282km, which is good. It has been such a pleasant change. It's simply beautiful being back in Europe. I enjoyed the scenery, the great roads. It was hot today – it is now 10.30 at night and it is still 25°C. I think it is going to continue to be pretty toasty until we are well north of Madrid. I sense this is going to be it from now on, the 4 a.m. starts and then pushing it a little bit later, just trying to get every possible hour off this record. And I hope the team are up for that – it is going to be a sleep-deprived push. I am just nervous about Spain. I know how hilly it is going to be, so it will be good to get the next couple of days out of the way. But for now, I'll get my head down for about four and a half hours.

Day 75

It's early doors day 75, and from here I hope to make it somewhere near Madrid today. Madrid is an important point, because one of the criteria for the Guinness World Record is to hit antipodal points, plus or minus a couple of degrees, and it's quite hard to find these points as most of the southern hemisphere is water. My route today goes eastwards, then starts to cut northeast, from the city of Ciudad Real. And it looks pretty punchy, up 800m at some points and well over 3,000m of climbing, plus it is going to be hot. It is over 20°C at four o'clock in the morning. So, a hot and hilly day, but that is what Spain is all about, so I am keen to get stuck into it.

The complete darkness started to lift soon into the graveyard shift. Even though the sun was a few hours coming, there was that gorgeous pre-dawn promise of a hot day as light escaped the horizon, fading into the consistent deep blue of a cloudless night sky. I was riding through wide, often fenceless fields of crops – golden blankets above which wisps of moisture hung in the still air, the faintest suggestion of mist above the damp earth, soon to evaporate into the warming day.

As the sun rose purposefully, this landscape started to change and became less open as I moved into the first ripples of foothills. The tell-tale sign was the field structure: smaller, less regular, fenced. After we'd cut on to a narrower road at Santa Amalia, where the RV had to breathe in to let anything pass, there were no road markings and almost no cars. Metal posts surrounded fields of sheep clustered around mangers of feed; the grasses were burnt brown and there was no greenness at all, except for the odd defiant weed along the verge.

By first break the wind was starting to pick up – a reassuring westerly, pushing me very gently in the direction of travel. I was in a very good place – alert, absorbed in the harsh beauty of this Mediterranean landscape, loving being sun-kissed and perfectly content with the easy riding. At break I had my usual ten-minute sleep and was up and eating second breakfast by the time Laura opened the RV door, then back on the bike in twenty minutes. Clockwork.

We had switched helmets – one carried the Bluetooth comms system, the other didn't – and for the next four hours I had back-to-back media calls. There had been a lot of back and forth with the team in Scotland about what the priorities were to allow me to keep focusing on the miles. But with the inevitable excitement building there was a lot to answer, and seeing as I was in a good place mentally and the conditions were fair, I was allowed to take priority calls. My tendency was always to say yes; Laura's, quite rightly, was always to ask, 'Do we need to?'

A live broadcast with *BBC Breakfast*, holding the phone on a selfie stick as I pedalled along, was not something I would condone, but I wasn't willing to stop, and the roads were quiet. Inevitably, all the journalists I spoke to were asking about what I was looking forward to and the emotions of Paris, questions that were hard to answer as I was so stuck in the moment. One, who will remain anonymous, went a step further, saying he would embargo this interview until I was in Paris, so could we have this conversation as if I were on the finish line? 'I can try,' I offered, realizing I still had 1,000 miles to go. Getting

ahead of yourself and making such assumptions is certainly a dangerous game.

Another 'don't try this at home' was my new practice of eating most
of my meals on the bike. Trying to get in 9,000kcal of food is hard
enough, even when your day lasts from 3.30 a.m. until 10 p.m., but of
course I was also now trying to sleep (or at least switch off) for a few
minutes each break, so my eating time off the bike was greatly
reduced. And we all knew that I would be pushing it late each day,
that we were no longer limited to sixteen-hours-a-day riding. To add
to the complicated fuelling strategy, my reflux was worse than ever,
and I was on omeprazole every day to pre-empt this, then Gaviscon
to settle it once it had started.

When the team posted a picture of me riding along spooning back
a bowl of porridge, it received an unexpected response from a minority who were angry at how terrible an example this was. I did feel like
pointing out that this wasn't going to become 'a thing', that kids
weren't about to be inspired by Mark Beaumont to pedal to school
eating their cereal. This practice, unsafe as it was, was born out of an
extreme situation – my inability to get enough calories onboard when
off the bike. This unexpected online response was fed back to me with
humour by the team, but we did decide to stop posting pictures of me
eating on the bike so that sensitive souls wouldn't get upset.

We would be getting less sleep up Europe, as we lengthened every
day on the bike in order to take every possible hour off the record, so
I wanted to keep the consistency of the naps during the breaks, even
if it was just five minutes' quiet time to hit reset and counter the tiredness. One advantage on this final stage was that we were not having to
account for any time zone changes, so this gave me an extra ten minutes each day compared to leg 3, which may sound daft, but believe
me, it makes all the difference.

Towards the evening I came across a familiar chap waiting for me at
the roadside. Niall Iain Macdonald was nomadically bike-packing his
way across Europe and, having followed my progress, had backtracked
by a day to find me. I first met Niall at the same time as Laura, at the
Kukri Adventure Scholarship, when he was fundraising to row solo
from New York to Stornoway. I had massive admiration for Niall's

dream but I worried about his campaign. He had been fundraising for the Scottish Association for Mental Health after suffering a breakdown in 2007, and having spent five weeks in the Atlantic without seeing dry land, I can tell you that it is not a good place to be if you suffer from mental illness; it drove me to the edge of my wits. Having said that, rowing the Atlantic is perfect if you just want to be left alone for a while!

I had met up with Niall a number of times over the years and unfortunately his North Atlantic bid had ended in a rescue after he suffered a back and head injury. But he was now in fine form, completely relaxed and enjoying exploring Europe, and it was nice to join someone on a journey that didn't have such a frenetic pace. I relaxed into his laid-back, unstressed company, and we pedalled along sharing stories in the golden light of a very warm Spanish evening. I very much enjoyed having a fellow countryman with me, reminiscing; this was really starting to feel like the homeward stretch, an easy spin into the sunset. In that moment, Paris felt like it was just over the horizon.

Then Niall punctured, and so mid-sentence I found myself carrying on alone.

After heading due east all day, the final 100km marked a turning point at Ciudad Real. We were momentarily disorientated in 'el centro', but after taking some wrong turns we then found our way out on a northeasterly tack. This 'Royal City', with its thirteenth-century roots, is on the modern-day commuter rail link to Madrid, 185km away. My task for the late shift was to split the difference, to get as close to the capital as possible.

The change in direction did nothing to alter the ascent, which continued until 335km into the day, then the final stint was a gradual and glorious descent. The wind was less helpful now but the terrain was fast, and spirits remained high. After the team's nerves about how tough Spain would be, this was a dream, and after nearly seventeen hours of riding we called it a day.

We have finished late, about half past ten, so I jumped straight into the RV off the bike, grabbed a shower, and am in bed as quickly as possible. It was a good day, about 2,700m of climbing, so slightly less than I expected – and absolutely beautiful. Despite the hills I have covered

260 miles (419km), which I didn't expect to do. I was definitely helped by a gentle tailwind and motivated by stunning riding. But also I was pushing it, I was really trying to get the miles in today. I feel that this is one of the last big milestones – let's just crack Spain. Get through what I remember from ten years ago to be a tough ride. Today was certainly easier than I expected. I felt good on the bike – I felt quite saddle-sore, but that is nothing to worry about. It feels crazy because I am hearing about my wife and friends, family, sponsors, all getting ready to fly to Paris, which makes the end start to feel pretty real!

Day 76

Early doors, start of day 76, just having a quick look at the map and we are very much heading northeast now. The plan is to skirt Madrid this morning – we are about 35 miles to our designated antipodal point, which has been agreed with Guinness World Records. And by the end of today we should really be pushing up towards the Pyrenees and the French border. We plan to cross the border pretty much on the most westerly point you can, so minimizing the climbs. In this final leg, my fear has always been about Spain, so today is crucial.

It was a very different day from the outset. We were already in the outer reaches of Madrid, busy commuter-ville. As we got closer to the capital we were diverted on to one road along the Jarama river that was little more than a track so our average speed suffered, despite it staying fairly flat along the valley. However, the biggest challenge was myself. Whether it was self-induced or unavoidable we couldn't figure out, but I was very unwell.

I rode out at 4 a.m. feeling fine, having managed some cereal and a coffee as usual. Then about an hour into the day, after having a large smoothie at 4.30 a.m., as always, I was sick. It came on pretty quickly, a wave of queasiness that gave me just enough time to pull on the brakes before I vomited into the verge. It was still pretty dark so the Follow Vehicle wasn't sure why I had stopped, and Laura and Alex would have assumed I had a puncture. Feeling better, as you normally do after such violent sickness, I carried on, but within twenty minutes another wave brought me to a halt, getting rid of whatever was left in my stomach.

I again managed to continue and rode into the outskirts of the pueblo of Arganda del Rey, my antipodal point outside the Madrid city centre. Following the Media Vehicle off the main road into the Plaza de la Alegría, I faced an oversized roundabout surrounded by apartment blocks. It took a few moments, in the shadows and orange glow of street lamps, to find the arrival party – Simon Manley, the British Ambassador to Spain. I'd expected him to be in his diplomatic car with a driver and perhaps an aide, but no, he had driven himself out, with his old mountain bike, and was kitted up in baggy shorts and white T-shirt with the slogan SPORT IS GREAT BRITAIN, ready to ride a few miles with me. What a wonderful effort at such an early hour.

Marcos Aroca and Daniel Fernandez from Menzies Aviation, still dressed in their high-vis vests, had driven out from Lisbon to find us at 6 a.m. with Laura's massage table, which had been left on the luggage carousel in our haste to leave the airport. I wasn't on top form for any of them but tried to share genuine thanks while Mike raced over with the official GWR paperwork to be signed, and the media boys captured the moment. I was no longer feeling sick, but I was very weak and unable to face food.

We pedalled back out, heading north, and I enjoyed a short descent with the ambassador, which was a blessing as his mountain bike had very soft tyres and he wasn't about to hold race pace. We enjoyed the best conversation I could muster on a day when at any other time in life I would have been tucked up in bed. By the time I was due east of Madrid, Simon had turned back; I was hugely grateful for his efforts to support me. And from then on it was a long, gradual climb for the next 230km, with a few saddles and false summits, but a solid eleven hours to the high point at 1,100m.

If, like the previous day towards Madrid, this had been ridden with a prevailing wind, it would have been similarly flowing; the road was never steep. But it wasn't. We had the double whammy – my being weak from sickness, unable to eat, and also facing a cracking headwind. The westerly had swung cruelly around to the north overnight, and while the graveyard shift had been fairly still, first light had turned on the switch.

By first break, Laura was pretty concerned: 'It's just typical. Today is the day Mark knows he is going into hills, one of the toughest days on the World. Last night we knew that the wind was turning north-east during the night, so it's straight on the nose and about fifteen knots. And to top it off he had projectile vomiting twice on the road, which is quite a concern for me, because he has a big hilly day, the headwind, and he needs his energy levels up. First thing I had given him a smoothie – that went down, followed by a wrap. Both foods he has had before, nothing was contaminated, we have all been drinking the milk, eating the eggs. Two bites into the wrap he threw up, then said he was full after the smoothie. Then I tried to give him electro-lytes. Fifteen minutes later he threw up again and then I gave him a tablet to try and settle his stomach. Then we went straight into climb-ing, and the problem is because we are in the Follow Vehicle we can't be right next to him and get food to him. He didn't have much in the tank. I've tried to give him jelly babies, or little biscuits made from oats and honey, which have stayed down – he has had eight small bis-cuits. Plus a peppermint tea and some mints to suck on. We then came into the outskirts of Madrid, lots of turns, lots of junctions, and he just hadn't eaten anything. My concern was that his blood sugar levels would be dropping, and I thought he was going to make a silly mis-take because his cognition is low. But we have made it to break time, and he is having a good sleep now.'

We were on the Meseta Central, the central Spanish plateau that rises to meet the mountainous north of Spain, and for well over six-teen hours I averaged less than 12.5 miles an hour. This woeful figure was somewhat skewed by a flying finish, 25km when I flew off the summit. I was hollow, running on empty, physically weak, mentally in neutral. I rode with my jaw limply open, slowly blinking, spinning my legs feebly into that mighty headwind. I was simply wishing time away. I no longer had the energy to be defiant. I was completely accepting, simply trying to limit damage by keeping any kind of momentum. I certainly wasn't putting up much of a fight, just not stopping, not for a second. I would put the time in, regardless of how far that took me.

At last, 300km into the day and already gone 9.30 p.m., I reached the high pass from Noviercas to Ólvega. It had been an incredibly slowly fought battle, into a gradient that should have been a breeze, with a favourable wind. I was already 85km down on an average day and my only hope now was to ride late and try and clear 200 miles. A pitiful target, but a triumph in a day from hell.

The descent was as open and gradual as the ascent, but enough to freewheel, pretty much for the first time in sixteen hours. In the darkness it was still warm, but nothing compared to being south of Madrid, so during the descent I cooled pretty quickly and couldn't wait to get off the bike and sleep.

I had kept my Garmin on the elevation screen, a graph of the climb, knowing I needed to reach 1,100m for the high point. Watching the screen showing speed, heart rate and power was too depressing, so a simple graph of height had been staring at me all day. But during the descent the lines were dropping steeply as I was going at three times the speed. I love descending in the dark, there is a heightened thrill to it. But this time I was shattered and just wanted it done. I was fixated on reaching 200 miles. That was all that mattered.

Coming off one of the steeper sections on to the flat, I was thinking, 'I don't know how far it is till the end of the day, till 200 miles.' So I took my left hand off the handlebars and was just flicking my Garmin screen off the descent graph and on to the distance screen when my front wheel hit something and I lost control.

I didn't go down immediately. The bike skittered out across the road as I tried to hold it, a tearaway ride as my front wheel violently speed-wobbled from side to side. I so nearly held it, but I didn't get my other hand back on the bars. Seconds after the impact, I went down.

The split second I hit the tarmac I was already clambering to my feet. I was in the oncoming lane and an HGV had been bearing down. Mercifully, it was on an uphill and had slammed on its brakes and come to a safe stop about ten metres away.

Laura, Mike and Alex were with me within seconds. After picking the bike up Mike waved a heartfelt thanks to the truck driver, and a minute later let him carry on, as I was guided over the crash-barrier out of harm's way. Our two motorhomes were parked in a dangerous spot, unable to pull off the road with crash-barriers on either side, but the media boys ran over to capture what was happening.

I leant on the barrier, legs shaking with adrenalin, with Laura looking after me. But I didn't stop long, a minute or two at most. I was so angry at the fall. Frightened, hurting, but mostly annoyed at myself, my carelessness in losing control of the bike.

'Is the bike OK, Alex?'

He was checking it over in the light of his head torch. 'Some scrapes, but it seems OK.'

'Right, let's go.'

'Please, just get into the RV and stop for a few minutes so I can check you over,' Laura asked calmly.

I was anything but calm. 'I'm fine, let's go.'

With that I grabbed the bike, swung it over the barrier back on to the road, mounted and freewheeled off. I felt very shaky as I clipped in. There was a scramble behind me as everyone raced for the RVs and followed. I hadn't checked anything, except pulling up my shorts for a quick look to see the road rash down my hip, and some stuff, including my phone, had fallen on to the road, but I simply rode off into the descent. It was pretty reckless.

Half an hour later we struggled to find an uneven lane to reverse the vehicles into, but it didn't matter – everyone was visibly shaken and relieved to be finally stopped. What a ridiculous day.

I'd been really lucky there wasn't anything coming the other way, or at least nothing closer than that truck. Nothing was really said about my reaction after the crash, but there were conversations about getting back to focusing on the short term. Whereas yesterday had been all about this flying victory lap to the finish, today had been a reminder that it wasn't over until it was over. There were definitely some hard miles still to be fought and this incident could have ended the 80 Days dream. It wasn't worth thinking about, but with less than five hours' sleep time left, some shut-eye was now the priority.

Alex gave me a hug, saying how much of a fright I had given him.

He had been at the wheel and directly behind me when I crashed. Laura gave me a hug too, like she often did at the end of the day, but this wasn't so much a well done as sheer relief that I was OK. Emotions were high, everyone was shattered.

It's the end of day 76, about half past ten at night, and it has been a really rough day, a hell of a day, especially when you compare it to yesterday when we flew and did 260 miles. I have covered 201 miles, and they were incredibly hard fought. I was sick first thing this morning, which is a first. I've had reflux but not full-blown sickness like that – and it just meant my energy levels were rock bottom. There were a lot of conversations about how to fuel me, how to get energy in, because I was fighting a hell of a headwind. Climbing, climbing, climbing – it would have been beautiful if it hadn't been so tough. And then by the end of the day, in the dark, I reached the high point and was descending, which would have been wonderful to finish the day, until I crashed. I am fine, but it could have been a hell of a lot worse. It has been a rough ride for everyone today. Not what I hoped for. What a hell of a battle, so hopefully tomorrow will be easier.

Day 77

It's hard to believe that my family fly out to Paris today. This fact makes the finish start to feel quite real. Considering the day that I had yesterday, I feel OK this morning. Just under four and a half hours' sleep and I feel all right; apart from losing a bit of skin on my right hip, there is no real damage from coming off the bike. This morning I am starting with a descent and another climb back up over the Pyrenees, just across from Pamplona and down to Biarritz, which is obviously back down to sea level. Then onwards across France into the Bordeaux region. To get into France – what a massive milestone, I can't wait. Today is Saturday and I hope we can finish this thing late on Monday, but we have Tuesday to play with as well if we need it. Yesterday was a great lesson about being consistent, keeping our focus short, because accidents and silly things can happen at any point. It's not done until it is done.

Eighty days from 4 a.m. on Sunday 2 July was anything up to 3.59
a.m. on Wednesday 20 September. We were on track for an evening
finish on Monday the 18th. But our block programme always allowed
for these small margins: seventy-five days of riding at 240 miles per
day, three days of flight time, plus two days of contingency – the
twelve hours per leg of 'faff' time. If the entire 18,000-mile plan had
gone perfectly, I would be finishing on 78 days and 0 hours. On this
'sprint finish' up leg 4 I hadn't yet hit the 240-mile-a-day average so I
was losing that advantage. But it looked close, very close, and I was
obsessed on the bike, transfixed by the idea of finishing on day 79, so
that the new record would be 78 days and whatever number of hours.
Finishing on day 80, the Tuesday, made my gut twist with fear that if
anything went wrong I might slip back over the 80 Days.

Richard Whitwell and Pete Latham from LDC had flown out to
ride with me today, with the help of Steve Foster behind the wheel.
Laura, as expected, was nervous about this, especially after riding on
the ragged edge from Madrid. I was obviously deep in the red and
needed to focus as best I could on the ride, to be alert and reactive. I
was more relaxed, as I knew both Rich and Pete would respect my
distance if I was struggling. I hoped that rather than distract me their
company would give me a change of focus. It wouldn't be the small
talk of strangers, which can be hard work when so shattered, it would
be the familiar company of friends. Plus, both are decent roadies.

However, they missed the early shift, a glorious 25-mile descent to
the Ebro river, out of the dark and into a heavily overcast but so far
still dry dawn. That bloody wind had died to nothing and while I was
pretty sore on the bike – a hangover from crashing – it was easy miles.

Pulling out of a lay-by near Cintruénigo, it gave me a real boost to
see their fresh and familiar faces. My crew were familiar, but far from
fresh – everyone bore the strain of getting it right on these final days
and was very sleep-deprived. After a brief spin across the well-named
'Depresión del Ebro' it was back into the hills, firstly up and over to
Pamplona, which coincided with about 100km and the first break of
the day.

By then the rain had started. It wasn't heavy to begin with, but
obviously settling in for the long haul. Pamplona is best known for the

running of the bulls, a fiesta known locally as San Fermín, and also for being a major waypoint on the Camino de Santiago, the famous pilgrimage across the north of Spain. Skirting Pamplona and nearby towns and villages with high medieval walls, Gothic-style churches and narrow wynds, it felt like we were pedalling through scenes from a picture postcard, albeit rather dark and wet ones on this occasion.

North of Pamplona we tackled the Pyrenees, though at one of its lowest passes – a mere 850m. The Carretera Pamplona-Behobia cuts through the valley on high bridges and tunnels, but cyclists are not allowed on this dual carriageway so we took to the old road which wove an intricate path of least resistance up and over the mountains, trying to hug the valley side, criss-crossing the highway at a few points. When we reached its high point just shy of Almandoz we considered ducking back on to the highway, which had very little traffic; it was a fast dash through a long tunnel or a punchy climb up and over the mountain, which would also add on quite a few miles.

The added miles I was less worried about as I had asked Mike to make sure we had at least 30 miles' buffer on the 18,000-mile target. Mike's aim was to cut it finer and finish as close to the 18,000 miles as he could get it, reasoning 'Why go further?' But I just couldn't face the risk of Guinness World Records turning around and questioning any miles, saying that we had come home just short of 18,000. There was no way to go back and do more!

A decade ago I had given myself a slightly ridiculous 300-mile margin of error for the same reason, but this time round with the level of planning and evidence I was happy with a 30-mile buffer. After all, what equated to a two-hour margin on about 1,200 hours of riding was still incredibly fine. With this current predicament, to fly through the tunnel or climb up and over despite the much slower progress, I couldn't face the guilt of knowingly breaking the rules of the road, so I was absolutely firm on this decision: we were going up.

It was a cracking climb, a real leg-sapping set of switchbacks on a narrow road that was rarely used – why would you drive this when there was a dual carriageway through the tunnel? The descent was sketchy, wet, with gravel on the corners, exciting and spectacular but not fast. Richard descended with a lot more confidence than Pete and me – I've always been timid on the big descents. It was very steep for 15km until we reached the Bidasoa river, which we then followed downstream, all the way to sea level and the border with France. In total it was over 50km of fast descending, meandering with every bend in the river.

The Bidasoa runs into the Bay of Biscay by the small town of Irun, between the better-known tourist meccas of San Sebastián on the Spanish side and Saint-Jean-de-Luz on the French. The border is the river itself for about 10km, so we zipped along very wet roads on the south bank, looking across at France, before crossing over a small bridge in the suburbs of Behobia.

Lunch stop had been a very wet affair, stripping off, changing and using a pile of talc powder to pull on new gloves. My fingers had still not recovered from the abuse of Around Britain back in April, and it didn't help my confidence on the descents having fingers with all the dexterity of a claw. Poor Rich and Pete had flown out thinking they would be basking in warm Spanish sunshine such as I had been boasting about west of Madrid at the time they had been packing their bags. They were not prepared for this inclement weather, but suffered it with smiles.

Through Saint-Jean-de-Luz we caught our first glimpse of the Bay of Biscay as we crossed the La Nivelle river with its rows of pleasure boats on their pontoons. Normally swarming with tourists, it was deserted, but the roads were busy and vehicles blasted us with jets of water to add to the stuff falling from on high. All in all it was comically wet, and I was glad for the company. Once we hit Biarritz we found our way inland to a bridge across the much bigger Adour river some distance upstream.

The Pyrénées-Atlantiques were not their normal beautiful self; it was a day of zinging along in the wet, watching your front wheel. Pete was getting visibly cold but doing a good job of pretending he was just fine. Tall and skinny, the chill got to him first, plus he just didn't have the right kit with him for this degree of foul weather. I eventually pulled up behind the RV and insisted, 'I've got enough kit to open a bike shop, just get in for a few miles and throw on some of my spare kit.' With that he agreed.

A short while later, riding with Rich, we crossed some train tracks on the diagonal. I took these at a wide angle.

Thud.

I didn't need to look back to know what had happened. I pulled up to see Rich in a tangle with his own bike, lying on the tarmac, trying to unclip a foot. He got quickly to his feet but I could see he was hurting physically and a tad embarrassed. Sophie Reed from LDC, who had coordinated their joining me, had made a big point about how they were here to support. At that moment we had a nearly hypothermic Pete in the van and Rich crashed in the wet. I had to laugh – not at Rich, but at the idiocy of the day.

Rich was fine – a bit of a sore hip and a few scrapes. And Pete soon rejoined us on the road.

'I got into the motorhome, we pulled away, and without even saying hello Laura told me to take my clothes off,' he told us. 'She is quite direct isn't she!'

'Yes, she is,' I laughed. I was used to Laura's no-nonsense ways.

The towns thinned out in the no-man's land of the Landes, an area of wetlands (which I can vouch for!) and pine forests we pedalled through in the growing dark. This was originally an inland sea, and the plateau that is left remains pretty featureless, an unfarmed and fairly infertile swathe. It was easy to tap out a steady pace in these perfectly flat, still conditions, encumbered only by the constant rain.

After exactly sixteen hours and two minutes of ride time we came to a stop in the parking area of a garage. The 2,300m of climbing had all happened in the first 90 miles, apart from a few coastal undulations, and we had made it just over 230 miles – disappointing, but triumphant, depending on how you looked at it.

That's the end of day 77, just gone ten o'clock at night, and I've covered about 130 miles and I am back in France. Just need to get back to Paris now.

'230 miles, Mark – you just said 130 miles!'

Ah yes, short-changed myself! It was beautiful coming through that last section of Spain, some big climbs over a small section of the Pyrenees then up the west coast of France, and it is now flat as a pancake. But it has been wet, very wet, as soon as we got back to France.

*

Rich, who had corrected me on my mileage, continued his piece to camera: 'An incredible day. I don't know how you have done that for another seventy-six days. My main reflection, apart from yourself clearly, is the incredible team you have got around you. The support and choreography is quite remarkable. There is some tremendous organization behind the scenes.'

'Did you enjoy it, Pete?' I asked. 'I know you got pretty cold and wet.'

'Yeah, suffered a bit with the cold and wet, but a beautiful ride, stunning scenery. Rained a heck of a lot today. But I echo what Rich says: it is amazing to see the team across two vans working seamlessly to keep Mark going. Mark is a cog in a big project; to get him there every day is staggering to see. Frightening to think that you have done that every day for two and a half months.'

I said goodbye to the guys, who would drive back to Biarritz and fly home to England. Unbeknown to me they were already discussing a quick turnaround to be in Paris. It had been the wettest day of the entire ride, but I was able to wind Laura up. 'I haven't crashed for ages' was an easy way to get her clambering around for something wooden to touch.

'Don't say that! Any last-minute disasters . . .'

She mothered me as I made a big puddle of my kit, pulled the compression pump on to my legs and tucked into a big bowl of pasta. Despite the conditions there was a different mood in camp. Twenty-four hours can make a world of difference on expedition and we were now in France, just shy of Bordeaux, within clear sight of the finish line.

From here I have another full day of riding and then things are looking good, barring any last-minute disasters, to arrive in Paris late afternoon on Monday. Last full day tomorrow.

Day 78

The rain woke me up in the night, and that is saying something. It's not too bad at the moment, but it's still wet air – it's going to be a pretty dreich day, as we say in Scotland. I'm going to leave the coast pretty quickly and head northeast towards Paris. And I've really left the big hills behind me now. The plan today, if I do a normal 240-miler, is to leave about 180 miles to finish off tomorrow. The wind is meant to come from the west, so it should be roughly helping me, or on my left shoulder – either way it won't hurt me. I am really hoping we can have some big rolling miles today; it should be quicker than yesterday morning for sure. All the team is pretty excited, but equally, last full day on the road, we just need to get up and going, to keep it consistent. There is still a long way to go and if we can get through today successfully we can start to think about the finish this time tomorrow.

As I stepped out at 4 a.m., someone turned the tap on: the graveyard shift was torrential rain. I didn't care, I really didn't. 'Give me all you've got!' I bellowed, grimacing as the water ran down my back and I pulled my fingers into a fist, wringing out the sodden gloves. It was bucketing down, but with every minute I was drawing closer to the end.

Dawn was an unconvincing event, light creeping in under the cloud base that shrouded the treetops. But it did slowly switch the tap off, and to my relief, having resigned myself to another sodden day, I found myself riding along quiet roads crossing the Gironde and the Dordogne.

Laura, normally pedantic about nutrition, seemed to be throwing caution to the wind. After a very successful raid of a boulangerie I was fuelled all morning on regular *pains au chocolat*, *pains aux raisins* and other delights. Goodness knows what Ruth McKean, my nutritionist, would have said about this strategy, but they certainly kept my spirits high.

Manni from MoonSport had raised his concern with Una that Johnny would be stretched capturing the finish, and they'd discussed the need for another media person. In turn, I was concerned that Johnny would be territorial about the photography, which was his real pride. It was decided that Johnny and Helmut should focus on the documentary filming and we should bring someone else in for stills.

A year earlier, when I had finished leading a London to Paris charity ride, I had asked a friend, Paul Brown, if he would be interested in getting involved. It was amazing to be sitting in Paris, having just cycled to the Arc with 150 others, and to hear his enthusiastic reaction. Paul's a professional drummer but also a passionate motorbike rider whom I had first met when I was leading Pro-Am races in the Alps. Starting as a motorbike marshal, he had developed his photo-moto responsibilities, carrying photographers and filmmakers on multiple cycle events. I wanted Paul on the final ride into Paris as he had an infectious enthusiasm and was a superb biker.

My second nomination was a chap called Johnny Cook. When I had cycled the North Coast 500, Johnny had come out off his own bat and photographed the whole ride. Considering I started at 6 a.m. on the Monday morning and finished at 8 p.m. on the Tuesday evening in diabolical weather, this was a serious commitment. I was lucky he did this as the official photos of the ride didn't turn out well, so I contacted Johnny, having not actually met him during the ride, to ask if I could pay him for his. They turned out to be an amazing set of artistic shots capturing the true grit of that journey.

Around the same time as Manni and Una were discussing the arrangements for the final push, another photographer called Jonny Verman had dropped me an email saying he would love to get involved in the end of the trip. Apparently, a few years ago at a talk this Jonny had come up to me to say he would love to come and photograph an expedition with me. I wasn't on my emails, but Mum was, and she assumed this was the same Johnny – Scottish Johnny, as Johnny Cook had become known over the preceding weeks, as a way to differentiate him from South African Johnny.

Jonny flew into Biarritz and the Media Vehicle shot off during the morning to pick him up. When I came in for my break, soaked through, I went straight into the motorhome to eat and change kit. Jonny came to the door to say hello and we had a quick chat. I was surprised that he didn't have a Scottish accent, as he was from near Inverness. Jonny was definitely English. But I honestly didn't think about it, I was too wrapped up in my own world. I just welcomed him to the team.

A few hours later the Follow Vehicle came alongside me and Laura called out of the window, saying that Una really needed to speak to me. The weather wasn't great and I just wanted to stay focused.

'Can it not wait?' I asked.

'I really think you should speak to her,' came the reply, and I could tell something was amiss.

I swapped helmets, so that I had the Bluetooth headset, and cycled ahead of the vehicle to make the call.

'I need to tell you something,' Mum started. 'Something really bizarre has happened. As you may have already realized, we have got the wrong Jonny!'

All afternoon this had built into an awkward situation in the vehicles – Mike, Laura and Alex suspected a mix-up, but couldn't say anything in front of Jonny. It was pretty obvious to everyone that 'Scottish Johnny' was not Scottish. Mike was worried that I would take the news very badly and seemed to be of the impression that English Jonny was going to be sent home.

I laughed. What else could you do? A few days from the finish, what a ridiculous mix-up! And I felt for poor English Jonny. I certainly didn't want him to think that he was unwanted.

'But this Jonny has never even ridden on the back of a motorbike,' Mum reasoned.

'Neither has Scottish Johnny, as far as I am aware. He is here now, he is a professional photographer, so let's just crack on. On the grand scale of everything, this is not a big problem. We will look back and laugh about it.'

So English Jonny stayed and knew nothing about the mix-up, for the time being.

By the 200km mark I was passing Angoulême, then cutting through the eastern reaches of the Cognac region. I was now in the heart of a well-populated expat community so I spent very little of the day cycling alone. Perhaps ten to fifteen cyclists joined me and there were many more roadside well-wishers. This level of attention made the day pass quickly and added to the growing sense of excitement. I could feel a magnetic pull towards Paris, a sense of finale, an agitation to get through today so that I could get on with tomorrow.

Some of the conversations as we cycled were wonderful and supportive; some were just bizarre. These riders, especially those who had retired to the area, obviously had time on their hands. There seemed little comprehension of how shattered I might be, that this was the culmination of 18,000 miles in the saddle; they treated their miles with me as a Sunday ride, either for nonsense small-talk or to bombard me with questions. I didn't have any enthusiasm to engage with all this. Obviously it wasn't their fault that I was so 'in the zone' that I couldn't tolerate waffle. But it amused me, this disconnect – their being a million miles from where my head was.

There were also quite a few press calls to be taken on the bike, although Laura and the team were doing their best to help with these, so I spent the afternoon answering the inevitable questions. What are you looking forward to most when you finish? What was your favourite place?

Having maintained such discipline for two and a half months, I was struggling to let go a little bit and allow myself to believe that I was getting to the point I had visualized thousands of times during the journey. It had always been about reaching this final run-in and I'd often imagined what it would feel like. Reality didn't match up yet. I was still focused on the road in front of me, yet I was pinching myself, saying, 'We are nearly there!'

It's the end of day 78 and I am just 180 miles from Paris, which is pretty ridiculous! I have done about 239 miles. There aren't many places to pull off this road, so we are stopped in a tiny parking bay. When we left the coast this morning it was absolutely bucketing with rain, so the first few hours were miserable. The rain has come and gone today, but I have not really minded it too much. I guess there was such a transition today – I sensed the team getting excited about the finish; there are so many conversations about the finish. Tomorrow is going to be pretty full on from the start. Tomorrow is going to be incredible. It's about a 180-mile roll-in from here, so I will start at 4 a.m. as usual, try and break up the day as normal with four-hour sets, and should finish five to six o'clock. Maybe I should be happier at this point, but there are still miles to ride. And this time tomorrow, if all goes well, it'll all be over. I will be back with Nicci and the kids, and Una, my mum, who has of course run Base Camp in Scotland, like she has for all my trips. And a lot of sponsors and friends are already in Paris, waiting for me.

It is going to be a lot of fun. It's about half past ten, so I will get about four and a half hours' sleep and I'll encourage the crew to get as much sleep as possible as well, as everyone looks a little bit cooked. Tomorrow is going to be massive – the end of 80 Days!

Day 79

It's day 79 . . . which is quite neat! Today is the last day I have to do this getting up at half past three. I'm quite looking forward to not getting up at half past three. How about you, Laura?

'Yeah, I don't mind!'

Rubbish! Since the second of July getting up at half past three has become the norm, but I don't think it ever becomes easy. It's 7°C outside with quite a clear start. I think it is meant to get wet later on, which is a shame. I'd love to finish in Paris in the dry, but I don't care, come rain or shine. I am sure once I have had a coffee and wake up I am going to start to become quite excited. It is going to be a busy old day with quite a lot of media from the start. I also hope there will be moments when I can stop and think about what is going on. Because this is obviously not just the last seventy-nine days, it's the last couple of years of planning, and it's also the culmination from me as a twelve-year-old boy pedalling across Scotland twenty-two years ago. Practising, going on lots of adventures, going further and further, and then this has been my ultimate dream. It's always been about the circumnavigation and the world record so . . . I really hope we can make it happen today. I don't think it will feel real until after I get to stop and get a different perspective on it all. I just want to get the wheels rolling for the last time and ride till dawn, ride till breakfast, get my power nap, follow the routines we have been doing for the last seventy-nine days, and then hopefully Paris should appear on the horizon. The whole team seem excited and there is definitely a lightness, a sense of anticipation, which is fantastic. I didn't know before this trip how I would deal with this close-knit teamwork, because I have never done it before. But I have absolutely loved it. The camaraderie has seen me through what has been by far the toughest expedition of my life, so it goes without saying that I couldn't have done it without the team. It is amazing to see them really starting to live the emotion of the finish, how much it means to all of them. So, let's get on the bike for the last time and get this done!

Counting down the lasts. That last morning smoothie, slightly warmed for the same effect as a hot-water bottle at 4.30 a.m.; the last dawn, creeping in slowly – which was one to remember. I was on tiny roads after passing Tours and crossing the Loire, heading to the east of Chartres. Despite the forecast it was a glorious foggy day, moody and utterly calm. Apt. Ahead lay mayhem, but for that hour I felt at peace, absorbed in the world around me. The phone hadn't started ringing, the world hadn't woken up yet, and I just spun my legs like I had since the start of July. It felt wonderful, trance-like. I shivered whenever I found pockets of cold air before cycling back into the warmth, knowing the sun would soon cut through. It climbed slowly over the bank of cloud until my foreground was clear and the sky was cloudless, the tree-lined valley silhouetted above me.

I kept my leg- and arm-warmers on. Despite the sunshine it felt like autumn as I pedalled into northern France.

Just 100 miles to go – the media boys came alongside excitedly, capturing the moment.

Now 50 miles to go – more photos, punctuating the countdown.

But on these tiny quiet roads I was given no sense of building towards Paris; there was just the odd bit of farm machinery or a van. I guess only local traffic would choose such a labyrinth.

Si Richardson was waiting for me soon before lunch break on a sweeping right-hander. He had driven out from Paris with his Global Cycling Network cameraman to capture the final hours. It had been a pleasure sharing the first day with him, and the team at GCN had done a royal job sharing the journey with a global audience. Out of those who had joined me through Australia, New Zealand and North America, the majority said they had first heard of the 80 Days through the weekly GCN coverage of my progress.

As I rode up and Si pedalled alongside, I was struck by the thought that I'd had my final solo moment on the World. From that point on it was given over to everyone around me who would share the excitement of the finish.

On those final 50 miles, the pressure grew and grew for my support team. English Jonny was now riding on the back of Paul's motorbike and it was a bit more complicated having a motorbike in the mix, and they were getting the blame for a lot of the uncertainty. Laura was in the back of the RV, quietly trying to calm Alex behind the wheel, and Mike was navigating, while also taking back-to-back press calls. It was similarly busy for me on the bike, and the miles flew by in a blur of conversations with journalists and, when possible, with Si.

In the small town of Saint-Arnoult-en-Yvelines, the Follow Vehicle turned left off the main street while Si and I carried on, having not seen them. I sensed something was wrong, so Si checked the Strava route on his computer and saw we were off course; meanwhile, Alex had abandoned the vehicle and run back to the junction. Helmut had set up an in-vehicle GoPro to capture the frantic intensity as the team fought its way to Versailles. From there, we were in the hands of professional outsiders whose job it was to give us a clear path to the Arc de Triomphe.

About 10km after we went off course, in the village of Bullion, I was doing a live Sky Sports News interview while riding behind the Follow Vehicle when the road got narrower, rougher, and then ended in a dirt track under some chestnut trees. Mike switched driving duties with Alex, who looked like he was about to explode. After reversing, we backtracked through town and found the correct road. It was annoying, unexpected complexity in these small roads. But I stayed relaxed: even if it took a few more hours than expected we were finishing today, there was no doubt. I could tell my team were shouldering the stress for me in this final run-in.

Twenty kilometres later we had the steep valley of Gif-sur-Yvette to navigate and reached a 'low vehicle' warning sign. Si and I made a quick decision to carry on while the motorhomes found the long way round. Rejoining the main D306, near La Croix de Fer, Si's route map saved us again as we shot past a left turn, did a U-turn and climbed steeply out of a valley. As we rejoined the road north to Versailles, we came across Mike and Alex standing at the roadside, looking relieved and surprised in equal doses. How had we possibly known the way?

Because those few hours were so confusing, so manic, it felt like Versailles was a very long time coming. I kept thinking of Harriet and Willa on the finish line in Paris, alongside the gathered press, none of whom would be very impressed if they had to wait around for hours. It was a ridiculous concern to have, considering the magnitude of the moment, but I was stressed about keeping people waiting.

As Rue Jean Mermoz joined Avenue de Paris we came to a halt and met quite an entourage. First there were the professionals – a car and three motorbikes set up to guide us quickly to the finish. Then there were about fifteen cyclists from KOGA who had ridden down over the past forty-eight hours from the north of Holland to ride in with me. Then there were lots more, a peloton of cyclists, all with their own stories about being there, all ready to ride that final 15km.

I nipped into the motorhome to take off my leg- and arm-warmers as Mike discussed plans with the guides and the media boys raced around setting up the cameras for the finish.

Laura jumped in: 'Are you ready?'

I took a deep breath, feeling a bundle of nerves. 'I think so.'

With butterflies fluttering in my stomach, I set out feeling pretty empty. I was so caught up in what was going on around me, the busy road and the mayhem of support vehicles and cyclists. I felt all alone on the gentle descent into the suburbs of Paris, which was effortless riding, because the others were keeping a respectful distance, bunched up twenty metres behind me. This felt bizarre, so I beckoned for them to come forward, to ride with me.

There were a few snatched conversations: with one guy who had cycled out from England to be there; with one of the designers from KOGA who had worked on my World bike; with Paul on the motorbike, beaming from ear to ear, encouraging me to soak up every moment. I nodded obligingly, but felt pretty overwhelmed by it all.

The lead guide was nicknamed 'Le Moustache' for very obvious reasons – he was the proud owner of what in the UK would be called comedy handlebars, but perhaps in Paris was just a rite of passage. Le Moustache was a retired Parisian policeman I had worked with before, and despite the chaos around him he was the epitome of chilled, chain-smoking his way to the finish, pulling his big motorbike alongside the guide car to be handed a lit cigarette through the window. A small lady on one of the other motorbikes was doing the lion's share of the work, racing forward to each junction to stop the traffic and doing her best audition for *Fast & Furious*.

More and more people joined in. My cousin Catie, who had been messaging pretty much every day of the ride, appeared at one of the only sets of traffic lights we didn't jump through for a quick selfie and hug. It was wonderful to see the efforts so many people had made to be there. Then in the final furlongs Neil Laughton and David Fox Pitt pitched up on their penny farthings. Old friends and supporters of all things adventure-related, Neil was aboard his black penny, adorned with a large brass horn, wearing tails and a top hat; David was on his bright red penny, wearing a tweed jacket and pith helmet. They had enjoyed a long, perhaps slightly liquid lunch and were ready to take on the unforgiving cobbles of central Paris. They fell a number of times on the way to the finish but did a fine job, adding to the sense of surreal madness.

Through Sèvres and across the Seine I was now back within the Périphérique, Paris's ring-road, so houses gave way to streets of shops and cafés – a bustling late Monday afternoon through Boulogne-Billancourt. Central Paris looks like a spider's web, with the Arc de Triomphe at its centre, and after turning on to Avenue Victor Hugo and kinking around the Longchamp racecourse on to the wide Boulevard Suchet, the final roundabout saw us turn on to Avenue Foch.

There, straight ahead, about a kilometre up a very gradual incline, was the Arc. The finish.

Those final metres, those final minutes, went on a lot longer than they should have as the road was rammed. Despite the best efforts of our guides, no amount of flashing lights and flashy driving was getting us through nose-to-tail traffic. I caught snatches of comments, glimpses of Alex's beaming face peering out of the windscreen of the Follow Vehicle, and breathed deeply, trying to take it all in, feeling overwhelmed.

We fought our way to the top of Avenue Foch and then I stopped with Jo at the zebra crossing, but with the constant flow of traffic there was no easy way to cross the road for what seemed a very long time. Then I saw Tony Humphreys. What was he doing here? He was stepping into the six lanes of traffic, with Mum behind him. Between the two of them and Jo they brought everyone to a stop and I made a dash for it. I needed to get to the finish line on the other side of the road, fifty metres away. There was obviously no way they could have set up a finishing line on the main road. Perhaps it would have been easier to dive into the mayhem of the Arc and go all the way around – that was the choice that the Follow Vehicle took. We instead eventually streamed across the road and, scooting my bike on to the pavement between the two converging avenues, I pedalled those final metres.

There was too much to take in, too many people, but the first person I saw was Lindsay Whitelaw from Artemis, holding one end of the finish line tape. I stopped and gave him a massive hug. Heather, my big sister, was on the other end. But where were Nicci and the girls? I turned around, scanning for them.

Harriet was dressed in a bright mustard dress, Willa in a smart green jacket. It used to be Harriet's – she had grown so much in the last few months. And Nicci, holding them both, beaming with happiness, looked absolutely beautiful.

I was oblivious to the cameras for a moment as I picked up the girls. Over their shoulder I spotted Mum, who joined in. Then, regaining my composure, I turned to a wall of press unlike anything I had ever experienced, a sea of flash guns and TV cameras. I didn't know where to look, what to say. When I did speak, I sounded hoarse, trying to answer questions that volleyed in all at the same time.

Amid this I felt a tap on my back, and turned to see Mum again, who was straight into the practicalities. It was so busy, everyone jostling around me, but Mum calmly introduced the Deputy Ambassador to France, Matthew Lodge, and Anna Orford, the official from Guinness World Records. I had forgotten that we still needed to verify the finish, which then reminded me that I hadn't yet switched off my Garmin to mark the end of the ride.

Matthew had a letter to sign on behalf of the British Embassy, marking the official finish time. After this was done, Anna gathered everyone's attention to announce the two new Guinness World Records, producing framed certificates.

The next few hours were a blur of interviews and photos. The hundreds who had made it to the finish all wanted to speak to me, to get a photo. I felt scrambled, trying to see everyone. Laura kept checking on me, wanting to keep this as short as possible, to get me back to the hotel quickly for some recovery. But I didn't want to let anyone down.

When we did get away from the press, it was time to thank the crew. The utter relief, the euphoria – you could see it painted on the faces of everyone who had been a part of this unbelievable journey. It was all too intense to take in objectively. This was the culmination of 18,035 miles of cycling through sixteen countries in less than eighty days. Popping champagne in the team huddle, Alex did a much better job than I did at showering everyone.

I tried to collect my thoughts.

Well, we are back where we started, at the Arc de Triomphe. What an amazing last day. My head was a bit scrambled riding into Paris, but the emotion definitely came at the finish there. It's just brilliant to be met by so many people, what a massive finale. And the new Guinness World Record for the fastest circumnavigation by bicycle is . . . 78 days, 14 hours and 40 minutes. So we made it – well done, team!

The taxi ride back to the hotel was where the finish line finally made sense to me. I was cuddling Harriet, I was back with my family, it was all over. I didn't have to get back on my bike. We had done it.

Around the World in 80 Days.

Day 80

I don't need to get on my bike . . .

I was about a hundred metres from the Champs-Elysées, a stone's throw from the Arc de Triomphe. And yes, it was a bizarre feeling to wake up and not have to ride my bike. When I say bizarre, I mean I felt about the worst I have ever felt after an expedition. Just that feeling where you physically hurt down to your toenails. When you finally let go mentally, it's amazing what the physical reaction is.

I had walked downstairs but was unable to go into breakfast, knowing that most people staying in the hotel were there to see me. I just couldn't face them. Instead I walked outside, hobbled down the street and sat on the steps of another building until Nicci found me and gave me a hug. I felt utterly broken. But the recovery process could finally start. The next few months were about coming down from this, normalizing my fitness – even walking up and down a flight of stairs hurt.

I said to Nicci that I was looking forward to catching up on all the social media comments, until I realized that the final Facebook Live had 300,000 views and over 4,000 comments. It was pretty nuts. I had seen a post from Mike Hall's mum, which meant a lot, and to which I had replied – he is the only other person who I know speculated about whether you could cycle Around the World in 80 Days.

Back at the hotel, just hours after the finish, we'd had a friends and family drinks party, hosted by Artemis. I had grabbed a quick shower, thrown on some smart clothes for the first time in months and hobbled along, really just wanting to sleep. But it was wonderful to have an hour to stop, look around and realize how much this journey had meant for so many people. Lindsay Whitelaw spoke, then Mum, then Mike, then Laura, and all said a few very kind words which meant the world to me.

That was my finish line, back with the people who had supported me, believed in the dream.

And after months of talking about it and imagining it, I got what I had been looking forward to – a glass of fine red wine.

It tasted absolutely disgusting.

Epilogue

From John Schnell in Canada: 'The day Mark finished in Paris, I finally rode my bike for the first time in fourteen years. It felt like I had been reacquainted with an old friend! I've been riding almost every day since then. I'm sixty-six years old now, so my aspirations aren't what they might have been thirty years ago. But hey! Mark Beaumont and the entire team have already inspired me to do something no one else has been able to, since my accident fourteen years ago. I'm riding my bike again! #inspiration Thanks, buddy!'

And of the thousands of comments I received after the finish line in Paris, here are a few which made me smile:

'When I heard you talking on the BBC about your plans I laughed, and my mate and I both agreed that this isn't possible. You have proven us wrong and we have been with you all the way. A privilege to be part of the impossible made possible.'

'Thankfully your biking is better than your rowing! Well done sir, top job.'

'Yey, the end! There are no words to sum up that achievement! To you and your crew.'

'Unbelievable stuff, Mark. Your rides and books inspire more people than you could ever know. I'm just one of the anonymous many who have been changed by your achievements.'

'Had a tear in the eye watching the live stream. Congratulations, chapeau. See you on the road.'

'Victory lap?'

Artemis World Cycle Statistics

A note on distances and data. The data from my Garmin Edge 1000s (the bike computers) was synced to my main Garmin account each evening, and the data from the 920XTs (the watches) was synced to a back-up Garmin account. The main Garmin account was auto-synced to my public Strava account. You can go online to see all my ride data for Around the World in 80 Days (strava.com/athletes/MarkBeaumont). The original data from my Garmin account was submitted to Guinness World Records and they were made aware of the following discrepancies.

In cycling and running circles it is a well-known yet confusing fact that Strava logs data slightly differently from Garmin – even though it is taking that data from the Garmin unit, as opposed to making its own recording. So, you can end up with the same day's ride looking slightly different on your Garmin and Strava accounts. The explanation given on the Strava website is as follows: 'Strava activity data may be different than what your Garmin displays because Strava analyzes all data independently once uploaded, regardless of the device used to record the file.' I am not sure this helps me understand how or why this should happen, and over the course of the World it seemed to make no difference in overall data for distances and time – discrepancies just seem to average themselves out. However, in my video diaries, recorded in the moment and featured throughout this book, I am referencing individual data points I read straight off my Garmin. In the main text and here in this appendix we have used the exact numbers as they appear on Strava. It should be noted that ride time measures time that wheels are rolling, as opposed to total time on the bike.

AROUND THE WORLD IN 80 DAYS

DAY	Date	DAILY DISTANCE		CUMAL.	RIDE TIME	ASCENT	SPEED (Kmph)	
		Miles	Km	Km		Metres	Avge.	Max.
1	02 Jul	247.3	398.0	398.0	15h 19m	1852	26.0	57.6
2	03 Jul	244.1	392.9	790.9	15h 09m	2177	25.9	59.0
3	04 Jul	248.9	400.5	1191.4	15h 24m	1345	26.0	58.7
4	05 Jul	245.5	395.1	1586.5	15h 32m	1192	25.4	48.6
5	06 Jul	242.6	390.5	1977.0	15h 33m	1806	25.1	44.3
6	07 Jul	243.5	391.9	2368.9	15h 45m	2224	24.9	52.6
7	08 Jul	245.6	395.3	2764.2	15h 31m	2213	25.5	49.7
8	09 Jul	261.7	421.2	3185.4	15h 06m	1615	27.9	51.5
9	10 Jul	228.0	367.0	3552.4	14h 16m	1516	25.7	57.2
10	11 Jul	244.9	394.1	3946.5	15h 20m	2594	25.7	68.4
11	12 Jul	239.2	385.0	4331.5	15h 39m	2785	24.6	54.0
12	13 Jul	248.1	399.3	4730.8	15h 12m	3034	26.3	64.1
13	14 Jul	240.4	386.9	5117.7	14h 46m	2567	26.2	62.6
14	15 Jul	249.1	400.9	5518.6	15h 24m	1703	26.0	52.6
15	16 Jul	252.2	405.8	5924.4	15h 12m	942	26.7	43.6
16	17 Jul	237.7	382.5	6306.9	15h 22m	578	24.9	34.6
17	18 Jul	228.4	367.6	6674.5	15h 28m	1524	23.8	49.3
18	19 Jul	234.5	377.4	7051.9	15h 53m	2521	23.7	66.2
19	20 Jul	246.0	395.9	7447.8	15h 41m	2695	25.2	60.5
20	21 Jul	239.4	385.3	7833.1	15h 25m	2436	25.0	58.3
21	22 Jul	239.3	385.1	8218.2	15h 57m	2282	24.1	66.6
22	23 Jul	230.0	370.1	8588.3	15h 52m	3768	23.3	72.4
23	24 Jul	238.5	383.8	8972.1	15h 54m	2027	24.1	67.0
24	25 Jul	199.0	320.2	9292.3	14h 29m	2972	22.1	66.6
25	26 Jul	264.3	425.4	9717.7	15h 45m	2429	27.0	70.2
26	27 Jul	219.5	353.3	10071.0	13h 41m	1474	25.8	61.6
27	28 Jul	188.8	303.9	10374.9	13h 48m	1263	22.0	69.5
28	29 Jul	217.9	350.6	10725.5	13h 44m	1602	25.5	67.0
29	30 Jul	119.0	191.5	10917.0	7h 40m	1392	24.9	53.3
30	31 Jul	252.2	405.8	11322.8	15h 28m	2445	26.2	65.2
31	01 Aug	237.9	382.9	11705.7	15h 42m	1429	24.4	54.4
32	02 Aug	233.9	376.5	12082.2	15h 39m	1087	24.0	47.2
33	03 Aug	249.1	400.9	12483.1	15h 18m	484	26.2	60.8
34	04 Aug	261.9	421.5	12904.6	15h20m	1299	27.5	49.3
35	05 Aug	261.4	420.7	13325.3	15h28m	1747	27.2	51.8
36	06 Aug	240.6	387.2	13712.5	15h33m	1220	24.9	48.6
37	07 Aug	224.6	361.5	14074.0	15h 45m	1529	23.0	57.2
38	08 Aug	245.4	395.0	14469.0	16h 10m	1502	24.4	57.6
39	09 Aug	191.8	308.7	14777.7	14h 21m	1858	21.5	55.4

🚲 Paris to Paris, 2 July to 18 September 2017 🚲

HEART RATE		START LOCATION		END LOCATION		NOTES
Avge.	Max.					
107	142	Paris	—	Bree	—	France/Belgium
99	137	Bree	—	Pattensen	—	Netherlands/Germany
98	134	Pattensen	—	Seelow	—	–
94	128	Seelow	—	Rogezewek	—	Germany/Poland
96	128	Rogezewek	—	Zventezeris	—	Into Lithuania
100	135	Zventezeris	—	Beksi	—	Latvia
97	127	Beksi	—	Mostovskoye	—	Russia
94	136	Mostovskoye	—	New Annino	—	–
97	136	New Annino	—	Lavrovka	—	*Tooth/elbow crash*
102	141	Lavrovka	—	Hentyh	—	–
100	135	Hentyh	—	Yakshur-Bod'ya	—	–
102	132	Yakshur-Bod'ya	—	Suksun	—	–
97	136	Suksun	—	Kamyshlov	—	–
96	125	Kamyshlov	—	Golyshmanovo	—	–
97	130	Golyshmanovo	—	Omsk	—	–
96	123	Omsk	—	Ubinskoye	—	–
100	131	Ubinskoye	—	Bolotnoye	—	–
100	135	Bolotnoye	—	Tyazhinskiy	—	–
101	135	Tyazhinskiy	—	Uyar	—	–
99	135	Uyar	—	Alzamay	—	–
100	132	Alzamay	—	Zalari	—	–
102	140	Zalari	—	Baikal Reserve	—	–
100	130	Baikal Reserve	—	Novoselenginsk	—	–
102	136	Novoselenginsk	—	Bornuur	—	Into Mongolia
101	132	Bornuur	—	Dalanjargalan	—	–
101	136	Dalanjargalan	—	Erenhot	—	Finish at Chinese border
109	139	Erenhot	—	ChaharYouyi Houqi	—	Into China
99	131	ChaharYouyi Houqi	—	Badaling	—	🚲 **END OF STAGE 1** 🚲
–	–	Perth	—	Darkan	—	Australia
97	135	Darkan	—	Jerramungup	—	–
97	138	Jerramungup	—	Salmon Gums	—	–
95	129	Salmon Gums	—	Balladonia	—	–
92	119	Balladonia	—	Eucla	—	–
94	130	Eucla	—	Mundrabilla	—	–
98	133	Mundrabilla	—	Bookabie	—	–
101	133	Bookabie	—	Moseley	—	–
101	141	Moseley	—	Middle Beach	—	–
100	136	Middle Beach	—	Willalooka	—	–
106	141	Willalooka	—	Taroon	—	*Support Vehicle written off*

| DAY | Date | DAILY DISTANCE | | CUMAL. | RIDE TIME | ASCENT | SPEED (Kmph) | |
		Miles	Km	Km		Metres	Avge.	Max.
40	10 Aug	209.8	337.6	15115.3	15h 36m	461	21.6	38.9
41	11 Aug	245.2	394.6	15509.9	16h 07m	1443	24.5	49.7
42	12 Aug	250.0	402.3	15912.2	16h 43m	1793	24.1	68.4
43	13 Aug	280.7	451.7	16363.9	18h 49m	3082	24.0	73.4
44	14 Aug	50.0	80.5	16444.4	3h 25m	388	23.5	55.4
45	15 Aug	223.3	359.3	16803.7	16h 16m	2982	22.1	69.5
46	16 Aug	227.5	366.1	17169.8	16h 52m	2832	21.7	61.2
47	17 Aug	176.8	284.6	17454.4	12h 10m	1188	23.4	64.1
48	18 Aug	249.4	401.3	17855.7	17h 58m	3286	22.3	77.8
49	19 Aug	146.1	235.2	18090.9	9h 56m	987	23.6	55.8
50	20 Aug	233.4	375.7	18466.6	15h 42m	3263	23.9	70.2
51	21 Aug	243.5	391.8	18858.4	15h 54m	2571	24.6	65.2
52	22 Aug	239.6	385.6	19244.0	16h 10m	2109	23.8	67.3
53	23 Aug	229.7	369.7	19613.7	15h 50m	3079	23.3	64.1
54	24 Aug	226.6	364.6	19978.3	15h 46m	3045	23.1	73.1
55	25 Aug	230.8	371.4	20349.7	15h 53m	3371	23.4	79.9
56	26 Aug	225.1	362.2	20711.9	15h 59m	3213	22.6	73.8
57	27 Aug	250.4	403.0	21114.9	15h 54m	2274	25.3	64.4
58	28 Aug	239.0	384.7	21499.6	15h 59m	2255	24.1	68.4
59	29 Aug	195.7	314.9	21814.5	15h 53m	1501	19.8	–
60	30 Aug	183.1	294.7	22109.2	15h 42m	1021	18.8	48.2
61	31 Aug	209.3	336.9	22446.1	16h 08m	542	20.9	40.3
62	01 Sep	269.8	434.2	22880.3	16h 29m	788	26.3	55.8
63	02 Sep	270.2	434.8	23315.1	16h 13m	859	26.8	49.3
64	03 Sep	243.7	392.2	23707.3	15h 57m	1503	24.6	64.1
65	04 Sep	249.6	401.7	24109.0	16h 01m	1620	25.1	68.4
66	05 Sep	238.7	384.1	24493.1	16h 01m	966	24.0	42.5
67	06 Sep	235.3	378.7	24871.8	16h 17m	1620	23.2	51.1
68	07 Sep	243.8	392.4	25264.2	16h 12m	2058	24.2	64.4
69	08 Sep	241.6	388.8	25653.0	15h 55m	1011	24.4	45.0
70	09 Sep	235.1	378.3	26031.3	16h 29m	1011	22.9	57.2
71	10 Sep	250.5	403.1	26434.4	16h 59m	2719	23.7	79.6
72	11 Sep	242.8	390.8	26825.2	16h 48m	2708	23.3	62.3
73	12 Sep	71.2	114.6	26939.8	4h 31m	830	25.3	64.1
74	13 Sep	175.4	282.2	27222.0	11h 44m	1603	24.0	67.3
75	14 Sep	260.6	419.4	27641.4	16h 47m	2760	25.0	65.9
76	15 Sep	201.9	324.9	27966.3	16h 32m	2599	19.6	58.0
77	16 Sep	230.3	370.6	28336.9	16h 02m	2316	23.1	56.5
78	17 Sep	239.3	385.1	28722.0	16h 17m	1654	23.6	58.7
79	18 Sep	188.2	302.9	29024.9	13h 16m	1432	22.8	51.5
80								

| HEART RATE | | START LOCATION | | END LOCATION | | NOTES |
Avge.	Max.					
— 102 —	127 —	Taroon	—	Broadford	—	–
— 99 —	132 —	Broadford	—	Dubbo	—	–
— 99 —	131 —	Dubbo	—	Moree	—	–
— 100 —	134 —	Moree	—	Brisbane	—	End of Australia
— 106 —	129 —	Invercargill	—	Lumsden	—	After flight to New Zealand
— 107 —	139 —	Lumsden	—	Haast	—	–
— 103 —	134 —	Haast	—	Reefton	—	–
— 104 —	137 —	Reefton	—	Picton	—	Inter-Island Ferry
— 105 —	141 —	Wellington	—	Ohakuri	—	*Morning crash*
— 99 —	131 —	Ohakuri	—	Auckland	—	🚲 END OF STAGE 2 🚲
— 113 —	144 —	Anchorage	—	Gakona	—	Alaska
— 105 —	136 —	Gakona	—	Central Yukon	—	Into Canada
— 103 —	132 —	Central Yukon	—	Whitehorse	—	–
— 102 —	133 —	Whitehorse	—	Watson Lake	—	–
— 102 —	133 —	Watson Lake	—	Muncho Lake	—	–
— 104 —	137 —	Muncho Lake	—	Prophet River	—	–
— 102 —	135 —	Prophet River	—	Hythe	—	–
— 99 —	130 —	Hythe	—	Mayerthorpe	—	–
— 115 —	127 —	Mayerthorpe	—	Three Hills	—	–
—	—	Three Hills	—	Kindersley	—	–
—	—	Kindersley	—	Tuxford	—	–
—	—	Tuxford	—	Portal	—	Cross into USA
—	—	Portal	—	Niagara	—	–
—	—	Niagara	—	Elrosa	—	–
—	—	Elrosa	—	Misha Mokwa	—	–
—	—	Misha Mokwa	—	Pensaukee	—	–
—	—	Pensaukee	—	Lake Superior	—	–
—	—	Lake Superior	—	Sudbury	—	Back into Canada
— *no data*	— *no data*	Sudbury	—	Arnprior	—	–
—	—	Arnprior	—	Chambly	—	–
—	—	Chambly	—	L'Islet-sur-Mer	—	–
—	—	L'Islet-sur-Mer	—	Newbridge	—	–
—	—	Newbridge	—	Oxford	—	–
—	—	Oxford	—	Halifax	—	🚲 END OF STAGE 3 🚲
—	—	Lisbon	—	Montijo	—	After flight to Portugal/Spain
—	—	Montijo	—	Anover de Tajo	—	–
—	—	Anover de Tajo	—	Tarazona	—	*Sick, evening crash*
—	—	Tarazona	—	Sanguinet	—	France
—	—	Sanguinet	—	Tours	—	–
—	—	Tours	—	Paris	—	🚲 END OF STAGE 4 🚲

78 days, 14 hours, 40 mins

AROUND THE WORLD IN 80 DAYS

SOME STATISTICS

Total distance: 18035.2 miles / 29024.9km

Total duration: 1197 hours 26 minutes

Average speed: 15.06mph / 24.24kph

Avg. heart rate: 100.6 b/m

Stage 1: 28 days – 6664mi / 10725km

Stage 2: 21 days – 45577mi / 7366km

Stage 3: 24 days – 5498mi / 8848km

Stage 4: 6 days – 1295mi / 2085km

Longest day: Day 43, racing to Brisbane Flight – 280.7mi / 451.7km, 18h 49m

Fastest day: Day 34, Nullarbor tailwinds, Australia – 17.1mph / 27.5kph average

Slowest day: Day 60, Canadian prairies, headwinds – 11.7mph / 18.8kph average

Hilliest day: Day 22, to Lake Baikal, Russia – 3768 metres ascent in 370.1km

Flattest day: Day 40, Central Australia – 461 metres ascent in 337.6km

Acknowledgements

Around the World in 80 Days was my dream and I turned the pedals, but for those coming to the story after the event it will be hard to appreciate the number of people and conversations and the amount of energy and good will it took to make this happen. I didn't have the capacity or skillset to do what the following people did, and I share the accolade of the first sub-eighty-day 18,000-mile circumnavigation by bicycle with everyone who had the vision and drive to join my team and see this through. It hurt a lot, but what a glorious journey.

These acknowledgements are not complete – every search of my emails brings up another contact who helped – but I have to stop somewhere. So, if you were a part of the 80 Days success but have not appeared in print, it is not intentional on my part. To everyone involved, my heartfelt thanks.

Family come first. Nicci and I have just celebrated our sixth wedding anniversary and since the moment we met she has supported my career brilliantly. We couldn't be more different in outlook and interests, which is a great strength. Harriet has learnt to ride her bike while I have been writing this book and will happily tell you that 'Daddy used to cycle around the world, but not any more.' Willa is very young, but early signs are that she will be very sporty and independent.

Mum, aka Una, aka Base Camp, was at the very heart of this expedition, as she has been since I was a twelve-year-old boy cycling across Scotland. Thanks, Mum, I'll never know all that you did, but your never-seeming-to-sleep commitment was legendary among the team on the road. I do appreciate the pressure you have been working under for years and the sacrifices you have made for me.

To Heather and Hannah, for always being there to support me and keep my feet firmly on the ground, as only siblings can! To Ron and Trish, Nicci's parents, and Tom, Michaela and the boys for being such a wonderfully supporting family, especially when I am away on expeditions. To cousin Catie and Auntie Fiona for hundreds of messages of support. And to Grampa, Daphne and Dad.

In the making of this book, it has been wonderful to work again with my friend and editor Giles Elliott, as well as copy editor Daniel Balado and my literary agent Mark Stanford. The team at Transworld have backed me since *The Man Who Cycled the World*, and for their continuing support I'd like to thank Henry Vines, as well as Hannah Bright for publicity.

Around the World in 80 Days simply wouldn't have happened without the belief and backing of Lindsay Whitelaw and Derek Stuart from Artemis Fund Managers. Thanks also for your friendship and advice over the years. Artemis and their PR team did a fantastic job, and included Caroline O'Donnell, Martha Braddell, Juliet Creggan, Catie Prosser, Grace Khare, Camilla Green and Tim Kelly.

I have worked with LDC (Lloyds Development Capital) for over a decade and the backing and personal support from Martin Draper, Sam Grey and Sophie Reed has meant a huge amount.

The dream machine was made by KOGA, another business I have worked with for over a decade, so thank you for the dedicated design work and financial support, led by Pieter Jan Rijpstra and Aloys Hanekamp. It was very cool that so many of you cycled down from Holland for the finish in Paris.

Other financial sponsors were Panaracer led by Jeff Zell and supported by Mark Okada; ZyroFisher led by Jon Sherwood with design and support work from the team at Altura including Daniel Leather, Warren Valentine, Helen Stevenson and Emma Robertson; Cardtronics/I-Design led by Ana Stuart with project work by Susannah Griffin, Nicki Robertson and Jack Vincent; Hiscox/Bikmo led by Ross Dingwall and David George; Visit Scotland led by Charlie Smith and supported by Ruma Cummins and Laura Mitchell; Edinburgh

Airport led by Rob Lang and Gordon Robertson, where one of the World bikes is now on display; and the Hunter Foundation, who generously backed the project from the very start.

My core performance and logistics team members on the road – Laura Penhaul, Mike Griffiths, Alex Glasgow, David Scott, Jo Craig and Tony Humphreys – committed a huge amount to this dream and understand better than anyone how tough the 80 Days was, how disciplined we were, and what 'Type 2 fun' really is! Huge thanks also go to crew members Claire Guthrie, Ry McGrath, Tim Spiteri, Fleur Royds and Nick Charlton, and to Hishgue Khishgdulam Tumurbaatar (translator), and Hajaa Khajidmaa, Sasha, Aleksandr, the two Dimitris and our four Chinese drivers.

A few more friends of the project, a list I could easily expand, are Sir Tom Hunter, Ewan Hunter, Sir Bill and Janice Gammell, Jeff Thomas, Tim Chevallier, Kevin Lyon, Alastair Laing, Michael Kennedy, Rob Wainwright, David Fox Pitt, James Mitchell, Bobby Burt, Grant Fraser, John Watson, Jonathan Lamont, Sarah Perry, Helen Sayles CBE, Sandy Kennedy, Calum McNicol, Damian Richmond, Adam Scott, Richard Curtis, Stewart Fairley, Jonathan Findlay, Rory Payne at Cocoa Loco, Jen Reynolds, Marshall Dallas at the EICC, Hugh Roberts at Sweetspot, Ian Kenworthy at the Reform Club, Duncan Sutcliffe at Sutcliffe Insurance, Rachel Paling and James Williamson at RJ Cycling Camps, Jerry Balloch for graphic design work, Stefan Morrocco and Kieran Duncan for filming in Scotland, and Carron Tobin for great advice and work on the charitable side.

For the years of planning and also those involved with Around Britain who then didn't come on the World, I'd like to thank Phil Mestecky, Justin Holt MBE, Leven Brown, Fergus McCallum, Katy Nicol, James Gravelle, Keith Walker and Angus Mill.

For medical support, testing and physiological preparation, a big thank you to my nutritionist Ruth McKean, sports physiologist Dr Lesley Ingram, friend and sports doc Dr Andrew Murray, bike fitter John Dennis at Physiohaus, the team at World Extreme Medicine including Mark Hannaford, Dr Sean Hundson and Burjor Langdana, Charlie Hampton at Isobar Compression Garments, Daniel Billington at RX Recovery Pump and Joe Dunbar at Soma Science saliva sampling.

Menzies Aviation were a generous financial sponsor, but also saved us untold hours at airports and a huge amount of money in excess baggage charges. The backing came from Forsyth Black, executive director, president and managing director, so proud of this Scottish yet global business. A huge amount of work (including during his holidays) was put in by David Liepins, General Manager Central Support; Alex Tan and Fook Ping Chen from Singapore Airlines; and from the Menzies Team globally: Stuart Key, Richard Bonner, Simon Hinman, Amy Woodcroft, Lloyd Thomson, Hussein Rawlings, Trevor Pickle, Johannes and Dustin, Mike Farris, Bal Dhesi, Sean McCool, Ramon Martinez, Ian Hutson, Michael Stratman, Marcos Aroca, Daniel Fernandez, Tomeu Mass and Matthew Johnson.

In-kind and smaller financial packages added up to a significant amount, and for these I would like to acknowledge John Clark Motor Group, led by Chris and Clare Clark supported by John Anderson; Phil Griffiths and Brian Tinsley from Yellow Ltd for Corima Wheels and Rudy Project helmets and sunglasses; Jo Taylor from Wiggle; XL Catlin led by Michael Wolfe; Highlander Outdoors led by Ramin Golzare, supported by Steve Christie; Boyd Tunnock from Tunnocks; rsk.co.uk; John Fisher at Firepot Foods; James Mayo at SOS Hydrate; Helen and Bill Cussen at Trident Sensors; Bryan McQueen at Dilglove; Chris Tatton at Saddleback; Sean Dines and Steve Davis at Mavic; Ingo Weiler at Profile Design; Spaceship Rentals; Jonathan Raggett from Red Carnation Hotels, London, and Doreen Hatier from Hotel California, Paris.

The expedition website artemisworldcycle.com and digital plan was completely sponsored by the amazing team at 80 Days Digital, led by Mark Forrester and David Gardner, with a huge amount of work from Chris McGuire, Sam Walker, Simon Boak and Douglas Hunter; markbeaumontonline.com remains the fantastic work of Jason Wagner at PING Creates. The team at Thorntons Law, led by Alastair Laing and supported by Kirsty Stewart, Amy Jones and Victoria McLaren, sponsored all of their legal support. Adam & Company private bank, led by Ryan Beattie with Jackie Walker, supported the ride by covering international bank charges and being very accommodating.

Muckle Media, led by Nathalie Agnew with project management from Ellie Wagstaff and support by Fiona Raynor and Annie Diamond, did a brilliant job of taking the 80 Days story to a global audience. PR was also supported on the LDC side by City Press led by Martin Currie, Mark Spence, Sophie Milward and Tom Parker. I'd also like to thank David Dick at the Trinity Group for media support.

GCN did a huge job of taking the story to their global audience of over 1.4 million, so thanks to Simon Richardson, Mike Rees and their team for riding with me and sharing the weekly updates.

The insanely hard-working media team on the road was Johnny Swanepoel and Helmut Scherz – the only two people who did every day of the ride with me. Well done, guys, you have my utmost respect. The filming and photography was coordinated by MoonSport Productions, led by Philip and Trent Key. The hardest-working member of the Cape Town team was undoubtedly Emanuel 'Manni' Ferreira, the production manager, who built a great collaboration and friendship with Una. Thanks also to L. J. 'Eljay' Rice (editor), Roxanne Lombard (social media) and Guy Macleod LLB (legal). Additional media support came from Jonny Verman (photography) and Paul Brown (media motorcycle), and thanks to Alain and Julie Cordier for the car/motorcycle escort into Paris.

The schools programme was brought to life by the team at Twinkl led by Imogen Wood and Gemma Barker, and also through the storytelling throughout the project on *Blue Peter*.

Logistics were at the heart of our success, and the team at Wexas have worked with me for a very long time, making sure I never miss a flight and take every hour off the world records. Thanks to the around-the-clock work of Alex Crosby, Jennifer Hartnett and Joanne Henderson.

Thank you also to the quick work of and promotion by Guinness World Records led by Doug Male and account manager Mark McKinley with support from Anna Ford and Amber-Georgina Gill.

British Embassy support came from Lord Ed Llewellyn (British Ambassador), Tess Mendbe and Matthew Lodge in Paris; John Hamilton, British High Commission, for making so many diplomatic connections; Rufus Drabble, Consular Regional Director, British Embassy, The Hague; Mark Rakestraw, HM Consul General, British Embassy, Moscow; Matthew Osbourne and Natalia Pietra at the British Consulate in Yekaterinburg; Kirsty Hayes, the British Ambassador to Portugal; and Simon Manley, the British Ambassador to Spain. Thanks also to Harry Leverment from the GREAT Campaign and the Foreign and Commonwealth Office's Global Response Centre.

The Man Who Cycled the World
Mark Beaumont

On 15 February 2008, Mark Beaumont pedalled through the Arc de Triomphe in Paris, 194 days and 17 hours after setting off on a mission to cycle around the globe. He had travelled 18,297 miles solo and unsupported, averaging 100 punishing miles a day, and smashed the Guinness World Record by an astonishing 81 days.

The Man Who Cycled the World is the story of that incredible feat of endurance. After battling broken wheels in Europe, then the hostile mountains and deserts of Turkey, Iran and Pakistan, a saddle-sore Mark crossed Asia. In Australia, the heat and a ferocious headwind threatened his resolve, before a terrible crash in America nearly ended the journey.

By the time Mark had raced night and day to reach Paris again, he had completed a remarkable adventure. *The Man Who Cycled the World* tells his epic story and provides an insight into many of the world's cultures from a unique perspective.

The Man Who Cycled the Americas
Mark Beaumont

One year after he became The Man Who Cycled the World, Mark Beaumont set off on a second record-breaking endurance adventure. It would involve another huge distance: 15,000 miles from the wilds of Alaska to the windswept southern tip of Argentina. But this time he faced a new challenge: scaling North and South America's highest peaks. Mount McKinley, otherwise known as Denali: 20,320 feet, technical, extremely cold, very dangerous. Aconcagua: the highest summit outside Asia. Tough at the best of times. Even harder after eight punishing months on the road.

The Man Who Cycled the Americas tells the story of Mark's incredible journey down the longest mountain range on the planet and of both the dangers and exhilaration that it brought. Full of his trademark charm, warmth and fascination with seeing the world at the pace of a bicycle, it is a thrilling trip through the diverse cultures of our most fascinating continents.

Africa Solo
Mark Beaumont

Seven years after smashing the record for cycling round the world and inspiring a generation of like-minded adventurers, Mark Beaumont set out on another epic record-breaking journey that would fulfil a dream – to cycle the length of Africa, as fast as humanly possible. But to make it from Cairo to Cape Town in one piece, a distance of more than 10,000 kilometres, unsupported, would prove the toughest solo challenge of his life.

After battling bureaucracy in Egypt and sandstorms in Sudan, then the unpaved roads and mountains of Ethiopia and rains in Kenya which turned dirt into mud, Mark often had to push his battered body and broken bike beyond the bounds of endurance. But as he sped further south, his astonishing daily mileages through grasslands and deserts would be accompanied by the roadside wonders that only this fascinating and complex continent can provide.

Africa Solo brings this all to life in glorious detail, from the warmth of the village hospitality and kindness of strangers to the utter joy of riding from the chill of a Zambian dawn to a pitch-dark Botswanan night with only the company of elephants.